The Changing Face of

The rapid development of Korean cinema during the decades of the 1960s and 2000s reveals a dynamic cinematic history that runs parallel to the nation's political, social, economic, and cultural transformation during these formative periods.

This book examines the ways in which South Korean cinema has undergone a transformation from an antiquated local industry in the 1960s into a thriving international cinema in the twenty-first century. It investigates the circumstances that allowed these two eras to emerge as creative watersheds and demonstrates the forces behind Korea's positioning of itself as an important contributor to regional and global culture, especially its interplay with Japan, Greater China, and the United States. Beginning with an explanation of the understudied operations of the film industry during its 1960s take-off, it then offers insight into the challenges that producers, directors, and policy makers faced in the 1970s and 1980s during the most volatile part of Park Chung Hee's authoritarian rule and the subsequent Chun Doo-hwan military government. It moves on to explore the film industry's professionalization in the 1990s and subsequent international expansion in the 2000s. In doing so, it explores the nexus and tensions of film policy, producing, directing, genres, and the internationalization of Korean cinema over half a century.

By highlighting the recent transnational turn in national cinemas, this book underscores the impact of developments pioneered by Korean cinema on the transformation of "Planet Hallyuwood". It will be of particular interest to students and scholars of Korean Studies and Film Studies.

Brian Yecies is a Senior Lecturer in Cultural Studies at the University of Wollongong, Australia.

Aegyung Shim is a past Korea Foundation Postdoctoral Research Fellow at the Institute for Social Transformation Research (ISTR) at the University of Wollongong, Australia.

Asia's Transformations

Edited by Mark Selden, Cornell University, USA

The books in this series explore the political, social, economic, and cultural consequences of Asia's transformations in the twentieth and twenty-first centuries. The series emphasizes the tumultuous interplay of local, national, regional, and global forces as Asia bids to become the hub of the world economy. While focusing on the contemporary, it also looks back to analyze the antecedents of Asia's contested rise.

This series comprises several strands:
Asia's Transformations

Titles include:

1 **Debating Human Rights***
   Critical essays from the United States and Asia
   Edited by Peter Van Ness

2 **Hong Kong's History***
   State and society under colonial rule
   Edited by Tak-Wing Ngo

3 **Japan's Comfort Women***
   Sexual slavery and prostitution during World War II and the US occupation
   Yuki Tanaka

4 **Opium, Empire and the Global Political Economy***
   Carl A. Trocki

5 **Chinese Society***
   Change, conflict and resistance
   Edited by Elizabeth J. Perry and Mark Selden

6 **Mao's Children in the New China***
   Voices from the Red Guard generation
   Yarong Jiang and David Ashley

7 **Remaking the Chinese State***
   Strategies, society and security
   Edited by Chien-min Chao and Bruce J. Dickson

8 **Korean Society***
   Civil society, democracy and the state
   Edited by Charles K. Armstrong

9 **The Making of Modern Korea***
   Adrian Buzo

10 **The Resurgence of East Asia***
   500, 150 and 50 Year perspectives
   Edited by Giovanni Arrighi, Takeshi Hamashita and Mark Selden

11 **Chinese Society, second edition***
   Change, conflict and resistance
   Edited by Elizabeth J. Perry and Mark Selden

12 **Ethnicity in Asia***
   Edited by Colin Mackerras

13 **The Battle for Asia***
   From decolonization to globalization
   Mark T. Berger

14 **State and Society in 21st Century China***
Edited by Peter Hays Gries and Stanley Rosen

15 **Japan's Quiet Transformation***
Social change and civil society in the 21st century
Jeff Kingston

16 **Confronting the Bush Doctrine***
Critical views from the Asia-Pacific
Edited by Mel Gurtov and Peter Van Ness

17 **China in War and Revolution, 1895–1949***
Peter Zarrow

18 **The Future of US–Korean Relations***
The imbalance of power
Edited by John Feffer

19 **Working in China***
Ethnographies of labor and workplace transformations
Edited by Ching Kwan Lee

20 **Korean Society, second edition***
Civil society, democracy and the state
Edited by Charles K. Armstrong

21 **Singapore***
The state and the culture of excess
Souchou Yao

22 **Pan-Asianism in Modern Japanese History***
Colonialism, regionalism and borders
Edited by Sven Saaler and J. Victor Koschmann

23 **The Making of Modern Korea, 2nd Edition***
Adrian Buzo

24 **Re-writing Culture in Taiwan***
Edited by Fang-long Shih, Stuart Thompson, and Paul-François Tremlett

25 **Reclaiming Chinese Society***
The new social activism
Edited by You-tien Hsing and Ching Kwan Lee

26 **Girl Reading Girl in Japan***
Edited by Tomoko Aoyama and Barbara Hartley

27 **Chinese Politics***
State, society and the market
Edited by Peter Hays Gries and Stanley Rosen

28 **Chinese Society, third edition***
Change, conflict and resistance
Edited by Elizabeth J. Perry and Mark Selden

29 **Mapping Modernity in Shanghai**
Space, gender, and visual culture in the Sojourners' City, 1853–98
Samuel Y. Liang

30 **Minorities and Multiculturalism in Japanese Education**
An interactive perspective
Edited by Ryoko Tsuneyoshi, Kaori H Okano and Sarane Boocock

31 **Japan's Wartime Medical Atrocities**
Comparative inquiries in science, history, and ethics
Edited by Jing-Bao Nie, Nanyan Guo, Mark Selden and Arthur Kleinman

32 **State and Society in Modern Rangoon**
Donald M. Seekins

33 **Learning Chinese, Turning Chinese***
Becoming sinophone in a globalised world
Edward McDonald

34 **Aesthetic Constructions of Korean Nationalism**
Spectacle, politics and history
Hong Kal

35 **Popular Culture and the State in East and Southeast Asia**
Edited by Nissim Otmazgin and Eyal Ben Ari

36 **Japan's Outcaste Abolition**
The struggle for national inclusion and the making of the modern state
Noah Y. McCormack

37 **The Market and Temple Fairs of Rural China**
Red fire
Gene Cooper

38 **The Role of American NGOs in China's Modernization**
Invited influence
Norton Wheeler

39 **State, Society and the Market in Contemporary Vietnam**
Property, power and values
Edited by Hue-Tam Ho Tai and Mark Sidel

40 **East Asia beyond the History Wars**
Confronting the ghosts of violence
Tessa Morris-Suzuki, Morris Low, Leonid Petrov and Timothy Yun Hui Tsu

41 **China**
How the empire fell
Joseph W. Esherick and C. X. George Wei

42 **The Political Economy of Affect and Emotion in East Asia**
Jie Yang

43 **Remaking China's Great Cities**
Space and culture in urban housing, renewal, and expansion
Samuel Y. Liang

44 **Vietnam's Socialist Servants**
Domesticity, class, gender, and identity
Minh T. N. Nguyen

45 **The San Francisco System and Its Legacies**
Continuation, transformation and historical reconciliation in the Asia-Pacific
Edited by Kimie Hara

46 **Transnational Trajectories in East Asia**
Nation, citizenship and region
Edited by Yasemin Nuhoğlu Soysal

47 **The Politics of Protection Rackets in Post-New Order Indonesia**
Coercive capital, authority and street politics
Ian Douglas Wilson

48 Coal Mining Women in Japan
    Heavy burdens
    Donald W. Burton

49 The Changing Face of Korean Cinema
    1960 to 2015
    Brian Yecies and Aegyung Shim

Asia's Great Cities
Each volume aims to capture the heartbeat of the contemporary city from multiple perspectives emblematic of the authors' own deep familiarity with the distinctive faces of the city, its history, society, culture, politics and economics, and its evolving position in national, regional and global frameworks. While most volumes emphasize urban developments since the Second World War, some pay close attention to the legacy of the longue durée in shaping the contemporary. Thematic and comparative volumes address such themes as urbanization, economic and financial linkages, architecture and space, wealth and power, gendered relationships, planning and anarchy, and ethnographies in national and regional perspective. Titles include:

1 **Bangkok***
   Place, practice and representation
   Marc Askew

2 **Representing Calcutta***
   Modernity, nationalism and the colonial uncanny
   Swati Chattopadhyay

3 **Singapore***
   Wealth, power and the culture of control
   Carl A. Trocki

4 **The City in South Asia**
   James Heitzman

5 **Global Shanghai, 1850–2010***
   A history in fragments
   Jeffrey N. Wasserstrom

6 **Hong Kong***
   Becoming a global city
   Stephen Chiu and Tai-Lok Lui

Asia.com is a series that focuses on the ways in which new information and communication technologies are influencing politics, society, and culture in Asia. Titles include:

1 **Japanese Cybercultures***
   Edited by Mark McLelland and Nanette Gottlieb

2 **Asia.com***
   Asia encounters the Internet
   Edited by K. C. Ho, Randolph Kluver and Kenneth C. C. Yang

3 **The Internet in Indonesia's New Democracy***
   David T. Hill and Krishna Sen

4 **Chinese Cyberspaces***
   Technological changes and political effects
   Edited by Jens Damm and Simona Thomas

5 Mobile Media in the Asia-Pacific
   Gender and the art of being
   mobile
   Larissa Hjorth

6 Online@AsiaPacific
   Mobile, social and locative media
   in the Asia–Pacific
   Larissa Hjorth and Michael Arnold

Literature and Society
Literature and Society is a series that seeks to demonstrate the ways in which Asian Literature is influenced by the politics, society, and culture in which it is produced. Titles include:

1 The Body in Postwar Japanese
   Fiction
   Douglas N. Slaymaker

2 Chinese Women Writers and
   the Feminist Imagination,
   1905–1948*
   Haiping Yan

3 Okinawan War Memory
   Transgenerational trauma and the
   war fiction of Medoruma Shun
   Kyle Ikeda

Routledge Studies in Asia's Transformations
Routledge Studies in Asia's Transformations is a forum for innovative new research intended for a high-level specialist readership. Titles include:

1 The American Occupation of
   Japan and Okinawa*
   Literature and memory
   Michael Molasky

2 Koreans in Japan*
   Critical voices from the margin
   Edited by Sonia Ryang

3 Internationalizing the Pacific
   The United States, Japan and the
   Institute of Pacific Relations in
   war and peace, 1919–1945
   Tomoko Akami

4 Imperialism in South East Asia*
   'A fleeting, passing phase'
   Nicholas Tarling

5 Chinese Media, Global Contexts*
   Edited by Chin-Chuan Lee

6 Remaking Citizenship in
   Hong Kong*
   Community, nation and the
   global city
   *Edited by Agnes S. Ku and
   Ngai Pun*

7 Japanese Industrial Governance
   Protectionism and the licensing state
   Yul Sohn

8 Developmental Dilemmas*
   Land reform and institutional
   change in China
   Edited by Peter Ho

9 **Genders, Transgenders and Sexualities in Japan***
   Edited by Mark McLelland and Romit Dasgupta

10 **Fertility, Family Planning and Population Policy in China***
   Edited by Dudley L. Poston, Che-Fu Lee, Chiung-Fang Chang, Sherry L. McKibben and Carol S. Walther

11 **Japanese Diasporas***
   Unsung pasts, conflicting presents and uncertain futures
   Edited by Nobuko Adachi

12 **How China Works***
   Perspectives on the twentieth-century industrial workplace
   Edited by Jacob Eyferth

13 **Remolding and Resistance among Writers of the Chinese Prison Camp**
   Disciplined and published
   Edited by Philip F. Williams and Yenna Wu

14 **Popular Culture, Globalization and Japan***
   Edited by Matthew Allen and Rumi Sakamoto

15 **medi@sia***
   Global media/tion in and out of context
   Edited by Todd Joseph Miles Holden and Timothy J. Scrase

16 **Vientiane***
   Transformations of a Lao landscape
   Marc Askew, William S. Logan and Colin Long

17 **State Formation and Radical Democracy in India**
   Manali Desai

18 **Democracy in Occupied Japan***
   The U.S. occupation and Japanese politics and society
   Edited by Mark E. Caprio and Yoneyuki Sugita

19 **Globalization, Culture and Society in Laos***
   Boike Rehbein

20 **Transcultural Japan***
   At the borderlands of race, gender, and identity
   Edited by David Blake Willis and Stephen Murphy-Shigematsu

21 **Post-Conflict Heritage, Post-Colonial Tourism**
   Culture, politics and development at Angkor
   Tim Winter

22 **Education and Reform in China***
   Emily Hannum and Albert Park

23 **Writing Okinawa: Narrative Acts of Identity and Resistance**
   Davinder L. Bhowmik

24 **Maid in China***
   Media, morality, and the cultural politics of boundaries
   Wanning Sun

25 **Northern Territories, Asia-Pacific Regional Conflicts and the Åland Experience**
   Untying the Kurillian knot
   Edited by Kimie Hara and Geoffrey Jukes

26 **Reconciling Indonesia**
Grassroots agency for peace
Birgit Bräuchler

27 **Singapore in the Malay World***
Building and breaching regional bridges
Lily Zubaidah Rahim

28 **Pirate Modernity***
Delhi's media urbanism
Ravi Sundaram

29 **The World Bank and the post-Washington Consensus in Vietnam and Indonesia**
Inheritance of loss
Susan Engel

30 **China on Video**
Smaller Screen Realities
Paola Voci

31 **Overseas Chinese, Ethnic Minorities and Nationalism**
De-centering China
Elena Barabantseva

32 **The Education of Migrant Children and China's Future**
The urban left behind
Holly H. Ming

Critical Asian Scholarship

Critical Asian Scholarship is a series intended to showcase the most important individual contributions to scholarship in Asian Studies. Each of the volumes presents a leading Asian scholar addressing themes that are central to his or her most significant and lasting contribution to Asian studies. The series is committed to the rich variety of research and writing on Asia and is not restricted to any particular discipline, theoretical approach or geographical expertise.

1 **Southeast Asia***
A testament
George McT. Kahin

2 **Women and the Family in Chinese History***
Patricia Buckley Ebrey

3 **China Unbound***
Evolving perspectives on the Chinese past
Paul A. Cohen

4 **China's Past, China's Future***
Energy, food, environment
Vaclav Smil

5 **The Chinese State in Ming Society***
Timothy Brook

6 **China, East Asia and the Global Economy***
Regional and historical perspectives
Takeshi Hamashita
Edited by Mark Selden and Linda Grove

7 **The Global and Regional in China's Nation-Formation***
Prasenjit Duara

8 **Decoding Subaltern Politics***
Ideology, disguise, and resistance
in agrarian politics
James C. Scott

9 **Mapping China and Managing the World***
Culture, cartography and
cosmology in late Imperial times
Richard J. Smith

10 **Technology, Gender and History in Imperial China***
Great transformations
reconsidered
Francesca Bray

* Available in paperback

The Changing Face of Korean Cinema
1960 to 2015

Brian Yecies and Aegyung Shim

LONDON AND NEW YORK

First published 2016 by Routledge

2 Park Square, Milton Park, Abingdon, Oxfordshire OX14 4RN
711 Third Avenue, New York, NY 10017

Routledge is an imprint of the Taylor & Francis Group, an informa business

First issued in paperback 2018

Copyright © 2016 Brian Yecies and Aegyung Shim

The right of Brian Yecies and Aegyung Shim to be identified as authors of this work has been asserted by them in accordance with sections 77 and 78 of the Copyright, Designs and Patents Act 1988.

All rights reserved. No part of this book may be reprinted or reproduced or utilised in any form or by any electronic, mechanical, or other means, now known or hereafter invented, including photocopying and recording, or in any information storage or retrieval system, without permission in writing from the publishers.

Notice:
Product or corporate names may be trademarks or registered trademarks, and are used only for identification and explanation without intent to infringe.

British Library Cataloguing in Publication Data
A catalogue record for this book is available from the British Library

Library of Congress Cataloging in Publication Data
Yecies, Brian, 1967–
The changing face of Korean cinema, 1960 to 2015 / Brian Yecies and Ae-Gyung Shim.
  pages cm. — (Asia's transformations)
Includes bibliographical references and index.
  1. Motion picture industry—Korea—History—20th century. 2. Motion picture industry—Korea—History—21st century. 3. Motion pictures—Korea—History—20th century.
  4. Motion pictures—Korea—History—21st century. I. Shim, Ae-Gyung, 1973- II. Title.
PN1993.5.K6Y428 2016
791.4309519'0904—dc23   2015025493

ISBN: 978-0-415-70765-7 (hbk)
ISBN: 978-1-138-60906-8 (pbk)

Typeset in Times New Roman
by codeMantra

This book is dedicated to Robert Shimhoon, Alex Kangho, and their grandfather Robert Yecies. It is also dedicated to filmmakers and cultural diversity advocates around the globe who continue to persevere against great challenges.

Research for large parts of this book was made possible through a research assistance grant from the Asia Research Fund (2003, Yecies), as well as a Korea Foundation Advanced Research Grant (2008, Yecies), Korea Foundation Research Fellowship (2005, Yecies), Korea Foundation Graduate Studies Fellowship (2007–2008, Shim), and Korea Foundation Post-doctorial Fellowship (2010–2011, Shim). Invaluable travel funds were also provided by the Australia-Korea Foundation, Academy of Korean Studies, University of Wollongong, and University of New South Wales. The book also draws on research being conducted in association with a 2014–2016 Australian Research Council Discovery project, *Willing Collaborators: Negotiating Change in East Asian Media Production* DP 140101643 (Michael Keane, Brian Yecies, and Terry Flew).

Contents

List of Figures   xvii
Abbreviations   xix
Foreword (by Director Byun Young-joo)   xxi

Introduction: Introducing "Planet Hallyuwood"   1

PART I
The Golden Age of the 1960s   17

1 Hypergrowth of the Propaganda Factory and the Producing Paradox   19

2 At the Crossroads of Directing and Politics   42

3 Genre Intersections and the Literary Film   62

4 Feasting on Asian Alliances: Hong Kong Co-productions and Japanese Remakes   81

PART II
The Dark Age of the 1970s and Hollywood's Domination in the Aftermath   105

5 Policy and Producing under Hollywood's Shadow in the 1970s and 1980s   107

6 Robust Invalids in a New Visual Era: Directing in the 1970s and 1980s   127

7 Weapons of Mass Distraction: The Erotic Film Genres of the
  1970s and 1980s   141

PART III
The Golden Age of the Post-censorship Era   155

8 The Rise of the New Corporate and Female Producers   157

9 The Rise of the Female Writer–Director and the Changing Face
   of Korean Cinema   182

10 Genre Transformations in Contemporary Korean Cinema   207

11 Korean Transnational Cinema and the Renewed
   Tilt Toward China   227

   Conclusion: Welcome to Planet Hallyuwood   251

   Bibliography   259
   Index   271

Figures

1.1	Film advertisement for *Rice*	28
1.2	Election campaign advertisement	29
1.3	Film advertisements for *The Red Scarf*	30
1.4	Film advertisements for *The Red Scarf*	31
2.1	Film advertisement for *Aimless Bullet*	47
2.2	Film advertisement for *Aimless Bullet*	49
2.3	Film advertisements for *The Empty Dream*	53
3.1	Film advertisements for *Deaf Samryong* (1964)	68
3.2	Film advertisement for *Seaside Village* (1965)	72
3.3	Film advertisement for *Mist* (1967)	75
4.1	Film advertisements for *The Last Woman of Shang* (1964)	86
4.2	Film advertisement for *Barefoot Youth* (1964)	95
4.3	Editorial cartoon: "This is how a Screenwriter Works"	98
5.1	Film advertisement for *The Testimony* (1974)	110
6.1	Film advertisements for *Homecoming to Stars* (1974) and *March of Fools* (1975)	131
6.2	Film advertisement for *Good Windy Day* (1980)	135
7.1	Film advertisement for *Youngja's Hey Day* (1975)	146
7.2	Film advertisements for *Madam Aema* (1982)	150
9.1	Film advertisement for *The Widow* (1955)	186
9.2	Film advertisement for *The Girl Raised as a Future Daughter-in-law* (1965)	187

Abbreviations

AFKN	American Forces Korea Network
BFA	Beijing Film Academy
BIFF	Busan International Film Festival
CDMI	Coalition for Cultural Diversity in Moving Images
CGV	CJ Golden Village
CJ E&M	CJ Entertainment and Mediaplex
DI	Digital Intermediary
ILRS	Import License Reward System
IMF	International Monetary Fund
IMDB	Internet Movie Database
KAFA	Korean Academy of Film Arts
KAMA	Korea Amateur Filmmakers Association
KCIA	Korean Central Intelligence Agency
KMDB	Korean Movie Database
KMPPA	Korean Motion Pictures Producers Association
KMPPC	Korean Motion Picture Promotion Corporation
KNUA	Korea National University of Arts
KOCCA	Korea Creative Contents Agency (formerly Korea Culture and Content Agency)
KOFA	Korean Film Archive
KOFIC	Korean Film Council (formerly Korean Film Commission)
MCPI	Ministry of Culture and Public Information
MPAA	Motion Picture Association of America (currently known as MPA)
MPAK	Motion Picture Association of Korea
MPEA	Motion Picture Export Association (currently known as MPA)
MPI	Ministry of Public Information
MPL	Motion Picture Law
NAK	National Archives of Korea
N.E.W.	*Next Entertainment World*
NFPC	National Film Production Center
NTR	Normal Trade Relations
PEC	Performance Ethics Committee

PRS	Producer Registration System
SAPPRFT	State Administration of Press, Publication, Radio, Film, and Television (PRC-China)
SARFT	State Administration of Radio, Film, and Television (PRC-China)
SCNR	Supreme Court of National Reconstruction
SIWFF	Seoul International Women's Film Festival
SQS	Screen Quota System
USAMGIK	United States Army Military Government in Korea
USIA	United States Information Agency
USTR	United States Trade Representative (Office of)
WIFK	Women in Film Korea

Foreword (by Director Byun Young-joo)

In 1997 the first Seoul International Women's Film Festival screened director Park Nam-ok's *The Widow* (1955) as the opening-night film. Still photographs of its production scenes were displayed in a corner of the festival venue. Seeing director Park in one of these photos standing behind the camera, wearing a *hanbok* (traditional Korean dress) and carrying her baby on her back was very intriguing to me. In the same year I watched director Kim Ki-young's *The Housemaid* (1960) at the Berlin International Film Festival. It was a marvelous experience and again strange.

At the end of the 1980s when my generation began dreaming of making films, we had no senior mentors to follow. Under decades of military dictatorship, all of the films we watched had been subjected to strong censorship before reaching us. It seemed impossible to make the kind of films we wanted to make in Korea. This was a difficult period when some university students were imprisoned simply because they had used their school holidays to produce 8mm short films containing content that was apparently "objectionable". We had no choice but to gather secretly in basements to watch these films and other "illegal" copies of foreign films shared by our university alumni who had studied abroad. Our covert but innocent activities were probably similar to those followed by the Dutch documentary filmmaker Joris Ivens' cinema club. We kept on dreaming, keeping our passion alive for making Korean films.

An older friend and colleague was among the first group of students to enter the national Korean Academy of Film Arts (KAFA) when it first opened in 1984. At that time, she was not allowed to touch the camera during cinematography workshops because she was a "female" student. The lecturer was uncomfortable with her touching the camera because he absurdly believed that a woman's touch was bad luck. However, my friend ignored this gender discrimination and continued to study the operation of the camera, persevering with her passion to become a filmmaker. I'll always be thankful for the days she patiently taught me how to operate a 16mm Arriflex camera.

It may be hard to believe, but this type of gender discrimination occurred in Korea's very recent past. Perhaps this is why I occasionally think of Korean film history with mixed feelings of strangeness and difficulty. For the past two decades, the Korean film industry has undergone significant transformation, and I too have matured alongside the industry. As a female writer-director, I have reached the same age and achieved the same level of development as the core industry people in Chungmuro (the symbolic and former geographic center of Korea's film industry), who in the past scoffed at my attempts and passion to become a feature film director.

For these reasons and more, it is a privilege to provide this note to Brian Yecies and Aegyung Shim for writing *The Changing Face of Korean Cinema, 1960 to 2015*, which offers invaluable insights from the past, up until early 2015. It covers so many stories we either heard about or directly experienced while making our own films. In this way, *The Changing Face of Korean Cinema* transcends the past by empowering us to contemplate where Korean cinema could and should lead well into the future. I hope that Brian and Aegyung will publish their book in Korean in the near future—so Koreans can learn fresh perspectives of their own social and cultural heritage.

Director Byun Young-joo, Seoul, July 2015

Introduction
Introducing "Planet Hallyuwood"

This book analyzes the dynamic ways in which the South Korean (hereafter Korean) cinema has undergone a transformation from an antiquated local industry in the 1960s to a thriving international cinema in the 2000s, right up to the present. First, it explains the understudied operations of the film industry during its 1960s takeoff. Analyzing the tensions that filmmakers confronted in the 1960s, it shows how the industry unexpectedly reached an apex in terms of both quantity and quality under the Park Chung Hee military government (1961–1979). The authoritarian Park regime used film as a propaganda tool to legitimize its rule and to stabilize its political leadership through censorship and other control mechanisms. In the process, the industry was transformed from a post-war cottage industry into a systematized dynamic industry that emulated studio practices from Hollywood.

Second, it offers insights into the challenges that producers, directors, and policy makers faced in the 1970s and 1980s during the most volatile part of Park Chung Hee's authoritarian rule and the subsequent Chun Doo-hwan military government. Case studies of the most popular commercial and arthouse genre films made during this period are used to trace the creative and cultural transformation as well as the strategies that these key players initiated in order to survive the industry's longest downturn after Korean cinema's rise in the early 1960s.

Third, the book investigates the film industry's professionalization in the 1990s and subsequent international expansion in the 2000s. It explains the pressures that filmmakers confronted in the 2000s and how the global spotlight fell on Korean cinema after the locally made blockbuster *Shiri* (1999) eclipsed the box office success of *Titanic* (1998) in the Korean market. This watershed event signaled the bursting of a bottleneck of creativity that had been restricted by government censorship before 1996. This precise moment marks the beginnings of Korean cinema's contemporary boom. Within a relatively short period, a group of talented writer-directors and producers began drawing local, regional, and international attention to a homegrown inventiveness and a host of new cinematic possibilities. This accomplishment demonstrated the new power of Korean cinema at home and then abroad. It was achieved not by replicating Hollywood films, but by mixing Hollywood elements with local values and indigenous notions of traditional and modern culture in ways that distinguish it from other Asian national cinemas.

By exploring the nexus and the tensions among film policy, producing, directing, genre, and the internationalization of Korean cinema during the 1960s and 2000s, that is, two of the most important periods in Korea's cinematic history, this book highlights the recent transnational turn in national cinemas. In so doing, it underscores the impacts that developments pioneered by the Korean cinema in the aesthetic, textual, industry, audience, critical, policy, and historical fields have had on the transformation of what we have come to call "Planet Hallyuwood". A fusion of Hollywood and *Hallyu* (the Korean Wave), "Planet Hallyuwood" delineates notable similarities and differences between the Korean cinema and Hollywood productions in terms of the use of universal story lines, genre construction, high production values and vertical integration across the production and distribution sectors.

The rapid development of Korean cinema during the decades of the 1960s and 2000s reveals a dynamic cinematic history running parallel to the nation's political, social, economic and cultural transformation. In this book we investigate the circumstances that allowed these two eras to emerge as creative watersheds, and demonstrates the forces behind Korea's positioning of itself as an important contributor to regional and global culture, and especially its interplay with the cinemas of Japan, Greater China, and the United States.

The Rise of Contemporary Korean Cinema

Since the late 1990s Korean cinema has become one of the most dynamic national cinemas in the world. This remarkable surge, occurring in the wake of the 1997 International Monetary Fund (IMF) crisis, was fuelled by the unexpected and extraordinary success of Kang Je-gyu's blockbuster action–spy drama *Shiri* (1999), which exceeded $25 million USD at the Korean box office and outsold Hollywood's mega-blockbuster *Titanic* (1997, released in Korea in February 1998). The success of *Shiri*, in which Samsung Entertainment was a major investor, was a key moment for Korean cinema and the domestic film industry as a whole. Making a successful Hollywood-style blockbuster with a Korean inflection put Kang at the forefront of the "New Korean Cinema", along with directors such as Kim Jee-woon, Park Chan-wook, Im Sang-soo, Hong Sang-soo, and Kim Ki-duk, who had all attracted local and international attention in the late 1990s.[1]

After the Korean Constitutional Court eliminated film censorship in 1996 under the government of Kim Young-sam (1993–1997), the first civilian president, conditions were ripe for the production and exhibition of an increasing number of domestic films.[2] New spaces for freedom of expression—held shut by decades of military dictatorship, preceded by three years of US military rule and 35 years of Japanese colonial rule—began to open and, although it has not disappeared completely, censorship is now considered a tool of the authoritarian governments of the past. After censorship was lifted, a small army of creative and cultural practitioners immediately set about developing one of the world's fastest-growing film industries. Filmmakers began telling new and arresting stories that quickly gained a following at international film festivals. It is no coincidence, then, that 1996 corresponded with the launching of the annual Busan International Film Festival (BIFF), which has become a key networking hub for the Asian film and digital media industry and a major showcase for both Korean and international films. The titles of Korea's internationally award-winning films are too numerous to mention here. Suffice it to say that since the installation of democratic government, powerful waves of Korean popular culture (aka 'the Korean Wave' or *Hanryu* or *Hallyu* in Korean)—initially driven by the export and popularization of television dramas and Korean popular music (K-pop) in Asia, and then by the production of fresh and diverse screen genres, story lines and aesthetic styles—have rippled out across the globe.

As part of this surge of media and popular culture, a bevy of rising stars and the proliferation of 'savvy' domestic film companies have helped the industry to win the lion's share of the domestic market. In 1991, 21.2 percent of all films screened in Korea were locally made, but that figure had nearly tripled to 61.2 percent by the end of 2006.[3] In 2008, the trend reversed briefly as local films released in cinemas decreased to 42 percent but quickly recovered to gain around 52 percent of market share in 2011—corresponding to a similar trend concerning box office takings. In 2014, domestic films retained their place at 50 percent, showing continuing strength in the market.[4] By global standards the dominance of Korean film in its own domestic market is an extraordinary cultural achievement, shared with only a few other countries—notably France, India, and the United States. Underlying this momentum is government support (in the form of a proactive film policy) and increasing ticket sales from local audiences. In terms of policy, the effectiveness of the Screen Quota System cannot be underestimated, even though the quota was halved in 2006. Since 1966, the Screen Quota System has shielded the domestic market from an onslaught of Hollywood films by requiring all cinemas to screen local films for a minimum of 146 days per year (reduced to 73 days after July 2006—albeit on paper).[5]

Between 2000 and 2005 this high-quality local product flowed outward to global export markets, enabling aesthetically provocative filmmakers and their genre-bending films—whether commercial, art-house, or independent productions—to connect with international audiences both in commercial cinemas and at major film festivals. The total value of Korean film exports in 2005 was almost $76 million USD—185 times higher than in 1996.[6] During this period, Korean cinema reached unprecedented levels of exposure, a phenomenon that was well documented in headlines in international trade magazines such as *Variety* and *The Hollywood Reporter*. By 2000, commentators began noticing that Hollywood distributors were taking the Korean film industry seriously enough to release American films in Korea at times that would avoid serious competition from Korean blockbusters.[7] This trend, particularly following Korea's increasing ties with the Chinese film industry, is still in force in 2015. The Korean wave had indeed broken, but on Korean terms and in a Korean way. Henceforth, all the major film festivals—Berlin, Cannes, Hong Kong, Melbourne, Rotterdam, Tokyo, and Venice—could not get enough of Korean films, inviting the industry's latest productions and scheduling special retrospectives, which were sold out within minutes, thus generating further interest in contemporary Korean cinema. Simply put, over the past decade it has been Korea's turn in the global spotlight, just as the national cinemas of Japan, China/PRC, Taiwan/ROC and Hong Kong had done in the past. In 2005 the Korean film industry attained the zenith of its new golden age to become what has been previously dubbed "Planet Hallyuwood".[8]

In 2015, Korean cinema is one of the most successful non-Hollywood cinemas, reaching far beyond its national and regional borders. However, since 2006 new pressures have been challenging the international stature and future development of the Korean film industry, giving rise to multiple cycles of downturn and recovery and creating a degree of uncertainty and instability. The number of films exported has shrunk, too: in 2008, a total of 354 films were exported, but this figure slipped to 279 in 2009 (although still a much higher total than the 38 films exported in 2000).[9] More recently, this figure has risen again; in 2014 total film exports reached 529, thanks to increasing sales of classic films and short animations, helping boost sales figures to over $26 million USD.[10] Thus, in recent times the Korean film industry has been experiencing the ironic problem of increasing global popularity alongside decreasing profits, although the most recent statistics show that the imbalance between the two elements is diminishing.

Korean cinema has experienced remarkable success on the domestic front, as well. An increasing number of viewers have flocked to the hundreds of new multiplexes that have been built since 1998, offering a variety of both Korean and foreign films, as well as catering to growing audience numbers and their demands for a comfortable viewing experience. The number of cinemagoers occupying the 362,657 seats facing these screens has risen from 50 million in 1998 to more than 150 million today.[11] Since 2004 several domestic films have for the first time surpassed the 10 million audience mark, becoming known as mega-box office hits or *cheonman yeonghwa* (10 million audience films). They include: *Silmido* (2003), *Taegukgi* (2004), *King and the Clown* (2005), *The Host* (2006), *Haeundae* (2009), *Masquerade* (2012), *Thieves* (2012), *Miracle in Cell No. 7* (2013), *The Attorney* (2013), *Roaring Currents* (2014), *Ode to My Father* (2014), *Assassination* (2015), and *Veteran* (2015).[12] In 2006 the industry celebrated gaining 63.8 percent—almost two thirds—of domestic market share, sealing a golden age of commercial success.[13] From 2011, domestic films have consistently maintained over a 50 percent share of the local market: 51.9 percent in 2011; 58.8 percent in 2012; 59.7 percent in 2013; and 50.1 percent in 2014.[14]

With these contemporary developments in mind, the book is divided into three parts in order to illustrate how history repeats itself, for this is not the first time that Korean cinema has experienced a *belle époque* or golden age in terms of market expansion. In the 1960s Korea as a whole enjoyed such a period under the Park Chung Hee regime, a time in which every facet of the country's growth and sustainability was being challenged. With this economic context in mind, Part one investigates the complex interplay between important developments in the film industry, major players, and policy initiatives that had a major impact on Korean cinema in the 1960s.

Previous studies have emphasized the outstanding performance of the Korean film industry during the 1960s, paying tribute to an active and innovative enterprise.[15] During this time, Korea underwent a process of rapid industrialization and development, and Koreans were exposed to the phenomenon of mass entertainment for the first time. The large number of films produced in this decade reflected the relentless energy and creativity of domestic filmmakers. Yet, what is missing from most existing studies is close attention to how policy development, industrial conditions, and aesthetic factors were intimately connected, and how each one contributed to this golden age of cinema. Although previous research has provided extensive information on the development of Korea's national cinema in aesthetic terms, and how it developed a 'unique (or undefined) form and style',[16] what one may call the politico-economic perspective has hitherto been neglected.

Few of these previous studies—many of which have been stimulated by the success of Korea's contemporary film industry—have seriously examined the dynamic linkages created in the 1960s between national film policy, the industry system, directorial practices and genre development, and audience reception, as well as the significant impact that all these elements had on the transformation of Korean cinema. Seeking to redress this imbalance, the first four chapters examine the golden age of Korean cinema from 1961 to 1970 with a view to gaining a new understanding of its politico-economic background in an epoch of rapid industrialization. For the nation as a whole, this period is best known for the experience of "compressed modernity", which involved rapid and large-scale industrialization, as well as the gradual stimulation of international trade, or what is generally called "internationalization".[17] For the cinema, the period saw filmmakers struggling—and very often succeeding—under the constraints of this accelerated growth, producing an average of 164 films per year. It was also a time that saw the first post-liberation film policy, new modes of production, the rise of master directors and the formulation of new film genres.

Despite these remarkable changes, previous studies of the golden age of the 1960s have focused on industry development in terms of output and the aesthetic achievements of a small number of directors including Shin Sang-ok, Yu Hyun-mok and Kim Ki-young. The dynamic and complex nexus of film policy, producers, directors and genres in the 1960s, which all contributed to its status as a cinematic golden age, has yet to be fully explored.

Chapter Overviews

One of the central claims made in all four chapters in Part one is that the cinematic golden age of the 1960s was the outcome of a combination of state control and a protectionist film policy, on the one hand, and the new production system (embracing directorial practices, genres, and international collaborations) that resulted from these circumstances.

With these connections in mind, Chapter 1 investigates the complex interplay between film policy and production under authoritarian President Park Chung Hee, whose all-controlling regime forced film producers to develop a range of survival strategies. To set the context for this complex environment and the comprehensive industrialization of the local film industry, we analyze the long-term role that the National Film Production Center (NFPC) played in the creation of a "propaganda factory". Next, we investigate the operational strategies initiated by a small but powerful cartel of producers, including Shin Film, Hanguk Yesul, and Donga Heungeop and the alliances that they formed with a larger cohort of quasi-illicit independent producers. Together, this producers' cartel and their coalition of willing subcontractors attempted to replicate the vertical integration system employed by Hollywood—primarily operating from studios in Chungmuro in Seoul, the cultural and artistic heart of the film industry. Despite the practical and financial limitations placed on them by the government's Producer Registration System (hereafter PRS), and despite their ultimate failure due to lack of capital and a disorganized distribution system, this cartel of registered producers enabled Korean cinema to achieve a golden age of productivity.

To examine the impact of film policy (and politics) on feature film production, Chapter 1 presents a case study of Shin Sang-ok's *Rice* (1963) and his *The Red Scarf* (1964). A propaganda production, *Rice* praises a compassionate, newly formed military government (a thinly veiled portrayal of the regime) for assisting farmers to create a public irrigation system for their rice fields, thus saving villagers from famine. An archetypal political endorsement film because of the explicit ways it portrays Park Chung Hee's vision for developing and governing rural communities, *Rice* was used in Park's 1963 presidential election campaign. A different kind of propagandistic filmmaking is depicted in *The Red Scarf*, a large-scale anticommunist war film based on a radio drama about the Korean Air Force. *The Red Scarf* was made as a "Hollywood style" visual spectacle blockbuster and enjoyed the biggest budget of any Korean film to date. Shin Films used technical features new to the Korean cinema including aerial shots, speed camera, and wide-screen techniques, and the film was packed with big stars—all extolling the virtues of the government and its development of the Korean Air Force.

By examining this period from the politico-economic angle, Chapter 1 provides a more complex discussion of national cinema and its links to policy and the production side of the industry than has previously been achieved. In so doing, its findings present a stark contrast to the professionalized ways in which the film business is conducted in Korea today.

Chapter 2 builds on the PRS story by focusing on the contribution that directors made to the film industry during its rapid industrialization in the 1960s. Specifically, we focus on Yu Hyun-mok (1925–2009), one of Korea's leading arthouse filmmakers and auteurs, and the strategies that he used to negotiate the challenges presented by a permanent political power struggle. We illustrate how Yu was able to do more than simply survive under duress. Whilst fellow directors Lee Man-hee and Shin Sang-ok achieved their reputations largely as commercial practitioners working in popular genres such as melodrama, war (action) films, and historical drama, Yu was one of a handful of filmmakers who established and then sustained a reputation as an arthouse filmmaker. He developed a unique stylistic repertoire while at the same time rejecting the lure of propaganda and commercial films in a hostile political environment (at least until the 1970s). Two of Yu's best-known films, *Aimless Bullet* (1961, aka *Obaltan*) and *The Empty Dream* (1965), are analyzed, showing how he developed a particular style that blended realist, expressionist and modernist elements, thus bringing a fresh face to Korean cinema. In addition, Yu's distinguished career shows how the Western auteur theory of film could be successfully adapted to a Korean context.

As a native Korean filmmaker who had survived the Japanese colonial period and the turmoil of the Korean War, Yu not only felt a patriotic obligation to reflect Korean culture onscreen, he was also dedicated to exploring the full limits of his chosen art form and his own creativity.[18] Responsible for directing a total of 45 films over a 40-year career, Yu believed that retaining control over both the directing and editing processes would help cement his status as an auteur filmmaker. By the time he had finished editing *The Empty Dream*, the fifth film that he both directed and edited, Yu had already established a reputation as one of Korean cinema's quintessential auteurs. Watching *The Empty Dream* today puts the viewer in mind of early French surrealism and German expressionism (in film and art), notable features of Yu's work that are especially evident in his masterpiece *Aimless Bullet* (1961). However, in *The Empty Dream* his exploration of these European avant-garde movements is even more pronounced than in his previous films. To the informed viewer, the most impressive aspects of this film are Yu's innovative blending of sound with montage and the surrealist-inspired production design. *The Empty Dream* remains one of Korean cinema's few feature-length experimental films that still feels ahead of its time today.

Chapter 3 explores the origins of the hybrid genre filmmaking traditions that have become a hallmark of Korean cinema. In particular, we examine the literary films that experienced a boom in the late 1960s. Influenced by the work of writers, and mindful of the social, economic, and cultural changes brought about by industrialization, directors began adapting novels for the screen as a way of offering their own critique of Korea's rapidly transforming society. This chapter shows how literary adaptation was used by both producers and directors as a vehicle for creating officially endorsed "cultural propaganda". The three feature films analyzed here—*Deaf Samryong* (1964), *Seaside Village* (1965), and *Mist* (1967)—promoted cultural nationalism, localized traditionalism, and depicted aspects of modernity, respectively.

After the Japanese colonial period ended in 1945, cultural nationalism became the cornerstone of Korea's cultural policy aimed at rehabilitating the nation's identity and heritage. *Deaf Samryong* was made as a showcase film, an attempt at visualizing Korean cultural identity on screen. Similarly, the "festival film" *Seaside Village* (1965) was used as a vehicle for promoting the notion of traditionalism—a quintessential "Koreanness" that represented customary ways of thinking and traditional values and sentiments. Finally, filmmakers also used the literary film and its sub-genres to explore issues of modernity, placing contemporary Korean society under the spotlight, a nation undergoing rapid industrialization and Westernization (aka "Americanization"). In its attempt to portray the bewilderment experienced by ordinary people living on the cusp of rapid and complex changes, *Mist* distinguished itself from other types of cultural propaganda films. As this chapter demonstrates, the literary genre provided Korean filmmakers with creative spaces in which to promote the nation's distinctive culture and traditions under the guise of "soft" propaganda, thus distancing their productions from the overt propaganda of government-backed anticommunist films.

To conclude our investigation of the 1960s, Chapter 4 underscores some of the pioneering interchanges involving Korea and Hong Kong and Korea and Japan that have had a major impact on their respective film industries. Our focus on a range of Korea–Hong Kong co-productions involving the Shaw Brothers, as well as Korean remakes of Japanese films, illustrates the internationalization strategies that filmmakers pursued not only to survive, but also to expand their personal and industry networks and indeed to change the fundamental identity and direction of Korean cinema. The filmmakers and films discussed here were influenced by a range of film types and genres—Hong Kong martial arts films, Italian/Spanish spaghetti Westerns and 007 James Bond action films, which were all popular with Korean audiences throughout the 1960s. These foreign genres were favored by registered producers-cum-importers as well as exhibitors because they consistently made heftier profits than domestic films—not to mention that foreign films contained superior story lines and aesthetic values compared to most domestic films.

To compensate for the falling profitability of domestic films, both registered and independent producers desperately (and creatively) strove to meet film policy requirements that rewarded them with import licenses for foreign films, enabling them to use the resulting box office profits to keep their companies afloat. However, given the strict policy environment at the time, this was easier said than done. To assist with meeting their production quotas, Korean producers supplemented their official collaborations with Hong Kong colleagues—such as the historical epic *The Last Woman of Shang* (1964)—with fake co-productions like *Monkey Goes West* (1966). At a time when Japanese cultural products were banned in Korea, producers also remade Japanese films, either by blatantly copying story lines or producing near-replicas of the originals. Our case study of director Kim Ki-duk's "youth film" *Barefoot Youth* (1964)—a copy of Japanese filmmaker Kō Nakahira's *Dorodarake no junjō* (1963)—illustrates how the local industry became embroiled in controversy surrounding the so-called plagiarism of Japanese films. Our concluding discussion shows how these interconnected activities contributed to the transformation of Korean cinema in both conspicuous and inconspicuous ways while strengthening strategic alliances with colleagues in Hong Kong and Japan, the two most active centers of the Asian film industry during this period.

Part II focuses on the interlude between the so-called golden age of the 1960s and the systematization of the film industry after 1992 by exploring the factors that brought about Korean cinema's "dark age", as well as its recovery between 1970 and the late 1980s. The three chapters in this section offer insights into the challenges that producers, directors, and policymakers faced during the most volatile period of Park Chung Hee's authoritarian rule and the military government of Chun Doo-hwan that followed. Case studies of the most popular commercial and art-house genre films made during this period are used to trace the strategies employed by these key players to survive the industry's longest downturn following its rise in the early 1960s, as well as the creative and cultural transformation of Korean cinema during this period.

Chapter 5 explores some of the key linkages between state policy and film production during the 1970s and 1980s and their effect on Korean cinema. Throughout both decades, the Motion Picture Law (hereafter MPL) was the government's chief tool for influencing and directing the domestic film industry, primarily through the PRS and censorship policy, supplemented by the Screen Quota System. Yet, while the national anticommunist agenda underlying the MPL under the Park Chung Hee and Chun Doo-hwan administrations had a great impact on domestic filmmaking, so too did the rapid growth in foreign films exhibited across the nation, making Korea an attractive market for Hollywood film distributors.

Against this background, we discuss the often fierce clashes between the MPL-backed cartel members of the Korean Motion Pictures Producers Association (KMPPA) and other industry leaders in the Korean Motion Picture Promotion Corporation (KMPPC, later the Korean Film Council [KOFIC]) with the US Motion Picture Export Association (MPEA, now known as the MPAA). The KMPPA and KMPPC proactively managed the balance between the domestic production of large-scale national policy films—such as *The Testimony* (1974), directed by Im Kwon-taek—and the influx of foreign films that the Screen Quota System effectively failed to block. Together, but not always in agreement, these two bodies shaped the complex environment in which the domestic film industry developed by devising means of limiting the economic and cultural impact of foreign films sourced principally from Hollywood. The story of how the government and the film industry struggled to overcome the effects of the market recession, widen the export market for films and promote national policy films to domestic audiences—while resisting encroachment by Hollywood—offers a pointed commentary on Korea's often painful experience of industrialization and aspects of globalization that accompanied the country's emergence as a major industrial and trading nation.

Chapter 6 shows how a new breed of directors challenged Korea's complex political and industrial system, a challenge that peaked after Park Chung Hee's government established the *Yushin* system in 1973. Although most filmmakers came under increasing pressure to make propaganda films for the government after 1973, a small group including director Lee Jang-ho sought outlets for their creativity through stylistic choices and by enlivening—perhaps subverting—their politically correct narratives with sexualized content and social realism. By way of contrast to the KMPPC's "national policy" films discussed in Chapter 5, Lee's films—*Heavenly Homecoming to Stars* (1974) and *Good Windy Day* (1980)—illustrate how his aesthetic choices and visual experimentation enabled him to speak for his generation and influence those who followed in his footsteps. Whereas the first film is one of Korea's earliest erotic "hostess" films, *Good Windy Day* depicts society's dark underbelly, a casualty of rapid social and cultural transformation. Both films represent Lee's relatively successful attempts to break free from the unfavorable conditions created by the MPL, a sterile and utilitarian production environment. In this way, Lee and the other directors discussed in this chapter formed part of a new generation of artists and filmmakers who opened up alternative pathways at a time when most filmmakers had lost their way as a result of economic and industry pressures.

Part II of the book concludes with sexploitation. That is, Chapter 7 demonstrates how filmmakers transformed the popular melodrama genre and attracted audiences away from their recently acquired home television sets back to the cinema through the inclusion of daring sexual content. In taking this approach, we throw new light on the so-called golden age of melodrama that began in the mid-1950s and continued unabated throughout the 1960s, 1970s, and 1980s, while also focusing on the key narrative conventions found in melodrama, the most prolific genre in Korean cinema. We explain how the "hostess" melodrama subgenre of the 1970s and the "erotic" (aka "ero") melodrama subgenre of the 1980s—more sexually explicit than hostess films—distracted audiences, filmmakers, and policymakers from their oppressive political environment while at the same time creating a cathartic—albeit misogynistic—release from the social pressures resulting from rapid industrialization. In short, our analysis of these two kinds of melodrama reveals fissures and ironies in the censorship process years before government censorship of films was rescinded in 1996.

Finally, Part III shows how the 1990s began with a sense of liberation and democratization after Kim Young-sam won the presidential election at the end of 1992. The domestic film industry began to transform itself in unforeseen ways through the business strategies employed by the entertainment arms of the Samsung and Daewoo *chaebols* or family-run conglomerates. However, the Asian financial crisis of 1997 and Korea's subsequent IMF bailout changed everything—particularly after Samsung and Daewoo restructured by selling off their entertainment divisions. Ironically, this pivotal moment occurred shortly after the successful release of the action–fantasy–romance *Ginkgo Bed* (1996) and the love story *The Contact* (1997)—and, of course, after *Shiri* had broken all records and far exceeded expectations at the box office.

Chapter 8 investigates the multiple waves of new producers and production companies that entered the film industry from the early 1990s and began contributing to the transformation not only of local industry practices, but of the very core of Korean cinema. Throughout the 1990s, but increasingly in the later half of the decade, *chaebols* such as Samsung and Daewoo began vertically integrating their entertainment arms across investment, production, and distribution channels, employing the kind of cost and market-control strategies for which Hollywood studios were well known in the 1930s. This changing environment saw the emergence of a fresh cohort of producers with aspirations to professionalize and diversify Korean cinema. The domestic film industry was fundamentally remodeled through the zeal and business acumen shown by this group of relatively young professionals as well as by the explosion in numbers of multiplex screens, which was happening around the same time. The result was the emergence of a generation of new directors, stars, and others engaged in all aspects of the newly industrialized filmmaking process. A virtuous circle was set in motion, enabling Korean cinema to achieve a renaissance comparable with the golden age of the 1960s.

Today, CJ E&M, Showbox, Lotte Cinema, and N.E.W. are the "big four" corporate (and dominant) players in the industry. Yet, as we discuss, a smaller group of previously unheralded female producers and their production companies are challenging the hegemony of these larger firms while developing new methods of collaborating with them in order to maintain the quality and creativity of domestic films. Chapter 8 addresses the rise of powerful female producers including Shim Jae-myung, Shim Bo-kyoung, Oh Jung-wan, Kim Mi-hee, Lee Eugene, and Ahn Soo-hyun and illustrate how these talented filmmakers began attracting attention from outside Korea in the 2000s. Together, and along with their male counterparts, the women discussed in this part of the book have played a significant role in Korean cinema's transformation from an industry suffocated by government censorship and dominated by foreign productions into a powerful and innovative vehicle for showcasing popular Korean culture and media to the world. Despite the continual relative neglect of their contributions—by producing arthouse successes as well as mainstream commercial hits, women producers have remained at the core of the domestic industry—often showing a willingness to work with new directors because they believe in them and their stories rather than solely in their potential commercial success. Their energy, vision, and dedication to exploring fresh stories and developing new talent has drawn local and global audiences alike to a constantly innovating national cinema that continues to expand along transnational lines.

Chapter 9 builds on this discussion of powerful female producers by showing how a number of female *directors* have made longstanding contributions to Korea's tradition of writer–directors—another ingredient that has contributed to the renaissance of Korean cinema. Despite the attention lavished on male "commercial auteurs", and despite the fact that most previous studies have failed to celebrate them, independent and commercial female writer–directors such as Lee Jeong-hyang, Byun Young-joo, Park Chan-ok, Lee Soo-yeon, Hong Ji-young, and Roh Deok have succeeded by building on the foundations laid by a small cohort of women filmmakers who preceded them. Our discussion of some of their films, including Park Chan-ok's *Paju* (2009) and Hong Ji-young's *The Naked Kitchen* (2009), shows how each filmmaker has contributed in her own special way to the changing face of Korean cinema and in so doing has issued a strong challenge to the gendered nature of the industry. Although not all of their films discussed in this chapter have been commercial successes, their invitation to audiences to reflect on and critique the dynamics of interpersonal relationships in Korean society—and, more specifically, the impact of traditional Confucian ideals on contemporary gender relations—makes them a source of inspiration for aspiring domestic filmmakers, regardless of gender. In short, the filmmakers discussed in this chapter have played a major part in rejuvenating and energizing the domestic film industry by introducing a range of stories that offer diverse representations of contemporary Korean life.

In Chapter 10, we focus on three contemporary feature films representing a variety of genres and genre traditions that have shone the global spotlight on Korean cinema. Together, *Mother* (2009), *Late Autumn* (2010), and *The Attorney*

(2013) illustrate the ways in which Korean cinema has succeeded in integrating both real-life and fictionalized story elements that stem from the nation's experience of accelerated development—or "compressed modernity" – that began in the 1960s. As one might expect, Korean filmmakers have frequently used their nation's "civilizational condition" as the backdrop for stories that transgress traditional genre boundaries. Although *Mother*, *Late Autumn*, and *The Attorney* represent different genres, the pathways taken by the main characters—inhabiting the fringes of contemporary society where moral ambiguities upset socially constructed boundaries of right and wrong—reveal a shared philosophical outlook. With this in mind, our analyses of these three representative genre films are presented as a guide to understanding contemporary Korean cinema from perspectives that have received little attention in previous studies, while revealing how these films push the boundaries of genre filmmaking in "glocal" ways.

The final chapter, Chapter 11, explores the previously understudied interactions of Korean film practitioners in and with Chinese colleagues and firms and investigate how these bilateral ventures are both feeding off and assisting the expansion of Korea's "soft power"—the export of Korean media and cultural products, also known as *Hallyu*. To shed more light on this important and growing trend in transnational filmmaking, we investigate the influential personal networks (aka *guanxi*) formed by a handful of aspiring Korean filmmakers while studying at the Beijing Film Academy during the early to mid-1990s. The contacts, friendships, and professional inroads made by these now major industry players have directly facilitated the increasing levels of co-operation in co-productions and post-production work that have marked collaboration between Korea and China in this area since the mid-2000s. The surge in personnel exchange, technological transfer, and overall co-operation between the two nations has unfolded on multiple levels, bringing together producers, directors, and actors as well as action, visual effects and post-production specialists and cinematographers on an unprecedented scale. Two aesthetically ambitious Chinese feature films, *Double Xposure* (2012) and *Blind Massage* (2014), are examined as quintessential examples of an evolving transnational cinema that is being created by a range of Korean and Chinese practitioners drawn from every corner of their respective industries. In turn, as we show, Koreans have contributed to the expansion of Chinese cinema in terms of the refinement of genres, themes, and story lines, as well as technical expertise, while Chinese film companies have enabled Korean cinema to increasingly internationalize its approach to overseas markets.

The book concludes by considering the complex circumstances of a national film industry attempting to do more than simply survive difficult times and overcome threats to freedom of expression, as well as the menace of piracy, illegal downloads, and intimidation by Hollywood's global market dominance. As the 11 chapters in this book demonstrate, the unfolding history of the Korean film industry has made it a "cinema of perseverance", one that has weathered complex political, economic, social, and cultural hardships, as well as the friction caused by conflicting interests and the risks involved in the forging of new opportunities.

While some areas have been well covered by previous scholars and critics, more detailed examination of Korean cinema between the 1960s and the 2010s is key to understanding the accelerated development experienced by Korea on its rocky path to full democracy. Without its persevering pioneers, the Korean cinema of the 1960s would not have been possible, nor would the so-called New Korean Cinema have flourished if filmmakers and policymakers had failed to challenge Hollywood's hegemony before and after the government eliminated censorship in 1996. Hence, the last five decades of Korean cinema should be appreciated not only for their aesthetic achievements, but also for the cultural and technical expertise that has created a burgeoning national cinema that has survived authoritarian, military—even democratic—administrations and their often hostile attitudes to the domestic film industry.

Methodology and Sources

In writing this book, we have utilized a variety of research methods including the collection and analysis of archive and library materials, as well as painstaking searches through decades of articles in the trade and popular press, industry press releases, and film annuals such as *Korean Cinema* (published by KOFIC) and the *International Motion Picture Almanac* (Quigley Publishing Company). This heterogeneous collection of materials has enabled us to achieve the dual purpose of "getting the story" while also understanding the ways in which "the story" has been shaped by domestic and international voices and perspectives that have changed over time. In other words, we have immersed ourselves in the historiography of Korean cinema while also contributing to the writing of its history. Having said that, the present manuscript is a companion to our first book: *Korea's Occupied Cinemas, 1893–1948* (2011).

Between 2000 and 2015, secondary source research and completed annual field research trips to Korea were conducted in order to carry out semi-structured industry interviews and participant observation at three major film festivals (Busan International Film Festival, Seoul International Women's Film Festival, and Bucheon International Fantastic Film Festival). Whilst in Korea, we also examined rare Korean-language archival film industry materials and films in institutions such as the National Assembly Library, Korean National Library, Yonsei University Library, Korean Film Council Library, Korean Film Archive, and National Archives of Korea (NAK) in Daejeon. Government documents held at the NAK reveal the Ministry of Public Information's (MPI) approach to film policy, showing that there were heated discussions over the MPL between the government and the film industry. In addition, editorials, news articles, reviews and advertisements in newspapers, as well as film magazines, were examined to gain a better understanding of how industry issues were discussed and how particular films were marketed and reviewed by the press. These journals include: *Chosun Daily*, *Donga Daily*, *Gyeonghyang Shinmun*, *Yeonghwa Japji* (*Movie Magazine*), *Yeonghwa Segye* (*Cinema World*), *Silver Screen*, *Shin Yeonghwa* (*New Films*), and *Yeonghwa TV Yesul* (*Film TV Art*). Nor was the secondary literature neglected;

journal articles and books in both English and Korean on Korean cinema, albeit few in number (but slowly expanding since we began writing many years ago), helped to broaden the scope of our analysis. Finally, viewing some of the most important genre films of the 1960s at the Korean Film Archive and also at the Busan International Film Festival was an important part of our research, revealing the distinctive aesthetics developed by individual directors as well as a range of international influences.

In addition, the book utilizes two qualitative forms of data collection: the semi-structured interview and (film) content analysis. Although these two approaches might be expected to produce very different—even incommensurate—data, they were specifically chosen as an illuminating and economical way of linking the reflections and experiences of representative directors, producers, and other practitioners from all sides of the film industry to a detailed consideration of their work. When put together, the two approaches offer deeper (and sometimes contrasting) insights into the filmmaking process than could be gleaned from articles in the trade and popular press alone—not just as responses to the various policy regimes that have shaped the film industry, but also in terms of the broader social setting.

We are grateful to the industry experts, scholars, researchers, directors, producers and other practitioners with whom we spoke informally or interviewed for this study—in Korea, China, Australia, and the US. While this approach was time consuming, and while it was often a challenge to collect accurate information given that people's memories fade and change over time (so that information gleaned from interviews had to be independently verified), their first-hand experience and diverse perspectives produced a rich understanding of the industry during this period in all its facets. Im Kwon-taek, Lee Hyeong-pyo, An Cheol-hyeon and Im Won-sik, who all began directing films in the 1960s, shared their invaluable knowledge of the production environment. Lee Jang-ho, a representative director from the 1970s and 1980s, shared his memories of working as an assistant director at Shin Film in the 1960s. Park Kwang-su, a well-known Korean New Wave director during the 1980s and the director of the Busan Film Commission, shared his personal views on the development of the industry.

Interviews with producers and policymakers elicited commentary on Korean cinema from the politico-economic viewpoint. Lee Woo-seok, the CEO of Donga Export Co. and a registered producer during the 1960s and 1970s, testified to the chaotic business conditions of the time. Kim In-gi and Hwang Nam, who both worked for registered production companies in the 1960s, spoke of the similar chaos surrounding the production process. Yu In-taek, today a producer with Kihoik Sidae, shared his analysis of the film industry environment of the 1960s. Interviews with policy experts such as Kim Hyae-joon, Kim Mee-hyeon, and Kim Hyeon-jung from KOFIC and Kim Tae-hoon from the Ministry of Culture and Tourism confirmed the significant role that film policy played in the process of industry development. Multiple discussions were also held with film scholars such as Kim Soyoung, Byon In-sik, and Yi Hyoin and researchers at the Korean Film Archive including Chung Chong-hwa and Cho Jun-hyeong. Other interviewees from a range of backgrounds included former BIFF Festival director Kim Dong-ho; a former MPEA representative in Korea, Cha Yun; screenwriters Baek Gyeol and Kim Ji-heon; and Seoul Cinema Complex owner Kwak Jeong-hwan. They shared their considered views and insights on the industry's evolution in the 1960s—invaluable information not available in either Korean or English-language published sources. Taken together, this unique body of information supplements, expands on, and sometimes calls into question interpretations of the period found in published materials.

Finally, a series of interviews was conducted with four prominent women active in the Korean film industry: writer–directors Byon Young-joo and Hong Ji-young; producer Kim Ji-yeon; and Chae Yoon-hee (aka Uni Chai), chairperson of the 600-plus-member Women in Film Korea industry group and president and CEO of All That Cinema, Korea's longest-running film publicity and marketing firm. This material was supplemented by interviews with other leading women filmmakers published in the leading Korean film magazine *Cine21* and three international trade publications, *Variety, The Hollywood Reporter*, and *Film Business Asia*, as well as a personal interview with a third writer–director, Lee Soo-yeon, conducted in 2003 following the screening of her debut feature film *The Uninvited*. Although a small cohort, we believe that the thoughts and feelings they expressed are representative of many female industry practitioners.

Special thanks go to directors John Woo, Kim Jee-woon, and Lee Myung-se, producers (Edward) Yi Chi-yun and Chloe Park, actor Song Kang-ho, Kevin Chang (Association of Film Commissioners International, AFCI), Darcy Paquet (*Koreanfilm.org*), Stephen Cremin (www.filmbiz.asia), Mark Russell (a writer for *The Hollywood Reporter*), former Megabox distribution manager Jang Kyung-ik, now president of Film Business at N.E.W., and Lee Ji-hyun. Finally, numerous post-production practitioners currently working in or with China, including Lee Yong-gi (HFR, Lollol Media), Ethan Park (HFR, Lollol Media, Forestt Studios), Chen Pei Yu (Tsui Hark's company), Peter Ahn (SK Independence, Dexter Digital Studios), Chuck Chae (Dexter Digital Studios), Lee Soo Kyung and Erin Kim (Digital Idea), Lee Se Hoon (MonEFF), and Zenith Seo, Kim Kimoon, and Shin Sangho (Digital Studio 2L), shared their experiences of working on Korean–Chinese collaborative projects—ventures that until now have gone largely unrecognized. Lastly, we are grateful for the long-term friendships with (and mentoring received from) colleagues Ben Goldsmith, Michael Keane, Roald Maliangkay, Tom O'Regan, Chang Kyung-Sup (Sociology, Seoul National University), Noh Kyung-hee, and Vivi Fan (Communication University of China).

For the romanizing of Korean words and names, the book generally follows the Korean government's Revised Romanization System, except where an alternative system was already established, such as for the term *chaebol*, the names of presidents Syngman Rhee and Park Chung Hee, director Im Kwon-taek and other film people whose names have been popularized through the Internet Movie Database (IMDB) or KOFIC publications. When referring to personal names, including those of directors, scholars and other industry practitioners, the family name usually precedes the given name, following established convention. All translations into English from Korean materials and interviews are our own work. The titles of Korean films and box office figures used in this book are sourced from the Korean Movie Database and maintained by the Korean Film Archive, as well as from other authoritative online sources such as *Box Office Mojo* and *EntGroup.cn*.

By combining and analyzing the information and insights gleaned from these rich and diverse sources in both Korean and English and drawn from many different countries, we hope to offer readers a new understanding of the complex development of Korean cinema during the "golden age" of the 1960s, the "dark age" of the 1970s, the rapid development of the industry during the 1980s and 1990s, all the way to the present day, which is witnessing a new golden age of Korean cinema.

Notes

1. See, for example, the chapters in Shin and Stringer 2005.
2. Before 1996, all domestic film scripts needed to be approved at the pre-production stage and all foreign films had to be examined by the Performance Ethics Committee, which had maintained these powers since its formation in the late 1970s.
3. *Korean Cinema 2000*: 265; *Korean Cinema 2006*: 495.
4. *Korean Cinema* 2014: 31.
5. In July 2006, the Screen Quota System was reduced by half as part of discussions over a free-trade agreement with the US—the result of four decades of relentless pressure from the Motion Picture Association of America.
6. *Korean Cinema 2004*: 297; *Korean Cinema 2009*: 42.
7. For example, see Segers, Frank. "Seoul Train: S. Korea Drives World Cinema". *The Hollywood Reporter* (April 18–24, 2000): 14–16.
8. For a more detailed discussion of "Planet Hallyuwood", see Yecies 2008.
9. *Korean Cinema 2009*: 42; *Korean Cinema 2004*: 297.
10. KOFIC. "2014 Korean Film Industry Overview (Hanguk Yeonghwa Saeop Gyeolsan)". KOFIC, 2015: 46. Although export sales figures from 2013 ($37 million USD) exceeded those of 2014, this can be explained by the sales generated by the locally produced international blockbuster *Snowpiercer* (2013).
11. Although the number of cinemas declined from 507 in 1998 to 309 in 2008, the number of screens rose from 507 in 1998 to just over 2,000 in 2010. See *Korean Cinema 2009*: 37–45.
12. At the moment of writing, only four foreign films have reached this mark: *Avatar* (2010), *Frozen* (2013), *Interstellar* (2014), and *Avengers 2* (2015).
13. See KOFIC 2007: 495; *Korean Cinema 2000*: 265; *Korean Cinema 2006*: 495.
14. *Korean Cinema* 2014: 31.
15. For instance, see Ho 2000; Min et al. 2003; Lee 2004; McHugh and Abelmann 2005; Park 2005; Yi, Jung and Park 2005.
16. Yi 2005: 148.
17. For more on this concept, see Chang 1998; Chang 1999.
18. Personal interview with Yu Hyun-mok, Busan, October 2005.

Part I

The Golden Age of the 1960s

1 Hypergrowth of the Propaganda Factory and the Producing Paradox

The material discussed in this chapter presents a stark contrast to the organized way in which the film business is conducted in Korea today. To develop a fuller understanding of the development of Korean cinema during the 1960s, it investigates the complex interplay between film policy and production under authoritarian President Park Chung Hee, whose all-controlling regime forced film producers to develop a range of survival strategies. A small but powerful cartel of producers, represented by leading filmmaker Shin Sang-ok—revered and reviled in equal measure—formed alliances with a larger cohort of quasi-illegal independent producers, thus—against all the odds—enabling Korean cinema to achieve a golden age of productivity. By examining this early golden age of Korean cinema from a political–economic angle, this chapter provides a more complex discussion of national cinema and its links to policy and the production side of the industry than has previously been achieved. One of the central claims of this study is that the golden age of the 1960s was the outcome of a combination of state control and a protectionist film policy and the new production system that resulted from these circumstances.

With the increasing power of the corporate producers in the contemporary Korean cinema in mind, this chapter focuses on a very different but pivotal period when a range of dynamic production strategies—including creative responses by filmmakers to government policy—contributed to an industry "boom" in the 1960s, the like of which was not to be seen again until the 2000s. This was a period when Korea experienced rapid progress in industrialization and policy development, as well as in the production of entertainment for the masses. A large number of productions that stemmed from a seemingly limitless store of creative energy placed a coterie of passionate filmmakers and their artistic achievements under the spotlight—all while facing the numerous challenges forced upon them under the Park Chung Hee government's national industrialization policy.

On 16 May 1961, General Park Chung Hee led a military coup and successfully seized control of South Korea. Within the first few months of its abrupt rise to power, his military government succeeded in systematizing its near-total administrative control over all film production, distribution (including both importing and exporting), and exhibition. This process began with the creation of the Ministry of Public Information (MPI) on 20 May 1961, the National Film Production Centre

(NFPC) on 22 June 1961, and the passing of the Motion Picture Law (MPL) on 20 January 1962. The MPI was tasked with the role of administering the NFPC and the MPL, which was modified significantly in 1963 and again in 1966 (see Table 1.1) and with coordinating all film, print, and radio broadcasting media campaigns on behalf of the government.

Almost overnight, the domestic film industry, which had been experiencing a new-found creativity since the end of Japanese colonial rule (1910–1945), turning out accomplished art films such as Yu Hyun-mok's *Obaltan/Aimless Bullet* (1961, discussed in the next chapter), was reduced to the status of a propaganda factory in which all productions were classified as either "hard" or "soft" propaganda.

Building a Propaganda Factory

The establishment of the National Film Production Center (NFPC) in June 1961 was part of this initiative. While the full story of the NFPC is yet to be told, suffice it to say that its goal was to produce newsreels as well as documentary and narrative "cultural" films containing specific political messages. It distributed these materials through commercial cinemas and community screening services. The NFPC was the nation's official propaganda generator, demonstrating the resources available to the government by producing newsreels and cultural films that were intended to supplement the domestic film industry.[1] While the NFPC produced overt hard propaganda, the rest of the film industry was expected to produce soft or subtle propaganda.

An analysis of *May 16 Revolution and Changed Society* (1961), one of the earliest NFPC cultural films made after the coup, illustrates just how directly these types of films were aimed at the public. This 31-minute black-and-white film starts with a montage of a rising sun, a parade of military trucks and soldiers and a phone ringing with the news of a baby born on the morning of 16 May 1961. The image of a new beginning is created through these connecting images, and Mr. Park, the protagonist of the film, explains the special meaning of this day. The film's purpose is to promote the 'revolution', which had promised to bring micro-changes to Korean society and macro-changes for individuals such as the Park family and their newborn baby. A scene showing Park holding the baby in his arms dissolves to a busy street scene, with people rushing to school and work. Finally, the film summarizes the new government's social policies and achievements; the happiness it has so clearly brought to the Park family makes life worth living in this brave new society.

May 16 Revolution interweaves Mr. Park's personal challenges with the government's economic and social policies. Thus his troubled business receives help from the newly established Industrial Bank of Korea, which we are told aims to support small-to-medium-sized enterprises. An explanation follows about the government's housing and unemployment policies. Park's brother, a wounded Korean War veteran, is shown getting a job at the Seoul Train Station with support from the Office of Veterans Administration. Park's father, a farmer, comes to Seoul by train and shares the news of a good harvest while praising his enjoyable and convenient train ride. At dinner, the family praises the revolution after listening to radio news about the new government's national reconstruction plan. They determine to do whatever they can to help build a new Korea. Assuring audiences that the government was making good progress on the nation's economic development and national security, "cultural" films of this type were produced throughout the early 1960s.[2]

While the productions of the NFPC represent hard propaganda, Shin's *Rice* and *The Red Scarf* fall squarely into the soft propaganda category. These and many other films of the period were to become key tools in what one critic has described as "campaigns of assault" and "campaigns of assistance", respectively.[3] The regime achieved these aims first by showing its power over the industry. It forcibly consolidated the number of feature film production companies from 76 to 16 in 1961 and then launched a major new initiative in the shape of the Motion Picture Law (MPL).

The MPL guided the production of propaganda feature films with a heavy hand. The MPL conveniently adopted the oppressive contents of the colonial-era Chosun Film Law including production control, the import quota system, script censorship and the producer registration scheme introduced in 1941 by the Japanese colonial government in Korea, applying them on a wide scale as a means to control Korea's burgeoning film industry.[4] This array of controls suggested that the government's ultimate intention was to construct a studio system that operated in similar ways to Hollywood studios, but with an authoritarian twist.

In January 1962, the military government promulgated its first film policy through the MPL, imposing 22 wide-ranging measures relating to censorship fees, screening permits, producer registration and importing, exporting, and exhibiting films. These measures applied to the entire Korean film industry, with heavy fines or imprisonment for non-compliance. The MPL comprised three main components: the Producer Registration System (hereafter PRS), import regulations and censorship guidelines. Relentless enforcement of these three elements enabled the MPI to gain effective control over the domestic film industry, dictating the genres and stories that the government wanted producers to develop by means of a system of "carrots on sticks". Throughout the 1960s, the government refreshed this "incentive program" by releasing a series of film policy amendments through this hierarchical legislative framework (see Table 1.1).

Through the PRS, the government compelled all producers, including those not subject to the forced consolidation of 1961 and others interested in joining this group, to register with the MPI. According to the MPL, each applicant for registration had to meet the specific criteria for the film equipment and experienced personnel identified in Table 1.1. These relatively liberal requirements enabled all 16 of the consolidated producers, plus an additional five that also met the criteria, to register under the new system.

However, in 1963 amendments to the MPL introduced stricter criteria, making it tougher for Korea's 21 existing producers to maintain their registration status. Each registered producer was now obligated to operate a permanent studio equipped with multiple cameras, lighting kits and a sound recorder. Contracts

Table 1.1 Summary of Changes to the MPL in the 1960s

Policy	1962	1963	1966
PRS	**Introduction** of registration requirements: • 1 x 35mm camera • 50 KW lighting kits • contracts with 1 engineer and 2 actors	1) **Reinforcement** of stricter registration requirements: • 3 x 35mm cameras • 200 KW lighting kits • 7,100 sq. feet studio • 1 simultaneous recording machine • contracts with 3 directors; 10 actors/actresses; 3 cinematographers; and 1 recording engineer • Mandatory annual production quota of 15 films for each company 2) Increased privileges: Merge of import/export under production	1) **Relaxation** of registration requirements: • 1 camera • 1 lighting kit • 1 studiocontracts with staff no longer necessaryMandatory annual production quota of 2 films for each company 2) *Daemyeong* banned
Censorship	**Inauguration:** 1) Pre-production stage: • Pre-production approval 2) Post-production stage: • Final product screening • Screening suspension	**Involvement of the Prosecutor's Office:** 1) Attendance at final product censorship 2) Application of anticommunist/obscenity laws	**Censorship Reinforcement:** 1) Pre-production stage • Pre-production approval • Script censorship 2) Production stage • Production suspension 3) Post-production stage • Final product/preview screening for screening permit • Screening suspension
Import Policy	**Launch of the Import Recommendation System**	**Launch of the Import License Reward System (ILRS)** Licenses awarded by 1) production results 2) export results 3) international film festival awards 4) quality film awards	**Modification of ILRS:** 1) Removal of production results 2) Addition of co-production results
NFPC's Films	Double bill screenings of cultural/feature films	Triple bill screenings of newsreels/cultural/feature films	
Screen Quota System			Launch of the law requiring a maximum of 1/3 of all films screened at cinemas should be domestic films

with a range of staff were also mandatory, which in turn gave registered producers control over production crews. Additionally, each company was required to maintain a rigorous production schedule of 15 films per year and to engage in the import and export of films (see Table 1.2).

Table 1.2 Number of Registered Film Companies as Mandated by the MPL (1961–1970)

Year	1961	1962	1963	1964	1965	1966	1967	1968	1969	1970
No.	65 merged to 16	16	21 merged to 6	10	19	26	25 merged to 12	17	19	23

Source: KMPPC 1977: 48.

This forced merger between its production and distribution arms consolidated the industry even further, an important development in view of the government's attempt to establish vertical integration within the system. While the PRS was born in 1962, it was at least another year before it established its position as the core mechanism for governing Korea's domestic film industry over the next two decades. Almost overnight, a "studio system" resembling a factory assembly line had been born. Korea now had six major film companies—a cartel—that suddenly found themselves in possession of exclusive privileges. The financial power and godlike authority of those in the inner circle increased over time as they became ensconced at the heart of all industry activities.

There were three types of registered (i.e., authorized) producers operating during the 1960s: producers in the traditional sense, producers with an importing background and short-term producers. Those in the first group, such as Shin Film, Geukdong Heungeop, Hapdong, Taechang, and Hanyang, followed the original prescription of the PRS to the letter, treating production as their primary business and film importing as a sideline.

The second group, represented by Hanguk Yesul and Segi Sangsa, which had both begun their import businesses as far back as 1953, prioritized importing over production. Yet, they too were at the mercy of the MPI, which allocated a limited number of foreign film import licenses—via Import License Reward System (hereafter ILRS, known in Korea as the import quota system)—at the beginning of each year and expected members of this group to use them within 12 months. As a policy instrument, the ILRS was designed to encourage local film production by rewarding registered producers with a permit to import a lucrative foreign film. These permits were awarded on the basis of a producer's: 1) production results; 2) export achievements; 3) international film festival awards and 4) government-approved best film award results. At the time, an import license carried a high monetary value because foreign films had gained in popularity, thus delivering increased box office returns. Despite the fact that tickets for foreign films were slightly higher than those for Korean films, audiences chose to watch foreign films over domestic films. In turn, import licenses were traded among registered producers on the black market with a premium, which the MPI acknowledged by classifying the permits as 'property value'.[5] In short, under the PRS seasoned importers had to transform themselves into producers to preserve their professional status. As a result of their limited production expertise, the firms in this category relied heavily on working with independent producers by illegally subcontracting and selling production rights to them. In the final credits of a film made in this way, the independent producer involved was styled as either *jejak damdang* or *chong jihwi,* both meaning producer-in-charge.

The third group consisted of smaller registered producers including Shinchang, Aseong, and Daeyoung. Although they were members of the Korean Motion Picture Producers Association, they struggled to maintain their registered status as government requirements became tougher. Their core business was working with the independent producers and administering the necessary paperwork for making films; thus, this third type of registered producer was often described as "a real estate agency".[6]

The two major industry groups at the time were the Korean Motion Picture Producers Association (hereafter KMPPA) and Motion Picture Association of Korea (hereafter MPAK). By around 1963 the KMPPA, which had been established in 1957, had become a powerful trade organization that advanced the business interests of its members—the privileged cartel of registered producers—while excluding independent producers from its membership. Although there was no ceiling set for membership of the KMPPA, the MPI controlled the organization's size by making frequent changes to the PRS, which kept the number of registered producers at a small but optimal level, resulting in constantly fluctuating numbers. On the opposite side of the industry, MPAK, established in 1962, represented all others involved in the industry including directors, actors, screenwriters, and technicians and worked to protect their rights against the KMPPA.

Rise of the Cartel and the Coalition of the Willing

The systematization of the PRS threw up a cartel of producers, who operated from the industry's center. It was an elitist system, enabling registered producers to maintain direct lines of communication with the MPI and other industry participants. Contributing covertly to the industry's productivity were a slew of unauthorized independent producers and importers who were more than willing to help the cartel manage their demanding workloads, in particular their ever-increasing registration requirements.

A small army of exhibitors (theater owners), operating across Korea's 13 separate provinces, played the role of investors, enabling these various practitioners—both elite and "illegal"—to keep the industry afloat by investing in productions through pre-sales. Both registered and independent producers tried to maintain a strong relationship with this network of exhibitor–investors, who were regularly invited to Chungmuro in Seoul—the cultural and artistic heart of the film industry—to listen to project pitches and enjoy being wined and dined in the big smoke. The quality of the script, the popularity of the cast and the reputation of the director were the winning combination for securing pre-sales, which went under the nickname of "provincial business" (*jibang jangsa*) among industry players. For all three types of producers, negotiating pre-sales became crucial for their survival.

In turn, these financing arrangements gave exhibitors across Korea's region-based distribution network (established in the late 1950s with the film market's sudden expansion) exclusive rights to distribute and screen a given film in their respective provinces, thus stimulating producers to increase their output with very little risk. Competition among these key regional players was fierce in this pre-multiplex era as by law only six prints of a film were allowed to circulate nationwide at any given time. Remarkably, this system lasted until 1988.[7]

In addition, these exhibitor–investors influenced the production environment in ways similar to the "New York Bankers" in Hollywood.[8] Usually exhibitors advanced about 60 percent of the production budget to producers in exchange for exclusive rights—paying up to a further 30 percent on receiving the film print. Under this system, with pre-sales funding acquired from multiple exhibitors across different provinces, a producer might only be required to contribute 10 percent or less of the total budget.[9] As a result of this practice, producers became overly dependent on pre-sales investments and thus failed to develop a range of other funding sources. On the surface, this close association between exhibitors and producers was beneficial for producers as it almost guaranteed a certain level of profit for a producer even before the cameras began rolling.[10] Nonetheless, exhibitors set screening dates for films prior to their wrapping-up, which effectively meant that questions of demand and audience responses were almost incidental—at least, this was how the system was explained to film industry representatives outside of Korea.[11] Hence, this common practice exposed the industry to undue influence by exhibitors in making decisions about favored film genres and styles in their role as investors.[12]

By the late 1960s, the film market was oversupplied with product, mostly "cheap second-rate domestic films".[13] These "quota quickies", which included anticommunist and literary films as well as fake co-productions with Hong Kong partners (which are discussed in Chapter 4), were tailored to attract import licenses rather than for box office success.[14] Faced with this flush of lower quality films, exhibitors struggled to recoup high yields on their investments. This situation was exacerbated by the fact that exhibitors began passing bad checks to producers.[15] As a result, the flow of funding for productions came to an abrupt halt, resulting in an unprecedented downturn for the industry.[16]

One of the most notable producers and directors of the time was Shin Sang-ok. Taking a closer look at his activities offers clear insights into how the industry worked at the time. His company Shin Film, founded in 1960, became Korea's largest film company during the 1960s, monopolizing around half of the industry's total capacity.[17] Shin Film's rapid growth represented the epitome of the Park regime's industrialization plan.[18] As a spokesperson for the KMPPA, Shin strongly advocated the benefits of industrialization, seeking to influence amendments to the MPL that would enable his own production company, Shin Film, to function more like Columbia Pictures. While Shin may have cited Columbia

Pictures as the kind of studio he wished to create, he also learned how Japanese film studios operated while forming relationships with two of them, Daiei and Toho. In the process, it became clear to Shin that the Japanese film industry was itself modeled on the Hollywood studio system.

Shin no doubt saw the benefits of the studio model through his working relationship with Daiei and Toho Studios in Japan, which taught him some important lessons. For example, in 1961 Shin exported his film *Seong Chunhyang* (1961) to Japan through Daiei, and used Daiei's advanced technology to complete the underwater scenes for *The Story of Sim Cheong* (1962). Even after he was "kidnapped" and taken to North Korea in 1978, Shin invited Toho's technical staff to the North and worked with them to complete his science-fiction quasi-Godzilla monster film *Pulgasari* (1985), a political allegory glorifying the unquenchable spirit of the North Korean people.

While other registered producers operated a single studio at best, Shin Film ran multiple studios that housed technology, planning, and art departments, editing room, acting studio and a directors' suite. By 1964, the company employed over 250 staff, including directors, assistant directors, and actors, spread over several large properties.[19] Hanyang, one of Shin Film's competitors, could muster only 80 staff members—less than one third of Shin Film's. Shin Film went on to become the parent company of three other registered production companies, Star (1965), Anyang (1967), and Shina (1968). Not surprisingly, underlying this remarkable growth was Shin's close relationship with the Park regime, which blossomed after Shin's release of *Evergreen Tree* (1961), a feature film that promoted rural development.[20] The film impressed Park, and he invited Shin to the Blue House, Korea's presidential residence. This was the start of a long relationship, especially in light of the fact that the film was used to promote Park's agriculture policy, which was focused on building infrastructure for the rural sector.[21]

One of the military government's revolutionary pledges was the eradication of poverty, and the rural development campaign was seen as an important means of achieving this. In the early 1960s, Korea was predominantly an agrarian society, with around 70 percent of its population living on farms. Chronic problems such as recurring famine and high unemployment blighted social development. The Park regime advocated new agricultural methods in order to increase the rice harvest, and *Evergreen Tree* served this agenda well.[22] Shin's visit to the Blue House was clearly instrumental in the eventual production of *Rice* (discussed below), which preceded Park Chung Hee's presidential election campaign in 1963.

During the 1960s, Shin Film rose to become an independent empire within Korea's film industry while overtly supporting the Park regime's industrialization agenda. While its rapid growth reflected its high production levels, it was also aided by unprecedented support from the government. Producer Shin had friends in high places, and his good relations with the Park regime made it easier for him to integrate his businesses vertically by streamlining production, exhibition, and distribution activities through his two cinemas in Seoul, Hollywood, and Myeongbo.

Before censorship tightened in the late 1960s Shin and Park remained close, and it was no secret that Shin and his companies continued to enjoy preferential treatment as a result of this relationship.[23] Shin Film's acquisition of Anyang Studio in 1966 is perhaps the best example of the close links between Shin Film and the political establishment.[24] Shin purchased Anyang Studio with financial assistance originating from Park Chung Hee's election campaign fund—a deal brokered with the help of Prime Minister Kim Jong-pil (the founder of the Korean Central Intelligence Agency, the KCIA).[25] In return for such favors, Shin actively promoted the Park regime by incorporating soft propaganda into many of his films. The most outstanding example of this was *Rice* (1963)—what we would now call a pure endorsement film.

The Archetypal Political Endorsement Film: *Rice* (1963)

A feature-length film produced and directed by Shin, *Rice* praises a group of young farmers who have created a successful irrigation system for their rice fields. It depicts a compassionate, newly formed military government sparing no effort to help villagers to overcome hunger, providing trucks and soldiers as well as explosives for the construction of this sorely needed public project. Because it portrays Park Chung Hee's vision for developing and governing rural communities in detail, the film was used as part of Park's presidential election campaign. As we will see, this was Shin's plan from the start. Although the claim is made in the prologue subtitles that the film was based on a true story—like Shin's earlier *Evergreen Tree* (1961)—the failure of the real-life irrigation project is turned into a success story, and the military government is congratulated for its assistance. This familiar story of struggling farmers attracted over 50,000 viewers in Seoul, and *Rice* received the Special Consideration Award at the 3rd Grand Bell Awards in 1964. It was later exported to Thailand.

The film's explicit propaganda message, and the brief opportunity it afforded for audiences to escape the realities of poverty, are hard to miss. At the core of this ideologically driven piece is a hero named Yong, who regards economic development as the shining pathway toward communal and national prosperity. He completes the irrigation system by overcoming physical difficulties, obstructive officials, superstitious villagers and an inhospitable environment. Yong's status as a war veteran with a permanent leg injury adds drama to the story.

As the film opens, we see glimpses of Yong's frustrated life in Seoul. His army friend Choi complains angrily to bar girls how wounded war veterans are cast aside and have difficulty fitting back into society. Having no peace living in Seoul, Yong returns to his hometown to care for his sick father. The beginning of the film, then, underscores the gloomy tone of life under the previous government.

Returning to his village, Yong encounters the grim reality of starvation in rural Korea. He is surprised to find children playing in the dirt, eating it as if it were rice. Back home, he is devastated to learn that his father is dying from malnutrition. At the funeral, Yong succumbs to his grief, scattering a handful of rice over the coffin. An innocent child asks him: "Are you crying because you are hungry? Don't cry. When you cry, you only become hungrier". After witnessing firsthand the level of poverty in his home village, Yong decides to stay and work to improve living conditions there. Since nothing can be grown because of the lack of water, he devises a plan for an irrigation system that will traverse rocky terrain and take water to the village's dried-up rice paddies. While most villagers support his plans in principle, they are hampered by numerous obstacles linked to local traditions.

First, landlord Song, who represents the old feudal class system, opposes Yong's plan because of the threat it poses to his economic and social position in the village. Second, corrupt and lazy government officials—representing the previous civilian governments of Syngman Rhee and Chang Myon—treat Yong as a fool and accuse him of being pro-communist because of his collaborative approach. Third, the female village shaman, who represents Korea's pre-modern legacy of superstition, is directly opposed to modernization and industrialization. She attempt to frighten the villagers from participating in Yong's project because of its potential to anger the mountain spirits.

All of these obstacles are presented as remnants of an older social, cultural, and political system that the Park government is determined to transform. Thus the new military government in the film—a thinly disguised version of the Park regime—actively supports Yong's project. One by one, the obstacles to progress are overcome. The power-hungry Song is imprisoned because of his corrupt connections with the previous government; the uncooperative bureaucrats are replaced by conscientious and efficient officials; and the shaman finally lends her support to Yong, joining the good cause and sharing in his eventual triumph.

Rice ends with an overtly positive message—not only about rural development and national progress, but also urging forgiveness of past wrongdoings under the former regime—all under the banner of a new military government. (Yong falls in love with Song's daughter, a strong woman dedicated to the irrigation project and national development, prompting him to ask the new local government to pardon Song.) Toward the end of the film, trucks loaded with soldiers and equipment arrive at the project site, demonstrating the efficiency and might of the military government. The closing shot of Yong and the villagers rejoicing over their abundant harvest in lush rice fields (also depicted in the film advertisement in Figure 1.1) stands in stark contrast to the melancholy atmosphere of the opening scenes and offers a message of hope and promise to the audience, regardless of their particular circumstances.

Figure 1.1 Film advertisement for *Rice*. *Gyeonghyang Shinmun* 15 November, 1963: 7.

The film was released strategically in September 1963, one month after the government had announced plans to hold an election and a month before it took place. Effectively, the film became a giant trailer for Park's presidential election campaign and his reform agenda. Even publicity materials for the film and the election were coordinated, as Figure 1.2 shows.

Figure 1.2 Election campaign advertisement. *Donga Daily* 2 October, 1963: 1.

The exhibition pattern for *Rice* was also noteworthy. In Seoul it was screened in the commercial Myeongbo Cinema as well as Seoul Citizen Hall, a venue for theatrical performances, exhibitions, and concerts. Given that most films were released in a single cinema in one region at a time, the screening of *Rice* in the Citizen Hall (in September 1963) guaranteed increased levels of exposure to a wider audience. Thus, audiences in Seoul must have numbered more than the reported 50,000 (according to KMDB), as this figure represented only its commercial box office. This so-called "message film" was also shown in remote villages, industrial complexes, and poor neighborhoods, where there was normally little access to film screenings. Such areas were well served by the 18 mobile screening teams that the MPI had established in June 1961 with free community entertainment programs comprising newsreels and cultural films and, increasingly, with selected feature films such as *Rice*.[26]

In retrospect, *Rice* makes no attempt to conceal Shin's subservience to the new Park government and its vigorous promotion of its rural development policies. Using the tools of soft propaganda, the military government is presented as a friend to the nation's farmers and indeed all citizens. In *Rice*, Shin's major concern is to emphasize the Park regime's success in assisting Korea's embattled farmers in contrast to the inefficient, bureaucratic, and self-serving efforts of the previous government.

Shin Sang-ok was a formidable industry figure throughout the Park era, not only for the sheer extent of his studios and the number of films that he produced, but also because of the influence (perceived or otherwise) he wielded in his dealings with the MPI and its promulgation of official film policy. While Shin acknowledged that he supported Park's ideas for industrialization, he consistently dismissed suggestions of excessive political influence, maintaining that his frequent meetings with President Park were simply friendly in character.[27] Although there is no clear evidence of Shin's direct involvement in the drafting of the MPL, there can be no question that Shin "collaborated" with Park and the MPI, thus ensuring maximum benefit for his own studios and his close associates in the production cartel.[28]

Following the election, in December 1963 the 3rd Republic of Korea was established with Park Chung Hee as president, thus cementing Shin's position as an industry leader. As the following analysis of the immensely successful film *The Red Scarf* shows, Shin's continuing production of propaganda films expanded his endorsement of government policy from an "escape from poverty" message to other ideological driven themes, notably anticommunism and nationalism.

The Red Scarf (1964) and the True Colors of Propaganda

The Red Scarf is a large-scale anticommunist war film and is based on a radio drama about the Korean Air Force written by Han Un-sa; it used technical features new to the Korean cinema including aerial shots, speed camera, and wide-screen techniques. *The Red Scarf* was made as a "Hollywood style" blockbuster with the biggest budget to date for any Korean film and was packed with visual spectacle and big stars (see Figure 1.3).[29] Before the film was released in March 1964, Shin Film ran a series of newspaper advertisements, informing potential audiences of the film's progress while reassuring investors that this highly ambitious project was taking longer to complete than expected.

Figure 1.3 Film advertisements for *The Red Scarf*. *Donga Daily* 17 March, 1964: 2.

The use of advanced technology, as well as a star-studded cast including Choi Eun-hee, Lee Min-ja, Kim Jin-kyu, and Shin Yeong-gyun, were the major marketing points of the film (See Figures 1.3 and 1.4.). Director Shin Sang-ok's international reputation also lured audiences to the cinema—just as it had attracted regional exhibitor–investors to the project. Shin's films had often been screened at major international film festivals such as the Berlin International Film Festival, the Venice International Film Festival, the Asian Film Festival, and the Academy

Awards. International critics had been drawn to his exploration of traditional Korean values and culture and magnificent landscapes depicted in films such as *Gate of Chastity* (1961), *Mother and a Guest* (1961) and *Deaf Samryong* (1964).

Figures 1.4 Film advertisements for *The Red Scarf*. *Gyeonghyang Shinmun* 4 March, 1964: 4; and *Gyeonghyang Shinmun* 26 March, 1964: 4. Author's own collection.

Set in the Korean War, the film focuses on the lives of combat pilots who show daring in both love and war. The red scarf of the title is part of the South Korean Air Force uniform worn by these glamorous flyboys. The film's theme song, also known as "The Red Scarf", which later became an official anthem of the Korean Air Force, lends an uplifting patriotic feeling to the flight scenes. Rookie pilots are dispatched to Gangryeung Air Force Base, close to the war zone. Under the tutelage of Wing Commander Na, by day they fly practice air raids and, after hours, they release their tensions over drinks at the station bar. During one such session, First Lieutenant Bae meets war-widow Ji-seon and instantly falls in love with her. They marry shortly before Bae is ordered to fly a series of missions over North Korea. In order to destroy a key bridge, Na heroically flies his plane into the structure, leaving his fellow pilots grieving his loss. The film concludes with a scene of pilots flying in formation with "The Red Scarf" playing in the background, glorifying the might and bravery of the Korean Air Force.

From a producer's and investors' perspective, *The Red Scarf* was a commercial success; perhaps surprisingly, its overtly propagandistic character had created "a feeling of national euphoria".[30] It became a box office hit after attracting audiences of 250,000 in Seoul and was exported to Japan, Hong Kong, and Taiwan.

Part of its success lay in its technical innovations; the aerial sequences, the first of their kind in a Korean film, were particularly praised in the popular press. These spectacular aerial shots included F-86 Sabre jet fighters flying in formation; parallel editing of aerial and ground attacks; emergency landings and escapes; a rescue by a Curtiss C-46 Commando transport aircraft; and Na's suicide attack on the bridge. Filming these sequences, for which a camera was mounted on an F-86 jet fighter, involved extended periods of time and a generous production budget. It is not surprising that four times as much film stock was used to shoot *The Red Scarf* than for a conventional production.[31]

Despite its propagandist intent and its numerous technical challenges—or, more precisely, because Shin was able to overcome them—*The Red Scarf* became a very successful entertainment film. The film won numerous domestic and international awards at forums such as the 11th Asian Film Festival, 4th Grand Bell Awards, and Blue Dragon Awards, taking prizes for best director, best editing, best actor/actress, best cinematography, best screenplay, and best supporting actor. *The Red Scarf* enhanced Shin's reputation as one of Korea's leading producers, and its success encouraged independent and smaller registered producers to continue reaping the benefits offered by the production cartel.

The Studio System and Its Subcontracting Game

Some commentators have viewed the introduction of the PRS and its compulsory character as a harmful influence on the film industry at a time when the Park government was aggressively pushing its industrialization agenda.[32] By contrast, other studies have linked the development of the PRS to the Hollywood studio system, showing how a small number of registered producers including Shin Film, Hanguk Yesul, and Donga Heungeop attempted to replicate Hollywood's vertical integration system—despite their ultimate failure due to lack of capital and a disorganized distribution system.[33] Both views offer food for thought.

In the US in the 1940s, a group of elite studio owners ran their Hollywood studios as "a system of corporations",[34] asserting their "creative control and administrative authority"[35] over all aspects of filmmaking. Similarly, the PRS model concentrated power among a small cartel of producers, and the KMPPA operated as an oligopoly similar to the US trade association, the Motion Picture Association of America (MPAA). However, in Korea, although producers had the right to distribute films, in effect exhibitors had much more say over the distribution process—that is, over the choice of films for public screening and their exhibition venues. Producers had to deal with at least six exhibitors when making decisions about the distribution of a particular film. These practical constraints illustrate the vulnerability and political impotence experienced by the Korean film industry under the authoritarian military regime of the 1960s. While the Hollywood studio system allowed major studios such as Fox Film Corporation, Paramount Pictures, Universal Pictures, and Columbia Pictures (all controlling members of the MPAA) to control the bulk of the US market, the KMPPA (and PRS) remained a much less stable and predictable entity than the MPAA.

Accordingly, the cartel or oligopoly that emerged out of the PRS was a mixture of two models: the family-business-oriented *chaebol*, native to Korea, and the Hollywood studio system. The *chaebol* concept grew out of Japan's prewar *zaibatsu* system and enabled a few large family-run vertically integrated business conglomerates—in the automobile, iron/steel, and heavy chemicals industries, for instance—to exert a significant influence on the nation's economy.[36] Resembling the *chaebol,* but on a much smaller scale, the PRS overemphasized the role of production to the detriment of the other arms of the industry, a direct outcome of developmental state policy.[37] Buttressing the film industry in this way reflected the ways in which Park "mixed the Japanese ethos of top-down mobilization and the U.S. ideas of technocracy with Korean nationalism in most un-Japanese and un-American ways to clear the way for economic growth".[38] Hence, through the PRS and comparable to initiatives launched by other countries such as Britain, Japan, India and China, the Korean government attempted to build a national film studio system based on current industry practices in the US.

Throughout the 1960s, the PRS served as the key mechanism for shaping and controlling the film industry. Members' registration status was kept current by meeting the new criteria announced with each policy modification. Producers seemed to be constantly catching up with these ever-changing requirements, giving rise to the oft-used metaphor of a carrot on a stick. Striving to strike a realistic balance between profit-taking and policy demands, registered producers engaged in three key strategies: trading rights to produce a film; trading rights to import a film (under the Import License Reward System, introduced below and discussed in detail in Chapter 4); and generating film pre-sales.

By continually introducing new industry specifications, the MPI was able to influence (and elevate) industry standards while regulating the number of producers and the day-to-day conduct of their activities. However, the MPI's influence in such matters was only partially effective, as a surprising number of unregistered (aka independent) producers found ways to circumvent the system. This was a relatively easy task given the industry's small size and collegiality; almost everyone knew everyone else.

Daemyeong jejak (hereafter *daemyeong*) was a widespread subcontracting system that emerged at the end of 1961. Almost all of the registered production companies engaged in this practice at some point for different reasons. For example, Shin Film, a very active company that prioritized the production of its own films, increasingly employed this measure in the late 1960s when it was experiencing constant cash flow problems. Producers with importing backgrounds such as Hanguk Yesul and Segi Sangsa were major users of this subcontracting system, making profits from selling production rights to these informal operatives. In essence, *daemyeong* enabled a registered producer to remain competitive by meeting stringent registration requirements while simultaneously facilitating—theoretically illegal—filmmaking opportunities for independent producers (deemed illegal after the PRS was launched in 1962). Subcontracting of this kind involved a four-step process.

First, in a move beneficial to both parties, a registered producer gave (and later sold) independent producers the right to make films by letting them use his name (registered status), which was necessary for filing paperwork and getting approval for production. Second, the independent producers—who included names such as Ho Hyeon-chan and Choi Hyeon-min and directors Yu Hyun-mok and Jeong So-yeong—made their films using their own or the registered producer's networks and equipment, opening the way to box office profits without the large investment necessary for official registration.[39] Third, the independent producer would return the favor by paying a commission to his registered counterpart, and the film's box office profits would go into the former's pockets.[40] When a *daemyeong* film was screened, the opening credits identified two types of producers: the "producer-in-charge" (referring to the independent producer), and the "producer" (referring to the registered producer). This acknowledgement suggested that the practice, albeit illegal, was widespread and recognized by those involved in the industry. Finally, the film in question was submitted to the MPI's film awards process, an arrangement that exclusively benefited the registered producer if successful as the "prize" was a license to import and distribute a foreign film—a sure formula for generating lucrative box office returns.

Whilst this semi-covert activity—initially conducted without the exchange of money—was an unintended consequence of the PRS and therefore fell outside the government's blueprint for the industry, it became critical to the sustainability of the producers' cartel and the industry as a whole. In 1963, the rate of *daemyeong*-funded productions increased rapidly following amendments to the MPL, which required registered producers to make a minimum of 15 films per year. In sum, it was a valuable tool that enabled registered producers to meet the increasing demands of the PRS. Eventually, the *daemyeong* system became so entrenched that the MPI acquiesced in its operation, demonstrating how at least those filmmakers with the right networks persevered by following multiple pathways for survival and success under the Park regime.

Table 1.3 Number of Domestic Feature Film Productions 1961–1970

Year	1961	1962	1963	1964	1965	1966	1967	1968	1969	1970
No.	86	113	144	147	189	136	172	212	229	209

Source: KMPPC 1977: 46.

As part of the frictions brought about in this changing environment, in 1964 the MPAK increased the level of its complaints against registered producers exploiting their independent colleagues.[41] Despite this, the *daemyeong* system continued to grow. Trade reports estimate that, in 1965, 130 out of 189 new films were *daemyeong* productions, meaning that two-thirds of all films produced in Korea at this time were completed by "dubious" means.[42] In reality, the figures in Table 1.3 suggest that few if any registered producers had been able to produce the statutory minimum of 15 films per year that the MPL required. Despite this bleak scenario, there were still opportunities for passionate independent producers such as Ho Hyeon-chan and Choi Hyeon-min who specialized in art-house films, which were rarely attempted by registered producers. Hence, the MPI did not hinder *daemyeong* because the practice was clearly beneficial in enabling many parts of the industry to reach a desired level of productivity, rising rapidly from 86 films in 1961 to 189 in 1965. However, this sudden increase in product overloaded the exhibition system: over 50 completed films produced in 1965 could not find outlets despite being scheduled for release in 1966.[43]

The end of the system was not far away and, in this sense, 1966 was a pivotal moment. In 1966, the same year that Korea's screen quota system was launched, the MPI formally banned *daemyeong* because it was no longer needed as a mechanism for generating productivity. The government was satisfied with current levels of productivity and set an annual production figure for the industry of 120 films—a target easily achievable by the registered producers alone (i.e., an average of 4.6 films per each of the 26 producers allowed to be registered according to the 1966 MPL).[44] Nevertheless, *daemyeong* continued in the black market, but with escalating costs for independent producers as a result of the lower number of productions permitted.[45] Few unregistered producers could afford to stay in the game, and a handful even took their own lives out of a growing sense of despair.[46]

After the external environment for the production system had been set, the MPI's focus turned to the control of content. Certain themes and styles were encouraged, and films that employed these elements were rewarded with import licenses.

Victim of Its Own Success

Whatever the resultant effect, Korea's official film policy substantially subsidized the industry while encouraging Shin and other registered producers to follow government guidelines as though they were chasing a carrot on a stick. However, in response to ongoing organized protests led by the MPAK—including many independent producers—over the new production regime, the MPI and the KMPPA agreed to eliminate the annual quota limit, and *daemyeong* was legalized in 1968.[47] In response, production numbers soared from 172 in 1967 to 229 in 1969.[48]

About 80 percent of the films produced in 1971 were *daemyeong* films, mostly low-quality "quota quickies", and in the same year all 21 registered producers were involved in *daemyeong* productions, with a maximum of eight films each, reaffirming the widespread utilization of the system.[49] Some registered companies such as Asung Film, Jeil Film Company, and Daedong Film Company even prioritized *daemyeong* as their core business. The government's loosening of controls, heeding the industry's call, showed that it lacked a clear understanding of how the industry actually worked. As a result, its actions effectively undermined the production environment, leading to the steady decline of Korean cinema throughout the 1970s.

In less than five years, the MPI's PRS, censorship guidelines, and import regulations enabled the Park government to shape and control the film industry as it had done for the automobile, iron, and steel industries.[50] The government wielded increasing power over the film industry, seeing the potential of cinema as an important vehicle for disseminating national ideology. Preventing the exhibition of noncompliant films was a key aspect of film policy during Park's tenure as president, thus completing the harnessing of film production, distribution, and exhibition to his political agenda as a propaganda tool.[51]

Despite the draconian system created by the MPI's policy structure, throughout the Park period members of the film industry—in particular the MPAK, representing those operatives not covered by the registered producers' body, the KMPPA—offered resistance wherever and whenever it could. Working on behalf of the great majority of the film community—including directors, cinematographers, actors, and independent (unregistered) producers—the MPAK consistently lobbied for the abolition of the MPL. In particular, it challenged the MPI over the PRS and *daemyeong* activities by appealing to the National Assembly as early as March 1964, on the grounds that *daemyeong* strengthened the privileged cartel of registered producers. The anti-MPL campaign was a bold sign of the industry's readiness to stand up to bullying from the MPI (and the Park government more generally). Resistance spearheaded by the MPAK continued sporadically throughout the 1960s and beyond, laying the groundwork for the Screen Quota protection movement in the 1990s.

Conclusion

Under the Park government's direction, the studio system in Korea flourished. In turn, this strengthened the government's control over the industry because studios had to work within its policy directives in order to stay in business. In the 1960s, the efforts of registered producers such as Shin Sang-ok were recognized in US trade reports, which considered the stage of development reached by the Korean film industry as "comparable to early Hollywood, with players under contract to the various studios".[52]

Perhaps the key link between the two film industries was the fact that in each case their films were rapidly turned out one after another, as if on an industrial assembly line. For example, according to the KMDB, in 1968 Shin Film produced a total of 17 films—five of which were made by trading production rights (*daemyeong jejak*), including *Over that Hill* (1968; a remake of 20th Century Fox's *Over the Hill* [1931]), the comedy, *A Male Housekeeper* (1968), and a melodrama about forbidden love called *Desire* (1968). Given the fact that films were generally completed within four weeks in the 1960s, this high number of productions completed in a single year suggests that Shin Film was working around the clock on multiple projects.

In the same year (1968), a total of 70 foreign films were imported into Korea. Four were brought in by Shin Film including the Italian-made sword-and-sandal or peplum epic *Hercules, Samson and Ulysses* (1963) and *The One-armed Swordman* (1967), a Hong Kong *wuxia* (swordplay) film produced by Shaw Brothers Studio.[53] As a result of their own export efforts and the production of award-winning films, registered producers including Shin received coveted import licenses, enabling them to gain access to these international money-spinners.

Despite some similarities between the structure of Korea's PRS and the major studio system in Hollywood (a "mature oligopoly—a group of companies cooperating to control a certain market"[54]), the effects of centralized policy intervention in Korea—and the resultant artificial shaping of the industry's development—made the Korean system very different from Hollywood. Paradoxically, given that the PRS had been designed as a production-centric industry system, the neglect of exhibition and distribution became a serious barrier to vertical integration, leading to a sharp decrease in the number of Korean films produced in the 1970s.

During the Golden Age of the 1960s, Korean cinema was largely defined by dynamic power struggles that brought the government and the film industry together in often-conflicting ways as producers, both registered and independent, sought to assert some measure of independence for themselves and the industry as a whole. Today, while some of the business strategies adopted by 1960s filmmakers may seem absurd and retrogressive, we can see that they were responding to specific problems and that their solutions were effective at the time. Their desire to achieve and retain their status as producers provided a dynamic motivation that gave a powerful impetus to the film industry as a whole. Money and the promise of prosperity drove productivity, allowing the local industry to enjoy its first true golden age.

Notes

1. The NFPC grew out of the Film Department of the Bureau of Public Information that had been established in 1948 under the Syngman Rhee government (1948–1960).
2. The genre of cultural films covered themes such as national security, hygiene, agricultural information, social issues, and social etiquette—the same types of categories found in Japanese "cultural" film productions of the Pacific War period.
3. Rubin 1971: 81.
4. Park's colonial experience is an important factor in these changes. Born in 1917, seven years after the Japanese had colonized Korea, he was trained as a military officer in the Imperial Army in Manchuria (a Japanese-controlled territory in Northeast China) in 1940 and served under Japanese colonial authority until 1945. As a military dictator, like the Japanese colonial authorities, he prioritized issues of national security and civil control above all else. It is no secret that Park deeply admired the Meiji imperial restoration, responsible for Japan's modernization, and also that he was profoundly influenced by Japanese colonial and military traditions. For discussions of Park's colonial experience and its influence on his thinking, see Yi 2002; Yi 2003; Moon and Jun 2011; and Park 1963.
5. This was a response to an enquiry made by Dongseong Film Co., whose registration was cancelled in 1965. Dongseong wanted to know if it was possible to sell its unused import licenses to another company. The MPI concluded that it was legitimate for Dongseong to transfer its import licenses under these circumstances. See KIM, G. (Legal Team of the MPI). "Answer to the Question Regarding the Motion Picture Law (Yeonghwabeop Jirui Hoesin)". (6 August 1965). Unpublished Report NAK document #_BA0136798.
6. "What's Going on with Each Company? (Gak Yeonghwa-ui Dongtaereul Arabopsida)". *Yeonghwa Japji* (January 1970): 148–49.
7. In 1989 the number of prints released for distribution was increased to 12, and between 1990 and 1993 this figure increased by one print per year. In 1994 this restriction was abolished, improving market conditions for both domestic and international films. See Ahn 2005: 296–97.

8. See Wade 1969: 10.
9. For a detailed historical overview of Korea's film distribution system, see Kim *et al.* 2003: 12–24.
10. A similar phenomenon occurred between 2003 and 2005 when Japanese distributors such as Shochiku, Comstock, and Gaga Communications rushed to purchase Korean films even before they were completed. This influx of capital for new projects such as *Now and Forever* (2006), *Once in a Summer* (2006) and *A Millionaire's First Love* (2006) accounted for 70 to 80 percent of all Korean film exports, leaving Korean producers happy but over-reliant on the Japanese market.
11. See Edwards, Bill. "South Korean Film Industry Blacklists Thesps Who Work in TV for Pay". *Variety* (17 April, 1968): page unknown. This was how registered producer Joo Dong-jin from the Yeonbang Film Company, who was visiting the US to study filmmaking, described the state of the Korean film industry to readers of this major American media and entertainment trade magazine.
12. During the 1960s a total of 1666 films were produced. The most frequently produced films (and also the most popular genres among regional exhibitors) were melodramas (831), action films (278) and comedies (160). See KMPPC 1977: 47.
13. Standish 1994: 73.
14. "News & Issues (Nyuseuwa Hwaje)". *Shin Donga* (September 1968): 414–15.
15. "What's Happening with Film, TV and Entertainment Industry (Yeonghwa, Yeonye, TV Bangsonggye Dongjeong)". *Geundae Yeonghwa* (December 1971): 44–45.
16. Other industries also experienced difficulties around this time. Between 1969 and 1971, more than 300 firms either went bankrupt or were on the verge of bankruptcy, desperately seeking state loans to bail them out. See Cumings 1997: 362–63.
17. Yi 2008: 46.
18. Shin Sang-ok recalls that Shin Film became so powerful that it caused a split in the industry: Shin Film on the one side and Chungmuro (i.e., everyone else) on the other. Lee, G. "Korean Cinema Retrospective Shin Sang-ok 12" (Hanguk Yeonghwa Hoegorok, Shin Sang-ok 12). *Cine21* (19 September 2003). Available: <http://www.cine21.com/Index?magazine.php?mag_id=20902>. Accessed 14 December 2012.
19. Director Lee Jang-ho, who began his career at Shin Film in 1965, describes the company in detail in: Lee, Jang-ho. "Korean Film Retrospective: Lee Jang-ho #34 (Hanguk Yeonghwa Hoego: Lee Jang-ho Pyeon #34)". *Cine21* (7 December 1999): 98.
20. This film was based on Shim Hun's novel *Evergreen Tree* published in 1935. This colonial novel dealt with passionate young college graduates coming to a rural village to teach farmers modern agricultural techniques and educate village children.
21. In accordance with this policy, the government introduced modern agricultural machinery and farming methods, established the National Agricultural Cooperative Federation (*Nonghyeop*) and a rural development administration and introduced the rural development law. See Han 1999: 112–28.
22. The film might also have influenced Park's conception of the New Village Movement (aka Saemaeul Movement), a rural community development campaign that he launched in 1970.
23. Shin benefited in other ways, too. For example, Shin Film received a relatively lenient penalty from the government after it was caught forging employment contracts and evading taxes in 1962. Moreover, rather than publically embarrass Shin for these transgressions, the police pardoned him and praised him for contributing to the development of the film industry during a press conference. Shin was also granted filming permits after failing to submit the mandatory production applications on time to the MPI—effectively creating a set of relaxed legal guidelines for Shin and a stricter set for everyone else. See Han, Bong. "Five Evils of the Film Industry (Yeonghwagye-ui Odae Akjil)". *Yeonghwa Segye* (July 1963): 50–51.
24. Anyang Studio was established by Hong Chan, president of Sudo Film Company, in 1957 with state-of-the-art facilities and supported by President Syngman Rhee.

However, within two years (in 1959), it was seized and its doors were closed by Korea's Industrial Bank due to financial difficulties resulting from poor management and a slew of box office failures.
25. Shin's actress wife, Choi Eun-hee, testified some years later that the money used to purchase the studio was given to Shin in this way. See Choi and Lee. "Oral History of Korean Arts—Choi Eun-hee (Gusulro Mannaneun Hanguk Yesulsa: Gongyeon Yesul—Choi Eun-hee)". Available: http://oralhistory.arko.or.kr/oral/main.asp. Accessed 12 September 2009.
26. "Mobile Screening Units Sent Nationwide (Jeonguge Sunhoe Yeonghwaban)". *Donga Daily* (28 June, 1961): 3. Mobile screening units visited various provinces with different programs and themes for four weeks at a time. Local police regularly assisted with these community screenings until the practice of "guidance for ideological enlightenment" was abolished in 2007. See "Removal of six outdated police regulations (Gyeongchal Sidaechagojeok Gyuchik 6 Jeon Pyeji)". *The Hankyoreh* (30 October, 2007). Available from <www.hani.co.kr/arti/society/society_general/246812.html>. Accessed 19 May, 2014.
27. After Shin Film's registration was cancelled in 1970, a large number of producers including Song Yu-chan and directors such as Yoon Bong-chun and Kim Su-yong publicly expressed their contempt for Shin and the ways in which he had influenced the content of film policy and the feelings of intimidation this had caused them. See "Film Empire Shin Film Gone from the Film Community (Yeonghwa Wangguk Shin Pilleumi Yeonghwagye-eseo Sarajida)". *Yeonye Japji* October 1970: 64; and Kim 2005.
28. According to senior Korean film historian Yi Hyoin (2008: 51), industry players hold differing opinions about Shin's contribution to the formation of the MPL in the 1960s; however, Shin was known to meet with President Park on a monthly basis, and Shin was also a close friend of Prime Minister Kim Jong-pil.
29. Berry 2003: 218.
30. Diffrient 2005: 171.
31. Shin 2007: 92–93.
32. See, for instance, Kim 1994; Park 2005.
33. Byon 2001a: 233.
34. Gomery 2005: 3.
35. Schatz 1996: 225.
36. See Yoo and Lee 1987: 96. Samsung and LG, which were formed in the 1950s, and other family companies such as Hyundai, SK, and Daewoo, founded in the 1960s, are representative Korean *chaebols*. Over the past five decades, these conglomerates have received massive government subsidies and preferential treatment in all facets of domestic business.
37. See Kim 2004: 206. Park and his government pre-selected *chaebols* and nurtured them as industrial elites loosely based on a combination of personal connections and past business performance. In return, the *chaebols* designed and executed business plans that relentlessly backed the government's drive to expand exports. This was one of the government's chief strategies for generating foreign currency, a primary aim of development policy under the Park regime.
38. Moon and Jun 2011: 115.
39. Veteran producer Kim In-gi, who worked for 160 different film production companies between the 1950s and 1980s, reported positive experiences with making *daemyeong* films in the 1960s. This subcontracting practice enabled his unregistered production companies to remain in business, thus advancing his career.
40. According to Park Haeng-cheol, a contracted producer with Shin Film, this commission was in effect an advance tax payment on future box office revenues—half was used to pay tax levied on box office gains and the other half went into the registered producer's purse. When box office returns were better than expected, an additional

fee was charged to the independent producer to pay for the increased tax bill. See Lee 2003: 195.
41. Director Yun Bong-chun, president of the MPAK, wrote a column in *Silver Screen* magazine accusing registered producers of being greedy and taking advantage of independent producers twice over by selling production rights and then taking up import licenses. See Shin, Bong-seung, and Bong-chun Yun. "Dispute over Film Law, Agree or Disagree (Yeonghwa Pyegibeop Chanban Sibi)". *Silver Screen* (January 1965): 110–11.
42. "Claims Surrounding the Film Law, Right or Wrong (Yeonghwabeobeul Dulleossan Chanban-ui Jujang)". *Chosun Daily* (3 February, 1966): 5.
43. See KMPPC 1977: 46; and Lee, Sun-geun. "Chronic Problems of the Film Community (Yeonghwagye Gojiljeogin Yoso)". *Yeonghwa Yesul* (January 1966): 107–108.
44. Shin's successful registration of Anyang (1967) and Shina (1968) as registered companies was a clever attempt to multiply his opportunities to make domestic films in response to this policy change. However, by mid-1968 the cancellation of the production quota system by the MPI impacted on Shin Film's production activities, leaving Shin financially over-extended. To ease this pressure, Shin Film began making more films in conjunction with independent producers, increasing the numbers of *daemyeong* films that he produced.
45. See Hwang, Un-heon. "Questions Regarding Korean Films: Best Ten Films, Best Performing Directors (Hanguk Yeonghwa Geu Gaunde-ui Munje: Gwangaekdongwon-ui Beseuteu Ten, Nuga Gajang Mani Yeonchulhaetna, Choedasan-ui Girok)". *Silver Screen* (March 1966): 57–60; and "News & Issues (Nyuseuwa Hwaje)". *Shin Donga* (September 1968): 414–15. In August 1966 revisions to the MPL banned *daemyeong* and declared that any registered producers involved in the practice would lose their registered status; following this directive, members of the KMPPA formally agreed to stop the practice of selling production rights to independent producers. However, some secretly continued to exchange their privileges with independent producers for high commissions, ranging between 40,000 and 50,000 won. Within two years, the commission charged to buy the rights to produce a single film had risen to an astounding one million to 1.5 million won. Average production costs were 5–6 million won in 1961, a figure that rose to 10–12 million won in 1968–1969 (Lee 2004: 329).
46. One such case involved the death of an established director, Noh Pil, in late 1966. Noh sought to shake off massive debts by making a profitable film but was unable to afford the production rights, and his efforts ended in suicide. See "Film Director (Yeonghwa Gamdok)". *Donga Daily* (2 August, 1966): 5; and "Tragic News of the Film Community: Director Noh Pil Killed Himself Pressured by the Debts (Yeonghwagye-ui Bibo: Bije Mollyeo Jasalhaneun Noh Pil Gamdok)". *Gyeonghyang Shinmun* (30 July, 1966): 7. Film magazines and newspapers made a martyr of Noh as a way of raising awareness of the human cost of the *daemyeong* system. The MPI's new annual quota system was blamed for the worsening situation, which had ultimately led to Noh's death. (According to the Korean Movie Database (KMDB), Noh (1928–1966) debuted in 1949 with *Pilot An Chang-Nam* and directed a total of 16 films, mostly melodramas.).
47. In 1968 the MPAK accused the registered producers of charging excessive *daemyeong* commissions and monopolizing import licenses and threatened a nation-wide strike of its members. More than 600 film industry members joined demands for an amendment to the MPL and abolition of the production quota system. It was the first action of its kind to demonstrate the collective power of the MPAK. See "News & Issues (Nyuseuwa Hwaje)". *Shin Donga* October 1968: 359.
48. KMPPC 1977: 46.
49. "Report (Ripoteu)". *Geundae Yeonghwa* (December 1971): 23–31.
50. Discussed respectively in Lee 2011; and Rhyu and Lew 2011.

51. One such "noncompliant" film that was heavily censored is *Seven Female POWs*, a story about the humane relationships between a male North Korean officer and five South Korean female POWs (four nurses and one prostitute whose clients are primarily US soldiers). Because the original print of the film was confiscated by the MPI (under pressure from an overzealous KCIA), we can only surmise how the narrative was constructed and what the original aesthetics were like. However, a number of newspaper and film magazine articles suggest that this film directed by Lee Man-hee endorsed the superiority of South Korea as a "better place to be" than the North. Despite this rosy picture, however, Lee was accused by the KCIA, intent on expanding its authority, of promulgating a "pro-communist" message in the film. Although Lee was arrested by the KCIA, he was eventually cleared of violating Korea's anticommunist laws. See "Director Lee Man-hee of *Seven Female POWs* Arrested (Yeonghwa Chirinui Yeoporo Gamdok Lee Man-hee ssi Gusok Giso)" *Gyeonghyang Shinmun* (5 Feb, 1965): 3; and "He Went Beyond the Freedom of Expression, Said Chief Prosecutor Lee of the Seoul District Prosecutor's Office (Yesuljayu Hangye Ital Lee Seoul Jigeomsajang Mal)". *Gyeonghyang Shinmun* 5 Feb, 1965: 5.
52. Edwards, Bill. "South Korean Film Industry Blacklists Thesps Who Work in TV for Pay". *Variety* (17 April, 1968): page unknown.
53. This popular Hong Kong martial arts film was later adapted by Korean producers into the *One-Legged Man* series in the 1970s. Inspired by the new generation of younger filmgoers who believed that foreign films had superior narratives and visual style to domestic films, Korean producers reshaped Hong Kong *wuxia* productions as Korean swordplay films—hoping to attract back audiences that had fallen away due to the advent of television.
54. Schatz 1988: 9.

2 At the Crossroads of Directing and Politics

This chapter focuses on a quintessential director from the 1960s who illustrates the complex relationship between filmmaking and the state, as well as investigate some of the strategies used by industry players to negotiate a pathway through the hazards created by an omnipresent political power struggle. It explores the tactics adopted by director Yu Hyun-mok (1925–2009), a leading arthouse filmmaker and auteur who was able to sustain his creative impulses under duress to enable him to do more than simply survive in this hostile environment. Yu's films *Aimless Bullet* (1961, aka *Obaltan*) and *The Empty Dream* (1965) are analyzed as case studies showing how he developed a particular style that blended realist, expressionist and modernist elements. Yu was one of a handful of filmmakers of the 1960s who developed personal styles that set them apart from the propaganda and commercial productions of the time. Despite the control over the industry exercised by the regime, this director developed a unique style and strategies for survival—at the same time bringing a fresh face to Korean cinema. In addition, Yu's distinguished career shows how the Western auteur theory of film could be successfully adapted to a Korean context.

The Challenge of Auteurship

Yu Hyun-mok (1925–2009) is regarded as one of Korea's leading arthouse filmmakers and auteurs. Whilst fellow practitioners Lee Man-hee and Shin Sang-ok achieved their reputations largely as commercial filmmakers working in popular genres such as melodrama, war (action) films, and historical drama, Yu Hyun-mok—and fellow directors including Kim Ki-young and Lee Sung-gu—established reputations as arthouse filmmakers by developing a unique stylistic repertoire while rejecting the lure of propaganda and commercial films.

Throughout the 1960s, the need for constant negotiation with government bureaucrats made it difficult for directors to balance the necessity of passing the censors with their desire to create films with their own unique style and aesthetic sensibility that reflected their often idiosyncratic view of society. Yu Hyun-mok sought to break free of this restrictive production environment by insistently advocating for a wider space in which to make arthouse films and at the same time freeing himself from the burden of having to direct propaganda and commercial films.

At the Crossroads of Directing and Politics   43

When the French critics writing for *Cahiers Du Cinéma* introduced auteur theory in the 1950s, they proposed the concept of the director as the creative center in the making of a film, like an author or a painter completing his artwork alone. In this sense, an "auteur" is a director whose experience and professionalism equips him or her to achieve a film's full artistic potential and is therefore the central figure responsible for a film's form, style, and meaning—which are seen as the ultimate expression of his or her worldview.[1] Among all Korean directors, Yu Hyun-mok best fits the auteur model because of the "signature" he left on his films. Yu developed his distinctive style by combining realist, expressionist, and modernist elements, creating an "aesthetics of devastation" through his exploration of the human condition in an age of despair.[2]

Yu frequently stated his admiration for foreign directors Ingmar Bergman and Robert Bresson and attempted to emulate their styles in his own films. Many of Yu's films were based on modern Korean literature, which often dealt with Korea's recent history including the Korean War, the territorial and ideological split between North and South, and the war's aftermath. Yu's work charts the influence of Western aesthetic movements in the pre- and post-war periods including French impressionist cinema and Italian Neo-realism, experimentalism, and existentialism. Exploring existentialist themes through experiments with sound and image construction were the main drivers behind Yu's aesthetic choices. In his autobiography, Yu described his ideal film style as a "cine-poem",[3] a choice that was probably influenced by the tradition of Korean realist cinema inaugurated by colonial filmmakers Na Un-gyu, Lee Gyu-hwan, and Choi In-gyu.[4] It came as no surprise, then, when he was dubbed "the Pathfinder of Korean Realism" by the organizers of the Busan International Film Festival in 1999.

Discussions of the idea of "auteur", and the differences between an auteur and a director, had appeared in the popular press since the 1950s. In the Korean context, commentators frequently discussed the dearth of "authorship" in relation to censorship and the PRS.[5] As we have already seen, directors had limited opportunities to develop a particular set of filmic styles and techniques because of the pressures they were under to make genre films of a kind they would have rejected in a more egalitarian environment. Given these special production conditions, previous scholars have sought to develop a localized auteur theory that emphasizes the importance of a director's worldview as a way of understanding his films and thus Korean film history as a whole.[6] However, while the need to create a new approach to "auteurship" in the Korean context is valid, most previous commentators have drawn exclusively on Western auteur theory and thus have overlooked the opportunity to draw out the similarities and differences between an indigenous Korean auteur theory and the Western concept.

The importance of understanding a particular director's view of the world has long been integral to auteur theory and its way of reconstructing a country's film history—particularly in regards to the US.[7] It has been said that an auteur will thrive in demanding production environments because "if auteurs exist in the most restrictive film-making system in the world, then they can exist anywhere".[8] Thus, in order to contextualize the auteur theory within the Korean environment, in what follows we seek to show how Yu—and two of his most important and well-known films—contribute to this localized understanding of the auteur.

The first case study, *Aimless Bullet* (1961), demonstrates the themes, choice of *mise-en-scene*, montage and sound effects, and the overall visual style associated with the "aesthetics of devastation" used by Yu to depict a society in decline. It then examines how Yu communicated his beliefs about auteurship through his efforts to spread his views on the art of film and freedom of expression. By advocating the role of the auteur in the media and through his teaching, and also by starting a film club, Yu sought to emphasize the importance of art filmmaking. As we show in the second case study, through the depiction of male sexual fantasy in a surreal, dreamy world in the rare experimental film *The Empty Dream* (1965), Yu put his theories into practice by confronting censorship head on. Both films are examples of the diverse aesthetic strategies he adopted from the mid-1960s to ensure his survival as a filmmaker. In addition to his well-known art filmmaking, Yu also made a number of popular genre films for political and economic reasons. He introduced and directed amateur films using 8mm technology, as well as producing independent cultural films. In adopting these various strategies in his filmography of 45 films, he gradually distanced himself from the restrictions imposed by the Producer Registration System (PRS).

Auteurship in the Korean Context

Yu was born and raised in Hwanghae province in North Korea, and he moved to Seoul following liberation in 1945. Influenced by his mother, who was a faithful Christian, in his youth Yu attempted to enter a seminary to train for the priesthood but failed the entry (English) test. However, his early interest in Christianity continued, becoming an important theme in his films. In 1947 Yu gained a place at Dongguk University to study literature and theater. Watching foreign films—such as *Crime et Châtiment* (1935)—a practice that had been banned since the late 1930s under Japanese colonial rule, Yu became interested in scriptwriting and directing. To learn more about filmmaking, he studied books on cinema and frequently visited production sites, including the location for director Choi In-gyu's *Hurray for Freedom* (1946).

In 1948, his second year at university, Yu organized a student film club, one of the earliest in Korea. That same year he directed and produced a 45-minute sound film, *Sea Wind*, with help from director Kim Seong-min and cinematographer Won Young-il.[9] This early attempt predated the establishment of film schools in Korea, so that Yu had to acquire the technical knowledge necessary for even rudimentary attempts at filmmaking on his own. (Korea's first film school, Seorabeol Art College, was established in 1953.) Following graduation, he started out in the industry as an assistant director on projects including Shin Sang-ok's debut film *Evil Night* (1952) and Lee Gyu-hwan's *Story of Chunhyang* (1955).

In 1956, Yu made his film debut with the family melodrama *Crossroad*, a story of twin girls who were separated when young and go on to lead very different lives. While this first film received little attention, within two years Yu had become an award-winning filmmaker. His fifth film, *The Seizure of Life* (1958), which deals with an unscrupulous businessman who fakes his own death to escape the consequences of his tax evasion, embezzlement and swindling, received the "best director" award and a host of other honors at the Second Annual Buil Film Festival in 1959.[10] At the time, along with other directors, such as Kim Ki-young and Lee Byung-il, Yu—with his uncompromising faith in film as art—was regarded as an exceptional creative talent who would lead the Korean film industry to new heights.

With the release of his eighth film, *Aimless Bullet,* in 1961, Yu achieved a watershed in Korean cinema through the film's realistic portrayal of a run-down post-war society—a rare achievement in an era when other domestic films, mostly melodramas, made little reference to contemporary events.[11] Yu's handling of aesthetic styling and his exploration of the human condition both achieved new heights in *Aimless Bullet*, marking him out as Korea's leading arthouse filmmaker and auteur. In the following analysis of the film, we explore his approach to questions of style and aesthetics, while also demonstrating how Yu's unwavering commitment to arthouse filmmaking challenged the censorship process.

The Auteur's Canvas: *Aimless Bullet* (1961)

The lofty reputation that Yu enjoyed throughout his career—and especially after Korean cinema had achieved new creative heights following the lifting of government censorship in 1996—largely stemmed from the domestic and international acclaim lavished on *Aimless Bullet*. Today, the film is routinely praised by domestic critics as the "best" Korean film of all time and has been consistently judged as the country's premier film, reminiscent of the position enjoyed by *Citizen Kane* in US film history.[12]

Aimless Bullet is based on Lee Beom-seon's short novel of the same name published in 1959. Like many post-war Korean novels, Lee's book dealt with issues such as poverty, the tragedy of a divided nation and separated families and posed fundamental questions about the meaning of life in an era of despair, frustration, and alienation.[13] Yu's unflinching depiction of post-war society is largely indebted to Lee's poignant novel. The fact that the film was produced at all was the result of the April Revolution of 1960, a democratic movement of students, teachers, and other citizens that brought about the collapse of the authoritarian regime of President Syngman Rhee. The new democratic government (the 2nd Republic of Korea) relaxed censorship during its eight months in office. For the first time in Korea's film history, the government handed over responsibility for censorship to a civilian authority, the Motion Picture Ethics Committee. Compared to the country's previous censorship regulations, built on the film laws inherited from the Japanese colonial era as well as the US occupation period, the new censorship apparatus created a liberal production environment. This newfound creative freedom—which was to be short-lived—enabled Yu to craft *Aimless Bullet* as a vehicle for expressing a critical view of society. Like the new democratic regime, the Motion Picture Ethics Committee disappeared following the military coup of May 1961.

46 The Golden Age of the 1960s

The film was produced by pioneer lighting technician Kim Seong-chun, as his first production following his establishment of the Daehan Film Company.[14] Drawing on his professional networks, Kim recruited rising director Yu and veteran cinematographer Kim Hak-seong, a cast that included seasoned actors Kim Jin-kyu, Choi Mu-ryong, and Moon Jeong-suk and other crew. So impressed were they by the screenplay that they all agreed to work on the film for free.[15] When *Aimless Bullet* was finally released in April 1961, it was praised for attaining a new level of artistry and for its bold attempt to reveal the "truth" about the dark side of life in Korea.[16] Among the film's technical achievements, the use of intensive sound effects, innovative camera techniques, and montage editing involving a sequence of short takes jumbled together were marked out for special praise.[17] Yu's status as a leading arthouse filmmaker was established by *Aimless Bullet*, which is still given high praise for its incisive exploration of the human condition, pioneering use of montage and sound effects and a *mise-en-scene* redolent of German expressionism.[18]

Aimless Bullet tells the story of a family of seven refugees from North Korea; crowded into a miserable shack in a district of Seoul known as Liberation village (*Haebang-chon*), they are trying to carve out a place for themselves in an impoverished post-war society. This poor neighborhood was established in 1945 following the liberation of Korea from Japanese occupation and is mostly inhabited by North Korean escapees. The film depicts characters whose lives are driven by social deprivation rather than positive desires and aspirations. Despite their grandly named village, family members are unable to liberate themselves from poverty. In their bleak weatherboard hut, the grandmother lies sick in bed, crying out deliriously, "Let's go; let's go". While not specifying any particular destination, and unable to go anywhere herself, the sick old woman symbolizes a nation that is profoundly lost and struggling to find a way out of its troubles. Cheol-ho, the first son and head of the household, is as an accounting clerk; financial hardship is chief among the many difficulties he faces. Even while suffering from constant toothache, he cannot afford to see a dentist. His malnourished wife is pregnant, and the second son, Yeong-ho, is a maimed ex-soldier who can't find a job. His sister Myeong-suk becomes a prostitute, consorting with foreign soldiers in order to support the family.

The future looks unrelentingly bleak for this family. Out of desperation, Yeong-ho robs a bank and is arrested. Cheol-ho's wife is rushed to hospital to deliver her baby but dies of complications during the birth. A motherless baby arrives into the world. After witnessing these deeply depressing events, Cheol-ho visits the dentist to have a tooth removed. Bleeding badly and stupefied by pain following the extraction, he hails a taxi but cannot decide where to go—Liberation village (where his mother is), the Central Police Station (where his brother is) or Seoul National University Hospital (where his wife is). The film ends with an out-of-focus night shot of Seoul, accompanied by a sigh from the taxi driver: "Such an aimless bullet, not knowing where to go".

A feeling of desperation and an urge to escape a hopeless way of life marks each character's journey, preparing the ground for the film's anti-climatic ending. Yu's experimentation with German expressionism, which had strongly influenced him, in his use of sound, lighting, and set design, intensified his depiction of a listless post-war society. At the same time, Yu's aesthetic choices effectively conveyed his characters' psychological states as they struggle with the circumstances of their lives—in ways reminiscent of Italian Neo-realist films such as *The Bicycle Thief* (1948). If Yu's goal was to portray the suffocating atmosphere of post-war Korea on screen, he was eminently successful.

At the time of its release in early 1961 (see Figure 2.1), *Aimless Bullet* received critical acclaim for its artistic achievement, but it failed to appeal to general audiences. In response to a run of poor houses, the Gukje Cinema pulled the film from its screening schedule early and replaced it with a more commercial title.[19] Nonetheless, Yu himself recalled that the Gukje Cinema had become a full house for about a week following opening day, albeit with more intellectuals than middle-class people in the audience. Although the film's potentially antagonistic title may have put off the cinema's regular customers, Yu recalled that those who did see *Aimless Bullet* were so impressed by the film that they gathered afterwards in bars near the cinema to discuss the film, its meaning, and its connection with their own experiences of suffering and deprivation.[20]

Figure 2.1 Film advertisement for *Aimless Bullet. Gyeonghyang Shinmun* 23 February, 1961:4.

48 The Golden Age of the 1960s

Despite Yu's positive memories of its reception at the Gukje Cinema, the film was a failure at the box office and was popular only with the so-called intelligentsia (*jisigin*), a group that included highly educated academics, scholars, and journalists—a very small proportion of the population. According to the National Statistics Office, in 1955 people aged over 25 with higher degrees (high school diplomas and above) comprised only 1.7 percent of the population. By 1966 this number had multiplied threefold to 5.6 percent—still an inconsiderable figure.[21]

To make things worse, the film became the first victim of the censorship guidelines promulgated by the new military government in July 1961. As discussed in Chapter 1, following the May 16 coup the regime required all cultural events and films intended for exhibition to pass censorship. *Aimless Bullet* was denied an exhibition license when submitted to the censors in July for re-release at second-run cinemas. In so doing, the Park government stifled the rising sense of freedom represented by *Aimless Bullet* and other films inspired by it. According to Yu's 1995 memoir, the film was banned for two seemingly feeble reasons. First, the sick grandmother's repeated shouting of "Let's go, let's go" ("*Gaja! Gaja!*") was interpreted by the censors as, "Let's go back to North Korea". Second, the social conditions portrayed in the film were regarded as too dark and abject.[22]

Perhaps a third reason for denying a permit was that the Park regime was concerned about the gathering of intellectuals and potentially subversive discussions about social conditions stimulated by the film. In reality, it was the intelligentsia who would have been concerned—essentially, they were revolutionaries who had succeeded in ousting the authoritarian Syngman Rhee regime and helped establish the short-lived democratic government that succeeded it. This aspect of the film's suppression was not publicized in newspapers and movie magazines, and the film did not receive a single award at any of the domestic film festivals held in 1961. The exhibition ban on *Aimless Bullet* lasted for two years.

In 1963, the ban was lifted unexpectedly with the help of American film scholar Dr. Richard McCann, a lecturer at the University of Southern California who was visiting Korea as a consultant for the National Film Production Centre (NFPC). During his four-month stay, McCann not only taught and advised NFPC staff, but also viewed numerous Korean films to enhance his understanding of the country and its film culture. Amongst them was *Aimless Bullet*, which he reportedly regarded as the best Korean film he had seen on account of its outstanding narrative structure, visual style, and technique.[23] McCann, who had connections with the selection committee of the San Francisco Film Festival, arranged a meeting with Minister of Public Information Im Seong-hee and director Yu at which he invited Korea to submit the film to the 7th San Francisco Film Festival, scheduled for November 1963. While the regime had hitherto denied the film to both domestic and overseas audiences, this foreign visitor convinced the government that *Aimless Bullet* should be valued for its outstanding creative qualities rather than its negative portrayal of Korean society. In fact, McCann strongly believed that *Aimless Bullet* was Academy Award material—especially considering that Korea's film industry was relatively new.[24]

At the Crossroads of Directing and Politics   49

To celebrate the exceptional international recognition generated by the film, the Daehan Film Company ran an advertisement for *Aimless Bullet* a few weeks before the start of the San Francisco Film Festival (see Figure 2.2). In it, a montage of positive reviews from six domestic newspapers (*Donga, Gyeonghyang, Seoul, Chosun, Hanguk,* and *Daehan Daily*), as well as a Japanese and an English-language paper, surrounds a portrait of the film's protagonist, Cheol-ho. The critical acclaim that *Aimless Bullet* had received following its release two years earlier is the obvious selling point of this advertisement. Although the original promotional campaign had lasted for only one week, this new advertisement reflected a renewed interest on the part of the producer, as well as the proprietors of the cinema (the Eulji Cinema) where the film was screened, to re-live and re-exploit the excitement generated by the film's original release.

Figure 2.2 Film advertisement for *Aimless Bullet. Donga Daily* 21 October, 1963: 4.

In November 1963 the film was screened at the San Francisco Film Festival, with director Yu and main actor Kim Jin-kyu (Cheol-ho) attending the event. In fact, the print sent to the festival later became the only copy of the film that is known to survive. This worn-out print with English subtitles was released on DVD in 2003.

The festival invitation and the lifting of the ban on *Aimless Bullet* occurred in the middle of a major political transition. The military regime was preparing to hand over power to a civilian government as it had promised in its revolutionary pledge. Park Chung Hee was running for president and the official presidential campaign began in September 1963. Given this political context, it could be argued that the positive press coverage surrounding the re-release of *Aimless Bullet* was intended as a "friendly gesture" by the military government toward the film and art community with a view to generating votes—just as politicians reach out to the film and cultural sectors for support today. The election was held on 15 October 1963, and Park Chung Hee became the new president of Korea.

Aimless Bullet marked a turning point in Yu's career. The critical acclaim that he received, the controversial banning of the film as well as its unexpected overturning all contributed to the elevation of Yu as Korea's leading arthouse director. Newspapers and magazines with a cultural bent sought him out to head up panel discussions and comment on industry issues, including censorship. At the same time, his interest in existentialism had deepened, and his next three films—*Kim's Daughters* (1963), *The Extra Mortals* (1964), and *The Martyrs* (1965)—were all "literary" genre films based on novels about people facing the challenges of social transformation, specifically postcolonial modernity and the war. *The Extra Mortals* was regarded as a companion piece to *Aimless Bullet* for its similar themes and critique of post-war society and its realist style. *The Martyrs*—Yu's first film after the establishment of his own (independent) production company, Yu Hyun-mok Productions, in 1964—explored weighty theological issues, questioning the presence of God in time of war. It was based on the Richard E. Kim (aka Kim Eun-guk) novel *The Martyred*, published in the US in 1964; the author explored the meaning of Christianity against the backdrop of the Korean War. After acquiring the copyright in late 1964, Yu relished the opportunity to explore a theme that had always interested him on the silver screen.[25]

While *Aimless Bullet* failed to garner awards at local film festivals, these mid-1960s productions won a slew of awards including best film, best director, best actor and actress, best art director, and best cinematography at various local film festivals. As an award-winning producer, these accolades entitled Yu—or, more specifically, Yu's production companies—to highly coveted film import licenses, compensating him for poor box office returns and also giving him a reputation for directing literary films—the quintessential art-house genre in Korea.

During this time, Yu actively shared his art filmmaking beliefs through opinion pieces in newspapers and magazines and speaking engagements at public seminars and private gatherings. In all these activities, Yu had three major aims: First, he urged students and directors to transcend conventional storytelling techniques and to develop their own anti-commercial film styles. As we show in our discussion of *The Empty Dream* below, Yu preferred to let sound effects, set design, editing, and montage lead and intensify his characters' emotions, rather than the storyline.

Second, Yu encouraged people to investigate the new film movements that were making an impact abroad. To lead the way, Yu founded the Cine Poem Club in 1964 with other film buffs such as literary critic Choi Il-soo and television producer Im Hak-song.[26] The club's regular activities included seminars and screenings of avant-garde and experimental films.[27] Together, Yu and his supporters introduced experimental filmmaking trends to students and other industry members, and explored ways of putting theory into practice. Through these activities, Yu encouraged others to join him in the search of new modes of cinematic expression, especially those that were popular in the West. Third, Yu was concerned about emphasizing the value of freedom of expression. As we show in the next section, he was dragged through the courts following the release of *The Empty Dream*. Yu chose to challenge the regime rather than submit to the censors' scissors.

The Empty Dream (1965) and the Vanguard of Art Filmmaking

While Yu had been interested in experimental filmmaking even before he began teaching at Dongguk University in 1963, his academic position lent additional credibility to his published opinions, in addition to giving him financial independence. Shortly after gaining his university post, Yu produced two short experimental films, *Lines* (1964, 13 minutes) and *Hand* (1964, 1 minute), both practical illustrations of the new ideas, cinematic expression, forms, and styles that had seized his attention.[28] The experience of making these two films gave him the basic knowledge necessary to complete his feature-length experimental film *The Empty Dream* (1965), which is regarded by contemporary film scholars as Korea's first avant-garde film production.[29]

The Empty Dream is a remake of the Japanese pornographic film *Daydream* (aka *Hakujitsumu* 1964), directed by Tetsuji Takechi, one of the leaders of the "pink film" movement that swept the Japanese cinema in the 1960s. Notorious as one of the first big-budget soft porn films of its kind to be made and released in Japan, *Daydream* explored male sexual fantasy in the setting of a dentist's office, showcasing a variety of sexual activities including rape and eroticized torture scenes as dream sequences. *Daydream* became a box office hit in Japan and was released in the US in the same year (apparently with new footage shot and added by US director Joseph Green).[30]

Korean producer Guk Kwae-nam, owner of Segi Sangsa, a Korean film company with an importing background, saw this very popular film during a business trip to Japan and recognized its box office potential for the Korean market. At the time, official cultural exchanges between Korea and Japan were banned, hampering the importation and release of Japanese films in Korea. With these restrictions in mind, Guk bought the remake rights to *Daydream* and, on returning to Korea, recruited Yu to direct the film. Guk was confident that Yu's reputation as an art filmmaker would help to get an adaptation of this striking and transgressive Japanese film passed by the censors.[31] Given that government policy prohibited the public screening of Japanese films, Korean filmmakers found it expedient simply to remake a variety of Japanese films. While *The Empty Dream* was an official remake facilitated through the purchase of its original copyright, many other titles were plagiarized, in whole or part, from Japanese films by unscrupulous screenwriters who simply lifted the original Japanese film scripts, which were regularly published in popular Japanese film magazines such as *Kinema Junpō*.

This widespread practice reflected a poor awareness of copyright in the film industry—not only among producers and directors, but also among MPI officials who showed little interest in curbing such activities. (A more detailed discussion about the media's heavy criticism of this prevalent practice is provided in Chapter 4.) Yet, Yu wanted no part in this cinematic charade, as it did nothing to encourage or develop native screenwriting talent. In an effort to avoid producing a replica of the original film, Yu edited the film himself, transforming *The Empty Dream* into an entirely experimental film that Yu believed veered off in directions undreamed of by the original filmmakers. Although Yu's version follows the structure of the Japanese original with an "almost unerring fidelity", it remains a far superior work in terms of art direction, cinematography, the use of montage, and other technical features—elements critics have described as reminiscent of early French surrealism or German expressionism.[32]

The film opens with a short children's play performed on a stage, prefiguring what will follow. In this film-within-a-film, two boys (one wearing a beard and carrying a cane, and the other wearing a beret) are shown dancing, chasing a girl in a white dress. This scene is followed by a four-minute montage sequence that juxtaposes close-up shots of whirling dental equipment, drilling machines in an iron foundry, and images of the watery, wide-open eyes and parted lips of the dentist and his patients. The screeching of industrial drills is played over these psychedelic images, amplifying the nightmarish atmosphere of the dental clinic. The absence of dialogue also aids in foregrounding visual imagery as a dominant element in the film's narrative trajectory. Subsequent shots are constructed from the patients' point of view as they undergo treatment, reflecting the psychological state of each in turn. For example, a child patient sees a fan that is transformed into an image of a propeller-driven aircraft. An elderly patient, who is advised by the dentist to avoid alcohol, imagines a beer glass in place of the rinsing cup. And in the case of the female protagonist, an overhead light morphs into a bunch of flowers. In each of these sequences, real-world objects are transformed into the things that each character imagines and desires, to the accompaniment of disconcerting sound effects and discordant music.

The montage sequence employed in the scene where the female protagonist is undergoing treatment suggests the awakening of sexual feelings in one of the male characters, who is observing her from the waiting room. Close-up shots of her lips, clenching fists, sweaty neck, and moving legs are intercut with images of a drill being inserted into her mouth. Water slowly drips into a cup during treatment, and her moaning and panting following her session in the chair intensifies these sexual undertones. As she rinses her mouth and winces in pain, the male patient waiting his turn becomes sexually aroused. Then, when it is his turn to sit in the dentist's chair, and he is sedated for an extraction procedure, we are witness to his fantasy in which he and the female patient join hands and escape the clutches of the villainous dentist.

Yu constructed this dream-like world using striking sound effects and a cubical set design that combines elements of German expressionist art and a Cubist painting by Salvador Dalí. His experimentation with expressionism, which was only hinted at in his previous film *Aimless Bullet* (1961), was brought to a new level in *The Empty Dream*. The sets designed for the dream sequences, including scenes set in a club and department store, utilized slanting poles and asymmetrical props with converging or diverging vertical and horizontal lines. The film's visual effects created a surreal atmosphere similar to that in *The Cabinet of Dr. Caligari* (1919), giving audiences a feeling of disorientation and lassitude. An audacious experiment, *The Empty Dream* marked an unparalleled turn in Korean cinema.

As producer Guk had anticipated, *The Empty Dream* passed the censors and was screened over the first two weeks of July 1965. Even the newspaper advertisements for the film oozed with overt themes of sexuality, with headlines announcing the film's main subject—"two bodies and their lusts", "sensuous physical paradise", and "completely exotic".

Figure 2.3 Film advertisements for *The Empty Dream* (from left to right): *Gyeonghyang Shinmun* 2 July 1965: 2; *Donga Daily* 3 July, 1965: 5; *Gyeonghyang Shinmun* 3 July, 1965: 8.

54 The Golden Age of the 1960s

Surprisingly, given this explicit promotion, reviews and other reports about the film were not forthcoming at the time of its release. In fact, for the next six months, very little about Yu appeared in Korea's news media. However, there was a frenzy of activity behind the scenes. The next thing that people read about Yu concerned his alleged violation of anticommunist and obscenity laws, and his subsequent arrest by the prosecutor's office in January 1966. A scene containing a naked body in *The Empty Dream* had turned the state interrogator's spotlight on Yu, forcing him to defend his filmmaking style and philosophy. Still, the real reason for Yu's arrest was probably his public opposition to the government's anticommunist campaign and his strong defense of freedom of expression. Yu's support for creativity in the film industry had led him to speak out on both issues, and he had also come to the defense of director Lee Man-hee in early 1965 after Lee was arrested for allegedly perpetrating pro-communistic ideals in *Seven Female POWs* (1965); many including Yu regarded Lee as a scapegoat who was being used to rein in artists under the control of the MPI.

In March 1965, Yu gave a public presentation on freedom of expression, raising awareness about the plight of director Lee Man-hee. At a seminar hosted by the International Conference for Cultural Freedom (Segye Munhwa Jayu Hoeui), Yu read a paper titled "Freedom on the Silver Screen" (Eunmak-ui Jayu). In his talk, he asserted that the Korean Constitution guaranteed every citizen the right to freedom of expression, as well as protection from attempts by the government to crack down on creative artists.[33] With his own censorship battles over *Aimless Bullet* no doubt fresh in his mind, Yu's speech was a bold demonstration of his support for Lee, gaining him much respect for being the only member of the film industry to take a public stand for freedom of expression. In response, the prosecutor's office turned its attention on Yu, triggering an incessant round of investigations. Prosecutor Choi Dae-hyeon, who was infamous for his hard-line anticommunist stance, was put in charge of the case, interrogating Yu and other filmmakers in an attempt to expose their "hidden agenda".

The release of *The Empty Dream* provided Choi with an ideal pretext to indict Yu for violating both anticommunist and obscenity laws—although the film only showed a glimpse of the actress's "bare" back (she was actually wearing a flesh-colored body stocking). The only other tangible evidence the prosecutor had to show for his efforts was a still picture of a semi-nude woman and scraps of film from the editing room floor. Despite the paucity of evidence, the case was sent to trial, symbolizing the government's intolerance of publicly expressed support for freedom of expression. As far as the regime was concerned, Yu (like Lee) was simply another convenient scapegoat.

Since Yu's public advocacy of freedom of expression was hardly a crime in itself, the prosecutor's office sought to prove that he had directed a pornographic film. Yu's defense was straightforward: all instances of full-frontal nudity had been cut from the completed film, and the actress had been wearing a full body stocking in the scene in question.[34] The trial lasted for more than 18 months, exhausting Yu physically and mentally as well as draining his financial resources. In the end, the court dropped the first charge of violating the Anticommunist Law but found him guilty of the second charge of producing a pornographic publication. As a result of this subsequent legal battle, *The Empty Dream* was withdrawn from cinemas, and for many years afterward it was believed by many—including Yu himself—to be lost. However, in 2004 the film was found quite by chance at the Korean Film Archive (hereafter KOFA) among its uncatalogued films. Following restoration work on the print, the film was publicly screened at the 2004 Buchon International Fantastic Film Festival.

Despite the personal toll the case had taken on him, the reversal of the most serious of these charges enabled Yu to reestablish and even strengthen his reputation as a director who had survived two major censorship battles without compromising his artistic or personal integrity. From this point in his career, Yu's stocks rose considerably, and once again he became a sought-after media celebrity and industry spokesperson. He resumed writing articles for newspapers and magazines and accepted invitations to give public seminars organized by the KMPPA (Korean Motion Pictures Producers Association) and the MPI on issues facing the domestic and international film industries. However, it seems that he never fully recovered from these traumatic experiences; as we will see, as Yu's career developed he struggled more and more to carve out a space for himself in the unequal battle between artistic integrity and complicity with the political establishment.

In 2006, researchers at KOFA together with a large panel of Korean film specialists placed *The Empty Dream* as 37th out of the 100 most significant Korean films produced and released between 1936 and 1996. (*Aimless Bullet* was ranked at 23.) After a wait lasting four decades, Yu had finally been given credit for his innovative exploration of themes and aesthetics that had proved so provocative in the mid-1960s. According to the KOFA website, "It is all but impossible to find a commercial film in Korea from the 1960s to the present day that has so boldly faced the problem of form as [did] *The Empty Dream*. In this sense, *The Empty Dream* is a film that marked a rare moment in Korean cinematic history".[35] Indeed, more rare moments were soon to be experienced—the kind that were sorely needed to draw Korean cinema out from under the shroud that had threatened to suffocate the industry throughout the 1970s.

The Aftermath: Following the Industry's Downward Spiral

Following his trial, Yu Hyun-mok's career followed a very different trajectory from those of his fellow directors. As a result of the government's support for film adaptations of domestic literary works through the Import License Reward System (ILRS) and the Producer Registration System (PRS), he was able to sustain and develop his position as an auteur. Constrained by political and commercial pressures to compromise his artistry and vision, Yu nevertheless found a pathway that would allow him to preserve his integrity. He was able to do so because literary genre films were essentially art films. As we saw in Chapter 1, in the 1960s Korean producers made increasing numbers of government-backed literary films to maximize their chances of winning an MPI award (for meeting their quota of films produced in this particular genre), thereby increasing their opportunities for gaining a lucrative import license. Yu understood how this system worked and exploited it to the full, profiting from the making of art films disguised as government-sponsored literary genre films—even if the completed film was shelved and never exhibited.[36]

While Yu's value as a commercial director was generally rated lower by registered producers than that of directors such as Shin Sang-ok, Kim Ki-duk, and Kim Su-yong, they were keenly aware of Yu's track record of winning awards, which brought highly coveted licenses to import and exhibit profitable foreign films in their train. For both parties, it was a partnership of convenience. Yu's award-winning films from this time include *The Guests of the Last Train* (1967) and *Descendants of Cain* (1968), both of which contain a strong social critique, as well as embodying his continuing exploration of existentialism and the human condition.

In *The Guests of the Last Train*, people are shown wandering aimlessly around the city until the curfew begins, when they board the last train for home. While commentators have seen the film as a modernist text that explores the impact of urbanization—similar to director Kim Su-yong's *Mist*—by showing how his characters' daily routines are circumscribed by the official curfew, Yu incorporated an element of social criticism, suggesting that Koreans were living in a stifling world in which all exits had been blocked by the regime. Ironically, the MPI, which had been partly responsible for his prosecution two years earlier, helped Yu make films of this type and at the same time sustain his reputation as an auteur throughout the late 1960s.[37]

Nevertheless, not all of the films in Yu's portfolio contributed to his status as an auteur. Like so many other directors concerned with keeping their heads above water, Yu became involved in projects that spanned multiple genres, including anticommunist films, comedies, and horror films—mostly to keep food on the table.[38] At the time, few if any filmmakers had the luxury of clinging to exclusive status as an auteur, and most were forced to make a number of commercial films that they would have preferred to avoid. However, in Yu's case, even if he had little choice in collaborating with the government, at the very least the practical realities facing the film industry enabled him to portray the multiple and diverse faces of Korean society in a variety of film genres and formats.[39]

In addition, within an increasingly over-regulated and restricted environment, Yu began to distance himself from the overbearing PRS by making a series of 16mm films that allowed him and his small production crews a measure of artistic freedom. Yu first became interested in 16mm filmmaking while on a trip to Europe in 1969, visiting studios and shopping for film equipment. He returned to Korea with a 16mm spring-wound professional Bolex camera that he had purchased in Switzerland and expressed an enthusiasm for the new wave of film trends sweeping over Britain, Czechoslovakia, France, Germany, and Poland.[40] In 1970, Yu established the Korea Amateur Filmmakers Association (KAMA), with film critic Byon In-sik, cinematographer Jeong Il-seong, and more than 80 others, with a view to making the achievements of these European film movements better known at home. (The KAMA is still active in the 2010s.) News of

Yu's amateur filmmaking activities spread quickly, raising questions among some industry people as to whether his involvement with projects outside the purview of the PRS would mark the end of his directorial career.[41]

Despite these misgivings, Yu's establishment of Yu Productions, a new cultural film production company, in 1972 effectively marked his independence from the PRS. Weary of endless negotiations with producers over projects that had to be either commercially successful or garner industry awards—and in contrast to other directors such as Lee Man-hee, Kim Su-yong, Kim ki-duk, and Shin Sang-ok, who were struggling to survive within the confines of the PRS—Yu decided to strike out on his own and produce independent cultural films. Ironically, this move involved a degree of compromise with the Park regime, for which "cultural" films were an effective propaganda tool.[42] Throughout the decade, the MPI was one of Yu Productions' largest clients, keeping Yu and his production crews busy with projects promoting government initiatives such as a national savings campaign and the New Village Movement.[43]

Conclusion

While today Yu Hyun-mok is remembered as one of Korea's leading filmmakers, until recently the contribution of the various strategies he developed for dealing with censorship to the success enjoyed by the domestic film industry in the 2010s has gone largely unrecognized. Part of a group of directors struggling to find ways of negotiating an ever-changing production environment, he achieved a measure of success, albeit temporary.

The MPI's developmentalist strategy of enlarging the scale of Korea's film industry seemingly worked. Money and the promise of prosperity boosted productivity, leading the industry to enjoy a Golden Age of Korean cinema. However, the next stage was not so bright. The 1970s was a time of radical downsizing for the industry, including the activities of registered producers. While the industry had expanded rapidly, its superstructure was flimsy, swayed by every small change in film policy. At the base, the Korean film industry was a victim of the developmentalist state policies of the 1960s. During the 1970s, television gained a poll position as the alternative national media, and film's usefulness to the Park regime decreased dramatically. The growth of the film market slowed at the end of the 1960s as production standards fell and cash flow within the film industry reduced to a trickle. Creativity and funding were both at a premium under the state's powerful censorship regime and tightly controlled PRS system. As we have seen, Yu fell foul of the censors when he attempted to challenge the political system. As the industry began its downward spiral in the 1970s, his own career followed suit. Just as his rise as the nation's leading director had represented the Golden Age of Korean cinema in the 1960s, his fall exemplified the industry's decline in the following decade.

For much of his career, Yu fought an uphill battle with a government that was determined to control the film industry through the PRS. At the same time, censorship rules became tougher, placing filmmakers under increased pressure.

Directors and producers had to make themselves subservient to the authorities, or at least appear to do so. Yu and many of his fellow directors each sought different pathways to liberate themselves from the demands of the PRS. Many of them believed in freedom of expression and sought to act as if they *were* free in a system that was clearly not. During the 1960s Yu stood out among his peers precisely for the ways in which he fought an oppressive system, one which had the final sanction of censorship at its disposal. As his legal battles demonstrated, his dogged perseverance and passion for the arts enabled him to overcome obstacles that would have cowed lesser spirits.

For an artist working in this environment, complying with the government was not a choice, but rather a survival strategy. As the regime's political leadership became entrenched, its quest for power and control of its citizens' activities increased. Yu was scapegoated by the MPI—and therefore the Park regime—at a time when the state was amassing total control over all aspects of society. Yu's censorship trial, which was advanced by the prosecutor's office as well as the KCIA (Korean Central Intelligence Agency), reveals the extent to which the state would go to assert its authority over Korean cinema.

Under the Park regime, artists were intimidated by overt physical threats, as Yu's arrest and trial show, as well as by more subtle means, such as the self-regulation that the film industry imposed on its members. Yu was a victim of both types of coercion. However, Yu's unyielding faith in art cinema and the ways that he put theory into practice were the foundation of his distinctive film style and sense of auteurship. Although in many ways shackled by the PRS, he took every opportunity to advocate creative autonomy and freedom of expression, extending the discussion of film issues well beyond the usual run of commercial imperatives, box office statistics, and government demands. His distinctive aesthetic palate, which blended realist, experimental, and modernist film styles, along with his trademark themes dealing with mortality, solitude, and religious belief, showed that auteurs could survive—even thrive—in Korea.

Creative expression of this kind, however, was severely challenged after the government tightened state surveillance in the mid-1960s. The ensuing censorship trial ultimately forced Yu to develop a new survival strategy. While continuing to make artfilms, he began experimenting with melodrama, using the sentimental love stories that were the staple of the genre to explore the human condition and as a vehicle for social criticism. In this way, Yu and others such as Lee Man-hee managed to slip away from control by Park's censorship regime. Yu outwitted the censors by creating and then defending a cinematic space that accommodated his creativity as an artist and his critical assessment of Korean society—a space the censors were unable to block. Yu's success in outflanking the PRS rewarded him with a loyal following and the confidence to continue making films for art's sake. Although his career as a feature filmmaker went into decline, until his death Yu was respected throughout the industry as a true auteur of Korean cinema and a devotee of art filmmaking.

However, while Yu survived the 1960s, he failed to maintain his integrity to the end—admittedly not an easy task in the circumstances he faced. As we have seen, in the 1970s Yu did an about-face, forming friendly relations with the Park government. His relationship with the authorities was formed on the pragmatic principle of "you scratch my back and I'll scratch yours", thus creating room for negotiation and compromise. In 1990 he directed *Nation's Light*, a documentary about Park Chung Hee that glorified Park's achievements to the accompaniment of an emotion-laden female voiceover—a total reversal of the political and artistic values for which he had fought so hard in the past. The circumstances—demanding filmmakers' complicity with political power—began to change in the 1990s with the political and social transformation of Korea, including the election of a civilian government in 1993 and the end of state censorship in 1996. A new era of arthouse filmmaking had arrived, enabling new talents like Kim Ki-duk and Hong Sang-soo to give free rein to their imaginations and unleash experiments of their own on the silver screen.

Notes

1. See Sarris 2004.
2. Lee 1995: 196.
3. Yu 1995: 109.
4. Kim 2003a.
5. "Any Problem with Censorship? (Yeonghwa Geomyeore Isang Eopneunga?)". *Yeonghwa Yesul* (May 1965): 60–67. At a panel organized by the magazine *Yeonghwa Yesul*, screenwriter Oh Yeong-jin and film critic Lee Young-il agreed that censorship and other restrictions placed on the industry by the Producer Registration System prevented directors from developing their individual styles and themes.
6. For example, see Kim Su-nam 2002 and 2003.
7. As notably attempted by Andrew Sarris 1962.
8. Nelmes 2003: 136.
9. According to Yu's memoirs, the film dealt with a fisherman's son who went mad after losing his father at sea (Yu 1995: 65). While this student effort is listed as Yu's first film in his autobiography and on websites such as the Korean Movie Database, the film is no longer extant, and there are no known references to it in newspapers or magazines of the period.
10. *The Seizure of Life* also won awards for best film, best actor, best supporting actor, best supporting actress, and best original score at the Buil Film Festival. Later in 1959 the film was submitted to the Sixth Asian Film Festival as Korea's official entry.
11. See "Watershed Films for Korea's Film Community (Hanguk Yeonghwagye-e Ildae Jeonggireul Maryeon)". *Chosun Daily* (28 April, 1961): 4. The other watershed film mentioned, along with *Aimless Bullet*, was director Shin Sang-ok's *Story of Chunhyang*, which was marked out for its unprecedented box office success. Audiences of 380,000 in Seoul broke previous box office records for both domestic and foreign films—a feat comparable to *Shiri's* (1999) outperforming of *Titanic* (1998) at the Korean the box office.
12. *Aimless Bullet* headed the list of the top 50 films of the twentieth century compiled by the Korean monthly film magazine *Screen* in 1998 and also headed *Screen's* 100 best Korean films in 1999. In 2014, the Korean Film Archive placed it at the top of its own list of the 100 most significant Korean films (tied for first place with *Housemaid* and *The March of Fools*).
13. Jeong et al. 2000: 67–69.
14. Kim Seong-chun (1903–1977) was Korea's first professional film lighting technician, often referred to by his colleagues as 'the master'. Having completed his training and apprenticeship in Japan in the 1920s, Kim returned to Korea in 1934, taking up work

60   *The Golden Age of the 1960s*

　　　in the colonial film industry. Beginning with *The Sprinkler* (1935), Kim worked on a total of 73 films as a lighting technician.
15. "Director Yu Quickens the Pace in the Making of Aimless Bullet (Pichi Ollineun Yu Gamdok, Obaltan Chwaryeong Kwaejo)". *Hanguk Daily* (8 August, 1960): 4.
16. "Watershed Films for Korea's Film Community (Hanguk Yeonghwagye-eh Ildae Jeonggi-reul Maryeon)". *Hanguk Daily* (28 April, 1961): 4; "Column: Horizon (Jipyeongseon)". *Chosun Daily* (14 April 1961): 1.
17. "New Film: *Aimless Bullet* is a Serious, Stimulating Film (Sinyeonghwa: Jinjihan Uiyokjak Obaltan)". *Gyeonghyang Shinmun* (17 April, 1961): 4; "New Film: Intensive Analysis of Pessimistic People (Sinyeonghwa: Bujeongjeok Inganui Jibyakjeogin Bunseok Obaltan)". *Seoul Newspaper* (20 April, 1961): 4.
18. Ho 2000; Lee 2004.
19. "Behind the Story of *Aimless Bullet* (Obaltan-ui Dwit Iyagi)". *Gyeonghyang Shinmun* (26 April, 1961): 4.
20. See PIFF 1999: 93.
21. National Statistics Office 1995: 80.
22. Yu 1995: 144–45.
23. "Future of Korean Cinema is Bright, Says Dr. McCann (Hanguk Yeonghwa-ui Apgireun Yangyang, Maekan Baksadam)". *Chosun Daily* (14 July, 1963): 5.
24. McCann's review is available on the festival website: http://history.sffs.org/films/film_details.php?id=116. (Accessed 26 November 2014).
25. "*The Martyred* being Made into a Film (Sungyoja Yeonghwahwa)". *Donga Daily* (9 February 1965): 8.
26. Byon 1995: 180.
27. "Weekly Update (Jugan Seunaep)". *Gyeonghyang Shinmun* (8 June, 1964): 5.
28. According to a story in the *Donga Daily* ["First Attempt of Making an Avant-garde Film (Jeonwi Yeonghwa Cheot Sido)" (9 June, 1964: 6)], *Lines* was about a war orphan looking for humanity in a world divided into arbitrary camps. As both films are lost, it is impossible to judge the level of experimentation they incorporated.
29. Kim 2003a.
30. *Daydream* became a box office hit in Japan and was released in the US the same year, with additional footage by American director Joseph Green. For more information, see Jasper Sharp's *Tetsuji Takechi: Erotic Nightmares* (2001) and *Review: Daydream* (2001), available at midnighteye.com, a website specializing in Japanese cinema. (Accessed 1 December 2010).
31. Yu and Cho, *Oral History of Korean Arts*. See http://www.daarts.or.kr/handle/11080/16560. Performing Arts—Yu Hyun-mok (Gusullo Mannaneun Hanguk Yesulsa: Gongyeon Yesul—Yu Hyun-mok). Available: http://oralhistory.arko.or.kr/oral/main.asp. Accessed 12 September 2009.
32. Sharp 2008:181.
33. The full text of Yu's speech was published in a newspaper article: "Freedom on the Silver Screen (Eunmak-ui Jayu)". *Gyeonghyang Shinmun* (24 March, 1965): 5.
34. The case turned Yu and producer Guk against each other. According to Yu, Guk had inappropriately filmed actress Park Su-jeong in the nude (and alone) under the pretext of shooting a "test reel". However, when was questioned under oath as a trial witness, Park admitted that she had been filmed naked during the actual production. Although the filming may have occurred without Yu's knowledge, Park's testimony damaged his case. (Park herself never recovered from the scandal and left the industry permanently after the trial). See Yu and Cho 2009.
35. See: *100 Korean Films (2006)*. Available: www.koreafilm.org/feature/100_37.asp. Accessed 10 September 2013.

36. Yu's *Son of a Man* (1980) is one such literary film that explored the meaning of religion through one man's quest for redemption. Although the box office takings were minimal, the film received the best picture award at the 19th Grand Bell Awards, enabling production company Hapdong to recoup production expenses due to the import license it was awarded as a result of the film's success.
37. As an experienced auteur and mentor, Yu also provided networking and paid work opportunities for younger filmmakers, including members of the Visual Generation group (*Youngsang Sidae*) and is remembered by colleagues (such as Byon In-sik) for his generosity and open door policy (Byon In-sik Personal interview 2005).
38. The list includes the anticommunist films *I Want to Be Human* (1969) and *Nightmare* (1968); comedies *The Three Hen-pecked Generations* (1967) and *I Will Give You Everything* (1968); and horror films *A Regret* (1967) and *Grudge* (1968).
39. Yu's financial situation was a major contributing factor in his decision to make these films. In the mid-to-late 1960s, he was almost bankrupt due to the box office failure of *The Martyrs*, which he had produced through the *daemyeong* system. In addition, his house had burned down while occupied by a tenant.
40. Yu 1995: 99.
41. "What's up with Producers? (Maker Sullye)". *Yeonye Japji* (October 1970): 33.
42. Cultural films were screened in double bills with feature films, a practice mandated by the Motion Picture Law in 1962 and continued until 1988. This measure was modeled on the 1939 Chosun Film Law enacted during the colonial era, which aimed to facilitate the screening of propaganda films in as many public venues as possible. The expression "cultural film" (*munhwa yeonghwa*) was originally adopted from the German Film Law under Hitler, translating the German term *Kulturfilm* (High 2003: 120).
43. Yu and Cho, *Oral History of Korean Arts*. See http://www.daarts.or.kr/handle/11080/6144. In 1973 the MPI established a new award category, best cultural film, for the Grand Bell Awards in order to encourage the production of these titles. In 1975, and again in 1976, Yu Productions received best cultural film award for *Dangerous Happiness* and *Deprived Desire* respectively.

3 Genre Intersections and the Literary Film

This chapter offers some new insights into the ways in which literary adaptation (hereafter the literary genre or literary films) was used by filmmakers as a vehicle for "cultural propaganda". It examines the understudied elements of cultural nationalism, as well as the interrelated aspects of traditionalism and modernism, that were central to the development of the genre. Compared to the overt propaganda of government-backed anticommunist films (which is discussed in detail elsewhere), the literary genre provided Korean filmmakers with a space in which to promote the nation's distinctive culture and traditions under the guise of "soft" propaganda.[1] To throw light on genre construction under the military regime—and within the context of changes made to the MPL in 1963 and 1966—we explore the complexity of the literary genre as its products developed into something more than "art films" pure and simple.[2] In so doing, we offer a new perspective on the workings of the government propaganda factory under the Park regime.

Korea's literary genre films have conventionally been treated in similar ways to literary films made in the West, where they are regarded as a "high art branch of cinema".[3] In Korea, this genre initially referred to films adapted from existing literary texts.[4] In the 1960s, literary films were categorized into two classes—colonial and post-war—according to the publication dates of the original texts; at the time, they were considered the cream of Korean cinema because they represented a "high level of artistic quality".[5] Based on the status accorded to literary films because of their level of artistic achievement, the genre has been seen solely in terms of its aesthetic contribution to Korean cinema and the expansion of the domestic film industry.[6] However, this assessment overlooks the important point that the literary genre was used extensively as a propaganda tool under the Park regime.

As this chapter demonstrates, because literary films were used for propaganda purposes by the government, the rise of this genre was the outcome of more than filmmakers' enthusiasm for making art-house movies. Previous studies have either limited their explanation of the genre to its role as a by-product of a policy instrument—namely the Import License Reward System (ILRS, discussed in Chapter 1)[7]—or discussed it in relation to the flood of low-quality "quota quickies" that appeared in response to Korea's changing policy landscape in the late 1960s.[8] These studies notwithstanding, the genre's critical relationship to government policy and its role as "soft" cultural propaganda has not hitherto been adequately investigated. Hence, in this chapter we investigate the history of the literary genre and the reasons behind its rise to popularity with filmmakers in the 1960s. Next, we analyze the genre's characteristics and explore the various impacts of the government, producers, and directors on the content of literary films.

In what follows, we illustrate the dissemination of soft propaganda through literary films through a number of case studies. First, *Deaf Samryong* (1964) is discussed in terms of the theme of cultural nationalism or the preservation of the nation's cultural identity. With the end of the Japanese colonial period in 1945, cultural nationalism became the cornerstone of Korea's cultural policy that aimed to restore the nation's cultural identity and heritage.[9] With its ability to project Korean national culture on the big screen, literary film was considered a primary vehicle for restoring Korea's cultural identity, offering audiences a powerful visual reminder of their cultural roots.[10]

Linked to the idea of cultural nationalism was the notion of traditionalism, which found a ready vehicle in "festival films" in the 1960s. The production of "festival films" demonstrates how the combined efforts of the government and filmmakers were channeled into creating "an imaginative landscape that draws on the shared history and values of the Korean people before the partition".[11] Festival films showcased a quintessential "Koreanness" that represented traditional ways of thinking, values, and sentiments. One such festival film, *Seaside Village* (1965), is analyzed below.

At the far end of the art filmmaking spectrum, directors were involved in an exploration of modernity, reflecting a desire to critique modern Korea, a nation on the cusp of industrialization, through literary films. Korea's modernization process in the post-war era reflected a number of influences—Westernization (aka "Americanization"), industrialization, and decolonization. As *Mist* (1967, aka *The Foggy Town*) shows, these modernist films sought to depict the disorientation experienced by ordinary people in the midst of these rapid and complex changes, thereby distancing this subgenre from other cultural propaganda films.

The Origins of the Literary Genre

The history of literary films dates back to the Japanese colonial period. According to the Korean Movie Database website, the first literary film on record is Lee Gyeong-son's *The Pioneer* (1925). Based on colonial author Lee Gwang-su's novel of the same name, this film celebrated the pioneering spirit of a scientist. However, the understanding of literary films as art cinema within the realist tradition was developed in the 1930s from the Japanese literary film movement known as *bungei-eiga*, from which the Korean name *munye yeonghwa* is taken. In an article titled "Japanese Films in Review 1938–9" in the *Cinema Yearbook of Japan 1939*, film critic Iizima Tadashi (aka Iijima Tadashi) outlined the character of the literary film as he saw it: "the spirit of seeking reality ... it is not a result of commercialism. We see artistic progress in the desire to make an *ensemble* of the motion picture and the realities of life".[12]

It has been claimed that, compared with other contemporary cinemas, Japanese literary films were "more faithful to real life, and by using them, filmmakers could move closer to the lives of ordinary people and achieve more realistic portrayals".[13] This description could also be applied to the literary films made in Korea in the colonial period, including *When the Sun Rises* (1927), *Deaf Samryong* (1929), *Omongnyeo* (1937), and *Altar for a Tutelary Deity* (1939). In the post-liberation period, literary films continued to be produced in a similar way; among the better-known titles are *A Hometown in Heart* (1949), *The Evil Night* (1952), *Dream* (1955), *An Idiot Adada* (1956), *Love* (1957), and *A Drifting Story* (1960).

Throughout this period a highbrow understanding of the literary film persisted, which excluded films based on popular fiction. For example, *Madam Freedom* (1956), based on the popular newspaper serial by Jung Bi-seok, was viewed as commercial melodrama by the press of the day, rather than as a literary film. At the time of its release, *Madam Freedom* caused controversy for broaching the taboo subject of adultery, inserting love scenes (including kissing), revealing the lure of materialism and the generation gap, and giving audiences an unsettling glimpse of the new Korean society of the post-liberation era. Kissing scenes in particular were regarded as unacceptable, according to Korea's traditional mores and were described as "premature for Koreans to see" and "vulgar".[14] Despite this controversy—or perhaps because of it—*Madam Freedom* became a box office hit in 1956.

These examples suggest the complexity of the links between literary films and "art film" in the Korea of the 1960s. However, few, if any, scholars have discussed the term and concept of "art film" as used by either the government or the industry. There are two major reasons for this. First, the genre conventions for art films were not firmly established in Korea during the 1960s.[15] Second, the MPI used the name *literary film* as a generic term for art films in general, thus suggesting all "art" films be included under a single genre category. Hence, in this chapter we use the term "art cinema" to mean a "mode of film practice" represented by the use of "realism, authorial expressivity and ambiguity".[16] This expanded description has much in common with the post-WWII art film movement that attempted to "turn its back on popular traditions and identified itself with experimentation and innovation in literature, painting, music, and theater".[17]

Bordwell's three characteristic features of art cinema are not hard to find in literary films from Korea. First, cinematic realism had a long history stemming from the colonial period. Represented by the nationalistic film *Arirang* (1926), which placed strong emphasis on local traditions and landscapes, this realist tradition continued into the 1960s. Quintessential literary films of the 1960s include *Aimless Bullet* (1961), *Deaf Samryong* (1963), and *Kim's Daughters* (1963). They dealt with the lives of people affected by social circumstances while conveying a strong sense of realism. Second, "authorial expressivity" is certainly present in the work of a handful of literary filmmakers such as Yu Hyun-mok, Kim Su-yong, and Lee Seong-gu. These directors developed their own styles and view of the world despite restrictive production conditions, thus reaffirming the reality of auteurship—the view of the director as the core creative element in the process of filmmaking—in a bleak social and political environment. (See Chapter 2 for a detailed discussion of auteurship in Korea.) Third, the theme of modernity was explored by portraying modernization as a process that embodied both positive and negative elements. Films such as *Mist* (1967) and *The General's Mustache* (1969) utilized technical and narrative features that were also found in the modernist film movements of the West such as Italian Neo-realism and the French Nouvelle Vague. For example, non-conventional storytelling techniques included devices such as the flashback, adding a studied ambiguity to film texts.[18]

However, Korea's art-house cinema added one more element to the mix: cultural propaganda, with a heavy emphasis on the promotion of nationalism. The rise of literary films in 1960s Korea was not a simple reflection of filmmakers' passion for making art-house films. The direction taken by the genre reflected the combined interests of the government, registered producers, and directors. However, the most immediate reason for the production of literary films was the policy support given by the ILRS. After 1963 the government began supporting propaganda filmmaking (divided into anticommunist, literary, and "enlightenment" genres) through the ILRS and increased its involvement over subsequent years. This provided a specific reason for producers to undertake literary filmmaking, leading to "a boom in literary films" in 1967.[19]

The relationship between art films and government subsidies was not unique to Korea. In a number of other countries, governments supported the making of such films to generate what might broadly be called cultural propaganda. In particular, after World War II ended in 1945, governments around the world championed domestic filmmakers and narrative films that expressed a fresh sense of cultural nationalism, thus creating new opportunities for non-mainstream filmmaking to succeed in the commercial arena.[20] In turn, the seemingly incompatible themes of cultural nationalism, traditionalism, and modernity could happily co-exist in the realm of art cinema thanks to new government policy initiatives. However, many of these films were less creative than perhaps expected or desired, as it was often easier for producers to accede to the state agenda and turn out a string of unimaginative mainstream feature films than work against the grain. Political support for art cinema made good sense in terms of promoting national pride and cultural identity, much of which is embodied in a nation's distinctive literary traditions.[21] In other words, through film the depiction of a nation's unique customs, manners, landscape, costumes, history, and cultural heritage—"ideas of coherence and unity and stable cultural meanings"—are combined in a process that differentiates it and its cultural products from the rest of the world.[22]

Second, members of the Korean film industry including directors, screenwriters, critics, and independent producers were committed to improving the quality of domestic films. According to reports in the popular press, literary films would raise the quality of local productions because of their emphasis on visual aesthetics. Screenwriter Shin Bong-seung described the literary film positively in terms of an enhanced "visual service" for audiences.[23] Film critic Woo Gyeong-sik also pointed out that literary films offered audiences a unique type of "explosive images".[24] Simply put, the making of literary films was perceived by young independent producers and directors as an opportunity to work with new and stimulating visual and narrative styles.[25] They were excited about the genre, associating it with a new film movement that would enable them to experiment with fresh visual styles and techniques while exploring a diverse range of subject matter that challenged conventional narrative methods.

Independent producers were a special group; they approached literary filmmaking for art's sake. As we saw in Chapter 1, these practitioners produced many award-winning films using the *daemyeong* system. Independent players such as Yu Hyun-mok (director), Ho Hyeon-chan (former film journalist), and Choi Hyeon-min (former theatrical director) made it widely known that they prioritized art-filmmaking over the pursuit of entertainment and commercial success. They lacked access to lucrative import licenses, and they did not make huge profits from box office takings, because art films by definition were not popular. Their literary filmmaking efforts were driven more by artistic ambition than by anticipated financial gains. By contrast, registered producers were interested in literary filmmaking only insofar as it gave them the opportunity to gain the import licenses attached to award-winning films. In the 1960s, the policy environment supported both approaches.

Apart from being an outlet for creativity, working on literary film projects had a number of advantages for directors. First, they had fewer worries about box office results. As long as their films received awards, they retained a certain amount of creative freedom. In addition, they had less censorship pressure when dealing with subjects that affirmed traditional values and national identity—the kind of cultural nationalism that the Park regime cultivated. The unique production environment, which prioritized the granting of import licenses before box office success, gave directors a strong hand in terms of aesthetics and technical experimentation. Looking back, veteran screenwriter Shim San, who is best known for *Beat* (1997) and *City of the Rising Sun* (1998), described the literary film genre as a niche market developed under special conditions.[26] As we saw in Chapter 2, director Yu Hyun-mok rose to fame as an auteur on the back of the literary genre in the 1960s.

Third, the scarcity of resources and manpower brought about by the nation's rapid recovery from the Korean War meant that the film industry was under pressure to produce high-quality scripts. The sheer effort need to rebuild the country— not to mention the film industry—made it difficult to develop new stories. In fact, Korea's ongoing difficulties in sourcing original screenplays can be dated back to the late 1950s.[27] Given that original film scripts (and screenwriters) were hard to find, filmmakers turned to Korea's ample supply of previously published literary works. And in some cases, it was simpler to remake foreign (primarily Japanese) films—an "internationalization" strategy explored in Chapter 4.[28]

Henceforth, the development of literary films was dictated by this double pathway, with the government's agenda on one side and the filmmakers' pursuit of art cinema on the other. In the outworking of this process three distinctive themes were explored: cultural nationalism, traditionalism, and the impact of modernity. While the first two subjects held the field throughout the 1960s, modernity and modernization became increasingly emphasized during the late 1960s.

If cultivating a newfound sense of nationalism was a strategy employed by the Park regime to guide the country's development and to legitimize its governance, the literary film was seen as an appropriate vehicle for expressing cultural nationalism and for rallying the public behind these objectives. As Park Chung Hee urged in 1962 following the coup that brought him to power, every Korean was bound by a "duty to fully explore and further develop our own culture and then to introduce it abroad".[29] In accordance with this goal, in January 1962 the Park regime announced the Cultural Properties Protection Law, allowing traditional performers to perform overseas and thereby help to "boost feelings of national pride".[30] In a similar way, the literary film genre helped strengthen the nation's depleted cultural identity and present positive images of the past by portraying the traditional morality, customs, and manners of a bygone era.

In *The Country, the Revolution and I*, a book he wrote and published in both Korean and English in 1963 to legitimize the military coup, Park Chung Hee set out his vision for the reconstruction of the nation and its traditional culture:

> We will establish a new concept of national society, a new view of Korea on the basis of our original traditions and sense of independence. ... We will make people feel proud of their new culture and their new social environment, and we will preserve that which has been traditionally "ours". We will eliminate the sense of loss of the self, a tendency to despise our own people, an emphasis on vanity and parasitism, and replace them with the spirit of a fresh start. ... We will increase our national strength, rejuvenate ourselves and advance toward the world proud and strong. (1963: 192)

Under the guidance of Park, the film industry produced literary films that enabled audiences to visualize a sense of what was "traditionally ours" so as to enable them to identify with their own culture. Perhaps surprisingly, many of the films that followed this prescription were based on colonial literature, work that was seen by contemporary critics as embodying the vernacular of cultural nationalism during the colonial period. Thus, literary films based on colonial novels such as Yi Kwang-su's *Heartless* (*Mujeong* 1917), Shim Hun's *Evergreen Tree* (aka Sangroksu 1935), and Kim Yu-jeong's *Spring, Spring* (Bom Bom 1935) consciously advocated a sense of cultural nationalism by emphasizing traditional values and ways of thinking, cultural norms that were fast disappearing with the rapid advance of industrialization during the 1960s.

The adaptation of colonial literature for the screen was popularized in the 1920s and the early 1930s. After the founding of March First Independence Movement in 1919, Japan introduced a softer cultural policy in order to appear acquiescent to Korean sentiment. This slight liberal turn provided "a catalyst for the expansion of the nationalist movement as a whole".[31] Novelists such as Yi Kwang-su, Kim Dong-in, Kim Dong-ri, and Hwang Sun-won began exploring the themes of independence and self-awareness as they applied to both individuals and the nation.[32] For example, shortly after the Japanese colonized Korea in the 1910s, Yi Kwang-su, one of the country's better-known colonial novelists and cultural nationalists, began exploring the connections between nationalism and modern writing styles and techniques.[33]

This type of overt nationalistic literature was easily adapted to film, resulting in the oblique representation of cultural nationalism through the portrayal of traditional values such as loyalty and the beauty and serenity of rural village life. The nationalistic sentiments of these colonial texts, which sought to explore notions of

68   The Golden Age of the 1960s

independence, self-awareness, and the value placed on tradition, were transferred directly to film, which in its turn attempted to recreate and restore Korea's threatened cultural identity and express it in visual terms. The best-known films based on colonial novels include: *Mother and a Guest* (1961), *Deaf Samryong* (1964), *When the Buckwheat Flower Blossoms* (1967), *Potato* (1968), and *Spring, Spring* (1969).

Another major source for literary films was the post-war literature produced by novelists such as Oh Young-su and Kim Seung-ok. These writers explored issues of modernization, existentialism, industrialization, and post-war living conditions, themes that are discussed later in this chapter.

Promoting Cultural Nationalism—*Deaf Samryong* (1964)

Korea's version of *The Hunchback of Notre Dame* (1939), *Deaf Samryong* (1964) was produced by Shin Film and directed by Shin Sang-ok. Its artistic achievements were recognized by the awards and invitations it received from a number of local and international film festivals between 1965 and 1966, including the Grand Bell Awards, the Buil Film Award, the Asian Film Festival, the Berlin International Film Festival, the Venice International Film Festival, the Sydney Film Festival, the Melbourne International Film Festival, and the San Francisco Film Festival.[34] At the time of its release, it was described in the domestic press as a highly stylish literary film with outstanding acting by Korea's representative actors Kim Jin-kyu and Choi Eun-hee (Shin Sang-ok's wife).

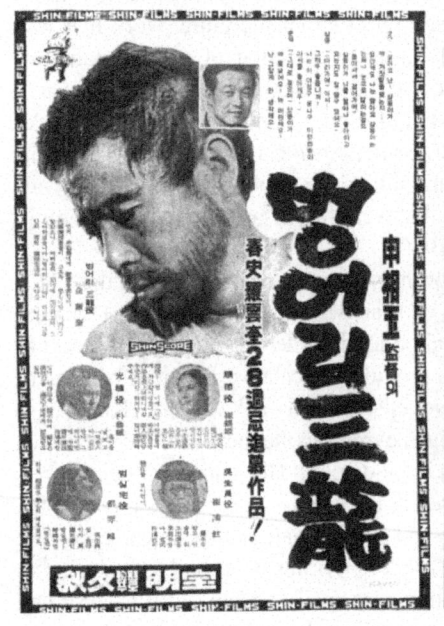

Figure 3.1 Film advertisements for *Deaf Samryong* (1964). *Gyeonghyang Shinmun* 10 September, 1964: 4; and *Gyeonghyang Shinmun* 21 November, 1964: 8.

Set in a rural village during the colonial era, the narrative revolves around four characters: deaf house servant Samryong, housemaid Chu-wol, newly married son of the house Kwang-sik, and his wife Sun-deok. Kwang-sik despises and abuses his wife, who belongs to a higher social class but comes from a poor family; she has married him for money. Instead of loving his wife, Kwang-sik is carrying on an affair with Chu-wol. Samryong respects Sun-deok, and sympathizes with her situation. When Man-soo, Chu-wol's husband, learns about her affair, he picks a fight with Kwang-sik, and Samryong steps in to defend his master. As a sign of appreciation for his act of loyalty, Sun-deok gives Samryong a gift, but Kwang-sik regards this as inappropriate, and he beats Samryong and ejects him from the house. That night, the cuckolded Man-soo sets fire to the house in revenge. Samryong returns and rescues Sun-deok from the burning house. However, during his attempt to save the ungrateful Kwang-sik, the roof collapses and both men perish.

As the film begins, we are led into a beautiful world of silence with a hand signing in the air on a wide black-and-white screen. Traditional Korean music is introduced, adding a note of sentimentality. The scene then shifts to an interior where Kwang-sik is seen placing something hot on the foot of Samryong, who is sleeping on the floor. Samryong is startled, but his tormentor is convulsed with laughter. Old master Oh comes in, comforting Samryong and scolding Kwang-sik. Samryong stops the old man shouting at his son, smiling at Oh and indicating that no harm has been done. Oh smiles back at him, saying "You're so faithful".

The virtues of loyalty and being "faithful" are indeed the main themes of the film. These traditional values are embodied in Samryong through his dedication to his masters Oh and Kwang-sik, and also to Sun-deok who is often referred to as Lady Oh. This loyalty, stemming from the traditional class system of master and servant, had its origins in Samryong's childhood memories of being taken under Oh's wing after being abandoned by his mother. Oh is a father figure for Samryong and occasionally expresses his affection for his disabled servant. After saving Samryong from Kwang-sik's anger, Oh tells him to run away, adding, "Just let me know where you've settled down. I'll visit you". Oh even pleads with Samryong to forgive him for having raised such a bad son. His unyielding loyalty to Oh's family is a product of these family circumstances. At the end of the film, Samryong sacrifices himself while attempting to save Kwang-sik, despite all the suffering he has caused.

However, the class system portrayed in *Deaf Samryong* is more complicated than the simple master–servant relationship represented by Oh and Samryong. The ruling class itself was traditionally divided into scholars (*yangban*), who enjoyed superior status, and wealthy landlords (*jiju*) who lacked a scholarly background and thus had lower status. In the film, this horizontal class conflict is represented by Kwang-sik, a rich farmer's son, and Sun-deok, the daughter of a scholar.

The traditional class system inherited from the Chosun Dynasty was officially abolished in 1894 after the government announced social reforms that disempowered the scholar class (*yangban*), who often acted as landlords who ruled over commoners and employed slaves.[35] Nevertheless, characters in the film including old master Oh still set a high premium on scholastic qualities; his reverence for such virtues led Oh to pursue Kwang-sik and Sun-deok's arranged marriage.

Sun-deok's family is described as culturally rich but financially poor. Although hers is a noble family that follows the lofty values of Confucius, it has no choice but to arrange a wealthy marriage for their daughter to lift the family out of poverty. For Kwang-sik, it is hard to tolerate a union with such a lady. He is already dallying with Chu-wol, who although a servant is outspoken and sexually attractive. Lady Oh lacks these qualities, and her gracious attitude toward him and others contrasts with Kwang-sik's bad behavior, which results in his physical abuse of his wife. Representing the traditional Confucian values of the past, Lady Oh is described as graceful, polite, elegant, and compassionate. Contrasting Kwang-sik's violence toward her with her own nobility of character, the film underscores the "radical destruction of Confucius values".[36]

Deaf Samryong depicts a world divided into two camps: the materialistic modern world of Kwang-sik and Chu-wol versus the traditional world of Lady Oh and Samryong. Samryong's loyalty and Lady Oh's Confucian values are shown as superior to those of the materialistic world. Although they are fast disappearing in a world of rapid modernization, traditional values are represented as worthy and honorable, compared to the shallow mores of the modern age, confirming that the nation's moral and cultural traditions are worth remembering and preserving. The film offers audiences a poignant glimpse of vanished values and norms, a nostalgic reminder of a way of life that is worthy of remembrance or even re-creation.

The mixed review of the film produced for the 1965 San Francisco Film Festival, written by critic Albert Johnson, is representative of the film's reception by Western audiences:

> The progress of Korean cinema has been exceptionally haphazard, and past Festival audiences have been bewildered by the naive treatments of melodramatic domestic triangles or sentimental epics. Therefore, Samryongi came as a surprise to the Berlin Festival and its delicate observation of a mute servant's love for his employer's wife revealed a tragic, lyrical sense that was entirely unexpected. Shin is a romantic, but he handles the subject matter with honesty and restraint; when the story bursts into violence, Western audiences may be dismayed by the rigor of the physical cruelties depicted, but one is left with the final impression of an Oriental folk tale, seen from a distance, wistful in attitude, half fancy and half truth.[37]

Despite Johnson's reference to "an Oriental folk tale", it may be that the film's central theme was not fully understood by overseas audiences. Korean film reporter Ahn Byeong-seop reported that following the film's screening at the festival it received harsh criticism in the US: its "local flavor" was interpreted as "old-fashioned" and "sentimental" rather than as something distinctive and different.[38] Given the fact that *Deaf Samryong* scooped the pool in Korea's own film awards, securing accolades as one of the best films of 1964, its largely negative critical reception in the foreign press was naturally disappointing to local industry players. However, Ahn concluded his report that the problem lay with the film's directorial style, not the subject matter, and encouraged Korean filmmakers to continue their pursuit of "local flavor".

Localizing Traditionalism in the Festival Film
Seaside Village (1965)

Closely linked to cultural nationalism, the notion of traditionalism was embraced as another crucial thematic element by literary filmmakers. The MPI encouraged producers to introduce elements of traditional Korean culture into their films by announcing its support for what it called "festival films" in January 1965. It seized the initiative, devising plans to submit a total of 39 domestic films to major international film festivals and distribute them through its embassy networks overseas.[39] This theoretical support for "festival films" was followed up in 1966 by new provisions in the revised MPL, which allocated additional import licenses to films invited to international film festivals. This encouraged producers to tailor their films in the direction of traditionalism and the representation of "Koreanness".

The presentation through film of Korea's unique culture and topography, which would differentiate Korean cinema from other national cinemas, was seen as a worthy goal. *Seaside Village* was one such "festival film" that succeeded in achieving these essentially political aims. As one commentator noted, this was the kind of film that could "transcend local issues and provincial tastes while simultaneously providing a window onto a different culture".[40] This view reflected the kind of exposure governments all over the world hoped to gain from festival films. The government's initiative to support festival films was welcomed by independent producers and directors. In Korea, independent producers such as Ho Hyeon-chan and Choi Hyeon-min and directors such as Yu Hyun-mok and Lee Sung-gu were already busy making literary films, which with a few adjustments could easily be turned into festival films.

As a producer with some experience of international film festivals, Ho Hyeon-chan favored a new approach to exploring broad human themes in order to maintain a universal appeal for modern audiences, while at the same time showing off Korea's unique landscapes.[41] In other words, while the depiction of distinctive landforms, culture, and mores would present a unique and exotic image of Korea, it should be coupled with universal themes in order to connect with overseas audiences. In the case of *Deaf Samryong*, the film's real meaning had been lost on overseas audiences, obscured by the film's complex representation of social class. Ho proposed the Japanese cinema as a model to follow because it had successfully showcased "exotic" subjects and oriental themes since the 1950s, receiving invitations to international film festivals as well as garnering numerous awards. *Seaside Village* represents Ho's vision of the ideal festival film.

Based on the novella by Oh Young-su, the film was directed by Kim Su-yong, who had made a name as a director of literary films. When *Seaside Village* was released, it was a box office success, attracting more than 100,000 patrons in Seoul (KMDB) and praised as a new form of poetic cinema by the press. As the film poster reproduced in Figure 3–2 shows, *Seaside Village* was promoted as an A-grade local film aiming to be the best picture of the year.

Seaside Village all but achieved this goal, receiving awards from domestic and international film festivals including the Grand Bell Awards, the Buil Film Festival,

Figure 3.2 Film advertisement for *Seaside Village* (1965). *Donga Daily* 18 November, 1965: 6.

and the Asian Film Festival.[42] With the success of this film, third-time producer Ho Hyeon-chan, who had previously worked as a film critic for the *Donga Daily*, announced his presence to the industry at large.[43] Many critics—including Ho himself—argued that *Seaside Village* set a precedent for the literary genre by achieving both commercial and artistic success, challenging the conventional wisdom that literary films were no more than arthouse productions made with an eye to gaining import licenses, and opening up a new and bright future for literary films.[44]

The film portrays the lives of villagers on an island off the coast of Korea. The shortage of working men is more than matched by the surfeit of widows who have lost their husbands at sea. The film follows the story of Hae-sun, a beautiful young widow who lost her fisherman husband after only three months of marriage. With no choice but to live alone and support herself, she joins the widows' diving community but is pursued by a village lad, Sang-su, and ends up having an affair with him. Hae-sun and Sang-su decide to go to the mainland but find that life there is tougher than on the island. When Sang-su falls over a cliff to his death, Hae-sun returns to the island and rejoins the diving widows.

As the film opens, the camera pans slowly across the fishing village, its inhabitants, and the ocean. Jeon Jo-myeong's camera captures the panoramic beauty and peaceful atmosphere of the village, almost turning it into a paradise. Complementing this breathtaking vista, a male voiceover praises the resilience of the village women who are well able to withstand the seasonal hardships that their harsh environment brings them.

Next, the camera follows the fishermen as they prepare for another day at sea. In the midst of their activity, there is talk of inauspicious signs and bad dreams. Despite these omens, and since fishing is their livelihood, family members—including a pregnant wife and a new bride—wave to the departing boats, wishing them a safe return. However, shortly after their departure, the weather turns wild. The arrival of dark clouds, strong winds, stormy rain, and bursts of thunder and lightning cause panic amongst the people. Women gather in front of the village's sacred tree and the Dragon God's altar, praying hard while being drenched and whipped by the storm. In the next scene, the villagers are shown crowded together at the cliff's edge, waiting for their men to return. The weather clears, and the boats pull into shore. The villagers rush down to the harbor cheering wildly, only to find that some of the fishermen are dead, and they begin to weep. This opening sequence sets the scene for what follows, explaining why and how the villagers continue to live on the island, persisting in this dangerous and unpredictable way of life.

The lives of the villagers are circumscribed by the sea, and the film portrays the unrelenting cycle of life on the island. Many village women, including Hae-sun's mother-in-law, have lost their husbands, but her brother-in-law still goes out to sea in order to make a living. The villagers show a degree of fatalism, accepting that their lives are at the mercy of the sea. The ocean is depicted as a mighty being that wields the power of life and death. As the opening scenes show, it is a thing to fear but also provides the villagers with a bountiful food supply, a means of livelihood, and a place where the island's many widows can ease their suffering. While some of the widows accept their lot and find ways of living with the ocean, others cannot cope with their fate. In one tragic sequence we are shown a woman walking out into the sea, leaving her baby behind. She is the young mother shown earlier who had lost her husband while pregnant. Her mind unhinged, she chooses death rather than a wretched life as a companionless wife and mother.

Complementing Hae-sun's story, the widows play an important part in the film. Gathering clams in order to support their families, they regard themselves as the real workers on the island. At one point, the male narrator asks rhetorically: "How come these mothers are all out working? Where are the fathers?" They establish a diving community, forming a strong sisterhood as compensation for their weak social status that condemns them to live and raise their families alone. These women come across as lonely but also as strong, honest, and compassionate. These characteristics come to the fore in a scene where the widows come down to the beach on a sleepless night, lying still and listening to the waves under the moonlight.

The sound of waves crashing on the shoreline accompanies a traditional lament sung by the widows. The camera pans, capturing the women scattered in small groups across the beach and further afield. Some are lying in each other's laps, some on a boat's deck, others gaze outside from their homes, while others again are washing clothes down at the river and sharing a cigarette. In Korea, leading a life as a widow was an enormous challenge. In Confucian tradition, a widow was expected to live with and support her husband's family. Remarriage was hardly a choice. As one of the widows says, they live alone to protect their social reputation, not because they choose to. While this dictum remains a fact of life in the film, *Seaside Village* gives this custom a new twist. What the film shows is not so much how the fishermen's widows follow the social norm, but how they cope with it, each in her own way.

The strong sisterhood that the women have built up through their diving community enables them to come to terms with their social vulnerability. Within the confines of the group they talk openly about sexuality, a taboo topic in traditional society. Among farming and fishing communities, sex was more openly discussed than was the case among the aristocracy, as many folk songs and folk stories attest. In the film, sexuality is celebrated as the origin of the women's being.[45] They actively pursue opportunities to meet their sexual needs rather than hiding their desires. Living on an island where sheer survival has a higher priority than strict observance of traditional customs and mores facilitates their exploration of sexuality. Thus, hauling in the fishing nets gives the widows an opportunity for physical contact with the strong, fit bodies of the village men. Hae-sun is offered practical advice by one widow who counsels her to keep seeing Sang-su and not to concern herself about village gossip. The scene of the widows lying on the beach in particular portrays their sexuality in a candid way, projecting the images of real women, not grieving widows, full of energy, passion and a lust for life.

According to Ho, in order to communicate effectively with overseas audiences a "festival film" should portray a country's unique cultural identity along with universal themes. *Seaside Village* succeeded in achieving this combination. The haunting beauty of the coastal landscape provided a fitting setting for a culturally specific story of fishermen's widows and their struggles, and the film's candid treatment of sexuality touched on universal themes. Similar literary films dealing with traditional themes and aimed at festival audiences were produced throughout the decade; they included *A Water Mill* (1966), *Stroller* (1967), and *An Old Potter* (1969).

Exploring Aspects of Modernity in *Mist* (1967)

While cultural nationalism and traditionalism were the dominant concerns of literary films, the notion of modernity was also explored by some directors. For example, in *Deaf Samryong,* director Shin Sang-ok explored the idea of traditional values being undermined and replaced by modern materialistic values. Similarly, Kim Su-yong compared life on an island with that on the mainland, where modernization was rapidly advancing. However, as we have seen, the idea of modernity became a major theme in the late 1960s when literary films began engaging more fully with post-war literature. Writers such as Kim Seung-ok, Yi Cheong-jun, and Seo Jeong-in were exploring the effects of industrialization on individuals' inner lives.[46]

Inspired by the work of these writers, and aware of the social, economic, and cultural changes brought about by industrialization, directors began adapting their novels for the screen, enabling them to offer their own critique of Korea's rapidly industrializing society. In addition to these new ideas, Korean directors experimented with the techniques used by European postwar modernist filmmakers, such as long takes and open-ended narratives and the innovative means they were developing to explore various states of mind, including subconsciousness.[47]

Films such as *Mist* (1967), *The Guests of the Last Train* (1967), and *The General's Mustache* (1968) offered similar critiques of the rapid pace of modernization in Korea. The release of these three films coincided with the completion of the Park regime's first economic development plan (1963–1967). The Korean people were becoming increasingly aware of the impact of industrialization after witnessing a large increase in exports, the restructuring of the agrarian system, and a runaway economic growth rate of more than eight percent per year. At the same time, the impact of modernization on society began to be noticed.

Mist, which was based on Kim Seung-ok's short novel *Mujin Travelogue* published in 1964, was adapted by director Kim Su-yong and produced by Hwang Hye-mi, one of only a few women working behind the camera at the time. (Hwang's story as female independent producer is discussed in Chapter 9.) To differentiate it from other films, Kim utilized innovative editing techniques such as flashbacks, montages, and long takes. It became the representative modernist film of the 1960s. Its focus on visual aesthetics and the creation of a surreal atmosphere, which was sustained throughout the film, were given heavy emphasis in the promotional material when the film was released. The Filipino film critic Jose Quirino, one of the jury members of the Asian Film Festival in 1967, noted that *Mist* was reminiscent of the works of Ingmar Bergman and *A Man and a Woman*, a French film directed by Claude Lelouch that won the *Grand Prix du Festival* (known today as the *Palme d'Or*) at the 1966 Cannes Film Festival.[48] Kim Su-yong received the best director award from the 14th Asian Film Festival and the Grand Bell Awards for his use of montage editing, amplified sound effects, and non-linear narrative structure, including the use of flashbacks.

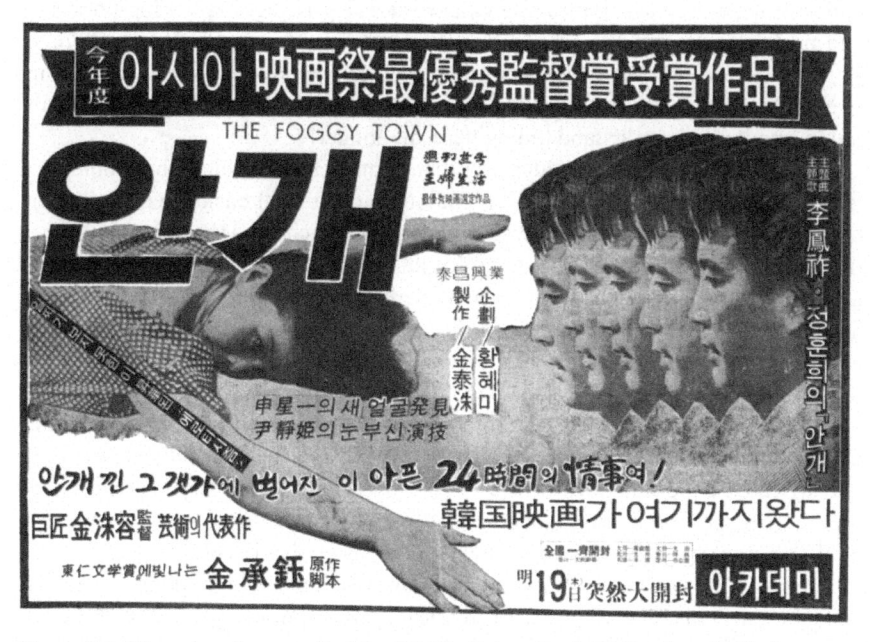

Figure 3.3 Film advertisement for *Mist* (1967). *Donga Daily* 17 October, 1967: 5.

The story line of *Mist* is simple. Yun Gi-jun, who is married to the daughter of the president of a big pharmaceutical company in Seoul, takes a short trip to visit his hometown of Mujin while his wife tries to close his promotion deal. During his stay in Mujin, he spends time with some old friends and has an affair with a music teacher. After receiving a call from his wife, Gi-jun heads back to Seoul. This rather simple story line is augmented by a complex narrative structure created by the clever use of interior monologue and regular flashbacks.

The film's opening sequence depicts the Seoul cityscape, seen through a window. The camera pans and pulls back, showing the interior of an office where Gi-jun is sitting at his desk, reading a book. Startled, he gets up from the desk. The camera shows us a close-up of the book, on which ants are crawling. Gi-jun swallows a pill with a mouthful of water. Next, an employee enters the room to get his signature on some paperwork. There follows a montage of close-up shots of typewriting, picking up the phone, and the employee opening and closing the office door, accompanied by salient sound effects. When Gi-jun opens a window, the traffic noise penetrates the office, mingling with the other noises entering from outside. All this suggests that Seoul is a modern urban hub, with rapid industrialization in progress. The strident mechanical soundscape, the hallucinatory effect of the crawling ants, and Gi-jun's responses all express his negative reaction to life in the crowded metropolis.

Sitting on the train to Mujin, Gi-jun's memories of his hometown unfold, and we listen in on an interior monologue deploring the town's poor economic status and the ugliness of the environment. He candidly admits that his biggest wish as a youngster was to leave Mujin as soon as he could. At this point, it becomes clear that *Mist* is not going to be another literary film dealing with cultural nationalism and traditional lifeways, portraying village life as a privileged space for innocence and nostalgia, as was the case with both *Deaf Samryong* and *Seaside Village*. Following Yun's stream of consciousness, the film unravels his memories. One memorable image shows the young Gi-jun emerging from the attic of his family home, shouting "I can't stand hiding here any longer!"

According to Gi-jun, the thick fog that permanently envelops his hometown is the only thing Mujin is known for. Although it is a rural backwater, Mujin harbors a secret desire to catch up with Korea's vibrant cities. *Mist* offers audiences the opportunity to think of Seoul and Mujin, not in terms of modern versus premodern, but modern versus want-to-be modern.[49] Returning to Mujin gives Gi-jun an unexpected occasion to reflect on his past, present, and future, offering him an opportunity to examine the real meaning of modernization. Tax official Cho, Gi-jun's friend, represents Mujin's opportunistic, authoritative, and condescending side—the negative aspect of modernity. Gi-jun's reunion with Cho takes place at Cho's house, where he is holding a card party. Later, a freeze-frame image of people playing cards is presented with Gi-jun's voiceover: "in Mujin everyone thinks people are snobbish". From this point on, an unflattering image of Mujin—a microcosm of all the problems that plague the modern city—is gradually constructed.

Visiting Cho's office workplace, Gi-jun discovers that Cho's life in Mujin is a carbon copy of his own life in Seoul. While Gi-jun is waiting in the office for Cho, an employee enters to get Cho's signature on some paperwork. The employee prepares Cho's approval seal for him, answers the ringing phone, and then hands the phone to Cho. The next shot is a close-up of Gi-jun's face, which shows a look of contempt. A second employee enters the office and repeats the same actions as the first employee. The clatter of typewriters grows louder, the camera tilts as Cho signs the second lot of paperwork, and a typing scene is shown in close-up. This is exactly how Gi-jun's own office life was portrayed at the start of the film. With some comic relief to break up the scene, the two employees bump heads as they pass each other. The mood is that of a black comedy, mocking bureaucracy in general. In the end, Gi-jun's disdain for Cho is directed back at himself.

Paralleling his discoveries about his hometown, Gi-jun encounters his own past through conversations with his former self and meeting the music teacher Ha, whom he sees as partly embodying his past self. Afflicted with a lung disease as a young man, at his mother's urging he hid himself in the attic to avoid being drafted during the Korean War; as a result, however, Gi-jun suffered qualms of conscience, accusing himself of being a coward. Putting his shameful past behind him, Gi-jun has sought to justify his existence by seeking security and success in life. While carrying on his affair with Ha, Gi-jun sees his present and past selves walking together before his eyes, talking and seeking reconciliation. Shown in close-up, his present self argues: "Look. I'm mature enough not to see the world through sentimental eyes. In the end, it was a good thing to marry a rich widow. What do you think?" His past self looks at him and sneers, without saying a word, and then spits contemptuously.

Whatever Gi-jun's moral standards were in the past, he has outgrown them now. In a sense, his trip to Mujin was a necessary rite of passage, acknowledging and vindicating his personal transformation. Toward the end of his visit, Yun sees a crazy girl, whom he met on the day he arrived, lying dead on the street and being carried away by the police. He sees that it is imperative that what happened in Mujin should stay in Mujin. Receiving his wife's telegram to come back to Seoul, Gi-jun boards a bus and heads back to the city. However, his final voiceover indicates that he has not yet fully closed the door on his past: "Once and for all, let's accept Mujin and its crazy loneliness, its popular songs, a bar girl's suicide, betrayal, and responsibility".

Conclusion

To sum up, despite their pretensions to high art Korea's literary films contained as much propaganda as the anticommunist genre. However, they presented their message in more subtle, covert ways. While the anticommunist genre was devised as an overt form of propaganda, literary films inclined toward themes of cultural nationalism, traditionalism, and modernism. As a result, the literary genre developed not into "pure" art-house cinema, but as what we might call "political" art cinema—a hybrid of propaganda and art film. This redefining of "art film" in the Korean context of the 1960s underlines the marked political character of the "literary films" produced as cultural propaganda during the period.

The literary films produced during the 1960s were unquestionably political. The government supported these productions in part because they offered an opportunity to promote Korea's artistic achievements to the wider world. As grateful recipients of the regime's largesse, and eager to gain coveted import licenses, producers tailored literary films to the government's prescription rather than to the refined tastes of art-house audiences. For filmmakers, literary films provided the opportunity to experiment with novel narrative structures, visual styles, and a range of themes and to court international fame. The themes of cultural nationalism, traditionalism, and the impact of modernity figured prominently, as exploring them enabled both parties to attain their respective objectives. Naturally, this involved political compromise and was a kind of collaboration in the unfavorable sense. Given the different agendas at work, the result was the creation of a *political* art cinema in Korea, one that was characterized by novel visual styles and technical experimentation achieved through innovative approaches to editing, soundscapes, and narrative architecture.

While the literary genre rose to prominence as the result of government backing, its decline was foreshadowed in 1969 when the MPI withdrew its support, ironically on the grounds that these films had met the government's envisioned quota for cultural propaganda.[50] In 1986 Korea's major film import policy instruments—the Import Recommendation System and the Import License Reward System—were permanently removed from the MPL. The literary genre had officially had its foundations removed. However, it has left a legacy worthy of re-evaluation in the light of our ever-growing knowledge of the Korean film industry.

Notes

1. See Shim 2011. The anticommunist film belonged to an explicit propaganda genre that shared close connections with government policy. Anticommunist films were encouraged and often coerced by the government because of their overt anticommunist stance, stemming directly from the regime's first national policy, which defined the political identity of the South Korean government under Cold War politics.
2. Previous scholars have differentiated literary genre films from other commercial films; see especially Lee 2000; Ho 2000; Kim 2002; Byon 2001a. In this chapter, we build on their distinctions by discussing representative literary genre films within a wider cinematic milieu.
3. Elliott 2003: 127.
4. Kim Nam-seok 2003: 5–6. Although previous scholars have argued that the literary genre should include films based on adaptations of a variety of source material including novels (both literary and popular), folk tales, radio dramas, and cartoons, citing the crucial role of the "adaptation process" in literary filmmaking, they have generally ignored the artistic conventions used in the adaptation process, which are central to the genre.
5. Lee 2004: 396.
6. Hyangsoon Yi 2002: 70.
7. Lee, Hyangjin 2000; Ho 2000; Kim Hak-su 2002; Yi, Hyangsoon 2002; Byon 2001a; and Kim 2006.
8. Baek 2002 and Hong 2003 refer to literary films from the late 1960s as "quota quickies" because they were used as bait to attract rewards from the ILRS.
9. For a useful discussion of cultural nationalism in Korea, see Yim 2003.

10. This was also the rationale behind bio-pics dealing with national heroes. For example, *Great Hero, Lee Sun-sin* (1962), a story about the navy admiral who outwitted the Japanese military during its invasion of Korea (1592–1598), was produced with government funding.
11. Doherty 1984: 846.
12. Tadashi 1939: 21. Tadashi also wrote the screenplay for *You and I* (*Kimi to Boku*, 1941), a Japan-Korea co-production that promoted the imperial ideology of Naisen Ittai ("Japan and Korea as one nation") through the story of a marriage between a Korean volunteer soldier and a Japanese woman.
13. Richie 2001: 95.
14. The film was released after the Ministry of Education had cut about 100 feet of footage containing kissing and dancing scenes as part of the official censorship process. See *Donga Daily*, 10 June 1956: 3. "Arguments over a Kissing Scene" (Kisseu Jangmyeone Daehan Sibi). Also see Lee 2004: 249–50.
15. Lee 2004: 296–97.
16. Bordwell 2004: 779.
17. Thompson and Bordwell 2003: 357.
18. For further information about the use of Western-inspired modernist film traditions in Korean films, see Lee 2001.
19. "Knocking on the Door of the Planning Department (Gihoeksil Nokeu)". *Yeonghwa Japji* (May 1968): 106–107.
20. Nowell-Smith 1996: 567.
21. Crofts 2006: 45.
22. Dissanayake 1994: xiii.
23. Shin, Bong-seung. "Smiling over Failures and Skipping Grades (Nakjewa Wolbanui Miso)". *Shin Sajo* (July 1963): 242–51.
24. "Last Month's News in Film Community (Jinandarui Yeonghwagye Nyuseu Ribyu)". *Yeonghwa Segye*. (July 1963): 120–21.
25. Ho 2000: 164.
26. Shim, San. "Father of 'Madam Aema' (Aema Buinui Abeoji)". *Cine21* #296 (3 April 2001). Available: <www.cine21.com/news/view/mag_id/1295>. Accessed 11 November 2014.
27. Ho 2000: 163.
28. Although official cultural exchanges between Korea and Japan were forbidden, Japanese film books and magazines were often smuggled into Korea using personal connections. According to screenwriter Shin Bong-seung, industry people used them to educate themselves about new film trends (KOFA 2007: 118–22).
29. Park drew attention to these words in his book *Our Nation's Path: Ideology of Social Reconstruction* (1970: 229).
30. Maliangkay 2008: 51.
31. Eckert *et al*. 1990: 279. After 1919, Koreans were permitted a limited degree of freedom of expression, leading to the rise of a cultural movement in the 1920s. For more information on cinema culture in this early period, see Yecies (2005).
32. Gwon 2006.
33. Yi Kwang-su also wrote the "Declaration for Korean Independence", the founding document of the March First Movement. However, in the late 1930s, Yi gained a reputation as a Japanese collaborator as a result of the numerous articles he published endorsing Japan's Naisen Ittai policy and its policy of replacing Korean names with Japanese names. Films based on Yi's novels include *Cool and Cold* (*Mujeong* 1962), *Great Monk Wonhyo* (1962), *A Sad Story of Danjong* (1963), *Affection* (*Yujeong* 1966), *Soil* (1967), *Dreams* (1967), and *Love* (1968).
34. The awards received by *Deaf Samryong* included best picture, best director, best music, and best producer at the 4th Grand Bell Awards in 1965, best actor and best screenplay at the Buil Film Award, and best actor at the 12th Asian Film Festival in 1965.

35. See Eckert *et al.* 1990: 222–30.
36. Ahn 2007: 63. In 2007 the Korean Film Archive published the Shin Sang-ok multi-disc DVD collection comprising *Seong Chunhyang Mother and a Guest, Deaf Samryongi, A Romantic Papa,* and *One Thousand Year Old Fox*. A booklet on Shin's filmography by Jin-soo Ahn was included with the collection.
37. Johnson's review is reproduced in the San Francisco Film Festival's history site: http://history.sffs.org/films/film_details.php?id=4345&searchfield=samyong. (Accessed 14 August 2011).
38. See Ahn, Byeong-seop. "Korean Cinema outside Looking in (Bakkeseo Boneun Hanguk Yeonghwa)". *Yeonghwa Yesul* (December 1965): 90–93. Film journalist Ahn Byeong-seop's article was based on film reviews published in the *San Francisco Chronicle* and the *San Francisco News-Call Bulletin*.
39. In January 1965 the MPI announced its annual film support strategy, which included the strict application of the MPL, support for 'sound' films (including literary, anti-communist, and cultural films), and support for international film festival submissions. See "News & Issues (Nyuseuwa Hwaje)". *Shin Donga* (February 1965): 352–53.
40. Nichols 1994: 16.
41. "Korean Cinema Has to Go Towards the Venice International Film Festival (Beniseuro Jinchulhaeyahal Uri Yeonghwa)". *Silver Screen* (August 1965): 65.
42. The awards won by *Seaside Village* included best supporting actress, best photography, and best editing at the 5th Grand Bell Awards (1966); best picture, best director, best supporting actress, best cinematography, best original score, and best new actors at the 9th Buil film festival (1966); best picture, best director, and best actor at the 2nd Korean Theatre Film Art Award 1966); and best black-and-white cinematography at the 13th Asian Film Festival (1966).
43. Before making *Seaside Village*, Ho had produced two films: *Only for You* (1962, directed by Yu Hyun-mok) and *Madam Wing* (1965).
44. Ho 2000: 139; Kim 2003b: 73.
45. Lee 1988.
46. Kang 2001: 105–10. Serious novels of the 1960s dealt with two main topics: war/ideology and industrialization. The latter was developed into two sub-themes: 1) the effects of rapid industrialization on society and 2) the alienation of individuals through the process of modernization (Kang 2001: 97–98).
47. A number of influential European modernist films, including Italian Neo-Realism and French Nouvelle Vogue productions, were screened in Korea after the 1950s. The list included *Eclipse* (Michelangelo Antonioni 1962), *La Ragazza di Bube* (Luigi Comencini 1965), *Les Parapluies de Cherbourg* (Jacques Demy 1964) and *Un Homme et Une Femme* (Claude Lelouch 1966).
48. Quirino's comments appear in newspaper advertisements for the film in *Donga Daily* (24 October 1967): 5.
49. Kim 2003b: 76.
50. In 1969 literary films were temporarily excluded from all ILRS categories, and in 1970 the ILRS was completely removed (for the first time) from the MPL. But, in 1973, with the 4th MPL revision, the ILRS was reinstated, producing a brief revival in literary filmmaking in the mid-1970s—until it was permanently removed in 1986.

4 Feasting on Asian Alliances
Hong Kong Co-productions and Japanese Remakes

In this chapter, we focus on the collaborative initiatives that Korean filmmakers pursued in the 1960s—before the film industry entered its 'dark age'—with the aim of expanding their networks and internationalizing Korean cinema. Given that the domestic industry was restricted in its operations by economic, political, and cultural factors, participation in international film festivals, co-production enterprises, genre adaptations, and remakes characterized this period. In what follows, we show how these interconnected activities contributed to the transformation of Korean cinema in both conspicuous and inconspicuous ways while strengthening strategic alliances with colleagues in Japan and Hong Kong, the two most active centers of the Asian film industry during this period.

A significant event in the early 1960s introduced Korean films (and the Korean film industry) to the international community: Korea's inaugural hosting of the 9th Asian Film Festival (launched in Tokyo in 1954 and now called the Asia-Pacific Film Festival). Held in Seoul from 12–16 May, 1962, the event concluded significantly on the first anniversary of Park Chung Hee's military *coup d'état*. The festival was organized by the KMPPA and coordinated by canonical director and producer Shin Sang-ok, president of the KMPPA and pioneer of the Park regime's industrialization program.

Industry members from across Asia attended the event and enjoyed live entertainment provided by the Hollywood star Rita Hayworth, a tour of the Panmunjeom demilitarized zone, and a private welcome from President Park Chung Hee at the Blue House.[1] At the festival three Korean films (all produced by Shin Film) shared seven major awards, including best film (*Mother and a Guest* (1961); best actor and actress (Shin Yeong-gyun and Choi Eun-hee in *Evergreen Tree* [1961]); best screenplay and best original score for *Evergreen Tree*; and best art direction (Jeong U-taek in *Prince Yeonsan* [1961]). The festival turned the spotlight on Korean cinema, with Shin Film at center stage, as well as boosting Korean filmmakers' self-confidence in front of their Asian colleagues. In particular, the festival helped Koreans overcome the inferiority complex that they held toward Japanese cinema, which had experienced a golden age since the mid-1950s.[2] The high-profile awards garnered at the 1962 festival displayed the fresh appeal of a largely unknown Korean cinema to a wide range of Asian film industry representatives, while also facilitating networking opportunities and cultural exchanges with Asian colleagues.[3]

In its turn, the Asian Film Festival resulted in two key internationalization developments. First, the event initiated a series of high-profile co-productions between Korea and Hong Kong—primarily between industry leaders Shin Sang-ok and Run Run Shaw, who had been one of the VIP guests at the festival. The Shin–Shaw alliance produced at least six co-productions and other joint projects between 1964 and 1969, including the box office hit *Last Woman of Shang* (1964).[4] Detailed discussions between Shin and Run Run Shaw, head of the recently built and expanded Shaw Brothers Studio in Hong Kong, provided the catalyst for re-invigorating this mutually beneficial partnership, which had begun three years earlier. Shin had been introduced to the Shaw brothers while working with Korean company Hanguk Yeonye in 1958 on the co-production *Love with an Alien* (aka *An Exotic Garden*).[5] His reunion with the Shaws in Seoul in 1962 enabled both sides to capitalize on their mutual interest in collaborative filmmaking.

As head of one of Hong Kong's rising media companies, established in 1957, and owner of the new Shaw Brothers studio, opened in 1961, Shaw was looking for ways to expand his company's presence in Hong Kong and the greater Asian region. Aiming to appeal to the Chinese diaspora throughout Asia, Shaw focused on producing epic historical dramas. By the mid-1960s, Shaw Brothers controlled more than 150 cinemas and an active distribution network that covered Hong Kong, Singapore, and Malaysia.[6] Simply put, Shaw Brothers needed a regular flow of films to exhibit, and collaborating with industry allies in Korea was seen as part of the solution. As the titles in Shaw Studio's catalog show, Shaw was particularly drawn to historical films. His interest only increased after seeing Shin's historical costume drama *Prince Yeonsan* in Seoul in May 1962, leading Shaw to express a keen desire to co-produce similar films with a Korean partner.[7] In addition, because Shin Film was Korea's largest production company, it was an obvious choice as a co-production partner.

Second, the 1962 festival offered Korean filmmakers unparalleled exposure to a number of Japanese feature and documentary films—five in each category.[8] This was an extremely rare opportunity—facilitated by interest on both sides to access each other's markets—to view Japanese media and cultural products that had been banned in Korea (along with music, magazines, and books) since Korea's liberation from Japan in 1945.[9] Korean filmmakers, along with other festival attendees and local media representatives, were deeply impressed by these Japanese films, which represented a range of genres and aesthetic styles that they had previously only heard or read about. Three films in particular enthralled audiences at the sold-out festival sessions: Toshio Masuda's *I Look up When I Walk* (1962, aka *Keep Your Chin Up* and Ue o muite arukō in Japanese); Yasuzō Masumura's *A Wife Confesses* (1961); and Akira Kurosawa's samurai film, *Sanjuro* (1962).[10] These Japanese film screenings especially opened Korean filmmakers' eyes to new ideas, leading to a flood of both illicit and licensed remakes of Japanese films. According to one newspaper report published in July 1963, at least half of the films made in Korea in 1963 were believed to have been plagiarized from popular Japanese originals, and to top it off, they performed relatively well at the box office.[11] Henceforth, this "remake" strategy was seen by the local industry (at least for a while) as a risk-proof method of staying afloat in terms of box office returns and ongoing investment.

With these inter-Asian linkages in mind, the year 1966 marked a major turning point for the Korean film industry, both in terms of the trend for plagiarized remakes and a dramatic shift toward the making of fake co-productions. At this time, and specifically after the MPI revised production quotas under the MPL, the industry was limited to making and/or distributing a total of 120 domestic films annually (to be shared equally by 26 registered companies at the time). Registered companies that had increased staff numbers and ramped up infrastructure to meet the MPI's previous requirements to produce 15 films annually were now forced to downsize. As a result, companies such as Shin Film, Anyang Film (also run by Shin Sang-ok), Asia Film, and Hwacheon Film began forging documents for bogus co-production arrangements, while others such as Geukdong Heungeop and Segi Sangsa gradually reduced their output of remade Japanese films. Although the MPI had now promised to initiate a thorough review process in order to crack down on unauthorized remakes, producers had already begun curtailing their activities in order to meet the reduced number of films that they were allowed to make.[12]

Through the combination of these various "internationalization" developments Korean filmmakers forged connections with a number of major players in (and films from) the region—particularly those from Hong Kong and Japan. Not only did these new links enable the Korean film industry to expand its network and scale of production, but they also generated new ideas and pathways for artistic expression, as well as questionable strategies for exploiting its new alliances in East Asia.

Converging with the Shaw Dynasty

In the late 1950s, Korea and Hong Kong were emerging markets that were attracting the attention of Shaw Brothers and Korean producers respectively. Players from both sides had engaged in a number of collaborative projects in order to explore the potential for international expansion. One of the earliest film collaborations between Korea and Hong Kong was *Love with an Alien*, the first Korean film shot on location in Hong Kong. This collaboration with the Shaw Brothers was produced by Hanguk Yeonye (aka Korea Entertainment Corporation), a pre-cartel production company established by rogue producer Im Hwa-su in 1954.[13] Its formation allowed members of the Korean film industry to gain access to Shaw-owned cinemas across Southeast Asia, while enabling the Shaw brothers to feed their expanding interest in property investment, regional film distribution, and the development of Shaw Brothers Studios.

Love with an Alien is a romantic melodrama about a handsome Korean composer (played by Kim Jin-kyu) who falls for a pretty Hong Kong singer (played by Lucilla Yu Ming). It is the oldest surviving color film in the Korean film archives, and was made six years before the Park Chung Hee government promulgated guidelines for official international co-productions (in 1963). The film was co-directed by Tu Gwang-qi (Hong Kong), Jeon Chang-geun (South Korea), and Mitsuo Wakasugi (Japan) and produced by Runde Shaw with co-financing from Korea's Hanguk Yeonye.

In an effort to "localize" the film—that is, to increase its appeal to audiences in Hong Kong and Singapore—Korean screenwriter Yu Du-yeon rewrote the script with assistance from Chinese writer Cheng Gang (based on the original story by Korean Kim Seok-min), transforming it from a serious drama with a tragic denouement into a light-hearted comedy.[14] Despite the filmmakers' best intentions, however, *Love with an Alien* failed to appeal to Korean and non-Korean audiences alike, mainly because it lacked the type of melodramatic story line that was so popular in Korea at the time.[15] And, because of its poor box office results, Shaw Brothers was reluctant to pursue further co-productions with Korean partners, particularly given the larger than average budget needed to complete this transnational production.[16] Few commentators at the time could imagine the commercial and creative merits of such projects outweighing the expenses incurred in their production.[17] Nonetheless, this inter-Asian collaboration was a valuable learning experience for both Korean and Hong Kong industry players, not least as a result of the advanced technology used in its production—in the form of Eastman color film—including the new skills demonstrated by its Japanese cinematographer Nishimoto Tadashi, who had been hired by the Shaw Brothers because of his experience with this new color format. (At the time, the press publicized that *Love with an Alien* was the Shaw Brothers' first production shot in Eastman color film, and it was a first for Korea too.[18])

While this first international co-production was unsuccessful at the box office, Hanguk Yeonye kept the collaborative momentum going, demonstrating the company's forward thinking and producer Im's commitment to international projects in Korea in the late 1950s. After *Love with an Alien*, Hanguk Yeonye co-produced *The Love of Shadow* (1958) and *The Affection of the World* (1958). Following in Im's footsteps, Gwangseong Film Co. produced *Love and Hatred* (1958) with Hong Kong International Films Ltd., while Shingwang Film Co. produced *Forever Only You* (1959) with another Hong Kong partner (whose name was not mentioned in press reports). Given Hanguk Yeonye's pivotal role in the industry, Im's dramatic fall in 1961 following a series of tumultuous political events including the April Revolution in 1960 and the military coup in May 1961 was a key factor contributing to the souring of relations between the Korean and Hong Kong film industries.[19] For a time the relationship hung in the balance.

In May 1963, the MPI established formal co-production guidelines that mandated a completed script and a signed contract or agreement with the foreign partner company before approving any collaborative project. However, the MPI was yet to address the problematical issue of film remakes, whether licensed or unlicensed, and the procedures they should undergo. In any case, Shin Film was the first company to jump through the new hoops set up by the ministry (a process that Shin Sang-ok was rumored to have had a major hand in), and duly received approval to co-produce a slate of new films with the Shaw Brothers.[20] Armed with a signed agreement, Shin Film and the Shaw Brothers aimed to produce large-scale historical dramas that shared stars, film crews, locations, funding, and their respective distribution and exhibition markets. They hoped that their co-productions would attract both local and international audiences with elaborate costumes, natural locations, and lavish props and sets. Their first film made under the new regime was the historical epic *The Last Woman of Shang* (1964, aka *Daji*), paving the way for further co-productions and the possible entry of Korean films into the US and East Asian markets that the Shaw Dynasty had been developing. By the time of its release, the legacy created by Im and Hanguk Yeonye had long been forgotten.

The Last Woman of Shang is a Chinese historical costume drama about the iron-fisted Emperor Zhou, the last Emperor of the Shang Dynasty, and his double-dealing queen Su Daji, who seeks revenge against Zhou for killing her father. After winning over Zhou and becoming his wife, Daji works to undermine his power and steal his vast wealth—all while hiding her true love for jailed nobleman Ji Fa. In the end, Ji Fa is released from prison and his rebel forces seize the palace, thus bringing the Shang Dynasty to an end. Many of the palace scenes in this "Run Run Shaw spectacular" (also described by one reviewer as a "pre-Columbian DeMille" production) were filmed at the Shaw Brothers' Clearwater Bay Studio in Hong Kong, while the extensive outdoor battle scenes were shot on location in the rolling fields of Suwon, Korea.[21]

On its release, *The Last Woman of Shang* was promoted as a big-budget blockbuster that had been three years in the making (including pre-production), involving over 15,000 extras and 3,500 horses (see Figure 4.1). With a reported total budget of $500,000 USD, *The Last Woman of Shang* was by far the most expensive and extravagant Korean film made to date. According to KMDB, the film attracted audiences of 150,000 in Seoul—a major achievement, given that during this period audiences rarely topped 100,000 (30,000 was considered to be a production's break-even point).[22] The film showcased a winning combination of Shaw Brothers' expertise in costume and set design and advanced filmmaking techniques, as well as Shin Film's experienced crews and expertise in utilizing natural locations in Korea gained through producing war and period films such as *Prince Yeonsan* (1961), *Seong Chunhyang* (1961), and *Tyrant Yeonsan* (1963). Well-known Korean actor Shin Yeong-gyun played the lead (Emperor Zhou) in both versions, and Queen Daji was played by leading Hong Kong actress Linda Lin Dai in the Chinese dubbed version and top Korean actress Choi Eun-hee (Shin Sang-ok's wife) in the Korean dubbed version. (The Chinese version was screened in the US; releasing a film in both Chinese and Korean was a strategy that had begun with *Love with an Alien*.[23])

Figure 4.1 Film advertisements for *The Last Woman of Shang* (1964). *Gyeonghyang Shinmun* 12 September, 1964: 8; and *Gyeonghyang Shinmun* 18 September, 1964: 8.

To maximize the momentum generated by his agreement with Shaw Brothers, and to remedy a lack of investment, Shin announced plans to expand his company and produce 40 low-budget domestic films per year.[24] (Most other producers aimed to make between 15 and 20 films annually.) If successful, Shin's assembly-line production strategy would be rewarded by the government with a corresponding number of licenses to import box-office hits from Hollywood. Given that exhibiting Hollywood films was a highly lucrative enterprise for local importers, these official licenses played a critical role in ensuring a company's profits.[25] By 1964 Shin Film was employing more than 250 staff members, including directors, assistant directors and actors—many of whom were under contract through agreements comparable to those used by companies in the US and Hong Kong film industries. However, although Shin Film ran one of the largest storage, equipment, editing, and studio production spaces in Korea, it was on a small scale compared to the Shaw Brothers' operation in Hong Kong, which in 1961 employed around 1,200 people.[26] Nevertheless, for most of the early to mid-1960s Shin Film was operating at maximum capacity, producing a steady stream of top-grossing films and looking for opportunities beyond Korea to further develop its operations.

Despite the buzz that Korean filmmakers and their use of natural locations had been generating in Hong Kong, the developing relationship between the Korean and Hong Kong film industries experienced a number of setbacks in 1966. Poor box office returns in Korea of some Shin Film co-productions handicapped the company in realizing the full potential of its international partnership with Shaw

Brothers. The Chinese-oriented historical dramas that formed the staple of their co-productions attracted smaller than expected audiences in Korea, making it impossible to break even, let alone make a profit, given the hefty production budgets involved. In addition, the lengthy production periods required to make these epics prevented Shin Film from offering its stable of contracted actors continuous employment. For instance, *The Last Woman of Shang* involved four months of production work in both Korea and Hong Kong, while most Korean films in the 1960s were produced in about four weeks.[27] This meant that the company's plans to make 40 films a year were next to impossible to achieve. Hence, in reality the inter-Asian collaboration envisaged by Shin Film and Shaw Brothers failed to benefit Korea's domestic industry in the long term. In addition, the terms of their co-production agreements were unbalanced as they provided a maximum of only six prints of a completed film for the Korean partner. This severely restricted the Korean party's international distribution opportunities, while the Hong Kong partner retained ownership of the negatives and thus could print unlimited copies at will.[28] The outcome was much more favorable for Shaw Brothers, which used its co-productions with Korea (and Japan) to expand its market dominance in Hong Kong, Singapore, and among the Chinese diaspora.

In addition, the new shared production quota system that the MPI initiated in 1966 through amendments to the MPL caused Shin Film unexpected financial difficulties as a result of interruptions to the company's cash flows. In an attempt to enable production companies and the market's 534 cinemas to accommodate a manageable number of domestic films, the MPI required that all registered companies produce an equal share of a combined total of 120 films per annum.[29] To get a larger piece of this pie, Shin Sang-ok established two new registered companies—Anyang Film and Shina Film in 1967 and 1968 respectively. However, despite the opportunistic growth strategy offered by these new arrangements, Shin began to experience accounting problems that threatened his business empire's market dominance—and even its very existence. When the MPI finally withdrew its new annual national production target in late 1968, the whole industry including Shin Film went into a tailspin from which it never recovered.

As a result of this complex mix of factors, companies such as Shin Film, Anyang Film (also run by Shin Sang-ok), Asia Film, and Hwacheon Film embarked on a series of fraudulent international collaborations as a strategy for increasing their cash flows as well as a mechanism for coping with the MPI's ever-changing policy amendments. After three years of working on a series of expensive and time-consuming co-productions that threatened to alienate local audiences, Shin realized that it would be easier—and vastly cheaper—to contrive a bogus co-production than to endure the risks entailed in producing a genuine collaboration. An early example was the Shaw Brothers' *Monkey Goes West* (1966), directed by Meng Hua Ho. Shin Film fronted Im Won-sik (a contracted employee with the firm) as the film's director when it was released in Korea in mid-1966. Close-ups of actor Park No-sik's face were inserted into the completed film to help it pass as a co-production. Nevertheless, after *Monkey Goes West* was released in Korea as a co-production, the MPI charged Shin Sang-ok with tax evasion. He was fined 16 million won (approximately $60,000 USD) for manipulating financial statements, a strategy that had enabled the company to save roughly 4 million won (approximately $15,000 USD).[30] (In the mid-1960s, the average production budget for a domestic film was between 5 and 6 million won.[31]) This underhand procedure had also enabled the company to avoid the immense costs involved in purchasing raw film stock, which was scarce in Korea at the time. Given his role as an industry leader, Shin's unethical and reckless behavior was a dark sign for the future of the local film industry and its potential to further inter-Asian collaboration. Once again, 1966 proved to be a seminal year, in this instance marking the time when signs of the so-called dark age of Korean cinema first emerged, prompted in part by the industry's taking the easiest—and least transparent—pathway for survival.

The release of *Monkey Goes West* set a precedent for the subsequent emergence of a slew of fake co-productions that became a conduit (albeit illegal) for importing (and exhibiting) Hong Kong films. Korean companies were particularly eager to profit from the growing popularity of Chinese martial arts (aka *wuxia*) films, which remained favorites of Korean audiences well into the 1980s. One early example is *Come Drink with Me* (1965, directed by King Hu), a *wuxia* adventure-crime film about a bandit gang that abducts the son of a small-town mayor and attempts to trade him for their jailed leader. When it was exhibited in Korea in 1967—after appearing as a wholly Hong Kong production in the 13th Asian Film Festival in Seoul in May 1966—*Come Drink with Me* unexpectedly achieved a wide appeal, offering importers a lucrative alternative to importing (more expensive) Hollywood films. Films such as *Come Drink with Me* earned the nickname of "a money piled cushion" (*don-bangseok* in Korean), meaning that they generated a pile of money high enough to sit on.[32] Simply put, for veteran producers such as Kim In-gi, "faking" a co-production was one of the simplest ways to import such desirable Hong Kong films without engaging in the lengthy and involved co-production process.[33] Because co-produced films were regarded by the MPI as local films, registered producers-cum-importers could count each such film as one of their 15 required annual productions, which in turn qualified them for a license to import an equally lucrative Hollywood film.

At the same time, the popularity of Hong Kong *wuxia* films encouraged Korean directors such as Chung Chang-hwa (aka Jeong Chang-hwa and Cheng Chang Ho) and Jang Il-ho to follow the internationalization path by looking for long-term opportunities in Hong Kong. Following an apprenticeship under famed colonial director Choi In-gyu, as well as spells with Shin Sang-ok and Hong Seong-gi, Chung debuted in 1953 with the Korean action-crime melodrama *The Final Temptation*, launching a filmography packed with action movies. Chung stands out for the mark he left on Hong Kong cinema in the 1970s and 1980s through the action films he made for Shaw Brothers and Golden Harvest. Chung began looking to Asia and beyond with his first Shaw Brothers film, *Temptress with Thousand Faces* (1968), which was exported to Europe.[34] Perhaps Chung's best-known Shaw Brothers kung fu film is *Five Fingers of Death* (1972, aka *King Boxer*), which was released in the US in March 1973 by Warner Bros.[35] The surprising box-office stamina of *Five Fingers of Death* not only contributed to the rise of a kung fu film craze in the US, but the critical acclaim it received earned Chung an important place in the annals of Hong Kong cinema. Truth be told, in Korea *Five Fingers of Death* was actually a "fake" co-production created by forging official documents through Shin's Anyang Film company. Thus, even busy directors such as Chung and Jang, best known for directing *Fists of Vengeance* (1972) and *Pil li Quan* (1972, aka *Saengsatu*), were implicated in this tempting get-rich-quick (and survive) scheme.

Shaw Brothers films directed by Chung and Jang were readily introduced to Korean audiences as co-productions. Short scenes and close-ups of Korean actors were often inserted into films to make them appear as official collaborations. This strategy often fooled the MPI—or at least the ministry failed to clamp down on this practice. Most of these films passed censorship without being discovered, enabling registered producers to continue exploiting the system and their links to the Hong Kong film industry. The year 1966 turned out to be a crucial one yet again. The MPI's establishment of the Screen Quota System in 1966, requiring that one-third of all films screened annually be of domestic origin, contributed to the increasing number of producers engaging in this faking practice; co-productions were regarded as local films, and thus they were exempt from the restrictions placed on foreign films.

The Korean industry's counterparts in Hong Kong (mainly Shaw Brothers at the beginning and Golden Harvest later) understood this situation and willingly signed co-production contracts and secret deals with registered producers. In many cases, the latter simply provided their Hong Kong partner with a list of Korean names to include in a film's credits in order to make it look like a collaborative production.[36] In turn, Korean companies such as Anyang Film and Shina Film—both sister companies of Shin Film—"transformed" a film made entirely in Hong Kong into a "co-production" by submitting forged contracts and supporting documentation to the MPI. At the same time, Shaw Brothers achieved a range of benefits by working with Korean partners, including access to a diversity of striking outdoor locations that were lacking in Hong Kong.[37] Old Buddhist temples, thick green forests, rocky mountains, open fields, island scenery, and impressive seascapes across all four seasons provided exotic landscapes that resembled mainland China but that were inaccessible to filmmakers from British-controlled Hong Kong (and other places) as a result of Cold War politics. As a result, many well-known Hong Kong directors including Han Hsing Li, Chang Cheh, John Woo, King Hu, and Siu-Tung Ching shot one or more films in Korea from the early 1960s.[38]

While filming on location, production crews from Hong Kong were exposed to a range of new techniques utilized by their Korean colleagues, including stunts, pyrotechnics, and martial arts skills used in taekwondo. Shaw Brothers' ultimate goal was to strengthen its branding and market position through an expanding catalog of local and co-produced films as well as by improving the production capabilities of their Hong Kong staff. To enhance these industrial–cultural exchanges, Shaw Brothers invited other Korean directors (besides Chung Chang Wha and Jang Il-ho) including Choi Gyeong-ok and Im Won-sik to shoot a series of historical *wuxia* films in Hong Kong.[39] In addition, Korean actors such as Hwang Jeong-lee, Kim Yong-ho (aka Casanova Wong, Ka Sat Fat, and Wong ho), and Dragon Lee—all three of whom were well known as taekwondo masters—extended their careers in the Hong Kong film industry. This flow of manpower and talent between the two countries—intended both to exploit and augment the collaborative momentum that *The Last Woman of Shang* had generated—occurred over a relatively short period. In turn, the names of these Korean stars and directors were promoted in the credits of Hong Kong films to further the illusion that they were genuine co-productions.

However, a backlash soon became apparent from within the industry itself. Negative responses to the ways in which these fake co-production films had been produced and the ease with which registered producers could exploit the co-production system threatened to outweigh any potential benefit for the Korean film industry. Critics, arthouse directors, and independent producers with limited access to funding, as well as Shin's international networks, protested the promotion of these Chinese-style swordplay films as "local" films, not least because they were transparent ploys to obtain import licenses, and their Korean content was miniscule. For practitioners keen to make genuine Korean films it was unacceptable for a Hong Kong-made martial arts feature to be classified as a local film through the 1966 Screen Quota System, which had been established to protect the domestic Korean market from domination by foreign films. Eventually, and painfully slowly, such complaints forced the Motion Picture Association of Korea (MPAK) to submit a petition to the MPI in November 1970, asking the government to curtail the approval and exhibition of bogus co-productions.[40] Although MPAK continued to advocate for reform, the MPI failed to implement any policy changes until 1975. However, by that time, significant and irreversible damage had already been done to the industry. Moreover, this and other strategies, including the unauthorized remake of Japanese films, continued over the next decade.[41]

Feasting on Japanese Remakes

Throughout the 1960s Hong Kong martial arts films, Italian/Spanish spaghetti Westerns, and 007 James Bond action films were popular with Korean audiences, and these genres consistently made registered producers-cum-importers heftier profits than domestic films. It was no secret that a new generation of young filmgoers believed that foreign films contained superior story lines and aesthetic values compared to domestic films.[42] As a result, the profitability of domestic films slipped lower and lower, sparking a frenzy among both registered and independent producers to secure increasing numbers of import licenses to keep their companies afloat. However, given the strict policy environment regulating the industry, this was easier said than done. To assist with meeting their production quotas, Korean producers began remaking films sourced from abroad, both copying story lines and producing near-replicas of the original films. Popular Hong Kong martial arts swordplay films, such as *One-Armed Swordsman* (1967), were adapted and remade as a local series, *One-Legged Man* (1974).

In addition to feeding off the popularity of *wuxia* films, Korean producers remade spaghetti Westerns such as *A Fistful Dollars* (1964) as localized "Manchurian Westerns", which portrayed Koreans fighting the Japanese Army and Chinese bandits during the colonial period in Manchuria.[43] Hoping to attract audiences that had waned in the early 1970s following the advent of television, filmmakers also adapted the 007 James Bond series into South vs. North Korean espionage films. Although they were banned by the Korean government, Japanese films, especially the youth rebellion "sun tribe" and soft porn "pink" genres, also became desirable targets for remakes, as we discuss in the following section.[44]

Ironically, while Japanese films were hard to find in Korea following the Japanese surrender in 1945, their scripts were often published in popular Japanese film magazines such as *Kinema Junpō* (founded in 1919). These were brought back to Korea by travelling businessmen as well as students studying in Japan who circulated these publications amongst film industry people on their return. Korean filmmakers thus found it relatively easy to acquire intimate details of the production of specific Japanese films and their actors (as well as the distribution and exhibition of foreign films in Japan)—knowledge that ultimately enabled them to remake many of these films. Many Korean screenwriters, cinematographers, and other industry practitioners were equipped with Japanese language skills. In the late 1930s and early 1940s the colonial government in Korea had replaced Korean language education with the learning of Japanese, banning the use of Korean in schools. Many members of the Korean film industry who were active in the 1950s and 1960s had studied under this colonial education system. They were also active readers of Japanese film magazines, which contained much valuable information about Japanese and global films. Essentially, although they were prevented from viewing Japanese films, Korean filmmakers had access to Japanese cinema by reading published screenplays and articles that gave them vicarious experience of filmmaking trends in Japan and other parts of the world.

As early as 1958, the Korean *Donga Daily* reported concerns over the "plagiarizing" of Japanese and French films, pointing to an absence of policy and industry measures that would proscribe such activities.[45] Yet, such practices flourished: in the first half of 1963, at least 35 out of 69 films made were appropriated from Japanese originals, and they attracted audiences of a notable size.[46] Henceforth, this "remake" strategy became a risk-proof means of internationalization, especially in terms of investment and box office returns.

For the domestic film industry, which had produced 86 films in 1961 and then 113, 144, 147, 189, 136, 172, 212, and 229 films in each successive year to the end of the decade, there was a choice between feast or famine.[47] To feed its needs, and particularly following the 9th Asian Film Festival, the industry increasingly drew on golden-age Japanese films as a source of inspiration and income. The screening of three festival films in particular fueled this drive. The first of these was the upbeat, angry, youth-oriented musical *I Look up When I Walk*, part of Nikkatsu Studio's collection of action crime films that contributed to the vigor and diversity of Japan's post-war golden age of cinema.[48] With its gritty portrayal of rival street gangs, it launched the international career of lead actor and singer Kyu Sakamoto.

The festival's 12-member jury, presided over by the well-known female Korean poet Mo Yun Sook (1910–1990), awarded it the prize for best color cinematography. The second of these influential Japanese films was the psychological mystery noir, *A Wife Confesses*, released by the major Japanese studio Daiei. This compelling courtroom drama unravels a complex case involving the murder of an abusive professor by his attractive young wife (Ayako) and her resulting trial. The film creatively employs sequences of jarring shots and disjointed edits, intricate flashbacks, and claustrophobic staging—evoking the techniques used by cinematographer and director Sidney Lumet for the classic Hollywood drama *12 Angry Men* (1957).[49] The third production was the samurai sword action film *Sanjuro*, the sequel to the critically acclaimed *Yojimbo* (1961); both films starred Mifune Toshirō, and both were distributed by Toho Studios, which had famously produced *Godzilla* (1954). *Sanjuro* explores the social, cultural, and political changes that threatened long-standing samurai traditions, including concepts of honor, loyalty, and justice that appeared in Japan in the mid-nineteenth century.[50] The film won the award for best sound recording at the 9th Asian Film Festival.[51]

As a result of the festival, Japanese cinema had a major impact on Korean filmmakers and cinephiles in general, despite the fact that access to screenings of Japanese films was severely limited. Conversely, Korean cinema gained the attention of some of Japan's top film industry representatives—particularly the Japanese festival delegation, which included film critic Ogi Masahiro, Daiei executive Nagata Masaichi, Shochiku's legendary president Kido Shiro, *Mainichi Shimbun* reporter Kyūshirō Kusakabe, and Toei executive Hiroshi Okawa, as well as 10 actors including Noriko Maki, Misako Uji, Keiko Nagawa, and Mieko Kondo.[52] They all hoped that the festival would be a step toward re-opening the Korean market to a new generation of Japanese films, the predecessors of which had filled cinema screens during the colonial period. Nikkatsu, Daiei, and Toho had all been highly active film distributors in Korea during the Japanese colonial period (1910–1945), with large numbers of films passing through their hands. Thus, for studio executives, the screening of their films at the Asian Film Festival in 1962 constituted a brief return to their glory days in the region.

As a show of goodwill, one week before the festival began Daiei announced plans to release Shin Sang-ok's drama *Seong Chunhyang* (1961) through its exhibition chain, making it the first Korean film to be released in Japan since the end of the colonial period.[53] *Seong Chunhyang* is based on a well-known traditional folk tale from the Chosun Dynasty, reflecting the unique qualities of Korean culture and society.[54] Given its distinctive cultural content, this film would have offered Japanese audiences a rare insight into Korean cinema.

In addition to the festival films that had created such a sense of excitement among Korean filmmakers, official government spokespeople such as Lee Won-wu, MPI Vice-Minister, sparked a cautious optimism about future industry and cultural exchanges between Korea and Japan. During the festival, Lee revealed details of unofficial discussions on this subject, including the interest shown by Japanese industry representatives in exporting films to Korea. However, further progress would be dependent on the direction taken by wider bi-lateral diplomacy, efforts that eventually resulted in the signing of the *Treaty on Basic Relations between Japan and the Republic of Korea* in 1965 after almost 15 years of discussions.[55] However, despite the delay in reaching this agreement, mutual interest in each other's film industries was now being pursued independently of formal government policy.

Capitalizing on this momentum and the apparent leniency the MPI was now showing towards the Japanese film industry, Korean film companies began exploring a range of new ideas and opportunities, in particular shooting on location in Japan and taking advantage of the advanced technical achievements exhibited by the Japanese film industry.[56] For example, in September 1962, only four months after the Asian Film Festival, the Seoul-based Sejong Film Company shot numerous scenes for *Black Gloves* (1963, directed by Kim Seong-min) at well-known Japanese locations, including Haneda Airport, the modern Western-style (old) Marunouchi Office Building in Tokyo, and the mountainous Hakone region of Kanagawa Prefecture—a stone's throw from Mt. Fuji and its pristine lakes. *Black Gloves* is an anticommunism film that portrays Korean–Japanese, and North Korean spies colluding to abduct unsuspecting Korean–Japanese and smuggle them into North Korea. According to the critics, the Japanese locations added a feeling of exoticism to the film.[57] In addition, Shin Film engaged the help of Toho and its technical staff to help it complete the spectacular underwater scenes shot for *The Story of Sim Cheong* (1962). Based on a classic Korean melodramatic tale, this film portrays a girl who sacrifices herself to the sea gods in order to provide for her blind father—whose sight is restored after being reunited with his daughter, who is spared by the sea deities.

Word of mouth and press publicity about such links with Japan made Korean producers and directors determined to open up the film market even further to Japanese films and joint productions. However, progress on the official front was slow, and in the context of a policy vacuum and resultant confusion about the best way forward, Korean filmmakers found their own ways of wooing Japanese film companies. One response involved the remaking of genre films that were popular in Japan, trusting that the ban on Japanese films would soon be lifted and hoping for an upturn in commercial links between the two countries.

In 1964, Korean filmmakers embarked on a series of "youth films", depicting a defiant and restless generation of young people lashing out in frustration against a conservative establishment with its rigid social hierarchies. Although they drew on outdoor locations in Seoul, including recognizable city streets, neighborhood markets, and bars, these productions were basically localized versions of Japanese "sun tribe" (*taiyozoku*) films. In other words, they rehearsed the same themes and story lines that characterized these Japanese films about rebellious urban youth. Sun tribe films depicted the post-war generation of young people in Japan, their anger, frustration, and disillusionment. Korean films that closely emulated Japanese sun tribe films include: *The Classroom of Youth* (1963), based on Ishizaka Yōjirō's novel *He and I* (1961) and the Japanese film adaptation *Aitsu to Watashi* (1961), directed by Yasushi Nakahira; *Private Tutor* (1963), based on Ishizaka Yōjirō's novel *A Slope in the Sun* (1958), which spawned a 1958 film of the same name directed by Tasaka Tomotaka; and *Barefoot Youth* (1964), closely based on Kō Nakahira's film *Dorodarake no junjō* (1963, aka *Mud Spattered Purity*). While some of these Korean adaptations were blatant and unauthorized copies of the Japanese originals, others were licensed remakes; not surprisingly, in some cases the dividing line between these two categories was blurred.

The term "sun tribe" originated from Ishihara Shintarō's award-winning Japanese novel, *Season of the Sun* (1955), which addressed a range of contemporary themes including "anti-establishment (and sometimes simply pointless) violence and casual morality, endorsing simple brutishness, cynicism, and abandon".[58] After the novel was adapted for the screen in 1956, the author's brother Ishihara Yujirō, who starred in the film, became known as the Elvis Presley of Japan and the iconic James Dean of Japanese youth.[59] In this way, Japanese sun tribe films became associated with—or were thought to be modeled on—international films that expressed the alienation of youth, such as Ingmar Bergman's *Summer with Monica* (1953) and Nicholas Ray's *Rebel without a Cause* (1955).[60] Ishihara Yujirō's regular co-star Kitahara Mie first appeared as his girlfriend in Nikkatsu's well-known sun tribe film *Crazed Fruit* (1956), which launched the couple's rise to stardom as well as their real-life relationship, which led to their marriage in 1960. It is not surprising that Korean youth films followed a similar path.

However, something more than creative inspiration was motivating Korean filmmakers, who openly based their films on specific Japanese sun tribe films—which themselves had no chance of being shown in Korean cinemas—as well as copying their visual styles.[61] Before long, this new and lucrative trend became an open secret in the Korean film industry as young, enthusiastic audiences flocked to cinemas, eager to take in as many of these stimulating youth films as possible. In fact, it was claimed at the time that local filmmakers would have a guaranteed box office hit if they matched lead actors Shin Seong-il and Eom Aeng-ran with an original Japanese story.[62] Like the Japanese pairing of Ishihara Yujirō and Kitahara Mie, Shin Seong-il and Eom Aeng-ran became popular icons while playing the lead roles in numerous Korean youth films including *The Classroom of Youth* (1963), *Private Tutor* (1963), *The Lost Sun* (1964), and *Barefoot Youth* (1964), all budget films made over a short period.[63] Like Ishihara and Kitahara, they married in real life in November 1964.

Through his numerous appearances as a good-looking and rebellious young man—just like Ishihara Yujiro's characters in Japanese films—Shin Seong-il became a role model for young Korean males, who copied his hairstyle and way of dressing as well as his unruly behavior.[64] In short, he became "Korea's Ishihara Yujiro", and thus "Korea's James Dean", through his screen persona, not least because in most of his films he adopted Ishihara's hairstyle, long on top and short on the sides.[65] Early in his career, Shin Seong-il had gained a following through appearing in the love story *Private Tutor*. However, his performance in the youth melodrama *Barefoot Youth* not only secured his reputation as the leading young heartthrob in Korean cinema, it also sparked a boom in Korean youth films.

Barefoot Youth was directed by Kim Ki-duk and produced by the registered company Geukdong Heungeop. The screenplay was written by Seo Yoon-seong, who had also adapted the screenplay for *Private Tutor*. Geukdong Heungeop was co-founded in 1959 by senior journalist Cha Tae-jin and director Kim Ki-duk, who together built the company into one of Korea's leading registered producers in the 1960s.[66] Until its bankruptcy in 1967—the result of financial difficulties created by changes to the MPL in 1966—the company had a reputation for introducing audiences to new and unusual genres and working with a range of well-known directors. Their productions included Kim Ki-duk's war films *Five Marines* (1961) and *South and North* (1965), his sports film *Buy My Fist* (1966) and the monster film *The Great Monster Yongary* (1967), as well as his family melodramas *I Will Be a King of the Day* (1966) and *Mother* (1967); Yu Hyun-mok's literary film *Daughters of Kim's Pharmacy* (1963); and Jeong Jin-woo's melodrama *Early Rain* (1966).

Barefoot Youth is a tragic love story involving a defiant hoodlum in his early twenties named Dusu (played by Shin) and a young woman (played by Eom) from a wealthy family. Both transgress their class boundaries to form a relationship. However, the pair's quest for everlasting love, which they seem at one point to have attained, ends tragically in a suicide pact. If these rebellious young lovers could find no place in Korean society, they believed, then their lives were not worth living. Dying in each other's arms—the ultimate romantic gesture—was seen as the only way they could remain together forever. While earlier youth films such as *The Classroom of Youth*, *Private Tutor*, and *The Lost Sun* dealt with a range of similar issues, they failed to capture and reflect the problems besetting Korean youth as effectively as *Barefoot Youth*.[67]

Figure 4.2 Film advertisement for *Barefoot Youth* (1964). *Donga Daily* 19 February, 1964: 6.

At the time of its release in early 1964, *Barefoot Youth* was exposed as a copy of Japanese filmmaker Kō Nakahira's *Dorodarake no junjō* (1963).[68] It seems that lead actor Shin, who was reveling in his rising popularity after starring in *The Classroom of Youth* one year earlier, had convinced Geukdong Heungeop president Cha Tae-jin to remake *Dorodarake no junjō*. Shin was keen to exploit his star appeal by appearing in as many youth films as he could, and the easiest way to do this at the time was to encourage Korean filmmakers to produce their own versions of popular Japanese films. Decades later, reflecting on his involvement with *Barefoot Youth*, director Kim Ki-duk claimed to have been unaware of similarities between the two films and even of the existence of the original Japanese screenplay.[69] However, according to Shin Seong-il the film's pre-production and production stages were completed simultaneously, suggesting that the plagiarizing of the Japanese original accelerated the filmmaking process.[70]

In sum, many of the themes and story lines used in films (and novels) about contemporary youth culture arrived in Korea via Japan, enabling Korean filmmakers to participate in an international trend that represented new and free-flowing ideas that reflected changes in youth culture around the world. At the same time, the proliferation of American fashion, culture, and ideas—introduced through the continuous exhibition of Hollywood films, the broadcasting of popular American music genres (i.e., jazz, rock, R & B) through the American Forces Korea Network (AFKN), and consumption of Western products such as Coca-Cola and bubblegum—also wielded considerable influence on Korean youth in the post-Korean War era (as they had done on Japanese youth in the postwar period).[71] Korean filmmakers often showcased these trends in the youth film genre (and contributed to their increasing popularity) by including American music (and popular dance styles like the mambo and twist) in settings such as jazz clubs, bars, and dance halls and also portrayed characters wearing American blue jeans and leather jackets. Their familiarity with representations of this international culture onscreen enabled Korean audiences to understand and identify with these modern trends because they were presented in a Korean context.

Despite their relative freedom regarding screen content, Korean filmmakers remained barred from including Japanese stars in their films. In an innovative attempt to appeal simultaneously to both markets—if and when they were finally opened up to each other—importer-cum-producer Segi Sangsa (under the aegis of registered producer Guk Kwae-nam) invited the young Japanese actress Michi Kanako to appear in his forthcoming film *Daughter of Government General* (1965). At the time, Michi was contracted with Nikkatsu, having recently gained attention for her role in Takechi Tetsuji's "pink film" *Daydream* (1964), which was the original inspiration for Yu Hyun-mok's *The Empty Dream* (1965)—discussed in Chapter 2. *Daughter of Government General* was a story about a Japanese girl and a Korean man (played by prolific actor Shin Yeong-gyun) who fall in love during the colonial period. However, the project failed to come to fruition because, despite Segi Sangsa's initiative, the official ban on Japanese actors appearing in Korean films was never lifted. In continuing this policy, the government was clearly motivated by genuine concerns over the cultural and economic implications of opening up the domestic industry not only to Japanese content, but also to Japan's robust film industry, which had completely dominated the Korean market throughout the colonial period that had ended only two decades earlier.[72] In response to these closed market conditions, surreptitious remakes of Japanese originals continued to hold the field. As discussed in Chapters 5 and 11, similar concerns were voiced when the Korean market was opened to the direct distribution of Hollywood films in the late 1980s and later to investment by Chinese companies in the mid-2010s. Despite these special circumstances, domestic critics condemned local remakes of Japanese sun tribe films because of their blatant plagiarism. Those speaking out against the practice included influential figures such as critic Lee Young-il, screenwriter Oh Young-jin, and director Yu Hyun-mok. Their concerns included the claim that the blatant copying of another country's films lowered the quality of Korean productions. Our own archival research has uncovered some of the illicitly copied films that irked these critics; they include Chung Chang-hwa's *Tell Me, Earth!* (1962, produced by Segi Sangsa), based on Gomikawa Junpei's six-volume novel *The Human Condition* (1956–1958), and director Kobayashi Masaki's remarkable epic (nearly 10-hour) trilogy (1959, 1959, 1961) about a Japanese conscientious objector living under extreme duress while serving in the Japanese army during wartime. Other offenders were Cho Keung-Ha's *The Colorful Rainbow* (1963, produced by Donga Film Co.), adapted from Genji Keita's novel *Katei no Jijo* (1962); Jang Il-ho's *The Ruffians* (1963, produced by Segi Sangsa), a close copy of *Yojimbo* (1961); and the Shin Sang-ok–Shaw Brothers co-production *The Bandits* (1967), largely taken from Japanese writer Yamada Nobuo's screenplay for *Bazoku*, which was published in January 1966 in *Scenario*, a monthly magazine run by the Japanese Screenwriters Association.

Plagiarism usually occurred during the screenwriting process, conducted under the auspices of a producer or head of a production company. In many cases, individuals combed through Japanese film magazines such as the popular *Kinema Junpō* seeking inspiration from the original scripts that were published in these outlets on a regular basis. Current and back issues of such magazines were easy to acquire, especially given that periodicals of this nature were not banned. With creative content from Japan so readily available, there was little incentive for Korean filmmakers to develop new and original material. Simply put, registered producers such as Geukdong Heungeop and Segi Sangsa, who were under immense pressure to meet annual production quotas, exploited remakes of popular Japanese films in order to turn a quick profit.

On one occasion, the respected film critic Lee Myeong-won made the sardonic comment in *Silver Screen*, one of Korea's most widely circulated film magazines, that all Korean screenwriters should have a working knowledge of Japanese and a good eye for imitation.[73] The cartoon shown in Figure 4.3 (pictured below), which appeared alongside Lee's comments, depicts the working style and key tools of a Korean screenwriter: a pen, scissors, glue, and a pile of Japanese screenplays. It was an open secret that this was a prevalent practice among some of the most active Korean producers in the mid-1960s.[74] Other concerned commentators such as film critic Lee Young-il, screenwriter Oh Young-jin, and director Yu Hyun-mok spoke up about this plagiarism "industry" and its negative effects on the quality of domestic films. Oh criticized registered producers in particular for exploiting the practice to make quick profits.[75] The unprofessional and lazy practice of copying already released films, whether this was done legally or not, short-circuited the creative process and discouraged younger filmmakers and industry hopefuls from developing the full range of their talents. Reputable screenwriters such as Han Wu-jeong (*Marines Who Never Returned*), Kim Ji-heon (*Late Autumn*), and Baek Gyeol (*Homebound*), known for their original work, seemed to represent a

Figure 4.3 Editorial cartoon: "This is how a Screenwriter Works". *Silver Screen* August 1965: 58.

minority of filmmakers who were recognized for their ability to create original stories that reflected the lives of real Koreans.

This being said, there was a small number of authorized remakes of Japanese films and script revisions during this period. Some of the better-known licensed remakes were *Dad, Please Get Married* (1963), based on Genji Keita's 1962 novel *Katei no Jijou* and Yoshimura Kōzaburō's film of the same title; *Private Tutor* (1963), based on Ishizaka Yōjirō's novel *A Slope in the Sun* (1958) and Tasaka Tomotaka's 1958 film of the same name; and *My Wife is Confessing* (1964), based on Murayama Masaya's novel *A Wife Confesses* (1961), which celebrated Japanese director Yasuzō Masumura made as a film in the same year. A number of Korean producers and directors had seen Masumura's *A Wife Confesses* (1961) when it was screened in Seoul during the Asian Film Festival in 1962. Arthouse director Yu Hyun-mok's *The Empty Dream* (1965) was taken with permission from Takechi Tetsuji's original script for the "pink film" *Daydream* (1964). (When we interviewed Yu in 2005 he claimed that while he had been very familiar with Takechi's salacious script, the difficulty of accessing Japanese films had prevented him from seeing the film itself.[76]) As we have seen, Korean auteur director Yu Hyun-mok's *The Empty Dream* (1965) still enjoys a reputation for the artistry he achieved through his re-creation of the original Japanese work. Despite their derivative nature, these adaptations challenged Korean filmmakers to develop an expanded range of aesthetic styles and story lines, elements that provided new and fresh approaches to the cinema for local audiences.

Conclusion

With the diverse approaches to co-productions and remakes discussed above in mind, we can conclude that Korean filmmakers of the 1960s had two primary aims: to explore some of the most recent international filmmaking trends (and genres) and—driven by the circumstances in which they found themselves—to make quick profits without investing time and resources in producing original scripts. In both cases, Koreans sought opportunities to work with and learn from Hong Kong and Japanese filmmakers while familiarizing themselves with their respective film industries, albeit from afar. Nonetheless, the most active East Asian filmmakers looked forward to a time in the near future when there would be increased opportunities for importing and exporting each other's films and promoting a regular flow of formal co-productions. The seeds that would potentially bring these varying types of collaboration to fruition were planted at the 9th Asian Film Festival.

During the 1960s the domestic film industry saw a rise in the number of cinemas, cinemagoers, new talent (actors, directors and experienced crew members), and annual film productions. From the creative perspective, canonical auteurs such as Shin Sang-ok, Lee Man-hee, Yu Hyun-mok, and Im Kwon-taek raised the bar in terms of aesthetic and narrative quality through their experimentation with visual styles and genres that were new to Korean audiences. Within a short period, Korea's melodrama-centric film industry had been transformed by these key players and their productions, which often mimicked popular genre films from abroad. Through a process involving both creative inspiration and cultural appropriation, a number of foreign genre films were adapted to Korea's distinctive political, social, and cultural milieu. Conversely, and to a minor extent, the larger film world was exposed to these new Korean genre films when they appeared in international film festivals, and a small number of them had been exported. Korea's interaction with the international film community increased as a direct result of the internal and external developments discussed in this chapter.

Notes

1. "The Blue House Full of Activities on 13th May (Hwagi Neomchin 13Irui Cheongwadae)". *Gyeonghyang Shinmun* (14 May 1962): 3. Hayworth was popular in Korea (and Asia in general) during the Japanese colonial and USAMGIK periods. Her films, including *Tales of Manhattan* (1942), were exhibited in Seoul for runs of several weeks, and she enjoyed constant publicity in film magazine and daily newspapers.
2. "Lessons from Asian Film Festival (Asia Yeonghwaje-ui Gyohun)". *Donga Daily* (18 May, 1962): 4.
3. Other events planned by the Park Chung Hee government in mid-1962, such as the Seoul International Music Festival and the Seoul Industrial Exposition, strengthened Korea's international links with its Asian neighbors by facilitating cultural exchanges among attendees, enabling Korean practitioners to showcase their talents, and marking the first anniversary of the military coup. In turn, these events enhanced the country's image by demonstrating the nation's "restored" stability to the region and the world.
4. *The Last Woman of Shang* paved the way for several subsequent official co-productions by Shin Film including the historical dramas *The Goddess of Mercy* (1966), *That Man*

in Chang-an (1966), *The King with my Face* (1966), and *The Thousand Year Old Fox* (1969), as well as the Manchurian Western *The Bandits* (1967, aka *Mounted Bandits*), and a horror film, *The Ghost Lovers* (1974, aka *A Woman with Half a Soul*).

5. Hanguk Yeonye company owner and producer Im Hwa-su hired Shin to direct *Independence Society and Young Syngman Rhee* (1959), a state-funded propaganda film designed to whitewash President Rhee's authoritarian style. The film extolled Rhee's role in Korea's fight for independence during the Japanese colonial period (1910–1945); it appeared prior to the March 1960 presidential election, which Rhee won. Working on this production opened Shin's eyes to the potential for inter-Asian collaboration. Following the advent of the April Revolution democratic movement in 1960, which was ignited by Rhee's questionable election result, and the eventual overthrow of the Rhee government, Shin re-established the Korean film industry's ties with Shaw Brothers.

6. Kar, Bren and Ho 2004: 221.

7. In a 1962 interview, Shaw expressed an affinity for Korean cinema and a strong interest in co-producing projects that would facilitate cultural exchange as well as shared investment. See "Co-productions with Korea Favored (Hangukgwa Hapjageul Huimang)". *Gyeonghyang Shinmun* (10 May, 1962): 4.

8. See "34 Films Entered In Asian Festival". *Pacific Stars and Stripes* (15 April, 1962): 7; and "6 Countries Enter Asian Film Festival". *Pacific Stars and Stripes* (9 May, 1962): 26.

9. Such materials, especially commercial films, were banned in Korea until as late as 1998. Takeshi Kitano's *Hanabi* (1997) was the first commercial Japanese feature film officially imported and exhibited in Korea since 1945.

10. The 13th Asian Film Festival in Seoul (5–9 May, 1966) offered audiences a second rare opportunity to see Japanese films, including Noboru Nakamura's *Springtime* (1966, aka *Danshun*) and Yasuki Chiba's *Night in Bangkok* (1966). According to Wade (1969: 7), some of Japan's entries were considered "second-string"; this may have been a deliberate strategy to prevent Japanese film industry representatives from winning too many awards and thus outshining their hosts. Alternatively, Japanese distributors may have wanted to reserve their best films for the larger and more famous Cannes, Venice, or Berlin international film festivals. The Seoul festival also featured three Shaw Brothers films: the melodramas *Blue and the Black* (1966) and *Love without End* (1961), and the *wuxia* martial arts film *Come Drink with Me* (1966).

11. "Half of Them are Copies—The First Half of the Year in Korean Cinema (Jeolbani Pyojeol Yeonghwa – Sangbangi-ui Banghwagye)". *Gyeonghyang Shinmun* (6 July, 1963): 8.

12. "Why Korean Cinema is in such a Perilous State (Hanguk Yeonghwaneun Jeolmang-ilsu Bakke Eopneunga)". *Gyeonghyang Shinmun* (22 January 1966): 5.

13. One of Korea's most experienced producers and exhibitors during the 1950s, Im was known as a thug with powerful political connections. As head of the Anticommunist Artists Association (a right-wing entertainers' organization), Im had a reputation for pressuring popular actors to star in his films and to attend political events hosted by President Syngman Rhee's Liberal Party (1951–1970).

14. "Difficulties in Making of Co-production Films (Hapjak Yeonghwa-ui Aero)". *Gyeonghyang Shinmun* (21 Feb, 1958): 4.

15. Kar 2004: 31.

16. Cho 2004: 16.

17. "Clever Policy Support Necessary for Making and Exporting Co-production Films (Hapjak Yeonghwa-ui Haewoe Jinchureun Hyeonmyeonghan Gukchaek Dwitbatchimeul)". *Donga Daily* (18 February, 1958): 4.

18. "Barriers to Making Co-production Films (Hapjak Yeonghwa-ui Aero)". *Gyeonghyang Shinmun* (21 February, 1958): 4.

19. Under Im's leadership, Hanguk Yeonye produced 19 films until it was liquidated in 1961 as a result of Im's premature death. Following the military coup in 1961, the Park Chung Hee government arrested Im and sentenced him to death for fomenting serious social and political unrest. See "Death Penalty for Im Hwa-su (Im Hwa-sue Sahyeong Eondo)". *Donga Daily* (23 August, 1961): 3.
20. "Another Co-produced Film (Hapjak Yeonghwa Tto Hana)". *Gyeonghyang Shinmun* (27 February, 1963): 8. Although advertisements for *The Last Woman of Shang* promoted it as the first official co-production involving Shin Film and Shaw Brothers, the historical drama *The Cloud Bridge of Gratitude* (1963), shot on location in Hong Kong the previous year, was probably their first collaborative project.
21. Although Korea's contribution was largely ignored in the US, well-known critic Bosley Crowther's *New York Times* review of the film was nonetheless colorful. See "Screen: Hong Kong's Run Run Shaw: 'Last Woman of Shang' Bows at 55th Street". *The New York Times* (15 December, 1964). Available: www.nytimes.com/movie/review?res=9D05E2DB123CEE32A25756C1A9649D946591D6CF. Accessed 12 November 2014.
22. See <www.kmdb.or.kr/vod/vod_basic.asp?nation=K&p_dataid=01064&keyword=%EB%8B%AC%EA%B8%B0>.
23. According to Kar (2004: 31–35), Shin Film maintained sole distribution rights for *The Last Woman of Shang* in Korea, while Shaw Brothers controlled the Hong Kong and remaining sectors of the Asian market through its established networks.
24. "Status and Analysis of Film Contents (Yeonghwa Sojae Balgul Hyeonhwang Bipyeong)". *Yeonghwa Segye* (June 1963): 51–52.
25. For example, in 1968 the number of domestic films screened was 204 while the number of foreign films was only 80. However, average audiences for foreign films were more than double those for domestic films: 107,269 and 40,271 respectively. See KMPPC 1977: 160.
26. See Shaw Brothers' official website: www.shaw.sg.
27. "Director Jang Directing from his Sickbed (Jang Gamdogeun Byeongsang-eseo Yeonchul Jisi)". *Gyeonghyang Shinmun* (21 December, 1963): 5.
28. "Losses all Around for Co-produced Films (Sonhaeman Boneun Hapjak Yeonghwa)". *Maeil Gyeongje* (9 February, 1970): 4.
29. Article 10 of the revised film law required producers interested in using foreign-sourced material to acquire the explicit agreement of the original copyright holder or their agent before applying to the MPI for permission to make the film. This policy amendment set the production of a 'remake' within a legal context, resulting in a near-immediate slump in so-called plagiarism cases.
30. "Shin Sang-ok Charged by Police (Shin Sang-ok ssi Ipgeon)". *Donga Daily* (16 July, 1966): 7.
31. "Admission Fees Hiked (Geukjang Ipjangryo Kkeongchung)". *Donga Daily* (22 February, 1967): 4.
32. "Chinese Martial Arts Films Expected to Ride High for Another Year (Junggukje Geomgaekmul 1Nyeoneun Deo Panchildeut)". *Donga Daily* (16 November, 1968): 5.
33. Personal interview with Kim In-gi. Seoul. October 2005.
34. Other films directed by Chung in Hong Kong include *Six Assassins* (1971), *Five Fingers of Death* (1972), *The Devil's Treasure* (1973), and *The Double Crossers* (1976).
35. See Desser 2004: 20–23.
36. Personal interview. Lee Hyung-pyo. Seoul. October 2004.
37. For further details, see Shim and Yecies 2012a.
38. Personal interview with John Woo. Beijing, November 2011. Through a combination of Korean and Hong Kong expertise, these Hong Kong filmmakers transformed well-preserved temples, leafy forests, snowy fields, and sea cliffs into dynamic backdrops for dozens of martial arts films and historical dramas including *The Magnificent Concubine*

(1962, directed by Han Hsing Li), *Four Riders* (1972, directed by Chang Cheh), *The Dragon Tamer* (1975, directed by John Woo), *Raining in the Mountain* (1979, directed by King Hu), and *Duel to the Death* (1983, directed by Siu-Tung Ching).
39. Choi directed *Sword of a Chivalrous Robber* (1968), *Five Assassins* (1968), and *Final Facedown in Cheonma Mountain* (1971), while Im is known for directing *Yeong* (1968), *A Wonderer* (1968), and *Armless Swordsman* (1969).
40. "Korea–Hong Kong Fake Co-production Dispute (Hanjung Hapjak Wijang Sibi)". *Donga Daily* (14 November 1970): 5; and "Stipulating Co-production Requirements (Hapjak Yeonghwa Jejak Jogeon Myeongmunhwa)". *Donga Daily* (8 February 1971): 5.
41. The details of these irregular collaborations are still unclear in many cases. When in 2004 the Busan International Film Festival showed a retrospective entitled "The Decades of Co-production between Hong Kong and Korea", *Duel to the Death* (1982) was screened as an official co-production. However, according to prolific Korean filmmaker Lee Hyung-pyo, while Hong Kong production company Golden Harvest listed his name as the director, the film was completed without his physical involvement. Personal interview with Lee Hyung-pyo. Seoul. October 2004.
42. *Korea Cinema* (September 1972): 99–103.
43. In the late 1960s, the further development of the Manchurian Western was partly inspired by Shin Sang-ok's *The Bandits* (1967), which was co-produced with Shaw Brothers and also partially copied from a Japanese screenplay written by Nobuo Yamada. See "Suspicions of Plagiarizing Japanese Screenplay (Ilgakbonseo Ilbu Pyojeol Hyeomui)". *Donga Daily* (26 September 1967): 5.
44. The post-colonial ban on Japanese films was so thorough that even Hollywood films containing Japanese elements were highly suspect. For instance, distributors had to mute the Japanese dialogue in *Sands of Iwo Jima* (1949) before it could be exhibited; *Heaven Knows, Mr. Allison* (1957) was initially rejected by censors because it contained Japanese extras; and the award-winning *Bridge on the River Kwai* (1957) was subjected to a lengthy censorship process because it starred Japanese actor Keiichiro Katsumoto. See "Films with Japanese Elements Cause Headaches (Ilbon Saekchae Yeonghwa Malsseong)". *Donga Daily* (18 October, 1962): 5; and "Japan Trouble #6. Spreading the Japanese Colors (Ilbon Teureoble #6. Beonjineun Waesaek Mude)". *Donga Daily* (6 February, 1964): 1.
45. "Looking Back on Cultural Life in 1958: Film Production Community Suffers Local Film Famine in Bumper Year (Ilguopalnyeon Munhwagye Gyeolsan: Pungnyeon Gigeun-ui Jejakgye Yeonghwagye)". *Donga Daily* (11 March, 1959): 4.
46. "Half of Them are Copies—The First Half of the Year in Korean Cinema (Jeolbani Pyojeol Yeonghwa—Sangbangi-ui Banghwagye)". *Gyeonghyang Shinmun* (6 July, 1963): 8.
47. KMPPC 1977: 46.
48. *I Look up When I Walk* is acknowledged by critics as a masterfully shot musical film about rebellious youth—perhaps inspired by the film version of the American musical *West Side Story*, which was released in Japan in December 1961 (about 4 months before *I Look up When I Walk* was made). See Wade 1969: 7.
49. The murder scene is set on a treacherous near-vertical rock face the married couple and Ayako's ostensible lover are climbing. During the trial, Ayako is accused of committing adultery and benefiting heavily from her husband's life insurance policy.
50. In *Sanjuro*, Mifune plays a burly, cunning, and outspoken *rōnin* (a samurai without a master) who, partly out of the goodness of his heart and partly out of boredom, helps members of a village clan rescue one of their elders who has been wrongly abducted by corrupt officials. A consummate swordsman, Sanjuro's eventual outsmarting of his adversaries helps restore order in the community.
51. At the 1966 festival, audiences were offered another rare opportunity to see Japanese films such as Noboru Nakamura's *Springtime* (1966) and Yasuki Chiba's *Night in Bangkok* (1966). The festival also featured three Shaw Brothers films: the melodramas

Blue and the Black (1966) and *Love without End* (1961) and the *wuxia* martial arts film *Come Drink with Me* (1966).
52. "Ten Japanese Actresses Visit Korea (Ilbaeu 10Myeong Ipgyeong)". *Gyeonghyang Shinmun* (9 May, 1962): 3.
53. "Seong Chunhyang to be Released on 13 May" (Yeonghwa Seong Chunhyang Nae 13Ilbuteo Sangyeong). *Donga Daily* (6 May, 1962): 4.
54. See Lee and Choe 1998: 36; and Yecies 2008. *Seong Chunhyang* portrays a love story involving a noble scholar and Chunhyang, the daughter of a *gisaeng* (*geisha* in Japanese), traditionally regarded as part of the lowest social class, to whom he is secretly married. The tale involves a corrupt official and a covert envoy sent by the king to inspect the regional bureaucracy. Seduced and threatened by the corrupt official, Chunhyang nevertheless maintains her fidelity to her husband. The scholar reveals his true identity, saves Chunhyang, and punishes the offending official. Both the 1923 silent version of *The Story of Chunhyang* (directed by Matsujiro Hayakawa of Japan) and the 1935 sound version of the same name—Korea's first successful talkie (directed by Lee Myung-woo)—were box-office hits, giving audiences glimpses of Korean landscapes and traditional ways of life.
55. "No Japanese Film Screenings before the National Relationship between Korea and Japan is Normalized, Says Vice Minister Lee" (Gukgyo Jeongsanghwa Gimi Boilttaekkaji Ilyeonghwa Sangyeong Andoe Lee Gongbogwan Eonmyeong). *Gyeonghynag Shinmun* (19 May, 1962): 3.
56. MPI Guidelines Established, Locations in Japan Permitted: (Ilbon Roke Heoyong Gongbubuseo Bangchim Surip). *Gyeonghyang Shinmun* (7 September, 1962): 8.
57. "Korean Film Locations in Japan" (Iguk Ilbon-eseoui Uri Yeonghwa Roke). *Donga Daily* (18 September, 1962): 5.
58. Goto-Jones 2009: 107.
59. Raine 2001: 223.
60. Chen, Lu. "NYFF Spotlight: Celebrating the Nikkatsu Centennial". *Film Society of Lincoln Center* (30 September 2011). Accessed 7 February 2015. Available at <www.filmlinc.com/blog/entry/nyff-spotlight-celebrating-the-nikkatsu-centennial>.
61. Reports in national newspapers such as the *Donga Daily* focused primarily on the negative aspects of remaking Japanese films. For example, see "Both Quality and Quantity Low" (Jil Yang Modu Sintongchanta). *Donga Daily* (12 August, 1964): 7.
62. "More than an Actor" (Yeongijaragiboda). *Donga Daily* (12 March, 1964): 7.
63. "Youthful Duo Shin Seong-il and Eom Aeng-ran at the Peak of their Popularity" (Gajang Jeomgo Ingijeoljeongin Kombi Shin Seong-ilgwa Eom Aeng-ran). *Gyeonghyang Shinmun* (7 January 1964): 5; "Shin Seong-il Starring in Thirteen Films at Once" (Muryeo 13Gae Jakpume Shin Seong-il Gyeopchigi Churyeon). *Donga Daily* (11 March, 1967): 5.
64. "Angry Apple" (Seongnan Neunggeum). *Gyeonghyang Shinmun* (5 November 1963): 8.
65. "Youth Goes Barefoot (31): Original Sports Hairstyle" (Cheongchuneun Maenbarida (31): Seupocheu Meori-Ui Wonjo). *Joongang Daily* (6 June, 2011). Available at http://article.joinsmsn.com/news/article/article.asp?total_id=5595366&cloc=olink|article|default. Accessed 15 November 2013.
66. See Kim, Sang-cheol. "Films by Geukdong Heungeop from Korea's Golden Age Cinema of the 1960s" (1960 Nyeondae Hanguk Yeonghwa Hwanggeumgi-reul Hamkkehan Yeonghwasa Geukdong Heungeop Jakpumi Hanjarie). *Film Paradise (Yeonghwa Cheonguk)* (6 February, 2013). Available at <www.koreafilm.or.kr/webzine/section_view.asp?Section=27&UpSeq=&downSeq=2574&intGroupNum=26. Accessed 26 Dec 2014.
67. For instance, *The Classroom of Youth* proved less than realistic for at least one reviewer; Shin's character was a university student who drove a car to school—most unusual for students at the time. See "*The Classroom of Youth* Reflects a Borrowed Reality" (Billyeo-on Hyeonsil Cheongchun Gyosil). *Donga Daily* (26 August, 1964):

7; and "Lives and Thoughts of University Students on and off Campus #4. Hobbies, Entertainment and Activities" (Kaempeoseu Anpak Daehaksaengdeurui Saenghwalgwa Uigyeon #4 Chuimi, Orak, Yongdo). *Donga Daily* (4 March, 1965): 5.
68. "Pure Love Born from the Mud – Barefoot Youth" (Jinheuk Soge Pin Sunae Maenbarui Cheongchun). *Gyeonghyang Shinmun* (7 March, 1964): 5.
69. Jeong, Hajong. "Barefoot Youth ... I Will Make my 70th Film When I Turn 80: Kim Ki-Duk at the BIFF Retrospecive" (Maenbareul... 80 Sejjeum 70 Beonjjae Yeonghwa Mandeul Geot: Busan Gukjeyeonghwaje Hoegojeon Yeon Kim Ki-Duk Gamdok). *Munhwa Daily* (19 Oct, 2011). Available: <www.munhwa.com/news/view.html?no=2011101901033630136004>. Accessed 12 Nov 2013. Also see KMDB: <www.kmdb.or.kr/vod/mm_basic.asp?pgGubun=06&tabmov=T&person_id=00001682>.
70. "Youth Goes Barefoot (32): Spy Operations (Cheongchuneun Maenbarida (31): Seupai Jakjeon)". *Joongang Daily* (7 June, 2011). Available at http://article.joinsmsn.com/news/article/article.asp?total_id=5597894&cloc=olink|article|default. Accessed 15 November, 2014.
71. See "20 Years' Report, Celebration of Liberation Series #4: Influence of American Culture" (Gwangbok Ginyeom Sirijeu (4) Amerikanijeumui Yeonghyang). *Donga Daily* (12 August, 1965): 5; and Kim and Shin 2010.
72. "Many Problems with Korean and Japanese Film Industry Exchanges" (Munjejeom Maneun Hanil Yeonghwa Gyoryu). *Donga Daily* (10 November, 1966): 5. In 1998, the ban on Japanese actors appearing in Korean films, and the release of Japanese films in Korea, was finally lifted. The first Korean film to cast actors from Japan was director Park Chul-soo's *Kazoku Cinema* (1998), based on the critically acclaimed 1997 novel *Kazoku Shinema* ("Family Cinema" in English) by Yū Miri, a Japanese author of Korean descent. The novel told the story of a family's break-up following a messy divorce and their reunion some 20 years later. Park's film was shot in Japanese and starred Japanese actors Isayama Hiroko, Matsuda Ichiho, and Nakajima Shinobu.
73. See the "Industry Panel Discussion" article, which included comments by critics Lee Young-il, Jeong Yeong-il, and Lee Myeong-won in *Silver Screen* (August 1965): 56–60.
74. Such practices were well documented and hotly debated at the time in numerous film magazine articles; see for example Han, Bong. "Five Evils of the Film Industry" (Yeonghwagye-ui Odae Akjil). *Yeonghwa Segye* (July 1963): 50–51; and Lee, Sun-geun. "Chronic Disease in the Film Industry" (Yeonghwagye-ui Gojiljeogin Pyosang). *Yeonghwa Yesul* (January 1966): 107.
75. Oh, Young-jin. "Let's Remove this Embarrassing Aspect of Korean Cinema" (Uri Yeonghwa-ui Chibureul Jegeohara). *Silver Screen* (January 1965): 55–57, 132.
76. Personal interview with Yu Hyun-mok. Pusan. October 2005.

Part II

The Dark Age of the 1970s and Hollywood's Domination in the Aftermath

5 Policy and Producing under Hollywood's Shadow in the 1970s and 1980s[1]

This chapter traces some of the major interconnections between state policy and film production during the 1970s and 1980s and their various effects on Korean cinema. Unquestionably, the methods used by the successive military regimes headed by Park Chung Hee and Chun Doo-hwan to enforce their national anti-communist agendas had the greatest impact on domestic filmmaking, as they did on society at large. Throughout these two decades, the Motion Picture Law (hereafter MPL) remained the government's chief means of harnessing the potential power and influence of the domestic film industry and of directing it, indirectly but emphatically, through two powerful agents: the Producer Registration System and censorship policy. Controlling the activities of film producers and directors through these two avenues for state pressure was made possible in practice with assistance from Korea's only quasi-government film industry administrative body—the Korean Motion Picture Promotion Corporation (hereafter KMPPC), which was established in 1973.

While the policy framework and the industry's production system remained the same, the external environment of the Korean film market was changing. During the 1970s and 1980s Korea experienced rapid economic growth, making itself known to the world as a contributor rather than a debtor country.[2] While its film market was declining in terms of total audience numbers, audiences for foreign films nearly quadrupled compared to domestic films in the 1980s. Along with a steady increase in ticket sales,[3] this made Korea an attractive and growing market to overseas film distributors, especially those in Hollywood, who maintained vigilant pressure to open the local market.[4]

Seeking to protect the domestic industry, both Korean producers and the government made multiple attempts to drastically limit the economic and cultural impact of foreign films. The story of how the government and film industry struggled alongside one another in their intersecting resistance to Hollywood's encroachment, as well as clashing on a host of issues, offers a poignant commentary on Korea's encounter with industrialization and aspects of globalization that accompanied the country's emergence as a major trading nation. Authoritarian state policy, that is the MPL, played a limited role in mediating these conflicts. The MPL, promulgated in 1962, ruled that *all* films, whether locally produced or imported foreign products, were liable to heavy government intervention. As previously discussed, a central plank of the MPL was the creation of the Producer Registration System (PRS), which required all film producers to register with the Ministry of Public Information (hereafter MPI) on an annual basis. However, the Screen Quota System that was created under the MPL in 1966 (discussed below) was near-completely ineffectual at maintaining an equitable balance between domestic and foreign films in the local marketplace, that is, until 1993.

Since 1945, with a hiatus during the Korean War, box office revenues generated by domestic films had been increasingly undermined by the rising popularity of foreign films—predominantly from Hollywood and Hong Kong. The Screen Quota System failed to protect producers of domestic films because exhibitors making lucrative profits from screening US films ignored the policy. Then in the 1970s, the equilibrium sought by the PRS was destabilized even further by new economic threats stemming from the expansion of Korea's three national broadcasting companies (KBS, MBC and TBC) and the swift diffusion of television, as well as a general increase in people's outdoor leisure activities—all of which resulted from Korea's rapid economic growth, stimulated by the Park government. Instead of going out to the cinema, a public space, Koreans stayed at home to watch soap operas on their television sets—part of a larger global trend.

In reality, there was little that the KMPPC or Screen Quota System could do to arrest the sharp decline of Korean cinema except to bolster its efforts to protect the domestic market from annihilation. Given this background, in this chapter we explore the ways in which government policymakers worked together to limit the distribution and exhibition of foreign—mostly American—films and to maintain control of the domestic market. Drawing on press releases, trade articles, congressional archive materials, and correspondence between the MPEA and the Office of the US Trade Representative (USTR) and the US Department of State, our study analyzes how Korean film industry representatives—namely the KMPPC and KMPPA—in their often fiery encounters with the Motion Picture Export Association (MPEA, now known as the MPA), lobbying tirelessly on behalf of Hollywood and US film distributors, played an important role in shaping the complex terrain on which the domestic film industry developed. In the course of this discussion, we present a detailed case study of the fate of one country's film industry under the long-term pressures of international trade. Penetrating the Korean market was simply business as usual for the MPAA and its members—just another example of Hollywood's highly organized export strategy.[5] There is of course another side to this story: the opening up of the film industry in Korea in the 1980s to the US market has helped key players in Korean cinema—producers and directors, as well as actors and technical specialists—achieve global reputations and attract international envy for their success.

Eventually in the early 1990s, Korea's Screen Quota System became a crucial factor in the gradual transformation of Korea's film market, contributing significantly to the ability of the Korean government and the film industry more generally to resist Hollywood's hegemony and maintain control of the domestic film market. Still in place today, but with less efficacy, Korea's Screen Quota System was a major achievement that has become the envy of film industries and arts and cultural advocates and policymakers around the globe.[6]

A New Agent in the Authoritarian Mix: The KMPPC

A new quasi-governmental film industry publicity organization, the Korean Motion Picture Promotion Corporation (KMPPC), was created by the 1973 Amendment to the MPL.[7] The KMPPC contributed to the government's comprehensive control over the film industry by: 1) immediately consolidating inactive and smaller production companies; 2) raising the financial operating and equipment requirements for registered production companies; 3) loaning registered production companies upwards of $80,000 USD; 4) collecting the $40,000 USD that producer-importers were required to contribute to the National Film Promotion Fund (which the KMPPC managed) for each government-rationed license that they obtained to import a foreign feature film; and 5) approving or rejecting particular genre films via an increasingly strict censorship process. All this was undertaken with the aim of developing and promoting the local film industry during a highly volatile period of large-scale industrialization in Korea.

Following the lead of the KMPPC, whose remit expired in 1999 when it was transformed into a less bureaucratic and more industry-run organization (but still under the aegis of the government) and renamed the Korean Film Commission (KOFIC, now called the Korean Film Council), producers were encouraged to turn out propagandistic material known as "national policy films" (gukchaek yeonghwa). This concept was by no means new to Korean cinema, as the anticommunist films and "enlightenment films" produced in the past were often utilized for the promotion of key national policies and pushed by the government since the early 1960s. The new name, "national policy films", merely underlined the ongoing urgency of the task in the government's eyes.

As if leading by example, the KMPPC itself produced six full-length films between 1974 and 1975, taking advantage of its power to recruit directors, actors, and film crews, as well as in-kind support from related sectors: *The Testimony* (1974), *Parade of Wives* (1974), *I Won't Cry* (1974), *The Wild Flowers in the Battle Field* (1974), *A Spy Remained Behind* (1975) and *The Taebaek Mountain* (1975). For the first time in Korean history, through the offices of the MPI and the KMPPC the government had become a feature film producer. Given the Park regime's hard-line policies and legal edicts against communism—with the ultimate aim of strengthening the country's national defense system—it was unsurprising that anticommunism was the leading theme of the KMPPC's national policy films.[8] Also unsurprisingly, the Korean War provided the ideal setting for these films. Although previous studies have largely overlooked national policy films in favor of the less propagandistic productions of the time, they illustrate an important facet of Korean cinema during a period when expectations within the industry were at a low ebb.

110 *The Dark Age and Hollywood's Domination*

The KMPPC aimed to present exemplary Korean films that would be a direct endorsement of the government's policies and be aimed at gaining audiences.[9] In other words, the KMPPC produced these large-scale films in an attempt to break through the market recession, widen the export market for films, and promote national policies to a domestic audience.

The Testimony (1974), directed by Im Kwon-taek, was the first national policy film produced by the KMPPC. There were few directors with experience making war films, which required heavy funding and extensive coordination between the producer and the military—a necessary partner in the making of such films. Lee Man-hee and Im Kwon-taek stood out as obvious choices to direct these films as each had directed multiple war movies during the 1960s, at a time when the average war film was prohibitively expensive. Veteran cinematographer Seo Jeong-min, who filmed many of Lee's pictures, remarked that the average budget for a war film was nearly double that for other genres.[10] If the in-kind support given by the military was to be translated into hard currency, the actual budget for a given war film would have quadrupled.

The Testimony was promoted as a "6.25" film, a reference to the date of the outbreak of war and a common name for the Korean War in Korea. The story follows the progress of the war from its beginning on 25 June, 1950, to the recapture of Seoul in September of the same year. The film depicts fierce attacks by communist soldiers from the North, and a series of relentless battle scenes that portray the communists as one-dimensional fiends. Intercut with the cruelty of these battle scenes are heartfelt stories of young soldiers from both sides of the conflict and their yearning for life. Concerned with educating the generation born after the war, and knowing little about it, director Im wanted to portray the strivings and longings of ordinary people in wartime in this film.[11] A promotional advertisement used at the time alludes to this, addressing the film's potential audience directly: "Do you remember the terrible destruction of the Han River Bridge? Did you experience how cruel they were? Can you say what caused this tragic war?—6.25 teaches an irrevocable lesson, written in blood".

Figure 5.1 Film advertisement for *The Testimony* (1974). *Gyeonghyang Shinmun* 1 January, 1974: 15.

Large-scale national policy films such as *The Testimony* were generously funded by the government and given a degree of support denied to privately funded projects. State funding for *The Testimony* totaled 70 million won (equivalent to about $85,000 USD, according to the real exchange rate for 1974), at a time when commercial films usually received no more than 10 to 20 million won. This large budget enabled the KMPPC to cast popular young actors such as Shin Il-ryong and Kim Chang-suk, and 500 extras were called in for location shooting. In addition, director Im had access to roughly six times the amount of raw film stock available to commercial filmmakers. To enhance the feeling of realism, real military uniforms and both small arms and large-scale weaponry were provided by the Korean Army, a remarkable contribution that was only made possible through the project's ties to the government. In all, *The Testimony* attracted nearly a quarter of a million viewers in Seoul, making it a big success at the box office.[12] And, in an unprecedented move, the KMPPC pulled some delicate diplomatic strings to invite a group of Japanese technical consultants including Akira Suzuki and Masao Yagi, from the special effects company EX Production, to Korea to aid in the design and execution of pyrotechnics and other live special effects such as air raids, bridge demolitions, and the creation of a large open film set of Seoul.[13]

Despite its heavy government backing and the inclusion of spectacular battle scenes, the national press considered that *The Testimony*'s overt anticommunism and its stereotypical portrayal of a relentlessly evil enemy undermined its entertainment value.[14] This was the same argument that industry members had reiterated over and over again in the late 1960s when the anticommunist film genre reached a saturation point.[15] In the 1970s, with the help of the KMPPC, the anticommunist film was given the opportunity to re-invent itself, but any new potential possessed by the genre remained unrealized. Because the primary demand for this type of propaganda film came from the government, the concerns expressed by filmmakers, businessmen, and audiences were considered of secondary importance, resulting in a "top-down" approach that had little respect for mutual contributions. Any sense of a "reciprocal" relationship between stakeholders—audiences, producers, and exhibitors, and the state—(Schatz 1981: 5) is missing from Korea's anticommunist genre. Despite its substantial financial and artistic support, not to mention the raw military power undergirding its rule, the government found that it was much more difficult to make "quality" films than it had imagined. This was the primary challenge facing the KMPPC throughout its production and sponsorship of "national policy" films.

In 1974, the KMPPC produced and released three further films: *Parade of Wives, I Won't Cry,* and *The Wild Flowers in the Battle Field*. They were unsuccessful with audiences, achieving paltry box office returns of 55,730, 31,913, and 27,065 in Seoul, respectively.[16] In 1975, the corporation produced and released *A Spy Remained Behind* and *The Taebaek Mountain*, which again achieved very poor box office returns—25,704 and 38,319 respectively. All five films performed much less strongly than *The Testimony*, casting doubt on the KMPPC's ability to produce message films of sufficient popular appeal. The MPI failed to recoup its investment, throwing into question its plans for producing further national policy films. In this context, a film's success was measured in terms of its takings at the box office, the true gauge of its utility to the MPI and the government's anti-communist campaign.

The KMPPC's direct involvement in film production had further unanticipated consequences, impacting negatively on the day-to-day operations of the industry. Because national policy films had priority over the production of all other films, as was also the case with the exhibition of films produced by the KMPPC, the production cycle that registered producers normally followed was significantly interrupted. Pre-existing contracts between a director and his star actors were suddenly rescinded if the corporation required that actor's services for one of its own films. In addition, working for the KMPPC meant that an actor had little time to become involved in other projects, let alone meet existing contractual obligations. On top of this, exhibition schedules pre-arranged between registered producers and cinema owners were overturned by the KMPPC if it considered that one of its national policy films needed to fill the slot occupied by another film. Free cinema screenings of its films were also arranged for middle and high school students under the direction of the MPI.[17] Naturally, this angered many exhibitors, who saw the influence they had previously wielded in the film industry, with the high levels of investment financing that they provided to producers, slipping away from them. Hence, both exhibitors and producers stood to lose considerable profits from their carefully scheduled, commercially attractive films, such as melodramas, over these unpopular national policy films.

As a result of low box office returns and the disruption caused to the industry in creating an adverse production and exhibition environment, the KMPPC's ambitious plans for producing its own films came to a rapid halt.[18] The corporation's strategy of releasing its films to coincide with major holidays, and taking over the pre-scheduled screening times of competing commercial films, had apparently failed to make much of a difference. Eventually, the KMPPC (and probably also the MPI) got the message after fielding complaints from across the industry. The lower than expected box office returns for its national policy films also hurt its cause. Hence, in 1975 the KMPPC ceased production of feature films, wrapping up all its outstanding projects.[19] In an attempt to appear more egalitarian, the corporation agreed to scale back its production activities and focus instead on developing support mechanisms and programs that could benefit the film industry as a whole.

Between this major change in the mid-1970s and the end of the decade, the government's film policy and the structures that supported it remained unchanged, as did the film industry as a whole, which remained in a downturn. During this time, and even after President Park was assassinated in 1979, the three-way negotiations among Korea, the US government, and the Motion Picture Export Association of America (MPEA) also tailed off. Nevertheless, advancing opportunities for imported films, including direct distribution, remained a long-term concern for the MPEA and became the leading issue in the Korean film industry in the 1980s.

Changing of the Guard

During the 1970s, the MPEA was relatively inactive in the Korean market. There was little it could do as the Park government refined its dual aims of supporting and controlling the domestic film industry. In any case, the local film market seemed insufficiently lucrative for the MPEA to take much interest in Korean affairs. Back in the US, Valenti and the MPEA were more concerned with the promise and performance of cable TV and the future role of American films in this new technology.[20]

Yet the Asian market was not neglected by Hollywood. Since the liberation of Korea from Japanese occupation in 1945, American film distributors had obeyed the adage that "trade follows the flag" and rushed stocks of their most popular films to the southern half of the peninsula.[21] Local cinemas were inundated with a range of genre films distributed directly from Hollywood (and a small number of countries outside the US) that the United States Army Military Government in Korea (hereafter USAMGIK, 1945–1948) believed would help the country reverse four decades of Japanese influence.[22] The MPEA operated in South Korea under the name of the Central Motion Picture Exchange (CMPE) and played a major role in promoting Hollywood's influence and increasing the foreign revenues earned by its member companies under a favorable trade and taxation regime.[23]

Most Korean commentators have been critical of the USAMGIK's approach to Korean art and culture including the dominance achieved by CMPE/Hollywood in the domestic market.[24] Indeed, at the time, both experienced and novice producers active in the Korean Film Union (KFU), such as Lee Byung-il, Lee Chang-yong, and Seong Dong-ho, strongly believed that US influence threatened their current and future filmmaking opportunities.[25] KFU member Kim Jeong-hyeok, a novelist and screenwriter, published an article in *Gyeonghyang Shinmun* condemning the organization's greed and attempt to dominate Korea's exhibition market, while enjoying zero-tax privileges at home.[26] For Kim, this was nothing less than an act of cultural imperialism.

The devastation wrought by the Korean War (1950–1953) retarded the growth of the film industry until Park Chung Hee took power in 1961. Following the war, in the words of one Warner Bros. executive, South Korea was a "ripe field for American pictures" because "the aftermath of war in any country leaves a great need for relaxation and entertainment".[27] While Hollywood's return to Korea in the post-war era got off to a promising start, it slowed dramatically when President Park limited the distribution and exhibition of all films through the MPL in 1962. Korea's contemporary Screen Quota System originates from the MPL; launched in 1966, it required every cinema to exhibit domestic films for a minimum of 90 days each year.[28] Cinemas also had to include a minimum number of locally produced films in their weekly schedule—a move that guaranteed screen time, but not box-office performance. The MPI further protected domestic producers, and the distribution and exhibition of Korean films, by establishing an annual quota—often referred to as an embargo—of imported films that limited the number of foreign films screened to a maximum percentage of domestic films released.

Throughout the 1960s, the MPEA, via the US Department of State, monitored Korea's trade regulations with great interest. Jack Valenti, one of the protagonists in this story, became president of the MPEA/MPAA in the same year the Korean screen quota was introduced.[29] Following their practice in other countries, on their visits to Korea MPEA representatives gathered information on the numbers of features, co-productions and foreign imports, cinema operating schedules, attendance records and annual box-office returns, and film rental receipts, all of which impacted on the distribution and exhibition of US films.[30] The country's rapid economic rise was another factor to add to the mix. By 1968 the US Department of State saw South Korea as a "promising and challenging" market and the "surprise package of the Far East", fundamentally because the country's imports had reached almost one billion US dollars.[31] South Korea was rapidly becoming a viable market for manufactured goods, in which the US, Japan, and Germany (to a lesser degree) were the primary competitors. If breaking into the Korean market was a difficult task, a primitive distribution system did nothing to encourage the MPEA. At this time, US films were first imported to offices in Japan, after which their distribution was inefficiently re-negotiated by middlemen for the Korean market, preventing Korean importers from dealing directly with the major US film companies.

In order to achieve its goal of further market penetration, the MPEA needed to find a way of dismantling Korea's robust trade barriers, which in 1965 allowed the import of only 53 foreign feature films, and also entice local producers. Valenti was disturbed by the situation he faced: many members of the powerful cartel of registered producers in the KMPPA were selling licenses to import US films on the black market to unregistered producers for $20,000 to $30,000 USD apiece.[32] As explained in a previous chapter, these heavily regulated import licenses provided both exhibitors and producers belonging to the KMPPA with a valuable opportunity to generate substantial profits from the screening of US films, which were extremely popular in Korea during the 1960s. At the end of the decade, the MPEA was concentrating its efforts on smashing the monopoly over film importation and the control of print rental prices held by the MPL and removing the "chicanery" surrounding import licensing practices followed by Korean producers.

Throughout the late 1960s, the Park Chung Hee government, especially through the Ministry of Culture and Public Information (MCPI, known as the MPI before 1968), seemed amenable to the MPEA's concerns. While the MCPI agreed in principle to most of the US film industry's requests, it balked at opening up its local market, presumably under strong pressure from President Park. The ministry sought to maintain the spirit and integrity of the MPL, which was designed to rebuild the Korean film industry on its own terms and by empowering the KMPPA in certain ways.[33] Nevertheless, in 1970, albeit for only a short time, the MCPI reduced the number of required screening days for domestic films to a minimum of 30, a move that temporarily appeased the MPEA. Thus, when the MPEA decided to get tough with foreign markets around this time, Korea was temporarily overlooked because the playing field for Hollywood films was deemed sufficiently level to allay its concerns.

Throughout the 1970s, the size of the local market shrank to new lows—as did the activities of nearly all registered producers. Profits from producing and exhibiting the dwindling number of domestic films fell sharply, as did the number of cinemas: Korea's 717 cinemas in 1971 dropped to 423 in 1981.[34] In fact, the sole growth area at this difficult time was the government's intervention in all aspects of the film industry, which, for all its good intentions, was ending up harming Korean cinema. In 1973, a fourth set of revisions to the MPL led to the creation of the KMPPC—a centralized non-profit industry support organization—as a way of further developing the film industry.[35] Under the new law, the MCPI increased mandatory screening days for domestic films to a minimum of 121, effectively guaranteeing a one-third screening ratio of domestic to foreign films. This was a bold attempt to protect the local market by resisting the aggressive advances of American film interests. At the same time, however, government and film industry representatives failed to agree on a unified approach to protecting the domestic market and limiting imports, a conflict that the MPEA would later exploit to its own advantage.

The Trade Wars Break out

After General Chun Doo-hwan became president in 1981, initiatives to protect the local film industry reached new heights. New regulations raised the required number of days for domestic films to be screened to a minimum of 165—Korea's highest quota yet. In turn, US distributors' frustration with the Korean market spilled over, jeopardizing trade relations between the two nations. Intense discussions on the subject of trade barriers to the US film industry were now taking place on an annual basis before various US Congressional Hearings. The implementation of bilateral trade agreements was seen as one of the most effective methods of liberalizing the film trade and expanding the rental income earned by US films in foreign countries. By making Korea's restrictions on US films a trading rights issue, the MPEA, whose core task was to protect the interests of its members throughout world markets, aligned its campaign with the US government's policies aimed at countering restraints on trade. In response, the Chun government realized the importance of catering to Hollywood's needs.

In July 1984, *Screen International* reported that the Korean government was terminating its film import quota while liberalizing the domestic production system, effectively abolishing the Producer Registration System (PRS).[36] Lifting the foreign film embargo had the potential to placate the MPEA by opening the floodgates to US films, barriers already ajar in the region as the result of the "very good" business enjoyed by Hollywood in Japan.[37] The *Screen International* report also suggested that these changes would increase Korea's chances of maintaining "Normal Trade Relations" (NTR) status (formerly Most Favored-Nation status) with the US. Chun's government was on the cusp of transforming the entire environment of the film industry in Korea, which between 1975 and 1984 had imported an average of only 33 foreign films per year, at the same time as it was being guaranteed lower tariffs for exported Korean autos, computer parts, and telecommunications equipment entering the US.[38] Korea was one of the world's fastest-developing film markets, predicted to yield upward of $40 million USD in rental billings per year.[39] The MPEA had gone further than simply enticing the MCPI to lift the foreign film embargo.

The abolition of the PRS in 1984 immediately resulted in a wave of independent filmmakers armed with an assortment of short, feature, animation, and documentary film projects arriving on the scene. Now anyone who wanted to produce a film could do so without having to seek approval from the MCPI. The distribution and foreign film import systems attached to the PRS were also dismantled, pushing the industry into an era of free competition. Korea's long-lasting oligopoly disappeared, opening up new opportunities for producers, directors, and importers alike. Almost overnight, and for the first time since the imposition of authoritarian rule, Korean cinema began to expand in a host of new directions involving both commercial and arthouse productions. In turn, this rapid increase in productivity gave the MCPI reason to re-think its plans to lift the embargo on foreign films or at least stall its negotiations with the MPEA to give the local industry the opportunity to show its full potential.

During this time, the MCPI was not alone in "hindering" the distribution of Hollywood films. Throughout the 1980s the Performance Ethics Committee (hereafter PEC), also held up the distribution of American films through its ruling that only one foreign film could be censored at any given time. Both domestic and foreign films were closely monitored by the PEC, Korea's primary censorship organization, which began censoring films in 1979, before their public release. The committee was a key tool used by the government to maintain centralized control over the flow of foreign media content. Since the PEC usually took between two and three months to approve a foreign film,[40] the MPEA regarded the Screen Quota System and the Performance Ethics Committee as significant obstacles to the export of US films and reasserted what it regarded as its right to greater access to the Korean market.[41]

On 11 September, 1985, following more than a decade of heavy restraints on imported films, the MPEA stepped up its fight against Korea's restrictive film regime by filing a formal complaint against the Screen Quota System with the Office of the United States Trade Representative (USTR) under Section 301 of the US Trade Act.[42] The USTR, which develops trade policies between the US and foreign nations, responded favourably to the MPEA's claims of "unreasonable" and "discriminatory" limitations on film distribution in Korea.[43] As a result, a window that would enable the direct distribution of US films—closed since the 1960s—was about to be forced open. Few in Korea could have predicted the effects this development would have on the local film industry.

In October 1985 the MPEA withdrew its formal complaints against the Chun government.[44] One month later, the MCPI proposed increasing the maximum number of annual screening days for foreign films from 200 to 245—in effect reducing the minimum number of screening days for domestic films. It also undertook to allow US film companies to open direct distribution offices and service cinemas, TV stations, and videotape rental businesses without restraint. This latest amendment to the MPL was also meant to allow Korean producer–distributors to import one foreign film for every four they made domestically.[45] Now playing hardball, the MPEA had exploited the USTR and its negotiations with the Korean government to influence the form of these policy changes.

However, the creative promise shown by Korean filmmakers after the PRS was scrapped had given the MCPI the ammunition to keep Hollywood at bay for at least a little while longer. According to Kim Dong-ho, former vice-minister of Culture and Public Information and former KMPPC president (as well as the founder and Director of the Busan International Film Festival, 1996–2010), the general consensus in Korea was to seek out a plan that would better protect the domestic film industry.[46] In late 1986 the Korean legislature failed to ratify the liberal agreements made in 1985. Once again, the MPEA was denied full access to the fast-growing Korean film market, one of Asia's leading "Cinema Tigers".[47]

The MPEA's resulting objections, most loudly voiced by Valenti, its leader, came at an opportune time because of the new prospects for contemporary art and transnational cultural exchange being opened up by President Chun's MCPI. In the lead-up to the 1988 Seoul Olympics, government spending on culture and the arts grew by leaps and bounds, a development that effectively diverted attention from the military dictatorship and improved the image of Chun's regime. Valenti's response was a barely concealed threat: he wanted foreign countries to know that US industries, including the film industry, believed in the expression "no pain, no gain" when approaching any type of market protectionism, potentially exposing foreign players to "some injury that they are not going to like".[48] The stakes were high because Hollywood saw South Korea as a "potential sleeping giant" for English-language films.[49] In addition, the 40,000 US military troops stationed in Korea at the time served as a potential captive audience for American films.

In 1988, US trade laws were revamped, giving the US government power to revoke a country's privileged trade status if any American industry or commodity was experiencing ongoing trade barriers.[50] Therefore, in order to maintain its trade position with the US, the newly elected Roh Tae-woo (1988–1993) government finally threw open the windows to Hollywood distributors, windows that had remained tightly closed as a way of protecting the local industry by shutting out external competition.[51] According to amendments to the MPL enacted in 1987, and new discussions with President Roh's government, MPEA member companies could now open branch offices in Seoul and distribute Hollywood films directly. United International Pictures (UIP), a collaborative sales operation involving Universal, Paramount, and MGM/United Artists, and 20th Century Fox were the first two distributors lined up to open local offices.[52]

Nevertheless, the Screen Quota System remained a powerful barrier (at least on paper) because the MCPI continued to mandate that every Korean cinema screen domestic films for a minimum of 106 days a year, or 29 percent of total screening days. Although the quota system had been retained, distributors of Hollywood films now had greater access to the Korean market. Their victory was seen as a hostile foray and would soon encounter aggressive and highly organized resistance, signalling pro-democratic protests against both Hollywood's dominance and the Roh government's "internationalization" of the Korean film industry in this way.

Snakes in the Aisles

In September 1988, shortly after UIP opened its direct-distribution office and just before the opening of the Olympic Games, hundreds of filmmakers, film stars, cultural protection advocates, members of opposition political parties, academics, and film students protested against Hollywood's penetration of Korea by marching in the Myongdong "peace district" area of Seoul. Leading the march were producers Lee Tae-won, Hwang Gi-seong, and Kang Dae-seon and directors Jang Sun-woo, Park Cheol-su, and Hong Gi-seon. This was the first of many well-organized events designed to attract the world's attention to the fight to protect Korea's film industry. One of the first directly distributed US films to be shown in Korea was Paramount's *Fatal Attraction* (1987). Protestors picketed Seoul cinemas screening the film, a violent story about adultery, demanding a boycott on *Fatal Attraction* and other directly distributed American films, which were seen as a cultural invasion as well as a direct threat to the domestic film industry. Protest signs daubed in red screamed: "Yankee, go home" and "Down with American Movies", drawing a frenzy of media attention.[53]

According to Cho Moon-jin, director of the Korea Film Directors Association, with more than 50 films to his credit made between 1969 and 1999, and a leader of the 27 October, 1988, demonstration in Seoul, the new laws would mean nothing less than a wholesale takeover of the industry: "Direct distribution of American films means that the US intends to totally put the Korean film industry into her hands, raking in all of the profits produced".[54] Cho and other industry stalwarts entertained the reasonable fear that US pictures would dominate the market: whereas in 1985 only 30 foreign films had been imported, in 1988 the figure increased five-fold to 176. The prospect of Korea's film industry falling into the grasp of US companies that would suck all profits out of the country, as well as gutting its creative livelihood, was too horrible to contemplate.

In a dramatic escalation of the conflict, in mid-September 1988 members of the Korean film industry threatened to release live snakes in cinemas screening *Fatal Attraction* and the teen-pic *Batteries not Included* (1987).[55] Then on 30 September and 1 October—during the final days of the Seoul Olympics—protestors carried out their threat in three cinemas. While snakes are worshiped as deities in Korean mythology and considered symbols of resurrection and everlasting life, the release of these snakes was purely functional, intended to frighten off patrons who might not agree with the protest or understand its ramifications. Many screenings were cancelled, and riot police kept protesters at bay as tensions among the KMPPC, the Ministry of Culture, and MPEA rose to new heights.[56]

Valenti immediately lodged a new round of complaints of "unfair" trade with the USTR, once again accusing Korea of hindering the distribution of US films.

For the US, creating obstacles to the importation, distribution, and exhibition of films in any foreign market denied the mammoth US film and television industry what it regarded as its rightful opportunities to maintain its $1.2 billion annual balance of trade surplus.[57] For Korea, there was a real fear that US pictures would take over the market, crushing the life out of the domestic industry. What both parties couldn't possibly foresee, however, was how the Roh government's open door policy for Hollywood would soon foster a new type of cultural exchange that would impact positively on the Korean film industry and on popular culture in general (see the conclusion on the next page).

Following weeks of intense negotiations, the Korean government reaffirmed that it would allow US film companies to distribute their products directly. The MPEA was doing everything it could to strengthen its access to the Korean market, which the organization considered to be a "gold mine",[58] with "the potential to become one of the largest markets for US motion pictures in Asia, second only to Japan where US motion picture companies now earn some $500,000,000 annually".[59] Valenti once again withdrew his organization's formal complaints as the Korean government capitulated, agreeing to a raft of concessions. These involved granting MPEA member film companies immediate access to the local cinema, television, and videotape markets; reducing film quota restrictions and censorship measures potentially limiting the number of films (and prints of each film, a maximum of 12 at the time) that US distributors could import; and implementing steps to prevent demonstrations and boycotts opposing the direct distribution of US films in Seoul and other cities.[60] The MPEA had finally captured a major piece of the Asian market, one that it had been pursuing since the mid-1960s. Although the agreement severely tested the government's support for the Screen Quota System, it remains in force to the present day and continues to protect the Korean film industry.

By global standards, the dominance of Korean films in their own domestic exhibition market is an extraordinary cultural triumph—one that few other countries, apart from India, China, and the US, have ever achieved. In 2006, the same year that the Screen Quota System was halved under pressure from the US, the annual domestic market share of Korean films soared to an astounding 61.2 percent, and in August 2013 it actually peaked above 90 percent for several days, driven by the commanding box office performance of four action-packed thrillers: *Snowpiercer*, directed by Bong Joon-ho and produced by Park Chan-wook (earning $53.6 million USD); *The Terror, Live*, by director Kim Byung-woo (earning $33.0 million USD); *Hide and Seek*, by first-time director Huh Jung (earning $17.7 million USD); and the disaster movie *The Flu* (earning $13.7 million USD in its opening week).[61] Despite the downturn suffered by the Korean film industry in 2007–2008—the result of factors such as the halving of the Screen Quota System, the collapse of the domestic DVD and other ancillary markets, and the loss of pre-sales to Japanese distributors—in 2014 Korean cinema has continued to dominate the local exhibition market, maintaining its status as one of the strongest local film industries in the world.

Conclusion

Throughout the 1990s, the number of imported films in the Korean market increased dramatically. With this onslaught of foreign films, new cinemas had to be built, and a whole new generation began attending the movies. In just over a decade, the number of screens grew by 326 percent (from 577 in 1995 to 1880 in 2006) in order to meet this demand. Unexpectedly, this new generation of cinema-goers became a crucial variable, making Korean films popular in their own domestic market. Hence, one could argue that the transnational circulation of Hollywood (and a smaller number of other countries') films in Korea had encouraged a new generation of cinema-goers—running into the millions—adding to a host of other factors that has seen contemporary Korean cinema take wing in the new millennium. Nevertheless, in the 1990s Hollywood's influential role in the domestic market was not a *fait accompli*, and in order to fully exploit their new "gold mine" MPAA members needed to remove numerous obstacles, including high import duties and what they saw as the continuing limitations imposed by the Screen Quota System, and spend money building modern cinemas to draw in new audiences. Although at first cinema-goers showed little support for domestically produced films, a new Golden Age of Hollywood in Korea had begun.

Following the MPAA's success in negotiating with the Korean government, members of the local film industry and other cultural diversity advocates were astonished at what they could accomplish once the heavy hand of government was lifted—particularly after the Kim Young-sam government (1993–1998) was elected. Korea's first civilian president since 1960, Kim initiated a wave of social, cultural, political, and economic reforms. Various sectors of the domestic film industry began testing the waters with new self-governing initiatives. One of their first accomplishments was the revitalization of the Screen Quota System in 1993 by the Screen Quota Watch Group (later known as the Coalition for Cultural Diversity in Moving Images, CDMI). The CDMI was formed by a group of young film industry workers in reaction to exhibitors refusing to screen the required number of domestic films because of the larger profits promised by screening imported product.[62] The CDMI, KOFIC (Korean Film Council), and other advocacy groups in the film industry in Korea and elsewhere argued, then as now, that bilateral trade negotiations are inappropriate vehicles for bringing pressure to bear on another country's audiovisual industry quotas and protectionist cultural policies.

Young producers who had entered the field after 1984 became active members of the film industry, looking for ways of making films with less restriction from government. With the changes in the industry environment, funding sources diversified. In addition to the traditional regional exhibitors and investors, new players such as Samsung and Daewoo arrived on the filmmaking scene in the early 1990s as investors and producers, introducing strict funding regimes and thus helping to establish clearer production protocols than had been in place in the past. These *chaebol* companies were keen to vertically integrate their operations and helped reorganize the distribution and exhibition system until they withdrew from the film market following the economic crisis that hit Korea at the end of the 1990s. Their business protocols were in turn inherited by new players—major Korean film companies such as CJ Entertainment, Showbox, and Lotte Entertainment.

In 1996, in a move that benefited the importation and circulation of US and other foreign films, as well as the production and distribution of domestic films, the Korean Constitutional Court ruled that the cutting of a film by the government-appointed PEC review board, which had been charged with censorship of both scripts and completed films, was unconstitutional. These changes led to filmmakers' experiencing a new self-consciousness and freedom of expression; censorship was now considered a mark of the authoritarian governments of the past.[63] The time was ripe for the production of more domestic feature films and a stable of new directors, including Lee Chang-dong, Kim Ki-duk, Lee Myung-se, Im Sang-soo, Kim Sang-Jin, Park Chan-wook, Jang Jin, Hong Sang-soo, Byun Young-joo, Lee Jeong-hyang, Yim Soon-rye, and Kim Jee-woon, rose to the occasion. They were assisted by highly competent production companies such as Cincine, Myung Film, Ikyeong Film, and Kihoek Sidae. The fruits of their labors, which have produced a second golden age of cinema in Korea, are discussed in the last four chapters.

Notes

1. Parts of this chapter appear in: Yecies 2010.
2. Between 1980 and 1986, Korea had overcome a significant economic crisis by generating elevated growth rates and a surplus in its balance of foreign trade payments. See Collins and Park 1989.
3. Total annual audience numbers for local and foreign films for selected years were as follows: 17,964,537 vs. 24,772,549 (1982); 16,425,345 vs. 31,672,918 (1985); 12,164,830 vs. 40,065,694 (1988); and 11,060,848 vs. 41,135,806 (1991). Statistics collected by the Korean Motion Picture Promotion Corporation (KMPPC), published in Choi et al. 1994: 328–31.
4. In 1969, the total number of the annual cinemagoers peaked at 173,043,272, decreasing over the following decade to 65,518,581 (1979) (KMPPC 1977: 167; Choi et al. 1994: 328). Audiences continued to decline throughout the 1980s and early 1990s, while the number of cinemas also dwindled: 63 local features were released in 1993, as against 347 imported films, causing the market share of domestic films in the Korean market to bottom out at 15.9 percent. See KOFIC 2001: 230.
5. Hollywood's overseas campaign has been thoroughly documented by Thompson 1985; Jarvie 1992; and Vasey 1997.
6. The "David and Goliath" story of Korea's resistance to the US film industry was spotlighted at the 2005 General Conference of UNESCO, meeting in Paris from 3–21 October. Korea's success in this arena was one of the primary catalysts for the development of an international policy instrument aimed at reinforcing cultural diversity and the protection of local cultural contents and artistic expression. At the meeting, this Convention was approved with overwhelming support, enabling Korea and other countries to bolster their fight to maintain autonomy over their own cultural, media, and communications policies and to foster cultural diversity in the face of pressure from international trade giants such as China and the US.
7. Before the formation of the KMPPC, the Film Support Union (Yeonghwa Jinheung Johap) was created by the MPI in 1970. It did not last long enough to make an impact on the running of the industry, and its general program was handed on to the KMPPC.

8. Korea's Anticommunist Law was established on 3 July, 1961, with the aim of suppressing all "potential" anti-government and pro-communist activities including having affiliations with communist organizations; praising or glorifying communist countries; and being in communication with communist parties in any country. The Anticommunist Law, which is still in force today, was significantly strengthened even before Park's Yushin Constitution took effect in 1973.
9. An 2006: 245.
10. Lee 2003: 256.
11. "*The Testimony*, to be Released on New Year's Day" (Jeungeon Sinjeong Gaebong). *Donga Daily* (21 December 1973): 5.
12. Production details of the film appear in "*The Testimony*: Reviving the Experience of the Korean War" (6.25 Gyeongheom Doesallin Jeungeon). *Gyeonghyang Shinmun* (20 December, 1973): 8; and "Shooting on Location with the Biggest Spectacle War Films" (Choedae Seukeil Jeonjaeng Jangmyeon Roke). *Donga Daily* (19 September, 1973): 5.
13. They began their relationship in 1967 when the Keukdong Film Company was producing Korea's first monster movie, *The Great Monster Yonggary*. Keukdong sought assistance from the Tokyo film company Toei Co. and through Toei were introduced to Akira Suzuki and Masao Yagi, who had designed the monster suits for Daiei's movie *Giant Monster Gamera* two years before. After working on *Yonggary*, the pair maintained their working relationship with the Korean film industry. See Chung et al. 2005: 41–44, 395–96. At the time, diplomatic and trade relations between South Korea and Japan were strained as a result of their recent colonial relationship; Japanese cultural products were banned in Korea until 1998.
14. "*The Testimony*: Exposing the Limits of National Policy Films" (Jeungeon Gukchaek Yeonghwa-ui Hangyeseong Deureona). *Donga Daily* (12 January, 1974): 5.
15. In March 1968 the MPI held a seminar aimed at promoting open discussion of the anticommunist film genre—its problems as well as ways of boosting production figures. See "Problems of the Anticommunist Film Genre" (Bangong Yeonghwa-ui Munjejeom). *Yeonghwa Japji* (March 1968): 66.
16. Among the national policy films produced by the KMPPC dealing with anticommunist and national separation issues, *Parade of Wives* stands out; it dealt with the government-sponsored economic development movement known as the New Village Movement (*Saemaeul Movement*), a major rural development initiative launched in 1972. One of the driving forces behind this movement was public education, facilitated through special classes, and a variety of publications (books, magazines, billboards) and broadcast media (radio, television, and cultural/news/feature films). In 1974 the MPI added a new category to the Grand Bell Awards—for National Policy/Saemaeul Film. A cash prize of one million won was award to the winner, in addition to an import license for one foreign film.
17. "Institutionalizing Screening of the KMPPC's National Policy Films for Students" (Yeongjingong Jejak Gukchaek Yeonghwa Haksaeng Gwallam Jedohwa). *Gyeonghyang Shinmun* (30 April, 1975): 4.
18. "A Poor Showing for National Policy Films" (Gukchaek Yeonghwa Jejak Bujin). *Gyeonghyang Shinmun* (26 August, 1974): 8; "The KMPPC Jumps the Cinema Exhibition Queue during the Holidays" (Yeongjingong, Myeongjeolttaemada Saechigi). *Donga Daily* (21 September, 1974): 5; and "Exposing the Limits of National Policy Films" (Jeongeon Gukchaek Yeonghwa-ui Hangyeseong Deureona). *Donga Daily* (12 January, 1974): 5.
19. According to a report published in 1988 by the Korean Board of Audits and Inspections, the KMPPC spent a total of 490 million won for making of six national policy films in 1973 and 1974. Due to their unsatisfactory box office results as well as a duplication in the work created by the NFPC, the KMPPC no longer produced films. See Shin,

Hyeon-su. "Audit Result Requiring Administrative Measures" (Gamsa Gyeolgwa Cheobun Yogu). Board of Audit and Inspection (7 June, 1988). NAK BA0070555: 69.
20. See Valenti, Jack. "Testimony regarding the role of congress in regulating cable television and the potential for new technologies in the communications system". *Hearings before the Subcommittee on Communications of the Committee on Interstate and Foreign Commerce. House of Representatives. 94th Congress, Second Session* (27 July, 1976): 634–65.
21. Self, S.B. "Movie Diplomacy: 'Propaganda' Value of Films Perils Hollywood's Rich Markets Abroad". *Wall Street Journal* (16 August, 1944): 6.
22. Most of the films screened in this period were talkies produced between the mid-1930s and the early 1940s. Action-adventure and historical biography films were the most prevalent genres, followed by melodramas, screwball comedies, musicals, Westerns, crime/detective thrillers, science fiction, and animated cartoons. The graphic imagery used in advertisements for these films, placed in local newspapers, also attracted non-Korean-speaking US troops—a welcome secondary audience. After May 1946, according to SCAP documents relating to the release of motion pictures in South Korea, American film distributors in the Korea/Japan-based Central Motion Picture Exchange (CMPE)—Allied Artists, Columbia, MGM, Paramount, Twentieth Century-Fox, United Artists, Universal, and Warner Bros.—began dominating South Korean screens. Although curtailed by the Korean War, this initiative constituted the first wave of direct distribution for US distributors who had to wait 40 years to regain the same rights.
23. See "MPEA Certificate of Incorporation – 5 June 1945"; "By-Laws of the MPEA"; "Inter-Office Memo Re: Export Trade Association", from Carl E. Milliken [MPDDA] to Will H. Hays, 9 March, 1945; and "Inter-Office Memo Re: Export Trade Association", from Carl E. Milliken to Will H. Hays, 3 May, 1945, all available at the Academy of the Motion Picture Arts and Sciences Library Archives (hereafter AMPAS), MPAA General Correspondence Files, Microfilm Roll #10.
24. For English-language discussions by Korean scholars of film culture during the USAMGIK period, see Lee and Choe 1998; Lee 2000; Kim 2002; Min, Joo and Kwak 2003; and Yi 2005.
25. Yi 2005: 24.
26. "The Cruel Stone-throwing of the CMPE" (Gahokhan Jungbae-ui Tuseok). *Gyeonghyang Shinmun* (6 February, 1947): 4.
27. See Cohen, W. 1953. 'RE: Korea'. Memorandum from W. Cohen to J. Dagal of Warner Bros. Pictures Japan. (15 September) File # Japan 16675A. USC-Warner Bros. Archives.
28. In January 1965, a year prior to the formal launch of the Screen Quota System, the Korean Ministry of Commerce and Industry promulgated Public Notice No. 3297, which regulated the importation of foreign films among other commodities. The import of foreign films was limited to a total value of $75,000 USD per fiscal quarter. See Department of State Airgram A-374 (1 February, 1965). General Records of the Department of State. Record Group 59. Central FilesPF, 1964–66. Box 1020. US National Archives and Records Administration, College Park, MD (hereafter cited as NARAII).
29. The MPEA/MPAA benefited greatly from Valenti's appointment because he had friends in high places. Valenti was special assistant to President Lyndon B. Johnson, and his political and advertising consulting agency, Weekly and Valenti, coordinated presidential press campaigns during John F. Kennedy's administration. Though he was no longer working in the White House on a daily basis, his position as president of the MPEA/MPAA kept him in frequent contact with President Richard M. Nixon as well as former President Johnson.
30. To collect these figures, the MPEA instituted a "sharp-edged industry intelligence system" with "swift communication", involving the distribution to its members of

more than 1,306 documents, reports, and bulletins dealing with problems in film markets around the world. See Valenti, Jack. "The 'Foreign Service' of the Motion Picture Association of America". *The Journal of the Producers Guild of America*. MPEA collection. MPEA-AMPTP 2000, Additions b.2. AMPAS (March 1968): 1–4.
31. Department of State Airgram A-629, 11 June, 1968. General Records of the Department of State. Central Files P Files, 1967–1969. RG59. Box 933. NARAII.
32. Here, the term "black market" is used with an obvious Western bias, one that was frequently perpetuated in trade headlines in *Variety* such as: "Korea's Black Market Films", (4 May, 1966): 143. The MPEA complained about these types of activity, which was business as usual for local producers, both because it circumvented the MPL *and* because they differed from the more formalized ways of doing business in the US.
33. Telegram from American Embassy in Seoul to US Secretary of State. General Records of the Department of State. CFPF, 1970–73. RG59. Box 1310. Inco Motion Pictures 17 Korea-US. NARAII.
34. Statistics collected by the KMPPC. See Choi et al. 1994: 330.
35. The KMPPC underwent a change of name to the Korean Film Commission (KOFIC) in 1993 and the Korean Film Council in 2004.
36. "South Korea Ends Film Import Quota". *Screen International* (21 July, 1984).
37. Baskin, Jeffrey. "UIP Topper Says Korean Pic Biz 'In The Dark Ages'". *Variety* (4 June, 1985): 6.
38. These figures are drawn from various issues of *Korea Cinema* between 1985 and 2003 (Seoul: Korean Motion Picture Promotion Corporation/Korean Film Commission) and *Korean Film Observatory* (2001–2004), the quarterly KOFIC trade journal covering the film industry and film policies in Korea.
39. Throughout the mid- and late-1980s, Valenti's optimistic profit projections appeared regularly in trade articles. In 1987 the commercial potential of Korea's film market was estimated at $15,000,000 USD, and less than one year later at between $20,000,000 USD and $40,000,000. See "Korea, Brazil Seen as Key O'seas Venues for U.S. Fare", *Variety* (28 October 1987); and Park, Seong-ho with Frank Segers, "Theater Rallies: Directors, Distribs Protest UIP Invasion of S. Korea". *Variety* (26 September, 1988).
40. The Performance Ethics Committee is today known as the Media Rating Board.
41. Memorandum from Peter G. Peterson to Secretary of State William P. Rogers, 25 June, 1971. General Records of the Department of State. CFPF, 1970–73. RG59. Box 1309. Inco. Motion Pictures-OECD. NARAII; and Department of State Telegram, 17 April, 1972. General Records of the Department of State. CFPF, 1970–73. RG59. Box 1309. Inco. Motion Pictures-OECD. NARAII.
42. "Film Makers Seek Action Against Korea". *San Francisco Chronicle* (11 September, 1985). This procedure is usually invoked when US rights under a foreign policy or practice are deemed restrictive for commerce. Section 301 gives the US President power to strike back at any country failing to open or liberalize its markets, including obstructing the export of US commodities such as autos, steel, agricultural products, computers, and films.
43. The MPEA's claims crystallized around four demands: 1) an increase in the number of imported Hollywood films and the liberalization of import license application procedures; 2) the opening of local distribution offices (direct distribution); 3) a reduction in the cash deposit ($800,000 USD) required by the KMPPC for each imported film; and 4) a decrease in the compulsory cash "contribution" ($170,000 USD) required of each imported film title and designated for a domestic film industry development fund. See Penny Pagano. "Probe Likely on Korea's Film Curbs". *Los Angeles Times* (25 October, 1985); and "South Korea Ends Film Import Quota". *Screen International* (21 July, 1984).
44. "Trade Complaint on Hold as MPEA, Korea Dicker". *Variety* (28 October, 1985).

45. Motion Picture Export Association (MPEA), News Release. 1988. (16 September): 1–3. Courtesy of the MPAA.
46. Kim Dong-ho. Personal interview. 14 October, 2004. Busan, Korea. The authors thank Kim Dong-ho, former long-time director of BIFF, for sharing his experiences as vice-minister.
47. For more on Korea as a so-called CinemaTiger, see Yecies 2010.
48. Valenti also stated that he wanted to bash the South Korean government "across the head with a 2 by 4" (a wooden plank). See Statement of Jack Valenti. "Testimony regarding trade reform legislation". *Hearings before the Subcommittee on Trade of the Committee on Ways and Means. House of Representatives. 99th Congress, Second Session* (15 April, 1986): 1003 and 1004.
49. Hollinger, Hy. "5-Day Event: AFMA Planning S. Korea Minimart". *Variety* (6 April, 1988).
50. Valenti, Jack. "Testimony regarding unfair foreign trade practices". *Hearings before the Subcommittee on Oversight and Investigations of the Committee on Energy and Commerce. House of Representatives. 101st Congress, First Session* (1 March, 1989): 77.
51. For a rare press article presenting balanced arguments on both the benefits and perils of keeping the Korean film industry a closed shop, see "Korean Movie Market to be Opened in July". *Economic Report* (February 1987): 26–27.
52. Hollinger, Hy. "A Switch: Yanks Set Up Shop In Korea". *Variety* (6 April 1988). At the same time, restrictions limiting the number of domestic producer-distributors and import licenses were relaxed. The number of local film companies immediately quadrupled from twenty to eighty. The Korean cinema was suddenly expanding from all sides.
53. Park with Segers, Op Cit. Other sources (such as *The Hankyeoreh*, 30 October, 1988: 12), pictured film industry workers demonstrating in front of the Congress in Seoul on 27 October 1988 – with banners carry slogans such as "Get Out US Films", and "Change the Film Law—Make a Law that Supports [Domestic] Film".
54. Park with Segers, Op Cit.
55. See Farhi, Paul. "Seoul's Movie Theaters: Real Snake Pits?" *The Washington Post* (17 September 1988): 14; and Kramer, Gene. "U.S. Film Exporters Charge Unfair Trade, Threat of Snakes in Cinemas". *The Associated Press* (16 September, 1988).
56. "MPEAA Raps Korea Threats vs. Distribs", *Variety* (28 September, 1988); Motion Picture Export Association (MPEA), News Release. 1988. (16 September): 1–3. Courtesy of the MPAA.
57. This figure was cited by Valenti in his testimony: "Trade Reform Legislation". *Hearings before the Subcommittee on Trade of the Committee on Ways and Means. House of Representatives. Ninety-Ninth Congress, Second Session*. (15 April, 1986). 989.
58. The Korean "gold mine" was not without its problems and obstacles for MPEA members, including gaining screen time (due to ongoing limitations imposed by the Screen Quota System), the need to build additional and more modern cinemas and high import duties. See Segers, Frank. "U.S. Indies, Majors find Korean Gold May Be Difficult to Mine". *Variety* (15 June, 1988).
59. "Testimony of Jack Valenti". Unfair Foreign Trade Practices, 256.
60. See Motion Picture Association of America (MPAA). "Motion Picture Industry Wins Victory on Korean Trade Practices". MPAA Press Release (28 October, 1988). Courtesy of the MPAA; and Harris, Paul. "Gov't 'warranty': Korea reaffirms open-door policy toward U.S. films". *Variety* (31 October, 1988).
61. See *Korean Cinema 2006*: 495; and Cremin, Stephen *Film Business Asia.com* "South Korean thrillers take 90% market share". (22 August, 2013) Available: www.filmbiz.asia/news/south-korean-thrillers-take-90-market-share. Accessed 10 September 2014.
62. The group, which had been founded in an outburst of enthusiasm at a time when countries such as France were engaged in fervent lobbying to incorporate their "audiovisual industries" in GATT and World Trade Organization negotiations, aimed to ensure

the survival of the Screen Quota System—as if it were the industry's most important safeguard (Yang 2004). The organization was successful with this aim until early 2006 when the Roh Moo-hyun government halved the Screen Quota System from 146 to 73 days per year. The efforts of the CDMI were significant insofar as their activities became a crucial support mechanism and confidence builder for aspiring as well as established Korean filmmakers.
63. Kim Hyae-joon 2002.

6 Robust Invalids in a New Visual Era
Directing in the 1970s and 1980s

In the late 1960s, the small number of people commentating on Korean cinema began recognizing the high level of productivity achieved by a handful of veteran directors, producers, and stars working under severe financial constraints and heavy government censorship. Despite this inhospitable working environment and the wider context of authoritarian military rule, Korean filmmakers succeeded in making more than 200 feature films per year between 1968 and 1971.[1] At that time, as we saw in Chapter 3, the Korean film industry had a reputation for relatively imaginative and well-made films of a standard equal to Japanese B productions—low-budget commercial films shot in less than four weeks and exhibited in a double bill where they supported the heavily promoted first feature.[2]

Despite this seemingly backhanded compliment, and amid hopes that the Korean film industry would maintain this level of productivity and continue contributing to the expansion of popular culture in Asia, in the early 1970s severe inflation caused an acute rise in production costs, drawing the industry into a downward spiral.[3] In 1972, the number of feature films produced fell sharply to 122, a mere shadow of the previous year's output. This period of reduced activity no doubt prompted the MPI's 1973 (fourth) amendment to the Motion Picture Law, which led to the formation of the powerful Korea Motion Picture Promotion Corporation (KMPPC), the predecessor of the Korea Film Council (KOFIC).

During this so-called dark age of local cinema, genuine creative expression dwindled as practitioners across the field began working with the government to produce promotional, feature, and cultural films that propagated the government's political agenda. Under tightened censorship regulations and increased political control, directors such as Yu Hyun-mok and Shin Sang-ok—masters from the golden age of the 1960s—found that opportunities for creative expression in their films were increasingly curtailed. As discussed in Chapter 2, Yu Hyun-mok, who had been well known as an arthouse director, vented his frustration with the restricted production environment in interviews, public lectures, and newspaper and magazine articles. As the result of financial and creative constraints, he shifted his emphasis to making cultural films, almost giving up his feature filmmaking. At the same time, Shin was experiencing inconsistent results at the box office; struggling with the same difficulties faced by Yu, films such as *Two Thieves in Love* (1971), *The Last Flight to Pyeongyang* (1971), *Sim Cheong* (1972), *Farewell*

(1973), and *The Han River* (1974) alternated between success and failure. While new directors appeared on the scene, few survived the decade.

Nevertheless, during this time, Korean directors were attempting to navigate their way through a complex political and industrial environment, which came to a head with the establishment of the *Yushin* system introduced by Park Chung Hee's authoritarian government in 1973. As a result of this development, the production environment became sterile and utilitarian, pressuring filmmakers to make films that served as a propagandistic mouthpiece for the government. In fact, the Emergency Measure No. 9 promulgated in 1975 barred anyone from criticizing the government through any public outlet, including but not limited to films.[4] The KMPPC had attempted to show leadership in this environment by producing "national policy" films that were aligned with this new directive. Yet, bridling under these constraints, other filmmakers sought ways to express their creativity through spirited stylistic choices and by spicing up their politically correct narratives. Out of the unfavorable conditions of the mid-1970s arose a new generation of hopeful artists and filmmakers who began contemplating new pathways for making movies.

One group of budding filmmakers in their thirties, calling themselves the "Visual Age" (aka Young Sang Shi Dae) and utilizing the British Free Cinema and the French New Wave (Nouvelle Vague) movements as models, created a manifesto distancing them from their predecessors. Despite—or perhaps because of—the lack of freedom of expression and the limited aesthetic and narrative models available, these aspiring filmmakers found creative new spaces for thinking about the form, style, and purpose of cinema. This group consisted of like-minded directors such as Lee Jang-ho, Ha Gil-jong, Hong Pa, Lee Won-se, and Kim Ho-seon and critic Byeon In-sik. Around the same time, cinephiles—including Chung Ji-young, Chung Sung-ill, Huh Moon-young, Jang Gil-soo, Kang Han-sup, Kim Hong-joon, Park Kwang-su and Shin Chul—were gathering at special screenings such as those held in Seoul in 1977 at the French Cultural Center and in 1978 at the German Cultural Center to watch and discuss new films.[5] These centers played an important role in exposing Korean intellectuals to a diverse foreign film culture and to cinema in general. Many members of this "cultural center generation" are to be found among Korean cinema's top directors, producers, critics, festival organizers, scholars, and policy and cultural diversity advocates today.

Similar to the New American Cinema movement and the French Novelle Vague, these celluloid adventurers were attempting to create something new by sharing ideas about filmmaking and exploring new techniques, styles, and ideas.[6] Together, they spearheaded some influential new filmmaking trends and were instrumental in revitalizing Korean cinema, which was stagnating under the dead weight of state intervention. Specifically, the Visual Age group sought to stimulate the arthouse scene by showing how a range of new film techniques and visual styles could be grafted onto the conventional filmmaking techniques widely used in commercial B-movies at the time.

Among the pioneering directors who not only thrived under the MPI's draconian regime, but who also made an enduring contribution to the rebellious creative power that underlay Korean cinema in the 1980s, Lee Jang-ho is pre-eminent. Regularly directing a mix of both commercial and arthouse films throughout the "dark age" of Korean cinema, Lee pushed the boundaries of quality filmmaking in a repressive era and continues to impact significantly on the domestic industry today. With his long-standing contributions to the Korean film industry, Lee's achievements have been widely celebrated; indeed a volume in the *Korean Film Directors* series on Lee Jang-ho was published by KOFIC/Seoul Selection in December 2009, around the same time as the books on Lee Man-hee and Lee Doo-yong. He captured the essence of youth culture in the 1970s and a society experiencing rapid materialism and changing sex roles in the 1980s and successfully evoked a society anguished by its turbulent past.[7] Yet, Lee's story and the films that he has made over the past four decades reveal a creativity and dynamism at work in Korean cinema that existed long before international critics and cinephiles turned the global spotlight on the new wave of Korean films that appeared after government censorship was lifted in 1996.

In the following section, we sketch the background to this remarkable filmmaker and analyze two of his most notable films—*Heavenly Homecoming to Stars* (1974), one of Korea's earliest erotic "hostess" genre films, and *Good Windy Day* (1980), to show how Lee's influential artistic voice and aesthetic experimentation enabled him to speak for his generation while serving as an inspiration to the younger Korean filmmakers who came after him. In essence, Lee's creative practices opened up an alternative pathway during a time when most filmmakers had lost their way as a result of economic and industry pressures.

The Visual Age

Between 1965 and 1973, Lee Jang-ho worked as an associate director under the formidable Shin Sang-ok during the making of *Thousand Year Old Fox* (1969, Cheonnyeonho), *Women of Yi-Dynasty* (1969), *The Evening Bell* (1970), *Sim Cheong* (1972), and *Three Days of their Reign* (1973). After shadowing Shin for several years, Lee made his directorial debut in 1974 with the erotic melodrama *Heavenly Homecoming to Stars*. Among all the directors he had known or worked under, Shin was the only one who had seriously encouraged Lee to think about filmmaking, learn new technical skills, and lead crews effectively on set. Shin's directorial style of balancing arthouse and commercial filmmaking had provided a good model for his own career. Thus, it is not surprising that Lee's first independent film was a hostess movie, a commercially appealing melodrama based on a bestselling book, which was nonetheless praised for its innovative repertoire of visual effects and editing techniques.

Before discussing Lee's films, it is helpful to understand something of the short-lived 1970s culture of which Lee was a part. Lee grew up and was educated in the post-liberation era (following Japan's surrender in 1945) under the heavy influence of Western (primarily US) culture. Like other members of his generation, Lee developed an interest in pop, folk, and rock music through radio, that is, primarily via the American Forces Korea Network (AFKN), which began broadcasting FM stereo radio programs of popular Western music in 1971. He also made weekly outings to the cinema to see Hollywood films. He experienced the civilian-led public demonstrations of 1960, the so-called April Revolution that led to the fall of Syngman Rhee's authoritarian government and the creation of Korea's first— albeit short-lived—civilian government that was ousted by Park Chung Hee's coup d'état in 1961. The events surrounding the public protests against Rhee and corruption in general exposed the younger generation to notions of democracy and freedom of expression. Unlike their parents' generation, they received higher education at high school and university and considered themselves different from their parents in their cultural habits and the creation of a distinctive youth culture.[8] They were the so-called April Revolution generation, and Lee was one of the "April Revolution generation of art lovers" (aka the *4.19 yesulin*). In the 1970s they surfaced as major players in the arts and culture.[9]

The blue jeans, acoustic guitars, draft beer, and pop songs affected by the youth culture of the 1970s marked them off from the 1960s generation, who wore old military uniforms, read serious philosophical journals such as *Sasanggye*, and drank makgeoli (Korea's traditional rice wine). This new movement was characterized as "nihilistic, experimental, humanistic, anti-standardization, and yearning for equality and freedom".[10] The youth generation of the 1970s was individualistic, defiant, and Westernized—traits also evident in the cinematic melodramas that characterized the decade. Compared to the melodramas of the 1960s that had mostly dealt with family issues, those of the 1970s focused on the changes occurring in an individual's life, with little attention paid to family background.

In an attempt to imbue Korea's stagnant film industry with new ideas and cinematic styles, Lee joined like-minded filmmakers such as ha Gil-jong, Hong Pa, and Lee Won-se, initiating a movement that they hoped would bear comparison with the New American Cinema and the French Novelle Vague. Lee and his friends called themselves the Visual Age, circulating their ideas and stimulating debate among their peers. They published a film journal, *Film Quarterly Young Sang Shi Dae*, which covered film theory and history as well as film reviews and industry news. The members of the Visual Age came to represent a generational changing of the guard in Korean cinema, focused especially on finding creative solutions to the challenges of censorship.

The directors who belonged to the Visual Age group are best known for capturing the essence of contemporary youth culture in their films. They frequently adapted the bestselling novels of the day, written by popular authors such as Choi In-ho (1945–2013) and Cho Seon-jak (1940 -). Lee's first film was based on Choi In-ho's novel of the same name, *Heavenly Homecoming to Stars*,[11] and two other directors from the group, Kim Ho-seon and Ha Gil-jong, adapted Cho Seon-jak's novel *Youngja's Heydays* (1975) and Choi In-ho's *March of Fools* (1975), respectively. They also worked with popular singers such as Lee Jang-hee, Song Chang-sik, and Im Hi-suk, utilizing their folk songs accompanied by acoustic guitar to convey their characters' feelings.[12] They focused on capturing the youth culture of the times—young people drinking beer and wearing bell-bottom jeans, dreaming of freedom, far removed from the restrictive social norms of contemporary Korea. It was for this reason that, despite their melodramatic story lines, film scholar Lee Ho-geol referred to the Visual Age group's films as "youth films" of the 1970s.[13]

Figure 6.1 Film advertisements for *Homecoming to Stars* (1974) and *March of Fools* (1975). *Donga Daily* 24 April, 1974: 6; *Gyeonghyang Shinmun* 29 May, 1975: 8.

One of the best-known Korean writers of the 1970s, Choi In-ho opened up new ground through his popular depiction of contemporary issues including sex, capitalism, and materialism. In the 1960s Korean novelists had concentrated on two areas: war and political ideology or industrialization—the latter theme often being subdivided into an exploration of the side-effects of rapid industrialization or the sense of alienation experienced by individuals in the industrialization process.[14] The popular novels of the 1970s also dealt with industrialization, but now the focus was on depicting the ways in which individuals and society had been transformed. Choi In-ho's *Heavenly Homecoming to Stars*, which attracted readers with its fast-paced narrative and overt sexuality, was the first of a stream of popular novels that came to be known as "hostess literature".[15] Lee, an old school friend of Choi's, successfully transplanted these popular elements from book to screen, attracting audiences of 460,000 to cinemas in Seoul, a ground-breaking record for a domestic film that became the model for the "hostess film" genre.[16] Members of the April Revolution generation of "art people", both Choi and Lee understood what contemporary audiences wanted to consume, presenting social issues and elements of youth culture in a way that was relatively undemanding and non-confrontational.

Lee's version of *Heavenly Homecoming to Stars* opens with the young male protagonist Mun-ho walking alone in a snow-covered field, holding a box containing cremation ashes. Mun-ho's memories of a girl, Gyeong-a, are presented in a flashback, itself interrupted by Gyeong-a's own flashbacks of the three lovers she had had before meeting Mun-ho. Mun-ho is presented as a loser, an artist devoid of ambition, a drinker and womanizer who suffers from bouts of sexually transmitted disease. In his first scene, he is shown hungover on the street and in the next he visits a clinic where he is diagnosed with an STD. He meets bar girl

Gyeong-a at her place of work and is attracted to her good looks, cheerfulness, and energy. They start dating, socializing in clubs filled with similar young couples enjoying lively music. When Mun-ho pressures her for a sexual relationship, we are offered flashbacks into her painful memories of previous men who had used and abandoned her: her first lover, an office worker, her second beau, who became her husband, and her third man, a bum. They all loved her body, but not her soul. When Gyeon-a becomes an alcoholic and falls into depression, Mun-ho abandons her, too. Alone again, Gyeong-a, who had once been a naïve office girl, becomes a prostitute before killing herself in a snow-covered field. The film ends as it began with Mun-ho scattering her ashes on the river.

Sexuality and sexual tension are the leading motifs in *Heavenly Homecoming to Stars*, testing the relationship and driving it forward. The film depicts a society where materialism is the dominant force, ensuring that relationships will be sterile. By showing how a young girl's life is gradually destroyed, the film illuminates the dark side of Korean society, rapidly—too rapidly—entering the brave new world of urbanization and industrialization. However, this dark backdrop failed to put off audiences attracted by lively songs accompanied by acoustic guitars, outbursts of poetry, stylish editing including the frequent use of flashbacks, and—last but not least—a melodramatic story of a beautiful girl who gave her all for love.

The success of *Heavenly Homecoming to Stars* was a cinematic phenomenon, demonstrating that a local film with content that pushed accepted boundaries could become a commercial box office success. Perhaps surprisingly, the film was selected as one of only three "quality films" nominated by the MPI, with its makers awarded a coveted license to import a foreign title. Given the MPI's selection criteria for "quality films", *Heavenly Homecoming to Stars* had somehow passed the tests of promoting national policy and containing "enlightening" elements and sound morality. Naturally, this official endorsement came as welcome news to Park Chong-chan of Hwacheon Gongsa, the registered producer who had hired Lee to direct the film. In 1974, only 13 films selected by the MPI as quality films were rewarded with an import license, which had a cash value of about 10 million won (roughly $21,000 USD at the time).[17] Given that the average production budget was at least 12 million won, an import license was a substantial financial incentive for a registered producer.[18] Ironically, *Heavenly Homecoming to Stars* was widely seen as a successful film in both commercial and artistic senses.

Despite this success, the 1970s youth culture of which Lee was a part was short lived. The political atmosphere of the time militated against anything that ran contrary to the authoritative rule of Park Chung Hee. Enjoyment of Western culture, with its emphasis on freedom and equality, and in which expressions of sorrow, pessimism and individualism were regarded as legitimate, sat uneasily with the rigid and forceful nationalism, anticommunism, and economic development promoted by the regime. For example, Mun-ho in *Heavenly Homecoming to Stars* is a painter, who lives day-by-day chasing girls without any aspirations for a better future. In *March of Fools*, the song "Whale Hunting" begins with the pessimistic lyrics: "Even after drinking, singing, and dancing, sadness still fills my mind. When I look around, wondering what to do, everyone has turned their backs on me". And Chang-su in *Youngja's Heydays* is a Vietnam War veteran who works in a public bathhouse as a professional scrubber (*ttaemiri*), scrubbing down customers. These characters and songs were hardly calculated to endear themselves to a regime with little tolerance for anything seen as deviating from the strict party line represented by the *Yushin* system.

The youth culture of the 1970s was thus not welcomed by the regime and, even before it had reached its peak, the government attempted to suppress it in the name of the "purification of society". From early December 1975, newspapers ran stories of popular entertainers being arrested for smoking marijuana. The Seoul prosecutor's office orchestrated highly coordinated spot checks on "suspicious" entertainers, arresting them on the spot.[19] Arresting prominent people for possession of "happy smoke"—as it was known at the time — and arraigning them through the prosecutor's office and the MPI, was seen by the regime as an effective way of ridding Korea of the "youth menace". Influential artists including singers Lee Jang-hi, Yun Hyeong-ju, Im Hi-suk, and Shin Jung-hyeon, actor Ha Jae-yeong, comedians Lee Sang-hae and Jeon Yu-seong, and director Lee Jang-ho were arrested, sometimes beaten and jailed, and their entertainment activities were suspended. The social and political significance of the campaign became clear when Park Chung Hee himself spoke out on the issue. Park declared that marijuana smoking, widespread among university students and entertainers, was not only "decadent", but "anti-social and anti-national", corroding young people's minds and Korea's national spirit.[20] (The contemporary drama-musical *Go Go 70s* (2008) dramatizes the lives of a 1970s Korean rock group and the impact that the military government had on them and youth culture more generally.)

Lee Jang-ho was one of the victims of the government's social purification drive. In April 1976, Lee and his brother, actor Lee Yeong-ho, were arrested for smoking marijuana. His arrest not only harmed his own career, but also affected the activities of the Visual Age group. Korea's nascent and rebellious youth counterculture had experienced a major setback. The spread of liberalism was stopped in its tracks, and entertainers came under increased pressure to comply with the government's nationalistic agenda in their activities. According to figures released by the MPI, between December 1965 and September 1977 a total of 137 entertainers were arrested and their careers suspended.[21] After continuing pleas from the detainees and their representative organizations to the government, they were gradually allowed to return to work from the beginning of 1978,[22] and following Park's death on 16 October, 1979, the remaining restrictions on their activities were lifted.

In the intervening years, Lee had all but given up filmmaking, preferring instead to watch as many films as possible, especially classic Korean films from the 1960s. One of his favorite movies was *Old Park* (1960), a heart-warming family melodrama directed by Kang Dae-jin, which deeply impressed him through the depth of its realism, especially in character portrayal. The film records the experiences of furnace repairman "Old Park", who represents pre-modern values, showing how he is challenged by and eventually reconciled with the contemporary world, represented by his children, via a series of episodic encounters and conflicts with them and other young people. Kim Seung-ho, a popular actor of the 1960s, received the Best Actor Award at the Asia Film Festival in 1961 for his performance as Old Park. Looking back on this cinematic era in the late 1990s, Lee recalled wishing that one day he could make a film in the same mold.[23] In 1980, the second stage of Lee's directorial career began following four years of exile.

New Wave Directing in the 1980s

After Park Chung Hee was assassinated in October 1979, a new military government led by Chun Doo-hwan seized power in a coup d'etat on 12 December, 1979. Under the new regime Lee Jang-ho and other blacklisted artists were no longer restricted by bans imposed by the previous government, and they were able to resume their careers. Lee marked his comeback with *Good Windy Day* (1980), a black comedy that differed strikingly from his previous films such as *Heavenly Homecoming to Stars* and *Yes, Good-Bye Today* (1976).

Good Windy Day, based on Choi Il-nam's novel *Our Vines*, starts with a 30-second animation showing three men being buffeted by a strong wind and end up clinging to each other for protection against the elements. The title, *Good Windy Day*, appears over their bunched figures. We then see open fields with farmers working; an old man and a young boy are shown sitting next to each other, watching over one of the fields. A train, a truck, and a bus are seen moving toward Seoul, carrying young men from the villages, among them three of the protagonists, Deok-bae, Chun-sik, and Gil-nam. Various locales—a junk yard, a market, a dumpster, and a taxi stand—are shown as black-and-white montages, suggesting the men's struggles to find places to live and work in Seoul.

In this opening sequence, Lee sets the context for the film by exposing the audience to the burning issues of urbanization and industrialization, the older generation left behind in the villages while young migrants struggle to make their way in the big city. To quote a statistic given in the film, of the 8 million residents of Seoul, fewer than 80,000 would have been born and raised there. Despite the pressures, Deok-bae, Chun-sik, and Gil-nam all find jobs—as a delivery man at a Chinese restaurant, a messenger at a motel, and an assistant in a barber's shop. Although all three work hard, they soon learn how difficult it is to "succeed" in Seoul. Chun-sik's girlfriend runs away with his savings—she has to support her younger brother, who wants to go to university. Gil-nam's girl strikes up a relationship with a wealthy real estate agent, leaving him for the older man; she has three younger siblings and a sick father to care for. Gil-nam ends up killing his rival in a crime of passion. Deok-bae, after being played by a wealthy socialite, begins a relationship with Gil-nam's younger sister, who has also arrived in Seoul to work at a factory. Following these domestic dramas, Chun-sik signs up for military service, while Gil-nam goes off to prison. Of the three friends only Deok-bae remains in Seoul, undertaking boxing training and preparing himself for the future.

Lee invests each character with a distinctive background, made up of elements drawn from a society wrestling with imported notions of developmentalism and capitalism. Shots of empty lots awaiting development are frequently shown, and stories of people losing their land through sharp real estate deals are heard. We hear the story of an old man who hanged himself after losing his property to a real estate agent and an unscrupulous developer. Lee shows how money has become all-consuming in this society, making some people miserable and others comfortable. Gil-nam's girlfriend dumps him for a much older man, hoping this will be a way of helping her family. Chun-sik's girlfriend steals money from him in order to support her brother. Under strong social pressure to support family members, especially younger siblings, young Korean women were often forced to set aside their own hopes and dreams. The film ends as it began with a short animation showing a group of three men breaking up and each going his own way.

Although the film's title may suggest otherwise, Lee's story explores the dark underbelly of society under the stresses of rapid transformation. The three protagonists represent three faces of Korean society, past, present, and future—linked together, on the one hand, by a driving ambition to modernize and catch up with the developed world as rapidly as possible, and on the other, by paying the price of striving to achieve too much too soon. The same capitalist system that is held up as a beacon of light in this modern Korea also traps its followers on a treadmill driven by their own lust for money and status. By using Korea's real-world attempts to hyper-stimulate economic development as the backdrop for his story, Lee depicts his characters struggling under the pressures exerted by the new world they are helping to create—what some sociologists have aptly called "compressed modernity".[24]

Figure 6.2 Film advertisement for *Good Windy Day* (1980). *Donga Daily* 22 November, 1980: 4.

Lee's adroit weaving together of these various social issues, even after a long break away from the industry, drew high praise from the critics.[25] Lee's fresh cinematic style in *Good Windy Day*, a film released during the "Seoul Spring"—a short period of political freedom between Park Chung Hee's assassination in October 1979 and the Gwangju Massacre carried out by the Chun Doo-hwan regime on 18 May, 1980—inspired a group of young filmmakers who became known as Lee Jang-ho's Team, including Bae Chang-ho, Park Kwang-su, Kim Hong-joon, Shin Seung-su, and Jang Sun-woo. Gathered around Lee, they shared ideas, consciously distancing themselves from established directors who had made their names in the 1960s such as Shin Sang-ok, Yu Hyun-mok, Kim Su-yong, Lee Seoeng-gu, and Jeong Jin-wu. They became part of the Korean New Wave in the late 1980s under Lee's tutelage. In the forefront of this movement, directors Park Kwang-su, Jang Sun-woo, and Bae Chang-ho were all socially committed and regarded realism as an essential aesthetic and narrative tool. According to Paquet, the background to the Korean New Wave was the government's relaxation of censorship and eventual abolition of the PRS (in 1984), thus enabling these directors and other independent producers to work more freely in the film industry than their colleagues could in the past.[26] Yet, the term Korean New Wave did not originate with this group, but was coined by overseas commentators such as Tony Rayns, who wrote about distinctive Korean directors and their films for the major Korean Cinema festival hosted in 1994 by London's Institute of Contemporary Arts.[27] Soon, others began to acknowledge their fresh attempt to explore "new content: new characters (the working classes, radical students), new settings (the factory, slum houses), and new problems (the north/south division, urbanization, industrial unrest, and family breakdown)".[28] These were the big issues of the 1980s, the age of democratic movements and rapid industrialization. The contribution of the New Wave directors and their relentless exploration of diverse visual styles and socio-political themes provided a firm foundation for the new face of Korean Cinema that emerged in the mid-to-late 1990s.[29]

With this successful "comeback" film, Lee won the Best Director Award in 1980 at the 19th Grand Bell Awards—South Korea's longest running and most prestigious film competition, the country's equivalent of the American Academy Awards. The success of *Good Windy Day* boosted Lee's confidence, stimulating him to a renewed exploration of social realism in his subsequent films. Given the strict social regulation and censorship policy carried over from the Park regime, this was no easy task.

Chun's censors did, however, introduce a more liberal approach to the depiction of sexuality on screen. For example, *Children of Darkness Part 1*, based on the novel of the same name by Lee Dong-cheol, dealt with the controversial subject of prostitution; its depiction of prostitutes offered a frank critique of life on the margins of Korean society. While its realistic subject matter and unflinching approach touched a raw nerve, at the time the film was considered an erotic melodrama—the publicity material spoke of actresses "revealing their bodies" on screen—helping to explain how the film passed the initial censorship hurdles and became a popular offering in cinemas.[30] Appearing in her first film, actress Na Young-hi became a star overnight, complimented by the press for taking the initiative in her many love scenes.[31] The social criticism element, however, proved a problem for the MPI as it later prohibited the commercial export and screening of *Children of Darkness Part 1* at overseas film festivals.[32] Appreciating the difficulties of working with the MPI and satisfying their requirements, Lee divided his time between social realist films and erotic melodramas—which were easier to recruit funding and attract audiences for—thus minimizing friction with the MPI and the censorship apparatus of the Performance Ethics Committee (PEC).[33]

In erotic melodramas like *Between the Knees* (1984) and *Eoudong* (1985), Lee substituted the sharp social commentary for which his previous films were known with a degree of attention to "bold nudity". As we will discuss in greater detail in next chapter, the 1980s saw the rise of the hostess melodrama, a type of erotic melodrama known as "ero films" (ero yeonghwa), in which sexuality was expressed overtly on the screen. *Between the Knees* drew nearly a quarter of a million cinema-goers in Seoul, becoming the second highest-earning film of the year.[34] Building on its success, Lee cast its female protagonist Lee Bo-hee in his next film, *Eoudong*, a historical drama about a famous *gisaeng* (known as a *geisha* in Japan) who seduced the king of the Chosun Dynasty. Posters for the film promoted Lee Bo-hee as the "incarnation of sexuality", arousing the interest of almost half a million people who saw the film in Seoul, making it the highest-grossing box office hit of 1986.[35]

Despite its authoritarian character, the Chun administration introduced policy initiatives aimed at forging a new national cultural identity by promoting excellence in the arts, cultural expression, and the expansion of international cultural exchanges.[36] The Producer Registration System was abolished by the MPI in 1984, making it easier for a wider range of people to produce films. Benefiting from this major industry change, Lee established his own production company, Pan Film Co., in 1986, which freed him from dependency on other producers and enabled him to make the types of films he wanted. No longer was his creative practice restricted by producers who were eager to distance themselves from him for political or artistic reasons.

One of the first commercial films produced by the Pan Film Co. was *Lee Jang-ho's Baseball Team* (1986) based on the popular comic book *Fearless Foreign Region*, written and drawn by Lee Hyeon-se. According to the KMDB, Lee's film attracted audiences of around 287,000 in Seoul, making it a moderate hit at the box office.[37] Although this first production was relatively successful, Lee lacked experience of the managerial and administrative skills necessary to run a film company. He might even have learned some bad business habits from Shin, who was notorious for mismanaging his own company, Shin Film (discussed in Chapter 1). Although Lee's later directorial efforts, such as *Miss Rhino and Mr. Korando* (1989) and *Myong-ja Akiko Sonia* (1992), and the films he produced, such as *Y's Experience* (1988) and *The Room in the Forest* (1991), were a diverse collection, demonstrating his willingness to experiment with new film styles and genres, all failed at the box office. As a result, Pan Film Co. became bogged down in serious financial difficulties—the kind of problems that Lee's mentor Shin Sang-ok had experienced with his own company in the late 1960s.

Conclusion

In the 1980s, Korean cinema benefited from a host of active directors who contributed a range of films across multiple genres and differing aesthetic and narrative styles that helped to fill the quota required for domestic films. Lee Jang-ho stands out among them as a director and producer working in both arthouse and commercial film. He is perhaps best known as the grandfather of the Korean "hostess" film. From his successful debut with *Heavenly Homecoming to Stars* in 1974, which made him a household name in Korea, an enforced exile of four years following his conviction for possession of marijuana, his film comeback with the social realist production *Good Windy Day*, and the box office hits *Between the Knees* and *Eoudong*, Lee's career has been nothing if not varied. The commercial failure of his production company Pan Film has done little to undermine the high level of respect that he commands today as a living legend of Korean cinema—one of the key figures responsible for changing the face of the domestic film industry between the 1960s and the 1980s.

Another aspect of Lee's pivotal role in the industry was his mentoring of young directors who went on to become part of the new wave of Korean cinema. Films like *Good Windy Day* and *Children of Darkness Part 1* shared the same strand of social criticism found in Korean New Wave films that appeared in the mid-1980s. Lee led a film movement (the Visual Age) in the 1970s and became godfather to a group of new directors including Bae Chang-ho, Jang Sun-woo, and Park Kwang-su, all associated with the Korean New Wave. Whether intentionally or otherwise, Lee inspired many of his peers as well as junior directors, making himself an indispensable link in the chain that brought about the transformation of Korean cinema starting in the 1970s.

The Korean New Wave of the 1980s was succeeded by another creative movement, the New Korean Cinema, represented by critically acclaimed directors such as Park Chan-wook, Kim Jee-woon, and Bong Joon-ho and including major industry figures Kang Woo-seok and Kang Je-gyu. This new generation of filmmakers became known as "commercial auteurs", experimenting with a range of genres and blurring the boundaries between arthouse and commercial filmmaking. This new breed of "local hitmakers" and "global provocateurs" are leading a cinematic renaissance inspired by directors such as Lee Jang-ho and the experimentation with style and genre that he initiated in the mid-1970s.[38]

Notes

1. This figure is taken from the KMPPC's 1977 yearbook (47): 212 domestic films were produced in 1968, 229 in 1969, 231 in 1970, and 202 in 1971.
2. Films in this category cited in Wade (1969), one of the few surveys of Korean cinema available in English at the time, include: *An Old Potter* (1969), *The General's Mustache* (1968), *Descendants of Cain* (1968), and *Women of Yi Dynasty* (1969).
3. At the time, Korea's economy was exceptionally vulnerable to external factors such as increases in the price of oil and raw materials and accordingly followed the rest of the world into recession. Inflation based on the consumer price index increased from 3.1 percent in 1973 to 24.3 percent in 1974, producing an average inflation rate of 16.8 percent for the 10 years between 1973 and 1982 (Collins and Park 1989: 9–11).
4. After the Vietnam War ended in 1974, the Park regime embarked on a thoroughgoing anticommunism drive. In 1975, in an affair known as the Inhyeokdang Incident, it made a high-profile example of 25 young men by arresting and brutalizing them for alleged involvement in antigovernment activities; eight of the group were sentenced to death. Anticommunist education was extended, and democratic movements led by university students were undermined through the disbanding of student clubs and the stationing of police on campuses. See Ma 1999 and Minkahyup *Human Rights Group* 2004: 27.
5. Shin 2007: 259.

6. "A Declaration of Forming a Visual Republic, Followed by Brief Criticism and Explanation" (Seukechi Bipan-gwa Haemyeong-i Eotgallin Yeongsang Gonghwaguk Seoneon). *Donga Daily* (4 August, 1975): 5.
7. See "Lee Jang-ho, movie director of everlasting youth" *HanCinema: The Korean Movie and Drama Database* (19 July, 2006). Available: http://www.hancinema.net/lee-jang-ho-movie-director-of-everlasting-youth-6594.html. Accessed 23 May 2014; and Paquet 2009: 12–13.
8. Lee 2003: 27–30.
9. Yi 2003: 17.
10. Byeong-ik Kim, "Youth Culture Marked by Blue Jeans, Acoustic Guitar and Draft Beer—and Rejection of Dishonesty, Inactivity, Mannerisms, and Silence" (Geojit, Anil, Sangtuseong, Chimmugeul Seulpeohaneun Beullujin, Tongita, Saengmaekju-ui Cheongnyeon Munhwa). *Donga Daily* (29 March, 1974): 5. Kim's article, an early exploration of the essence of the youth culture of the 1970s, prompted serious discussion on the subject among scholars and journalists.
11. *Heavenly Homecoming to Stars* was based on a popular novel by Choi In-ho, serialized in the *Chosun Daily* between 1972 and 1973. When the book version of *Heavenly Homecoming to Stars* was published in 1974 it became an instant bestseller, selling over 100,000 copies (at a time when half that figure was considered a bestseller in Korea). See "Bestseller" (Beseuteu Selleo). *Maeil Gyeongje* (30 April, 1974): 7.
12. Lee's song "I Give You All" in *Heavenly Homecoming to Stars,* Im's "Shadow in Youngja's Heydays", and Song's "Whale Hunting" in *March of Fools* all became popular when the films were released, and are still loved by many as classic 1970s tunes.
13. Lee 2003: 244.
14. Kang 2001: 97–98.
15. Kim et al. 2003: 80–81.
16. "Previews of Films for New Year Release" (Sinjeong-e Seonboil Yeonghwa Jisangsisahoe). *Gyeonghyang Shinmun* (24 December, 1974): 8.
17. "Thirteen Films Competing against Getting Import Licenses with High Cash Value" (Gunchimdoneun Oehwa Suipgeum Usuyeonghwae 13Pyeon Gyeongjaeng). *Donga Daily* (5 October, 1974): 5.
18. "Local Films Repeatedly Fail in Box Office" (Champae Geodeup Banghwa Heunghaeng). *Gyeonghyang Shinmun* (1 October, 1975): 7.
19. "Arrest of Three Singers Lee Jang-hee, Yun Hyeong-ju, and Lee Jong-yong" (Lee Jang-hi, Yun Hyeong-ju, Li Jong-yong Gasu 3 Myeong Gusok). *Gyeonghyang Shinmun* (4 December, 1975): 7; "Compilation of 30 'Happy Smoker' Entertainers List" (Haepi Seumokeo Sangseup Heubyeon 20 Yeonyein Myeongdan Ipsu). *Donga Daily* (8 December, 1975): 7; and "Entertainers' Organizations on Alert to Stub out Marijuana" (Marihwana Yeongireul Kkeora Yeonhyeop Bisang). *Gyeonghyang Shinmun* (12 December, 1975): 8.
20. Park Chung Hee described marijuana smoking as a "national peril". See "President Park Demands Maximum Sentence for Marijuana Smoker" (Park Daetongryeong Daemacho Heubyeonja Choigohyeon-eul). *Gyeonghyang Shinmun* (2 February, 1976): 1; "President Park Visits MPI, Orders Promotion of Independent National Culture" (Park Daetongryeong Mungongbu Sunsiseo Jisi Jucheseong Batang Minjokmunhwa Changdal). *Donga Daily* (5 February, 1976): 1; and "Crackdown on Decadent Entertainment" (Park Daetongryeong Toepyejeok Munye Dansok). *Maeil Gyeongje* (6 February, 1976): 1.
21. "Marijuana-smoking Entertainers Rise to 137" (Daemacho Yeonyein Modu 1 Baek 37 Myeong). *Donga Daily* (13 October, 1977): 7.
22. "20 Marijuana-smoking Singers Permitted to Perform, Except on Television" (Daemacho Gwallyeon Yeonyein 20 Yeomyeong Bangsong-oe Ilbanmudae Churyeon Heoyong). *Gyeonghyang Shinmun* (15 February, 1978): 8. However, the 20 singers

mentioned here still had difficulties finding employment, as many club owners no longer wanted to work with them.
23. Lee's insights about the industry's transformation between the 1960s and 1980s appear in the weekly film magazine *Cine21*. See Lee, Jang-ho. "Korean Film Retrospective: Lee Jang-ho (Hanguk Yeonghwa Hoegorok: Lee Jang-ho)". *Cine21* #34 (7 December, 1999): 98; and Lee, Jang-ho. "Korean Film Retrospective: Lee Jang-ho" (Hanguk Yeonghwa Hoegorok: Lee Jang-ho). *Cine21* #35 (14 December, 1999): 96.
24. For more on this concept, see Chang 1998 and 1999.
25. "Lee Jang-ho Directs Again" (Lee Jang-ho Hwaldong Jaegae). *Donga Daily* (20 September, 1980): 5.
26. Paquet 2009: 21.
27. Rayns, T. 1994. Seoul Stirring: 5 Korean Directors, Institute of Contemporary Arts, London.
28. Standish 1994: 77.
29. Scholar Yi Hyoin points out that because directors were still hampered by heavy censorship regulations, the level of social criticism and realism found in these films was comparatively low. See Yi 2003: 142. Nonetheless, the inclusion of even small amounts of social criticism and realism enriched their film texts, adding a certain dynamism to a cinema that had until then been dominated by melodramas and action films.
30. "A Trend for Exposing Bodies—Film Directors Become Bolder" (Ot Beotgigi Yuhaeng Hwakkeunhaejin Yeonghwa Gamdokdeul). *Donga Daily* (23 June, 1981): 12. Other films mentioned in this context include *Mulberry* (1981, Ppong), *The Maiden Who Went to the City* (1981, Dosiro Gan Cheonyeo) and *Three Times Each for Short and Long Ways* (1981, Sebeoneun Jjalkke Sebeoneun Gilge).
31. "Who is the Better Actress? No Teasing, But Bold Exposure of Bodies in Love Scenes" (Yangnyeomjeok Gaenyeom Beotgo Daedamhan Hwamyeon Wiro Jiteojin Reobeusin, Eoneu Yeowuga Jalhana). *Gyeonghyang Shinmun* (9 April, 1982): 12.
32. See Lee, Jang-ho. "Korean Film Retrospective: Jang-Jo Lee". *Cine21* #44 (1 February, 2000): 90.
33. At the time, all domestic film scripts had to be approved at the pre-production stage by the MPI, and the final prints of both domestic and foreign films had to be reviewed before their release by the PEC, which had maintained these powers since its formation in 1979.
34. "*Whale Hunt* No. 1 Film for Largest Audiences and Biggest Stars—Lee Mi-suk and Ahn Sung-gi" (Gorae Sanyang Gwangaek Dongwon 1 Wi, Choedae Churyeon Lee Mi-suk Ahn Sung-gi). *Donga Daily* (18 December, 1984): 8.
35. "Cinemas Getting Ready for Chuseok Special Programs" (Gak Yeonghwagwan Chuseok Teukseon Peuro Junbi). *Donga Daily* (18 September, 1985): 12; and "Eoudong Attracting 480 Thousand Audiences, Becoming #1 Box Office Film" (Eoudong Gwangaek 48 Man Dongyo Heunghaeng 1 Wi). *Gyeonghyang Shinmun* (16 December, 1986): 12.
36. Yim 2003: 40–41.
37. See <www.kmdb.or.kr/vod/vod_basic.asp?nation=K&p_dataid=03967&keyword=%EC%99%B8%EC%9D%B8%EA%B5%AC%EB%8B%A8>.
38. Choi 2010.

7 Weapons of Mass Distraction
The Erotic Film Genres of the 1970s and 1980s

One of the biggest changes in the mediascape in the 1970s was the advent of television, which threatened the exclusive status of film as a visual entertainment medium and one of the government's most useful tools for the dissemination of information. On the commercial front, as in other countries such as the US, the UK, and Japan, television in Korea was seen as a strong potential competitor to the film industry. Acknowledging the threat they faced, throughout the 1960s film companies in these countries sought "convergence at all levels".[1] For example, Korea's neighbor Japan was one of the first to restructure its media industry, opening up a new era of collaboration between film and television.[2] These changes caused by the advent of television, however, came to Korea belatedly in the 1970s.

As far as Korean cinema was concerned, the introduction of television meant not just the arrival of a dangerous opponent, but also a potential substitute for the unique position film had enjoyed as a propaganda tool. By the end of 1972, the number of television sets in South Korea had reached one million. A fall in the quality of domestic films, along with a lack of new talent—the result of a significant number of popular film actors switching to television drama—undermined the status of the film producer as a major voice for the government's national ideology project.[3] With increased accessibility and nationwide diffusion, television rapidly replaced film as the most powerful means of spreading official propaganda. In fact, the Park regime always showed an interest in supporting the broadcasting industry as part of a broader push for technological advancement. In 1961 the government distributed 20,000 television sets on installment plans. Then, the Electronic Industry Promotion Act (1969) boosted the growth of the electronics industry by encouraging the nation-wide dissemination of television sets, a move followed up by the introduction of lower taxes on new television sets.[4] Given this competing force, it was little wonder that the newly established KMPPC launched its own plans to produce "national policy" films around this time.

In the 1970s, people began referring to television as "bedroom cinema" (*anbang geukjang*). TV serial melodramas became popular, drawing middle-aged female audiences—the mainstay of local cinema in the 1960s—away from theaters. This was the beginning of a love affair with television drama that continues undimmed. Today, Korea is well known in Asia as a producer of so-called "Hallyu" dramas—now regular television fare in countries such as China, Taiwan,

Japan, and beyond—not to mention major streaming content for Internet-based non-English video drama providers such as Viki.com and Dramafever.com.

In this chapter we focus on the major narrative conventions found in melodrama, the most prolific genre in Korean cinema during the 1970s and 1980s. Beginning in the mid-1950s, the so-called Golden Age of melodrama continued throughout the 1960s, 1970s, and 1980s. Yet, with a television set in every Korean home, filmmakers faced the challenge of transforming the genre to attract audiences back to the cinema by showing more—and more daring—sexual content on screen. Thus, the "hostess" melodramas of the 1970s and the "erotic" melodramas (usually known as "ero films") of the 1980s were born. In what follows, we explain how these two erotic subgenres provided audiences, filmmakers, and policymakers alike with a welcome distraction from authoritarian military rule, while creating a cathartic—albeit misogynistic—release from the social pressures resulting from Korea's rapid industrialization. Both the "hostess" and "erotic" species of melodrama made their own distinctive contributions to the changing face of Korean cinema and society. Their development revealed fissures and ironic predilections in the censorship process well before government censorship of films was abandoned in 1996.

A Golden Age of Melodrama?

In many ways, melodrama provides the key to understanding the complex historical development of Korean cinema. As both a genre and a thematic thread, melodrama has long been a favorite form of visual entertainment for Koreans, dating back to the beginnings of the nation's film history. Its popularity reflects the universal appeal of the melodramatic, what Thomas Elsaesser described as the use of an "exaggerated rise-and-fall pattern in human actions and emotional responses, a from-the-sublime-to-the-ridiculous movement, a foreshortening of lived time in favor of intensity".[5] Throughout cultural history, the arts, including literature and theater, have embraced melodramatic elements, features that gradually coalesced into a popular genre in the West through the use of "heightened emotionalism and sentimentality"—frequently by placing characters in harm's way in order to stimulate the audience's emotions.[6]

As other commentators have pointed out, these basic storytelling elements and traditions had also existed in pre-modern Korean art forms and texts, including dramatic performances such as *pansori* (Korea's traditional musical storytelling). Thus, for filmmakers, incorporating melodramatic themes and conventions into their work was a relatively easy and natural process, also providing a sense of familiarity for audiences.[7] In the 1960s, according to the Korean Movie Data Collection, domestic melodramas were so popular that between 1961 and 1970 about 45 percent of all films produced in Korea belonged to this genre (725 out of 1,637).[8]

Given that the tragic aspects of women's lives was the leading theme of the genre, melodrama was particularly attractive to female audiences because it mirrored their lives on the silver screen. Women went to the cinema in droves to see melodramas, sympathized deeply with the heroines, and shed bucket-loads of tears.

Tear-jerking titles endorsing conservative morals were particularly popular in the late 1960s—they were dubbed *shinpa* melodramas on account of their excessive emotional expression. While the melodramas popular in the early 1960s praised family values and family relationships, in the late 1960s they began focusing more on the tensions between modern family life and Korea's traditional Confucian and patriarchal family systems. Motherhood was held up as the ultimate domestic value; a mother's sacrificing of her own desires was the unquestionable social virtue binding family members together. These cinematic stories were charged with poignant emotion and pathos surrounding female protagonists struggling to overcome a variety of hardships and premarital or extramarital sexual temptations—thus inviting identification by their overwhelmingly female audiences.

Most film critics and commentators agreed that women were the mainstay of the domestic cinema, dismissing the female audience as "rubber shoe cinemagoers" (*Gomusin gwangaek*)—a contemptuous reference to the feminine footwear frequently left behind in cinemas after screenings. When the television industry was established in Korea in the early 1970s and began broadcasting daily soap operas, women stayed at home to follow these alternative melodramas and rapidly became a significant and reliable television audience. This development in turn severely undermined the film industry, exacerbating existing falls in production and in cinema and audience numbers throughout the 1970s. At the same time, television was the reason behind the genre's transformation in the 1970s and 1980s.

As the genre developed, Korean cinematic melodramas came to focus primarily on family matters and thorny love relationships, often reflecting wider social issues. In the process, perhaps to a greater extent than in other national cinemas, women were portrayed as victims, sacrificing themselves—either voluntarily or through coercion—for their family or (if unmarried) their male partners. The postcolonial (post-1945) and Korean War (1950–53) periods—times when the nation was deeply affected by personal hardship and family tragedies—have provided seemingly endless inspiration for the makers of melodramas. The rapid industrialization and urbanization that followed, and their impact on the social, cultural, and political fabric of Korea, also provided filmmakers with the raw material for emotionally engaging stories. Many of these tales also deal with the interpersonal conflicts resulting from the clash between traditional patriarchal and Confucian values, on the one hand, and modern, Western ideas that flowed in following the "opening up" of Korea, on the other. The exhibition of thousands of Hollywood genre films seems to have played a significant role in this process of social, cultural, and political transformation.

For more than a century, Korea has been valued as a lucrative market for cultural content emanating from the US (and the UK), and then more directly from the global entertainment center of Hollywood.[9] As a result of this international presence, many local filmmakers grew up watching an endless flow of Hollywood films and dreaming of becoming Hollywood directors. One notable Korean film in particular, *Aimless Bullet* (1961), directed by veteran filmmaker Yu Hyun-mok, was heavily influenced by the plethora of Hollywood movies exhibited in Korea. The story of a poor family trying to survive in the aftermath of the Korean War, it combined "Hollywood melodramatic tropes and realist South Korean aesthetics".[10] Yu, who is today regarded as a representative Korean auteur, was one of many directors who attempted to invest their melodramas with "palimpsestic traces of Hollywood's tropes and iconography".[11] By emulating Hollywood in this way, Korean directors such as Shin Sang-ok, Kim Su-yong, Jeong So-young, and Jeong Jin-wu contributed to a golden age of melodrama—one that included the vast majority of films produced between 1955 and 1972.[12]

Titillation and Political Distraction: The Hostess Films of the 1970s

During the 1970s, the film industry in Korea experienced a downturn in terms of both the quality and quantity of films produced, resulting in a loss of support from local audiences. In place of the domestic films that audiences avoided *en masse*, an increasing interest in foreign (primarily Hollywood) films became evident. This was in spite of the MPI's limitation on the number of imported titles—reaching only between 31 and 43 films per year between 1974 and 1980—about half the number of foreign films permitted for exhibition in 1971. According to a survey conducted by the KMPPC in 1972, a new generation of young filmgoers believed—with good reason—that foreign films contained more arresting narratives and superior visual aesthetics than local productions.[13] Melodrama, already a very popular film genre, was transformed by the leading directors and producers discussed above as a way of coping with these major changes in the film market. A slew of dramas hit Korean cinemas, portraying a new type of female "professional" working in bars at night. The "hostess" film was born—melodrama with a twist. The barroom "hostess"—a term that appeared in the 1970s—was a young woman who served alcohol to male customers, a new role linked to the rise of the adult entertainment industry in Korea.

Although the Park regime policed public morality strictly—for example, regulating the length of men's hair and women's skirts, and clamping down on marijuana smoking—in an attempt to limit Western influence, it was relatively relaxed about the depiction of sexuality on screen. This reflected a major change to the way the censorship laws were applied. In the mid-1960s, the government's censorship rulings were closely associated with the criminal law, especially anticommunist and obscenity legislation, and often involved the prosecutor's office. While the Park government's hard-line policies opposing communism formed the regime's legal foundation, aiming at strengthening anticommunist ideology and securing the national defense system,[14] the obscenity law served to reinforce traditional morality based on the patriarchal family system and to discourage liberal expressions of sexuality. If films were suspected of having transgressed these laws, directors would be hauled up before the prosecutor's office.

The first case where the obscenity law was applied to a local production involved director Yu Hyun-mok and his film *The Empty Dream* (1965) (discussed in Chapter 2). Though the film showed only a glimpse of the back of an actress wearing a flesh-colored body stocking, this scene gave the prosecutor's office sufficient reason to charge Yu. The case against Yu symbolized the government's intolerance of anyone attempting to push the established boundaries around freedom of expression. A few years later, in 1969, three other established directors—Shin Sang-ok, Park Jong-ho, and Lee Hyeong-pyo—were arrested for violating the obscenity law, indicating a tightening up of censorship. The films targeted included Shin Sang-ok's *Eunuch* (1968) and *Women of Yi-Dynasty* (1969), Park Jong-ho's *A Woman in the Wall* (1969), and Lee Hyeong-pyo's *Your Name is Woman* (1969). Both the completed films and material cut during the editing process were subject to investigation, as "producing obscene materials" was considered a crime by the prosecutor's office regardless of whether or not they had been exhibited in a public context. As a result of these investigations, all three directors were arrested on charges of violating the obscenity laws. After being brought to trial, they were all sentenced to pay fines.

According to film critic Ho Hyun-chan, the "hostess" genre emerged when it did for two reasons. First, the government may well have acknowledged that the rigid political situation represented by the *Yushin* system required an easing of strictures in the arena of public morality. The obscenity law was eased to such an extent that *Heavenly Homecoming to Stars* was selected by the MPI as a "quality film", enabling production company Hwacheon Gongsa to gain a coveted import license.[15] Second, developments in the Korean cinema were simply paralleling what was happening in the outside world in the 1970s, such as "Roman porno" in Japan and the "sexploitation" films coming out of Hollywood.[16] On top of these, three further factors were at work in the rise of the hostess genre. First, the adaptation for the screen of a number of popular novels published in the 1970s also played a part in ensuring the success of these films. Second, the enduring popularity of melodrama provided fertile ground for the growth of the new subgenre. And last, the young directors who had grown up in the post-liberation era and were part of the youth culture of the 1970s were making films that reflected their own experience and differed markedly from the entertainment offered to their parents' generation.

The hostess genre was born with Lee Jang-ho's directorial debut *Heavenly Homecoming to Stars* (1974), which attracted audiences of more than 460,000 in Seoul and launched him on a path that saw him become one of the leading directors of the period. As discussed in the previous chapter, *Heavenly Homecoming to Stars* is the tragic story of Gyeong-a, a bar girl who commits suicide following a series of failed relationships. The intimate life of a young woman presented in a series of flashbacks proved especially attractive to audiences, offering the type of voyeuristic experience that television could never provide.

Lee's first film proved that the industry's fears of television killing the film exhibition market were unfounded, despite the reality that this new medium was in the process of being rolled out across the nation. The number of television sets in Korean households increased from 43,684 in 1966 to 2,809,131 in 1976, a more than 60-fold increase within the decade.[17] Three broadcasting companies were operating during the 1960s: the government-run KBS (Korea Broadcasting System), from 1961, and two commercial stations, TBC (Tongyang Broadcasting Company) and MBC (Munhwa Broadcasting Corp), from 1964 and 1969, respectively. MBC showed daily dramas from the outset, gradually attracting a large female audience. With the advent of TBC's *My Lady* (Assi), all three broadcasting companies were producing daily soap operas. It seemed that television had stolen the audience for melodrama, even encroaching on the evening session or "golden hour" at the local cinema, traditionally the favored time for city workers to take in a movie.[18]

Hard on the heels of *Heavenly Homecoming Stars* came *Youngja's Heydays* (1975, Youngja-ui Jeonseong Sidae), which was also a box office hit, inspiring other filmmakers to try their hand at the genre. The link between the two titles was directly stated in the advertising poster for the latter film: "From Gyeong-a's time in 1974 to Youngja's heydays in 1975" (see Figure 7.1). Echoing Lee's film, *Youngja's Heydays*, based on the novel by Jo Seon-jak, portrays a young girl from the countryside who is callously taken advantage of by the men she encounters in the big city. Only 19, Youngja's first job in the city is as a housemaid for a wealthy family, a sought-after position. Yet, within days of landing the job, she is raped by the family's son and fired without compensation. Alone in the city and lacking social networks, Youngja accepts a series of menial jobs, including positions as a factory worker and bus conductor. While working as a bus conductor, she falls from the overcrowded vehicle, losing her left arm. Her inability to cope with this physical disability causes her much suffering. Feeling that she has exhausted all other options, she becomes a prostitute.

The film's title forms a cruelly ironic commentary on Youngja's experiences in the big city. Her deep sense of alienation and the harsh reality of her situation make it difficult to imagine her having the interest or energy to reflect on her rural upbringing. The audience is left to imagine the simple pleasures of country life, a fictitious rural idyll reflecting a gentler, kinder, more innocent Korea of the distant past. However, the use of a brazen realism to portray the negative effects of runaway capitalism through Youngja's eyes received critical acclaim by the press—who also labeled it "a truly adult movie".[19]

Figure 7.1 Film advertisement for *Youngja's Hey Day* (1975). *Gyeonghyang Shinmun* 8 February, 1975: 8.

The "adult" orientation of *Youngja's Heydays* is evident in the film poster, which shows Youngja sitting on a chair wearing lingerie and high-heeled shoes. Her legs are spread wide, her lingerie inches high up her thighs, her shoulder strap hangs loosely, and she is wearing a suggestive smile. Although many critics praised the film's implied social criticism,[20] the publicity surrounding it was focused mainly on the film's adult content and gossip surrounding actress Yeom Bok-sun, who became an overnight star. According to popular media magazine *Monthly TV*, Yeom was having an affair with Korean playboy Park Dong-myeong, who was allegedly involved with many other actresses at the time.[21] Taking advantage of the publicity surrounding this scandal, and against the wishes of those involved in the film, after *Youngja's Heydays* was released black-market comics with the same title and containing erotic stories and over 70 images from the film were put on sale.[22]

Youngja's Heydays attracted audiences of 398,000 in Seoul, making it the top picture of the year at the box office—no small feat, given that only six of the 75 films produced in 1975 received audiences of more than 50,000. A sequel, *Chang-su's Heydays*, was made very quickly and released at the end of the same year; it followed the career of Young-ja's first love in *Youngja's Heydays*, Chang-su, and his faithful love for her. Only three films released in 1975 attracted audiences of more than 100,000: *Youngja's Heydays*, Ha Gil-jong's *March of Fools*, and Lee jang-ho's *It Rained Yesterday*—all directed by members of the Visual Age group and illustrating the industry's precarious situation. Thus, the success of *Youngja's Heydays* gave rise to numerous copy-cat films, adding to the growing number of so-called hostess or "Youngja" films.[23] Common to all these films is the convention of portraying the female protagonist as a sexual object and constructing the camera's point of view as a voyeur. Whatever its moral and aesthetic deficits, this strategy had the practical outcome of selling tickets in bulk during a period marked by a dearth of domestic successes at the box office.[24] The hostess film held the field until a type of melodrama with added erotic content, the so-called *ero yeonghwa*, surfaced in the early 1980s.

Other well-known hostess films produced in the 1970s were *Cuckoo's Dolls* (1976), *Blue Days* (1976), *Winter Woman* (1977, Gyeoul Yeoja), *Do You Know Kkotsuni* (1978), and *I Am Lady Number 77* (1978). In each of these films, the female protagonist becomes a hostess at a bar at some point in her life. Compared to the female leads of the 1960s, who starred in productions that celebrated family values and prioritized motherhood, the girls in these 1970s melodramas flaunted their sexuality on the silver screen. They offered a seductive combination of attractiveness, innocence, compassion, and an openness to sexual encounters that was exploited both willingly and also through coercion. This was both a heady and a dangerous mix. As Lee Ho-geol observes, when these young women lost their "virginity" (i.e. their innocence) and became prostitutes, they were no longer protected by a society where patriarchal norms prevailed.[25] Despite such powerful social sanctions, hostess films treated young girls as objectives of desire. As traditional virtues and conventional morality were increasingly questioned in the 1970s, the time was ripe for a new generation of filmmakers—including Lee Jang-ho, Kim Ho-seon, and Ha Gil-jong—to implement new strategies to attract local audiences to domestic films on show at suburban cinemas.

Professional Ladies of the Night in 1980s Erotica Films

From the 1950s, political and sexual themes had been identified as major targets of official censorship, especially material that showed communism or North Korea in a positive light. Nevertheless, ironically—or, as we have suggested, because sexual themes enabled audiences to momentarily escape the reality of living under a dictatorship—film censors generally overlooked eroticism and overt sexual material (including rape scenes) across various genres. A liberal attitude to the portrayal of sex in "hostess" films, and its more explicit counterpart, "ero" films, was part of the government's overall approach to cultural policy, which became known as the "3S Policy"—"sports, sex, and screen"—and which eventually secured the 1988 Olympics for Korea.[26] Chun Doo-hwan's military regime, which came to power following a coup in December 1979, maintained absolute and ruthless control over all aspects of society, an approach seen in the national army's violent quashing of democratic protests on 18 May, 1980—within six months of seizing power—in the city of Gwangju, an event known as the Gwangju Massacre.

The 3S policy—the so-called sexing and athleticizing of the nation—also had the effect of drawing public attention away from the bloody Gwangju Massacre and subsequent criticism of the government. Under the Chun regime's cultural policy, Sex, Screen, and Sports were the "bread and circuses" offered to the masses in an attempt to divert their attention away from politics.[27] As early as 1983 the press was discussing this policy and the rationale behind it in terms of "stupifying", "hypnotizing", and "relieving the stress" felt by the public.[28] The 3S program was rapidly rolled out. Color television was launched nationwide in 1980. Professional baseball and soccer leagues were launched in 1982 and 1983 respectively. At the same time, freedom of expression was suppressed, particularly in the media. In 1980, a total of 64 newspapers and broadcasting companies were either forced to close or were merged into 18 state-approved organizations, leaving 172 defunct periodicals and over 1,000 journalists jobless.[29]

Against this backdrop of political terror, accompanied by tanks, bullets, and bloodshed in the streets of Gwangju, and the ruthless suppression of the media, a slew of "ero" or erotic films appeared to soothe frayed nerves. Screenwriter Shim San recalls this bleak period as a grotesque mix of oppression and liberation.[30] The many soft pornography films made and released in the mid-1980s included: *Mulberry* (1981), *Three Times Each for Short and Long Ways* (1981), *Red Cherry* (1982), *Madam Aema* (1982), *Women Don't Fear the Night* (1983), *The Stolen Apple Tastes Good* (1984), *A Night of Burning Bone and Skin* (1985), and *The Woman Who Lives on Night* (1985). Actresses such as Jeong Yun-hi, Yu Ji-in, and Jang Mi-hi became popular because of their willingness to display their naked bodies on screen. Under the more "liberal" censorship regime—at least as far as sexual expression was concerned—directors well understood that making a "pink" film would give them a better chance of success at the box office. First used in the Korean context by an anonymous director in a newspaper article, the term "pink" implied a link between domestic ero melodramas and Japanese soft porn films.[31]

Since the 1960s, Korean filmmakers had acquired a considerable knowledge of developments in the global film market including Japan—even though they were not able to view any of these films on screen. They obtained Japanese film magazines such as *Kinema Junpō* from friends and family members visiting Japan and studied them for information about the film market and conditions in the industry as well as devouring screenplays of Japanese films. A few favored individuals, including importers and producers, were able to keep their finger on the pulse through attending overseas events such as the Asian Film Festival. When we interviewed him, Lee Woo-seok, a producer and representative of the Dong-A Export Co. since the 1960s, commented that Korean producers would slavishly copy any overseas genre film that had been a big hit at the box office. The boom in spy action and martial arts films in the late 1960s followed this pattern, as did hostess films and erotic melodramas. According to an interview we held with director Lee Hyeong-pyo, this was an accepted way of creating a new trend in filmmaking.

As a result of the Chun government's lobbying for hosting rights to international athletics events, the Asian Games and the Olympic Games were held in Korea in 1986 and 1988, respectively. In 1982, the government relaxed the regulations governing school uniforms and men's hairstyles and abolished the nighttime curfew (24:00–4:00) that had been in place since 1945 under the United States Army Military Government in Korea (hereafter USAMGIK). Bars were permitted to stay open all night and film censorship regulations were relaxed to allow stronger sexual content on screen. This latter reform was welcomed by some industry members who were considering making adult films as one way of giving a boost to the local industry.[32] With the curfew lifted, theaters like the Seoul Cinema quickly sought to benefit by launching midnight screenings. Erotic films were seen as the best fit for this new slot.

The best known of these cheaply made erotic films is *Madam Aema*—also the first midnight movie to be screened in Korea. *Madam Aema* attracted younger audiences with its powerful eroticism—much bolder in its sexual expression and more daring in its crossing of moral boundaries than any of the hostess films of the 1970s. One newspaper advertisement clearly stated that the film was for "adults only" (see below), and a review in the *Donga Daily* described it as presenting an affair conducted by a married woman in a positive light.[33]

In reporting the film, the media focused heavily on the glamorous figure of lead actress Ahn So-young and the amount of flesh exposed on screen. In *Madam Aema*, the heroine is having an affair with her old lover while waiting for her husband to be released from prison but is also drawn to a young university student. Bored by her lover's taste for sexual perversion and tired of waiting for her husband, but touched by the student's genuine feelings for her, she dreams of accompanying him to France. Nevertheless, she stays at home and is reunited with her husband on his release. A pure sexploitation film, *Madam Aema* was clearly crafted to indulge male sexual fantasies and made explicit use of voyeuristic camera techniques.

Despite its near-pornographic intent, critic Yi Hyoin praised the film as "advanced" insofar as it stripped away any pretense from a scenario in which a

150 *The Dark Age and Hollywood's Domination*

Figure 7.2 Film advertisements for *Madam Aema* (1982). *Donga Daily* 4 February, 1982: 4; and *Maeil Gyeongje* (24 February, 1982): 14.

married woman and her lover engage in pure sexual indulgence.[34] Screenwriter Shim San also made the point that unlike the women in hostess films, who are depicted as being forced into prostitution, the female protagonists of erotic melodramas actively seek fulfillment of their sexual desires.[35] Such themes were reflected in the promotional posters for *Madam Aema*: "Madam Aema's whole body is running toward you"; "Minors cannot watch Madam Aema". Although Madam Aema is shown returning to her husband at the end of the film and thus giving a nod to conventional morality, she is not punished for her wayward sexual behavior. She is neither forced into prostitution nor driven to kill herself. In this way, the erotic films of the 1980s marked a significant departure from traditional social norms rooted in Confucianism—a feature that may explain Yi Hyoin's reference to the film as "advanced".

The very basic story line of *Madam Aema*—little more than a vehicle for a series of sexually provocative scenes—succeeded in attracting audiences of 315,738 in Seoul, making it the top-grossing film of the year.[36] A flow of similar movies capitalized on the success of *Madam Aema*, including: *Mountain Strawberries* (1982), *The Woman and the Rain* (1982), *Mrs. Kim Mari* (1983), *The Lover of a Friend* (1983), *Between the Knees* (1984), *A Night of Burning Bone and Skin* (1985), and *Woman, Woman* (1985). While not all were successful at the box office, they were all later released on videotape, seen as a relatively easy way of recouping profits. With the videotape market expanding in the late 1980s, some of these films such as *Madam Aema* and *Mountain Strawberries* were released straight to videotape as part of franchising deals. Filmmakers became bolder in terms of the subject matter presented, and in the late 1980s prostitution and Korea's lucrative sex industry became common subjects of ero films. *Prostitution* (1988), which audaciously showcased the film's subject matter in its title, was representative of this trend, featuring the luxurious lives of professional call girls.

Amid all the explicit sex, melodrama still proved a powerful draw-card. For *Madam Aema* screenwriter Lee Mun-wung, part of the film's popularity could be explained by the fact that it was the story of a married woman and so succeeded in attracting female audiences—largely married and middle-aged—back to the cinema.[37] Eroticism was seen as a sure-fire solution to the problem of declining theater audiences. Big-budget spectacle films, while different from anything television had to offer, were too risky to make in a moribund market environment. Science fiction films, with their elaborate costumes and sets involving aliens and spacecraft, were out of the question because of the technical problems involved. Eroticism was seen as an accessible and affordable alternative that required less investment and offered something "visually different". And, of course, sex sold.

Despite these ambitious plans, the Golden Age of the erotic movies took a sharp dive after the market was fully opened to foreign film imports in 1988. With the influx of Hollywood films such as *Fatal Attraction* (1987) and *Basic Instinct* (1992), which were far more confronting than Korean productions in terms of sexual expression and daring story lines, domestic erotic films slowly disappeared from cinemas. Hampered by a conservative Confucian moral code and a patriarchal social system, Korea's home-grown erotic films could not compete with their Hollywood rivals. Hence, while Korean producers continued to make erotic films, they increasingly targeted the rapidly growing videotape market.

Conclusion

The 1970s unfolded under the shadow of Park Chung Hee's *Yushin* system, much more strictly enforced than before, and the Chun Doo-hwan government that succeeded it in the 1980s. Even under a severe censorship regime employed to thwart social and political dissent of any kind, a remarkable license was given to the onscreen expression of sexual behavior in order to divert attention away from Korea's repressive political and social environment. The "hostess" and "ero" films produced in the 1970s and 1980s constituted a major part of the country's mainstream film industry during these two decades. The downturn that hit the industry and its struggle to compete against the new medium of television were the two most important factors motivating producers to make the voyeuristic sexploitation films that succeeded in luring large audiences to late-night sessions in cinemas across Korea.

Despite the march of the years, melodrama has remained one of the most popular film genres produced in Korea and has remained largely unchanged in its essentials. While elements such as settings and the characteristics of the female protagonists have changed as a result of the social, cultural, and political transformations experienced by Koreans, the celluloid melodrama—or, at least, films containing melodramatic narrative conventions—dominated all other genres until the 2000s, when action and thriller films and hybridized genre films outstripped them in popularity.

Notes

1. Hilmes 1996: 466.
2. Reacting to the drop in cinema attendances and the associated fall in profits, six major film companies, led by Toei, reversed their initially hostile attitudes toward television and joined forces to set up a new broadcasting company, exploiting the new medium as a fresh revenue stream. See Anderson and Richie 1982: 255.
3. In its analysis of the state of the Korean film industry in 1972, the popular film magazine *Yeonghwa Japji* concluded that television was set to thrive at the expense of the film industry. See: "Film Ousted by Television: The Future of the Korean Film Industry After 1972" (TV e Millyeonan Yeonghwa Pando: 72 Nyeondokkaji On Yeonghwa-ui Unmyeongeun?). *Yeonghwa Japji* (December 1972): 140–42.
4. See Jo 2003: 151–54.
5. Elsaesser 1991: 76.
6. Singer 2001: 37.
7. Abelmann 2005: 47.
8. KMPPC 1977: 47.
9. From the mid-1890s, foreign missionaries used magic lanterns and outdoor slide shows to educate and entertain Koreans as well as American, British, Chinese, and Japanese expatriates living in and around Seoul, and regular screenings of commercial entertainment films sourced from the US (and also from France, the UK, and Japan) occurred in and around Seoul from the 1910s. Between the mid-1920s and mid-1930s, Korea became a major market for US films, outperforming Japan for a time. See Yecies 2005 and 2008; and Yecies and Shim 2011.
10. Chung 2005: 119.
11. Chung 2005: 123.
12. See McHugh and Abelmann 2005.
13. *Korea Cinema* (September 1972): 99–103.
14. Korea's Anticommunist Law was passed on 3 July, 1961, in order to suppress all "potential" anti-governmental activities. The so-called pro-communist activities outlined in the legislation included affiliation with communist organizations, expressing admiration for communist countries and regimes, and any communication with communist parties. The law was strengthened following the consolidation of the Park regime's political leadership during the mid-1960s.
15. "Ministry of Public Information Selects 'Quality' Films Including *Heavenly Homecoming to Stars*" (Mungongbu Choewusu Yeonghwa Byeoldeurui Gohyang Deung Seonjeong). *Maeil Gyeongje* (25 April, 1974): 8.
16. Ho 2000: 199.
17. KMPPC 1977: 156.
18. "Cinema's Golden Hour Seeing Declining Audiences" (Geukjangga Goldeun Awo Jeonyeok Gwangaegi Julgoitta). *Gyeonghyang Shinmun* (12 March, 1975): 5. Cinema owners even discussed the possibility of introducing an evening session discount to attract more customers.
19. "Youngja's Hey Day" (Yeongjaui Jeonseong Sidae). *Donga Daily* (22 April, 1975): 3.
20. Kim and Jeong 2001; Kim 2005; Byun 2007.
21. Yeom sued *Monthly TV's* editor Nam Dae-hwan for defamation. "Miss Yeom Bok-sun to Sue Magazine Editor" (Yeom Bok-sun yang Japji Pyeonjipjang Goso). *Gyeonghyang Shinmun* (16 July, 1975): 7.

22. "Overview of Korean Cinema during the Past 30 Years" (Hanguk Yeonghwa 30 Nyeon Gyeolsan). *Gyeonghyang Shinmun* (8 July, 1975): 5. Two further sequels were made in the 1980s: *Youngja's Heydays II* (1982) and *Youngja's Heydays 87* (1987).
23. "Local Films Continue to Fail" (Champae Geodeup Banghwa Heunghaeng). *Gyeonghyang Shinmun* (1 October, 1975): 6.
24. "Local Film Boom—Renaissance for High School Films and Adult Film Audiences Also Grow" (Banghwa Bum Je 2 Jeonseonggiro Gogyomul Tago Seongin Yeonghwado Gwangaek Neureo). *Gyeonghyang Shinmun* (15 September, 1977): 5.
25. Lee 2003: 239.
26. See Lee 2007b: 277–79.
27. Lee 2007a: 271–72.
28. "What is Significance of Medicare Pledge?" (Uibo Illeonhwa Gongyak Eotteoke Dwaettna). *Donga Daily* (2 November, 1983): 4; "Lack of Balance in Public Relations" (Hongboui Bulgyunhyeong). *Donga Daily* (24 October, 1984): 3; and "Need for a Space to Relieve People's Stress" (Seuteureseu Pureojul Gonggan Ashipda). *Gyeonghyang Shinmun* (7 November, 1984): 5.
29. For further details regarding the Chun government's clampdown on press freedom in 1981, see the press release issued by Korea's Truth and Reconciliation Commission: "Press Release Regarding the Consolidation of the Press and the Journalists Who Were Forced to Quit in 1980" (1980nyeon Eollon Tong Pyehap Mit Eollonin Gangje Haejik Sageon Bodojaryo) (7 January, 2010). Available at: <www.jinsil.go.kr/Information_Notice/article2/read.asp?num=190&pageno=3&stype=&sval=&data_years=2015&data_month=>. Accessed 20 December 2014.
30. Shim, San. "Father of 'Madam Aema'" (Aema Buinui Abeoji). *Cine21* #296 (3 April, 2001). Available: <www.cine21.com/news/view/mag_id/1295>. Accessed 11 November 2014.
31. "A Trend for Exposing Bodies—Film Directors Become Bolder" (Ot beotgigi Yuhaeng Hwakkeunhaejin Yeonghwa Gamdokdeul). *Donga Daily* (23 June, 1981): 12.
32. "Quality of Film Stagnant Due to Censorship" (Geomyeore Geollyeo Jireun Jejarie). *Gyeonghyang Shinmun* (23 March, 1979): 5.
33. "Increasing Feminism Voices in TV/Films" (TV/Yeonghwa Yeoseong Haebang Giryu). *Donga Daily* (16 January, 1982): 11.
34. Yi 2003: 251.
35. Shim, San, Op Cit.
36. The top-grossing foreign film of the year was *Body Heat* (1981), attracting audiences of over 350,000 in Seoul. This Hollywood film was compared with *Madam Aema*, underscoring the trend in genre films released in 1982. "Local Films Still Neglected, Only 4 Box Office Hits" (Yeojeonhan Banghwa Oemyeon Olhae Hiteu Gyeou 4 Pyeon). *Gyeonghyang Shinmun* (8 November, 1982): 12.
37. "Boom in Films about Married Women" (Gihonnyeo Sojae Yeonghwa Jejak Bum). *Maeil Gyeongje* (1 March, 1982): 9.

Part III
The Golden Age of the Post-censorship Era

8 The Rise of the New Corporate and Female Producers

This chapter investigates some of the representative producers and production companies that have made important contributions to the expansion of the Korean film industry since the early 1990s. It addresses the key roles they have played in its transformation from an industry suffocated by government censorship and dominated by foreign productions to a powerful and innovative vehicle for showcasing popular Korean culture and media to the world. As part of this discussion, we chart the rise and impact of major industry players and explain how the varied business strategies they employed triggered a paradigm shift that challenged the traditional filmmaking system in Chungmuro—the symbolic (and former geographic) center of Korea's film industry.

Whilst each of the producers discussed below has followed one of many—often risky—pathways and faced numerous challenges along the way, the collective capacity they have built over the past quarter-century by achieving operational efficiency and economies of scale, as well as an international standard of business transparency, has enabled early twenty-first-century Korea to enjoy a cinematic golden age—in terms of maturity and diversity, as well as the quality and quantity of films produced. Each participant has played a uniquely important role in defining the stories, styles, creative talent, and audience tastes that have made Korean cinema what it is today.

To bring these developments to life, we build on several earlier but limited studies by focusing on female industry leaders, whose numbers now equal—if not exceed—those of their male colleagues.[1] This group of leading women producers has changed the face of Korean cinema in the post-censorship era by creating successful small-to-medium (SME) production firms and producing a diverse array of critically acclaimed films with strong appeal to both local and global audiences. In addition to their business prowess, each of the producers and SMEs discussed in this chapter has been able to work effectively with the flood of talented directors, actors, and production technicians who flocked to the industry following the lifting of censorship restrictions by the Kim Young Sam administration (1993–1998) in 1996.

Systematizing the Entertainment Factory

Following the inauguration of President Kim Young Sam, Korea's first civilian president, in early 1993, a new era began to open up for the domestic film industry. Even before the Kim government eliminated script censorship in 1996, but increasingly afterwards, a slew of savvy producers and large corporations began turning out a diverse range of domestic hits as well as films made for and with Hollywood, China, and beyond, boosting the industry to new heights of optimism and self-confidence.

Today's filmmakers face a very different situation from that of the producers and companies that sought to function under the draconian Producer Registration System (PRS) of the 1970s and 1980s. As we have seen, this generation of producers focused their activities heavily on the importation, distribution, and exhibition of Hollywood blockbusters and Hong Kong martial arts films rather than on making films of their own. Nevertheless, new personnel and fresh production ideas emerged from remnants of the old PRS oligopoly system after it was formally abolished in 1984. Underpinning their activities and business strategies was an unfamiliar level of transparency and efficiency. This is precisely what most industry sectors—including the family-run conglomerates known as *chaebols* in Korea—have been required to maintain as part of the International Monetary Fund's (IMF) bailout package granted to Korea following the 1997 Asian economic crisis.

During the mid and late 1980s, bilateral concessions agreed to between the Chun Doo-hwan administration (1980–1988) and the US government paved the way for an onslaught of Hollywood films to enter the Korean market. Capitalizing on the holding of the 1988 Olympics in Seoul, Hollywood distributors gained direct rights to distribute American films in cinemas and vast numbers of videotapes destined for the shelves of rental outlets across urban and rural Korea. At this time, the videotape market was dominated by a number of small and medium-sized *chaebol*-owned regional distributors including Wooil Yeongsang (Daewoo), SKC (SK), Saehan Media, and Dreambox and Starmax (both owned by Samsung).[2] The domestic and (licensed) imported film businesses controlled by these networks were worth an estimated $30 million USD per year and were expected to continue expanding with the increasing dissemination of VCRs.[3] To capitalize on the growing popularity and consumption of Hollywood videos in the domestic market, Samsung, Daewoo, and LG ramped up the production and diffusion of locally made VCRs. Samsung and Daewoo in particular were keen to develop this aspect of their activities, as it blended seamlessly into the national rollout of multi-channel cable television in the early 1990s. The entertainment business began to appear to be a good investment to numerous *chaebols* and their vertically integrated subsidiaries.

These *chaebols* optimized their investment in the entertainment industry by aggressively seeking the full rights to a particular film in order to provide their ancillary business interests with content such as video, which began arriving in Korea in the mid-to-late 1980s, as well as cable (i.e., pay) television, which entered the domestic market in the early-to-mid 1990s. For example, both Samsung and Daewoo had created entertainment arms to produce films, and both had obtained cable channels—Catch One and DCN (known today as OCN). To a lesser extent, they also began investing in the exhibition side of the industry, seeking to establish their own cinema (multiplex) networks. However, before this goal could be achieved, in 1999 both Samsung and Daewoo were forced to relinquish their stake in the film industry in the aftermath of the Asian financial crisis, which cut a swathe through Korea's economy in 1997. The vacuum left by these two major companies was eventually filled by a handful of firms including Cinema Service, CJ Entertainment, Showbox, and Lotte Entertainment, which were in turn followed by newcomer Next Entertainment World (aka N.E.W.) in late 2008.

Among them, CJ Entertainment arrived on the domestic scene following its role as a founding investor of US production company DreamWorks in 1995, thereby securing regional distribution of DreamWorks' films in Asia. Less hampered by the financial crisis than its rivals, CJ Entertainment moved quickly to expand its film industry holdings; the company launched the multiplex era in Korea in 1998 when it opened its first CGV (short for CJ Golden Village) multiplex in Seoul's eastern districts. In 1999, CJ Entertainment also acquired the cable channel Catch One; 12 years later it acquired OCN from Orion Group, which had originally purchased it from Daewoo. In 2011, CJ Entertainment changed its name to CJ E&M (Entertainment and Mediaplex), and today it is Korea's largest media conglomerate—operating across all the major entertainment sectors, including film, broadcasting, music, and gaming (CJ E&M is discussed in greater detail below). Here it is sufficient to note that the new energy, ideas, and funding that infused Korea's mediasphere in the mid-to-late 1990s enabled the stagnant film industry to experience an unprecedented paradigm shift.

The irrevocable entry of *chaebols* into the film industry created new funding sources that enabled the industry to overcome a number of problems associated with its limited size. It also allowed it to overcome the financial hardships that filmmakers had been experiencing for decades—particularly after the mid-to-late 1980s when the local film market became dominated by Hollywood companies that were distributing US films directly. The *chaebols* introduced stable, long-term funding strategies that resulted in enhanced production values. Although many of the smaller companies were concerned that these large, vertically integrated conglomerates might engulf them, there was a perceived need to resuscitate the underperforming local industry, and the *chaebols*' extended hands provided a ready means of achieving this.[4] Until major venture capital began flowing into the film industry in the early 2000s, in concert with generous public film funding schemes, these corporate players effectively retooled the industry by implementing comparatively transparent management and accounting systems, standardized box office tracking procedures, cross-platform marketing campaigns, and planning and internationalization strategies. "Going global" was familiar territory for many *chaebols* and their management teams, which had successfully developed consumer electronics and other goods for international markets.

In particular, Samsung's entertainment arm became Korean cinema's first real-world "training academy" for film production planning and management. (Film production courses at KAFA, for example, became available only in 1995, while most university film programs focused on directing and the study of film theory.) Samsung and other *chaebols* also attempted to remedy the dearth of Korean films that had come about due to a long-standing preference for foreign films (and a growing dissatisfaction with the derivative genre films discussed in Chapter 7). At the same time these corporate managers, who now took on the role of "executive producers", were positioned outside of the film industry and looked to new sources of inspiration to rejuvenate Korean cinema. Thus, the *chaebols* and their organizational approach to the film and entertainment business via their entertainment subsidiaries played a major role in enabling Korean cinema to become the international success story it is today.

With the domestic industry now subject to a systematic regime—another way of saying that professional practices in Korea were becoming aligned to those common in the US film industry—a new type of 'planned film' (*gihoek yeonghwa* in Korean) emerged. These were commercial "concept films" that combined funding from a *chaebol* with expertise provided by a new generation of producers who managed the entire filmmaking process from financing and pre-production to line producing, post-production, and marketing. Some of the best-known planned films of the 1990s include ShinCine Communications' *Marriage Story* (1992), *Mr. Mamma* (1992), *The Fox with Nine Tails* (1994), and *Gingko Bed* (1996); Kang Woo-seok Productions' (later known as Cinema Service) *Two Cops* series (1993, 1996); Myung Film's *Contact* (1997); and of course Kang Je-gyu Film and Samsung Entertainment's record-smashing hit *Shiri* (1999). These genre-specific and commercially oriented films explored a wider range of stories than Korean filmmakers had attempted before; they set new trends that became a major hallmark of the "New Korean cinema".

As we discussed in detail in Chapters 1 and 5, before the early 1990s films were mostly designed and planned under the careful eye of a director or director–producer, often with input from a film company owner (filling the role of an executive producer whose major task was to recruit funding), and thus were lacking the professional production and marketing expertise that the *chaebols* were able to offer. Between the mid-1950s and the early 1990s, most film projects were small relative to today's standards, and production companies usually lacked a planning department. The choice of films to be made was determined by the company president and the individual directors. During this period, most film companies generally consisted of a president who arranged funding and maintained a broad overview of production; a producer who managed the entire production process; a line producer who assisted with practical tasks such as shooting schedules, equipment preparation, managing the production crew, and logistics; a production manager who was responsible to the line producer; and a bookkeeper.

As one of the earliest domestic 'planned films', the 1992 production *Marriage Story* holds a significant place in Korean film history. Directed by Kim Ui-seok, *Marriage Story* is a socially engaged romantic comedy that follows the marriage, divorce, and re-coupling of a young urban professional couple who work in the same broadcasting company. While executive producer Ikyeong Films controlled business and legal matters and mobilized funding from Samsung and other regional distributors, ShinCine Communications (hereafter ShinCine) established in 1988 by Shin Chul managed the day-to-day production process. Not only was *Marriage Story* a box office hit, but ShinCine became a seedbed for Korea's next generation of producers, including Oh Jung-wan (aka Oh Jeong-wan), Ahn Soo-hyun, Kim Mu-ryeong, Yu In-taek, Cha Seung-jae (aka Tcha Seung-jai), Kim Sun-ah, Lee Mun-myeong, and Kwon Byeong-gyun. In an unprecedented decision initiated at the script development stage, ShinCine undertook market research and focus group interviews with a group of newlywed couples living in Seoul. The plan was to develop a story that would appeal to its target audience of young urban dwellers between their late teens and thirties.[5] The effort paid off; *Marriage Story* was a huge success, becoming the top cinema box office hit of 1992 and attracting audiences of more than 500,000 in Seoul (and many more when Dreambox released it on videotape). Until the late 1990s, *Marriage Story* remained among the biggest box office draws of Korean cinema.

Compared to more familiar offerings, *Marriage Story* was fast-paced and had a fresh visual style and sense of humor, features that impressed audiences and critics alike.[6] Shim Jae-myung, who went on to found Myung Film, adopted some innovative techniques to market the film, including running a series of newspaper advertisements with suggestive taglines such as 'Sleep, No Sleep, Light off, Do it?'—an obvious reference to the couple's sexual preferences. Dreambox, Samsung's videotape company, funded this production, which was one of the earliest projects to receive investment from a *chaebol*. This type of corporate funding differed significantly from the ad-hoc and random funding sources previously pursued by influential regional distributors—who in any case were badly out of touch with younger audiences. In turn, this innovative funding system enabled a host of new producers to make films that appealed to Korea's large pool of cinephiles under 40. Moreover, *Marriage Story* and its many successors became vehicles for promoting household and leisure products such as Samsung's white goods, which in the 1992 production were used as set props in the couple's house. The longstanding tradition of product placement in Hollywood films, to which Korean audiences had been exposed as far back as the 1920s, now became a key production feature of domestic films. In sum, all of these elements, which reflected the new commercial foundations of the industry, signaled the rejuvenation of Korean cinema.

A major turning point occurred in 1995 when Samsung established Samsung Entertainment, a subsidiary charged with leading the company and film industry into uncharted territory. From then on, all of Samsung's cultural and entertainment ventures—Naises (live events and music), Starmax (a videotape company), Dreambox (a videotape company that merged with Starmax in 1996), Catch One (a pay/cable TV channel), and Cheil Communications' Q Channel (a documentary cable television channel)—would be organized under a single umbrella. Samsung Entertainment now took its place as a major entertainment company with a widely diversified portfolio.

The continuing expansion of this major corporate player, as well as the operational efficiency and economies of scale achieved—not to mention the international standard of business transparency that it and other *chaebols* introduced—signaled a paradigm shift for Chungmuro. As the previous three chapters have shown, heavy-handed government control throughout the 1970s and 1980s had kept Chungmuro wrapped in a suffocating blanket of parochialism from which producers (and directors) could not escape. These "old-school" film representatives had little choice but to maintain their narrow focus on preventing the local film market from being overwhelmed by the direct distribution of Hollywood films (and videos). However, thanks to an influx of capital and the experienced business managers who accompanied it, from the early 1990s producers had access to increased budgets and sophisticated accounting systems that enabled them to approach filmmaking as a well-organized and transparent manufacturing process. The fact that projects were now backed with adequate funding facilitated access to state-of-the-art equipment and experienced technicians (who in turn trained novice crew members)—all elements necessary to develop the systematic production methods and international standards that have contributed to the robust health of the contemporary Korean film industry.

As discussed earlier in the book, before the intervention of the *chaebols* into the film industry, Korea's distribution network fell along regional boundaries, and individual exhibitors played a crucial role as investors by providing producers with shoestring budgets in return for guaranteed pre-sales of a given film. Such practices were heavily dependent on special deals made through personal networks, as well as the volatile box office performance of one-off film screenings. However, in the 1990s, the arrival of wealthy new players led to the creation of national distribution networks that were either built from scratch or acquired from regional exhibitors and consolidated subsequently. Ironically, major US distributors such as UIP also benefited from these newly formed national distribution networks—especially after the Korean government began allowing the circulation of more than six prints of a particular film title. Shortly afterwards, as a result of CGV's introduction of multiplexes in 1998 (followed by Lotte Cinema in 1999 and Megabox in 2000), the total number of screens underwent an exponential increase—from 507 in 1998 to 588 in 1999, 720 in 2000, 1,132 in 2003, through to 1,648 in 2005, leveling off at around 2000 in 2007.

In the middle of this upheaval in the industry, Kang Je-gyu, director of the fantasy–horror film *Gingko Bed* (1996), made the spy action–melodrama *Shiri* (1999) which sent shock waves across the local industry and beyond; the ripples created can still be felt today. The last film to be funded by Samsung Entertainment, *Shiri* was an outstanding success in Korea, drawing over six million admissions nationwide. In fact, it broke all existing box office records—even those set by the Hollywood mega-blockbuster *Titanic* (1998). One newspaper toasted director Kang Je-gyu and Samsung Entertainment's triumph with the witty headline, 'Little Fish Shiri Sank the Titanic'.[7] *Shiri*'s success heralded many broken box office records to come, marking the beginning of a new age of Korean cinema. Thanks to the commercial success of *Shiri*, investment continued to flow from a number of new producer–distributors and venture capitalists who had had their eyes on the film industry for some time, including some former Samsung and Daewoo employees who created their own successful film companies following the industry's shake-up in 1999.[8]

As a result of these positive synergies, a production boom ensued. The market began to expand as increased investment issued in the making of new and exciting commercial entertainment films and the emergence of a host of creative and adventurous directors bent on breathing a spirit of universality into their narratives and characters while maintaining a distinctive Korean voice. The *chaebols* paved the way for the vertical integration of investment, production, distribution, and exhibition—a new phenomenon for the Korean film industry.

Samsung and Daewoo dominated the film and video sector until they offloaded their entertainment businesses in 1999, after the Kim Dae-jung government (1998–2003) required *chaebols* to reorganize and sell off some of their smaller subsidiaries. This major initiative was part of government efforts to rescue Korea from the 'IMF crisis', which paralyzed Asian financial markets in 1997. As part of this restructuring process, the *chaebols* offloaded their entertainment arms in that same year—ironically at the pivotal moment when *Shiri* had broken all records and far exceeded expectations at the box office. Out of the ashes emerged a fresh cohort of producers and other industry players who were eager to occupy the newly industrialized playing field.

The New Industrialized In-crowd

At the turn of the 2000s, the Korean film industry continued to be transformed through a number of key developments. First was the establishment of a handful of producer–distributors, the earliest of which included Cinema Service, founded in 1995 by Kang Woo-seok, who since 1989 had been busy directing popular dramas and romantic comedies including *Two Cops* (1993), *How to Top My Wife* (1994), and *Two Cops II* (1996). Kang Woo-seok was joined by Kim Ui-seok and Kim Seong-hong, the directors of *Holiday in Seoul* (1997) and *The Hole* (1997), respectively. With a view to producing commercial films, this filmmaker–producer trio pooled their personal funds and other financial resources to form a new company. They teamed up with Kwak Jeong-hwan, aka Chungmuro's Godfather, the powerful and seasoned owner of Seoul Cinema who controlled the capital and distribution channels necessary for developing an effective vertically integrated film company. Kang Woo-seok's alliance with Kwak, who had acquired the Seoul Cinema in 1978, enabled Cinema Service to capitalize on the powerful industry networks and exceptional business acumen that Kwak had developed since the 1960s.[9]

Over three decades, Kwak had formed a loose distribution network with dozens of local cinemas, including the Daeyeong Geukjang in Seoul, Busan Academy Cinema, and Daegu Chungang Cinema. In addition, Kwak had negotiated lucrative direct distribution contracts with UIP around the time of the Seoul Olympics in 1988, enabling him to release memorable hits such as Paramount's *Ghost* in 1990. Similar distribution contracts with 20th Century Fox, Warner Bros., and

Walt Disney followed soon after, cementing Kwak's position as one of Korea's most powerful exhibitor–distributors. The Kang–Kwak alliance enabled Cinema Service to become the most influential production and distribution companies of the late 1990s—particularly after Samsung and Daewoo unexpectedly exited the industry in 1999 in the wake of Korea's economic crisis.

During its first decade, Cinema Service, which also invested in Primus multiplex cinemas in 2002, produced and distributed a regular stream of hit films including writer–director Jang Jin's noir gangster comedy *Guns and Talks* (2001); Kang Woo-seok's spy drama *Silmido* (2003), the first Korean film to draw audiences of 10 million; and director–producer Kang Woo-seok's detective action thriller *Another Public Enemy* (2005). Unquestionably, the scale and success of these films, as well as Cinema Service's distribution of Hollywood mega-hits such as *Lord of the Rings: The Fellowship of the Ring* (2001), *Lord of the Rings: The Two Towers* (2002), and *Terminator 3: Rise of the Machines* (2003), cemented Kang Woo-seok's status as an industry heavyweight. In fact, he was selected by *Cine21*'s annual survey as the industry's "number one powerhouse" for eight consecutive years (1997–2004) for his capability as a commercial director, producer, and investor, as well as his commitment to social activism.

In 2005, Kang Woo-seok's influence began to wane when CJ Entertainment acquired Cinema Service, after which CJ Entertainment's CEO Park Dong-ho assumed Kang Woo-seok's mantle as industry leader. This major move confirmed CJ Entertainment's dominant position in the industry while signaling the arrival of a second wave of large conglomerates (including Showbox and Lotte Entertainment) that were vertically integrated across all aspects of production, distribution, and exhibition. Ownership of their own multiplex cinema chains (CGV, Megabox, and Lotte Cinema, respectively) separated these newcomers from their predecessors. Today, while Cinema Service, as a subsidiary of CJ Entertainment, continues to release a steady stream of films, it has scaled back its operations after experiencing a string of box office failures, including *Hwang Jin Yi* (2007), *Kidnapping Granny K* (2007), and *Modern Boy* (2008), confirming the adage that audiences do matter.

In 2002, the Orion Group, one of Korea's most senior conglomerates, added the film production and distribution company Showbox to its Megabox chain of multiplex cinemas (launched in 2000) and On Media cable channels as a vertically integrated competitor to the CJ Group—and CJ Entertainment more specifically. (The Orion Group vice-chairperson behind Showbox and Megabox was Lee Hwa-kyung, the company founder's daughter.) For five years, the Orion Group, which also owns confectionery and snack companies (including the famous Choco Pie chocolate-covered marshmallow and biscuit treat) and restaurants as well as sports teams, was a fierce competitor of the CJ Group, but following the film industry's peak year in 2006 it sold Megabox to the Australian financial firm Macquarie Group, thus signaling a partial retreat from the entertainment industry. The sale of On Media to CJ Entertainment in 2010 all but removed Orion Group from the entertainment playing field.

Lotte Group became a more serious competitor in 2003 when it established the film production and distribution company Lotte Entertainment to service its multiplex chain Lotte Cinema, which had opened in 1999. With its aggressive vertically integrated business model, by 2015 the Lotte Group, which is known for its department stores and shopping malls, had become the number two player in the industry behind CJ Entertainment.

Finally, in 2008, Kim Woo-taek, the former CEO of Showbox and Megabox—shortly after the multiplex chain was sold to Macquarie Group—launched the production and distribution company Next Entertainment World (aka N.E.W.). As the newest player on the block, with interests in the film, music, live performance, and ancillary rights sectors, N.E.W. is already making a major contribution to the Korean film industry, not least in its role as a leading independent film distributor. N.E.W. became a major player in the Chinese market virtually overnight at the end of December 2014 (see Chapter 11) after one of China's biggest production studios, Zhejiang Huace Film & TV (controlled by Chinese billionaire Fu Meicheng), acquired a 15 percent stake in N.E.W. for around $52 million USD. This deal suggests that N.E.W. is set on a path that will diverge from those taken by Orion Group and Lotte Group but is already crossing with CJ Entertainment in China.

Since acquiring Cinema Service, CJ Entertainment has become the most senior of a number of producer–distributor companies that have left their marks on the local film industry. (CJ Entertainment began as a subsidiary company formed in 1995 by the *chaebol* Cheil Jedang—now known as CJ Group, primarily a food company.) In early 2011, CJ Entertainment became Korea's largest media conglomerate after the CJ Group consolidated its broadcasting, film, gaming, music, and performance arms under the single banner of CJ Entertainment and Media (aka CJ E&M), with Samsung founder Lee Byung Chull's granddaughter, Miky Lee (aka Mi-Kyung Lee), at the helm as vice-chairman of the restructured organization. (In 1993, Miky and her brother Jay Hyun Lee—currently CJ Group's chairman—took over CJ from their father Lee Maeng Hee, the son of Samsung's founder.)

Miky Lee's longstanding involvement in Korea's entertainment industry began in 1995 when she successfully negotiated an exclusive distribution deal with DreamWorks after CJ invested $300 million (roughly an 11 percent founding share) in the then new Hollywood studio created by Steven Spielberg, Jeffrey Katzenberg, and David Geffen. This arrangement opened up an unprecedented pathway into the US for CJ, giving it exclusive rights to distribute some of the most popular and profitable Hollywood films throughout Asia (outside Japan). Overnight, this deal catapulted CJ to the top of the domestic film industry, providing the company with a regular supply of US blockbusters and enabling it to open Korea's first multiplex cinema in 1998: the CGV Gangbyeon cinema in Seoul. (In early 2006, following a highly profitable 10-year relationship with DreamWorks, CJ sold its stake in the US company to Viacom, the parent of Paramount Pictures.) At the end of 2010, CJ Entertainment established Filament Pictures, a subsidiary with the dual aim of distributing international films and investing in low-budget domestic films costing between $175,000 and $850,000 USD to make. Distributing films from as far afield as Japan, China, and India, in addition to its low-to-middle budget Korean films, the new company aimed to entertain local audiences with a diverse mix of films drawn from popular domestic and Hollywood genres.

Today, CJ E&M's vertical and horizontal integration across the sectors of film, broadcasting (CJ Media; On Media, a multiple cable channel company merged with CJ E&M in 2014, previously owned by the Orion Group), music (Mnet Media), and gaming (O Media Holdings; CJ Internet), have enabled the company to maintain a leadership role in both local and international markets. At home, CJ E&M nurtures new talent by supporting training academies such as the prestigious KAFA and the Korean National University of Arts (KNUA). It also sponsors a script treatment competition at KNUA for current and graduate students. Female writer–director Jeong Ju-ri's *A Girl at My Door* (2014) is an exemplary beneficiary of this competition; the film was invited to the Cannes Film Festival following its success in this CJ E&M-sponsored program.

For the CJ Group, advancing its global enterprise and accelerating globalization has included forging new markets in China since late 2005—in part by opening a branch office in Beijing—while expanding its corporate network in the US. (In 2005 it also set up its US entertainment headquarters in Los Angeles, thereby augmenting its established position as a leading manufacturer of food and consumer products.) In 2006, CGV opened its first Chinese multiplex in Shanghai in partnership with Shanghai Film Group. CJ E&M began co-producing films in China with the romantic comedy *Sophie's Revenge* (2009), starring leading Chinese actresses Zhang Ziyi and Fan Bingbing and Korean actor So Ji-seup and created with China Film Group and Perfect World Pictures. One Western critic familiar with Asian cinematic tastes characterized *Sophie's Revenge* as "a thoroughly entertaining (in a brain-checked-in-at-the-door way) slice of colorful romantic escapism".[10] Although this and subsequent co-productions have been slow to attract the huge audiences anticipated, CJ E&M's Chinese endeavors produced a dividend in 2013 with the box office success of *A Wedding Invitation*, a romantic comedy the company produced using local and Korean crews.

A Wedding Invitation, directed by Korean rom-com master Oh Ki-hwan and produced by CJ E&M, is an example of a pan-Asian collaboration designed to appeal to Chinese audiences from conception to script development, through to production, marketing, and exhibition. This tear-jerking melodrama is loosely based on Oh's Korean film *Last Present* (2001), with assistance in "localizing" the story provided by Chinese screenwriter Qin Haiyan. The characters and settings in the original version—the early 2000s in Korea—were altered to reflect life in contemporary China. Distributed by the state-run China Film Group, the largest national film distributor, *A Wedding Invitation* generated almost $32 million USD (200 million Yuan) in mainland China, making it the highest-grossing Korean–China co-production at the time of its release.[11] The same collaborative strategy has been employed in the Chinese production of *20 Once Again* (2015)—a remake of CJ E&M's Korean fantasy–comedy hit *Miss Granny* (2014), which topped China's box office charts in January 2015 ($59 million USD), breaking the previous record held by *A Wedding Invitation*. Simply put, CJ E&M's modus operandi is to work closely with Chinese actors and local production crews while reserving core creative positions (and IP) for Korean nationals, in particular the roles of producer, director, cinematographer, chief editor, costume designer, visual and special effects (post-production) specialist, and make-up artist. It has been placed as the top ninth grossing rom-com in China.[12] As we argue in Chapter 11,

China has become the open frontier on which CJ E&M and many Korean firms and practitioners have set their sights.

While the commercial sector of the East Asian production scene is dominated by a powerful, vertically integrated group of investor–distributors—CJ E&M, Showbox, Lotte Entertainment, and N.E.W.—several small-to-medium production companies run by both male and female producers are also flourishing. The so-called "power of the producer"—as opposed to the power of writer–directors such as Im Sang-soo, Kim Jee-woon, Hur Jin-ho, Lee Chang-dong, Park Chan-wook, Bong Joon-ho, and Kim Ki-duk—has reached new heights through this group's willingness to finance globally marketable films and encourage talented young directors to make them. This cohort has been responsible for initiating innovative business practices and producing a long list of critically acclaimed commercial and independent feature films that, taken together, have given a powerful impetus to the fundamental re-orientation of the industry over the past 20 years.

The Rise of the Female Producer

One of the most significant signs of the changing face of Korean cinema is the rise of powerful female producers, such as Shim Jae-myung, Shim Bo-kyoung, Oh Jung-wan, Kim Mi-hee, Lee Eugene, and Ahn Soo-hyun, talented filmmakers who began attracting attention from outside Korea in the 2000s. While helming CJ Entertainment, major player Miky Lee has inspired them all in one way or another—primarily by encouraging them to follow a different pathway from the one blazed by CJ itself (and Korea's other major integrated corporate producers, Showbox and Lotte Entertainment).

To take the list in order, Shim Jae-myung (aka Jaime Shim, 1963 -) represents the first generation of film producers (of both sexes) who emerged in the reform era of the early 1990s and who remain active today. Since Shim's founding of Myung Film, she has produced many of the innovative and successful genre films that have created and sustained Korean cinema's reputation as a vibrant national cinema. Her extensive and varied filmography includes Kim Jee-woon's *The Quiet Family* (1998); *Happy End* (1999); Park Chan-wook's *JSA* (2000); Kim Ki-duk's *The Isle* (2000); Im Sang-soo's *A Good Lawyer's Wife* (2003); and *The President's Last Bang* (2005), both co-produced with Shin Chul; and *Forever the Moment* (2007). Myung Film was also responsible for the internationally successful children's feature animation *Leafie, a Hen into the Wild* (2010)[13] and *Architecture 101* (2011), both of which were made in collaboration with Lotte Entertainment, which handled investment and distribution. Shim's productive career and the strategies adopted by her company offer important insights into the industry's larger trajectory.

While studying literature at Dongduk Women's University in the mid-1980s, Shim followed in the footsteps of the aspiring Visual Age group of filmmakers, a movement heavily influenced by 1950s and 1960s French New Wave films and the New American Cinema of the 1960s and 1970s. (Members attended regular film screenings at the French Cultural Center in Seoul, opened in 1968.) In her mid-twenties, Shim entered the industry in 1988 with a public relations and copywriting position at Seoul Cinema, working under one of Korea's most powerful regional investor–exhibitors, industry veteran Kwak Jeong-hwan. During her stint at Seoul Cinema, Shim developed an expanding network of contacts, including directors Lee Joon-ik and Kang Je-gyu, critic Jeong Seong-il, and producers Shin Chul and Seok Myung-hong, who have all gone on to become some of the most active members of the contemporary film industry. In 1991, she moved into the pre-production and production area after landing a job at Geukdong Screen, a production and importing company with a reputation for introducing Korean audiences to Hong Kong action films such as John Woo's noir action–crime drama *The Killer* (1989), starring Chow Yun-fat and produced by Tsui Hark. This phase of her career impressed Shim with the necessity for incorporating formal marketing (i.e., planning) strategies into the film business.

In 1992, Shim established the film marketing agency Myung Planning, which was renamed Myung Film in 1995. At this time, firms that employed marketing strategies of this type were new for Korea, despite the fact that major American and Japanese studios and distributors had introduced extensive advertising and promotional campaigns—including celebrity endorsements, product tie-ins, product placement, contests, ornate lobby displays, outdoor signage, and radio and print campaigns—to the Korean market as early as the 1920s. Nevertheless, Myung Planning was a local pioneer in this area, which began to make up an increasing share of a film's total budget following ShinCine's success with *Marriage Story* in 1992.

In 1995, Shim and her sister Shim Bo-kyoung, along with Lee Eun, whom Shim Jae-myung had recently married, joined forces to change the face of Myung Film. Shim Bo-kyoung had been working in advertising, and Lee was a director of independent films such as *The Night before Strike* (1990), a drama set in the democratic labor movement of the 1980s. Lee also had production management and budgeting experience acquired through his involvement with the Jangsangotmae independent film group, which made feature-length independent films (as opposed to commercial films). More than a name change, Myung Film was now a full-fledged film production company. Shim Bo-kyoung became head of planning and, following the formation of MK Buffalo in 2004, she took on the role of the new joint company's planning director. In these early days, the professional planning skills displayed by rival industry practitioners, in particular producer Shin Chul (and his company ShinCine), provided positive models for the trio to follow.[14]

By 2001, the small number of critically acclaimed and commercially successful films produced by Myung Film had made the company one of the top Korean producers on Hollywood's watch list. Rewarded with critical success and lucrative box office returns for well-crafted, commercially oriented art films such as *The Contact* (1997), Kim Jee-woon's *The Quiet Family* (1998), Kim Ki-duk's *The Isle* (2000), and Park Chan-wook's *Joint Security Area* (2000, aka *JSA*), Shim and Lee (Shim's partner and husband) developed a reputation for wielding "commercial and artistic success with grace, class and humility".[15] Myung Film was positioned squarely at the center of Korean cinema's boom, the result of an increase in the total films produced annually since the success of *Shiri* in 1999 (up from 49 in 1999 to 80 in 2003) combined with the right mix of commercial and artistic qualities, all presented to eager audiences on an expanding number of multiplex screens. All of these elements converged to push the total share of domestic films released in the Korean market from a respectable 39.7 percent in 1999 to a sterling 53.49 percent in 2003.[16] Although the entry of venture capitalists created new funding sources during this period to replace the previously dominant *chaebols*, there was still a shortage of funding to cover the costs of the increasing number of films in production.

In response, with the aim of providing a steady stream of funding for new projects—and to cash in on the industry boom—in 2004 Myung Film and Kang Je-gyu Film strategically merged to form MK Buffalo, becoming a listed company on the Korean stock market. At the time, floating a production company was a popular strategy, intended to compete with the increasing dominance of large investor–distributor firms in the film market by creating joint producer–investor–distributor initiatives.[17] In 2005, MK Buffalo was renamed MK Pictures, and both companies retained their names in order to pursue separate projects that reflected their respective interests. (Eventually MK Pictures changed back to Myung Film in 2010, three years after the company was delisted from the stock market.) Meanwhile, other companies that were floated publicly at this time include Sidus in 2004; Tube Pictures and Spectrum DVD in 2005; and Prime Entertainment in 2006.[18]

MK Pictures differentiated itself from other companies by backing diverse and creative projects and maintaining a focus on what it called its "exclusive producer system". This was at a time when the industry was becoming increasingly dominated by three vertically integrated mega-companies—CJ Entertainment, Showbox and Lotte Entertainment—that produced mainstream commercial films for generic audiences. MK Pictures offered the type of personalized service and commitment the three industry giants could not—or were unwilling to—provide. Director Im Sang-soo, for instance, benefited from MK Pictures' services when his film *The President's Last Bang* (2005) became the subject of legal action by the family of former authoritarian president Park Chung Hee. By contrast, CJ Entertainment responded to the negative publicity and political pressure generated by Park's family by reneging on its investment (20 percent of the total production budget) in *The President's Last Bang* and withdrawing its pre-arranged distribution deal for the film.

The President's Last Bang, the first film produced by the newly formed MK Pictures, sets out to recreate President Park Chung Hee's last night on earth before KCIA Director Kim Jae-gyu (played by Baek Yun-shik) shot him at close range with a revolver. In its depiction of these events, the film offers a subtle critique of Park's 18-year rule, treating the night the assassination took place as a microcosm of the rule of a man who was—and still is—revered by many of his countrymen and loathed by others. Scenes in which Park's political opponents are imprisoned and tortured, and socialists and liberals are accused of being North Korean spies, serve as acute reminders of the realities of Park's regime. We are also given an intimate view of his sexual proclivities and indulgences—for example, in the opening scenes where bikini-clad women expose their supple breasts for the president's pleasure. Later, we see call girls lined up (with their mothers), eager to give President Park—in the words of one of the characters—'what made him happy'. No holds are barred on the political front, either, as the audience is exposed to Park's coercive ideals and policies that became a means of inculcating his version of patriotism, his pro-Japanese leanings (he had been an officer in the Japanese army during the colonial period), and finally his extreme right-wing views on nuclear armament and Korea's relationship with the US.

Fluid cinematography by veteran cameraman Kim Woo-hyung takes the audience on an emotionally charged journey as KCIA Chief Kim decides that 'tonight is the night' to kill the president—ostensibly in the name of 'democracy'. We follow KCIA Chief Agent Ju (played by Han Suk-gyu) and another KCIA operative, Colonel Min (played by Kim Eung-soo), as they collude to carry out the killing at a private dinner. A bloody gun battle ensues between Park's bodyguards and the rebel agents after Director Kim shoots the president, splattering his blood across the dinner table. Following the assassination, chaos breaks out among the Korean military as senior officers jockey for position and attempt to maintain civil order. The film offers a sardonic yet indirect portrait of Park Chung Hee, who significantly remains nameless throughout the film and is often simply referred to—with massive irony—as 'the highly respectable one' (*gakha*).

With its excessive portrayal of violence and frequent use of vulgar language, Im's film depicts a 'dirty old man' who sent students, pro-democracy leaders, and other alleged communist sympathizers to be brutalized and humiliated in the KCIA's torture cells. In *The President's Last Bang* Im ventured into highly provocative and uncharted waters, with full knowledge that he was broaching what had hitherto been a taboo subject. It might be thought that a developed country with a maturing democracy, in which censorship was longer an issue, would have encouraged such exercises in self-examination—or at least would have the confidence and self-reflexive skills to face up to critical, albeit painful, portrayals of its recent history.

Nevertheless, on 31 January, 2005, only three days before the film's scheduled public release, the Seoul Central Court ruled that parts of the film be cut. This decision was prompted by litigation by Park Ji-man, the son of the late President Park, who attempted to get the film banned by arguing that the inclusion in the opening and closing credits of stills and footage of protest marches and of his father's funeral ceremony blurred the boundaries between fact and fiction. Im and MK Pictures immediately appealed the court's ruling. Although the court stated that the film was a fictional treatment that audiences would interpret as a creative work, Park Ji-man was successful, at least initially, in getting the film censored. Im and MK Pictures (producers Shim, Lee, Shin, and Kang) were left with two legal options: either cut scenes from the film or to pay $30,000 USD in fines each time the original version was commercially screened in cinemas or on television. The filmmakers chose the first option and deleted scenes containing documentary footage. To put the matter plainly, the court feared that the film would violate the privacy—and privilege—of the Park family. Im Sang-soo's deconstruction of the mythical aura surrounding President Park was perceived as audacious and even insulting, given the high profile enjoyed by Park's daughter Park Geun-hye as chairwoman of the center-right opposition party (and, as of 2013, president of Korea).[19]

The damage done by the court case was minor compared to the new hurdle that MK Pictures was confronted with in January 2005 when its domestic and international distributor (and co-investor) CJ Entertainment abruptly withdrew its distribution arrangements through its CGV cinemas as a result of the court case and the controversy surrounding the film. As a result, when *The President's Last Bang* was eventually released (during the Lunar New Year holiday season), it attracted smaller audiences than expected both in Korea and overseas, although the sensation surrounding the court case and its dark portrayal of Park Chung Hee had lent the film a degree of notoriety at home. Its poor box office performance was partly the result of restricted screenings in smaller multiplex cinemas not affiliated to CGV. It was released on around 190 screens with 31,000 seats, only half as many screens as the top five domestic films released in the same year (keeping in mind that the total number of screens in 2005 was 1,648). By comparison, *Another Public Enemy* (2005) opened on 370 screens (with 85,000 seats) and *Marathon* (2005) on roughly 300 screens (with 66,000 seats), while *King and the Clown* (2005)—made on a budget of $4 million USD like *The President's Last Bang* but co-distributed by Cinema Service and CJ Entertainment—eventually sold more than 10 million tickets, becoming the kind of commercial success known in the industry as a *cheonman yeonghwa* or "10 million audience film", which is discussed in greater detail in Chapter 10.[20] In short, the 10-million audience mark has become a key indicator for Korean cinema's expansion and vitality.

As a result of these constraints, *The President's Last Bang* failed to attract large numbers of cinemagoers in their 20s and 30s—the prime target audience for new releases in Korea. In addition to being influenced by the negative hype surrounding the film, audiences may have failed to identify with the story, or even comprehend why President Park had been assassinated, an understandable response given the lack of open discussion of this troubled period in the nation's recent history.[21]

In a counter-protest against Park Ji-man's legal actions, the filmmakers appealed the Seoul Central Court's 2005 decision and Park's efforts to discredit the film. In August 2006, MK Pictures was successful in overturning the censorship decision: the appeals court took the side of freedom of expression. Although the deleted documentary footage was restored, the producers were directed to pay Park Ji-man around $106,000 USD for defaming his father's character.[22] The case was finally settled in 2008; Park was required to return the settlement sum to MK Pictures provided that the company add a caption to all film prints stating that *The President's Last Bang* was an imaginative work of fiction.

After selling the majority of their shares in MK Pictures in mid-2007 to Kangwon Networks—a cable company seeking opportunities to expand its activities into production and exhibition—Shim and Lee sought to restore Myung Film's reputation for innovative filmmaking; they acquired it after producing Park Chan-wook's

JSA (2000) and female writer–director Yim Soon-rye's *Waikiki Brothers* (2001). Whilst MK Pictures capitalized on new opportunities in production and distribution, aided by venture capital from Lotte Entertainment, the company now found that it was overburdened by an increasing number of projects, which had multiplied from one or two films per year to eight films per year.[23] The company was expanding faster than expected and was hard put to meet the demands on its resources, especially after the departure of Shim Bo-kyoung. After departing Myung Film in 2005, Shim Bo-kyoung established BK Pictures, building on the marketing and production skills and strategies that she had honed while working at Myung Film. In 2009, MK Pictures produced several notable films directed by women filmmakers, including Park Chan-ok's *Paju* (2009), which is discussed at length in the next chapter.

After *Paju*, Myung Film produced *Cyrano Agency* (2010), *Leafie, A Hen into the Wild* (2011), *Architecture 101* (2011), and *Venus Talk* (2014)—all films notable for exploring familiar subjects in unconventional ways. After drawing a massive 4.1 million viewers to the cinema, *Architecture 101* became the top-grossing domestic melodrama romance in Korean cinema history. *Leafie* was Myung Film's first feature-length animation, achieving unprecedented box office results for a film of its kind, primarily because of its high production values and outstanding story line. In addition, *Leafie* is one of only a handful of feature films officially exported to China and was Korea's first feature-length animation to play on China's growing number of multiplex screens. More recently, Myung Film has produced veteran director Im Kwon-taek's *Hwajang* (2014)—his 102nd film—and Jeju Island-born female director and Korean Academy of Film Arts graduate Boo Ji-young's *Cart* (2014). (The Korean word *hwajang* has the dual meaning of cremation and make-up.) A medium-budget production (generated through crowdfunding), *Cart* tells the story of female supermarket workers who form a union to combat labor exploitation—a scenario reminiscent of Martin Ritt's *Norma Rae* (1979), which portrayed the daily struggle of mill workers and the poor treatment of women in 1970s America. In 2015, Myung Film is actively pursuing the Chinese market with the strategy of remaking its hit Korean films for a whole new (and very large) generation of fans.

Although previous studies have glossed over the longstanding impact of her work in local and international circles, Shim Jae-myung's status as one of Korea's most influential female producers is undeniable. In December 2012, Shim Jae-myung was selected by *The Hollywood Reporter* as one of the world's 'International Power Women: The 12 Execs Making Waves Worldwide', being described as 'The Godmother of Korean Cinema'.[24] And in 2015, Shim was selected by peers and critics alike as the second most powerful member of the Korean film industry. In a survey conducted by *Donga Daily*, more than 30 of Korea's leading film industry professionals awarded Shim second place to CJ E&M, Korea's uncontested global movie conglomerate.[25] Better than anything else, the award illustrated Korea's David-and-Goliath division of producers, with Shim Jae-myung and SME companies like Myung Film on one side and the giant CJ E&M on the other.

Oh Jung-wan is another outstanding female representative of Korea's first generation of film producers in Korean Cinema. She entered the film industry after graduating in sociology from Yonsei University in 1987 (around the time that directors such as Im Sang-soo and Bong Joon-ho were studying there). In 1988 Oh married Shin Chul and joined ShinCine as a founding member after first working in advertising for about a year. Through the leadership and experience provided by the company's CEO and founder Shin Chul, Oh learned vast amounts about producing a film and the inner workings of the newly rationalized industry, including planning and marketing. Oh's first production (with a formal credit) was the socially engaged romantic comedy *Marriage Story* discussed above. In 1997, Oh left ShinCine and became a freelance producer before establishing her own company, BOM Productions, in 1999 (the year in which she and Shin Chul divorced).

After striking out on her own, Oh recruited likeminded creative colleagues and began producing a diverse body of stylish commercial–art films. Within a relatively short period, BOM had earned a reputation as a successful boutique production company after making a series of critically acclaimed and profitable films, beginning with Kim Jee-woon's *Foul King* (2000), followed by Kim's *A Tale of Two Sisters* (2003) and *A Bittersweet Life* (2005), and E J-yong's *Untold Scandal* (2003). (At the time, *Untold Scandal* was one of only three Korean projects to receive support from the Hong Kong Asia Film Financing Forum.) Oh also showed early involvement in international co-productions through her work on the Korea–Japan–Hong Kong omnibus films *Three* (2002) and *Three Extremes* (2004). Not only did these early efforts include box office successes and critically acclaimed films with high production values, but they also boosted the careers of directors Kim Jee-woon, E J-yong, and Hong Sang-soo, who have all been central players in the changing face of Korean cinema. BOM's more recent productions include Hong Sang-soo's *Woman on the Beach* (2006) and *Night and Day* (2007), *You Are My Sunshine* (2005, with Oh as executive producer), the action film *Countdown* (2011), Lee Yoon-ki's *My Dear Enemy* (2008), and *Come Rain, Come Shine* (2011).

The third veteran female producer to be discussed, Kim Mi-hee, also deserves mention. In 1988, after graduating from Danguk University with a BA in Korean language and literature, she began working in the film industry as a copywriter and then a marketer at Hwacheon Films, a production company founded in the early 1970s. She also worked as a film promoter for Dong-A Export Co., which had been active in the industry since the late 1960s. During this time Kim was exposed to the conventional approaches and techniques espoused by Korea's previous generation of film companies. Then, when Kang Woo-seok established Kang Woo-seok Productions in 1993 (renamed Cinema Service in 1995), Kim joined the company as a planning director and worked on three films—*How to Top My Wife* (1994), *Two Cops II* (1996), and *Two Cops III* (1998)—under the mentorship of Kang Woo-seok.

In 1998 Kim Mi-hee founded her own production company, FnH Pictures (short for Fun and Happiness), with director Kim Sang-jin (of *Two Cops III*); her company soon became linked with Cinema Service and Kang Woo-seok's strategy for filling the gap created by the withdrawal of the *chaebols* from the local industry. FnH's first film (which Cinema Service distributed) was *Attack the Gas Station!* (1999)—a seminal genre-bending film that showcased the talents of up-and-coming stars Lee Sung-jae, Yoo Oh-sung, Kang Seong-jin, and Yu Ji-tae and attracted global attention to Korean cinema. Kim also produced the erotic drama and debut feature film *Ardor* (2002) made by well-known female documentary filmmaker Byun Young-joo, which grossed over $2 million USD in Korean cinemas. She also dabbled in action films including the urban martial arts drama *Arahan* (2004) and the historical detective film *Bloody Rain* (2005), thereby enlarging the scope of domestic genre films and expanding her company at the same time. At the end of 2005, during a peak in the fortunes of the industry for which Kim was owed much of the credit, FnH merged with industry heavyweight Sidus, owned by Cha Seung-jae, and the new Sidus FnH company was promptly listed on the Korean stock exchange.

This period coincided with the entry of Korean wireless and mobile telecommunication companies into the film industry and the new funding sources they brought with them. In 2005, as Korea's wired/wireless telecommunications and high-speed Internet giants such as Korea Telecom (KT) and SK Telecom (SKT) were commercializing Digital Multimedia Broadcasting (aka DMB), they jockeyed to underwrite the production of new media contents and acquire existing media archives (TV programs and movies) for their DMB channels. While SK Telecom acquired iHQ, investment from KT led to the merger of Sidus and FnH and the purchase of the new company, Sidus FnH, by KT. Despite the new owners' intentions to create an effective synergistic organization (comparable to Myung Film), Sidus FnH failed to produce the type of box office hits under the executive leadership of KT that Kim and Cha had achieved in their former separate companies.[26] The pair left Sidus FnH in 2009.

Since 2012, Kim has reclaimed her place in the spotlight with her new company Studio Dreamcatcher. The company debuted with *Pacemaker* (2012), a sports drama about an injured runner who overcomes his limitations and transforms himself from a racing team's pacemaker into a marathon contestant in his own right. Although *Pacemaker* failed commercially, Studio Dreamcatcher's second film, *Hide and Seek* (2013), a thriller about an intruder who torments a family in their own home, made a big splash at the local box office, attracting audiences of 5.6 million nationwide. *Hide and Seek* became the top Korean thriller of all time, surpassing the previous record holders *Memories of Murder* (2003, 5.24 million) and *The Chaser* (2008, 5.02 million). With this outstanding success, Kim has reinvigorated not only her own seasoned career, but Korean cinema in general.

Female producer Lee Eugene (aka Lee Yu-jin), the fourth on our list, has also made a significant contribution to the transformation of Korean cinema. Lee and Ahn Soo-hyun (discussed below) are two of the most active members of Korea's so-called second generation of film producers; they received their training in the 1990s at the hands of first-generation producers such as Shim Jae-myung, Oh Jung-wan, and Cha Seung-jae. This younger cohort established production companies in the mid-2000s, going on to create a fresh crop of critically acclaimed and commercially profitable films.

After graduating in education from Ehwa Women's University, Lee worked as a copywriter and then creative director for the major Korean advertising firm Korad (1991 to 1997). In 1998, she joined the film industry where one of her first tasks was to develop the marketing campaign for E J-yong's *An Affair* (1998). Between 2000 and 2005, she worked for BOM Productions under the leadership of Oh Jung-wan, producing films such as E J-yong's *Untold Scandal* (2003, with line producer Cho Neung-yeon) and female writer–director Lee Soo-yeon's *The Uninvited* (2003). She then went on to produce Kim Jee-woon's *A Bittersweet Life* (2005) and Park Jin-pyo's *You Are My Sunshine* (2005). By the end of 2005, high-profile productions such as these had given Lee the experience and confidence she needed to form her own production company, Zip Cinema, which was modeled on international firms such as Working Title Films and Focus Features—well known for their expertise in producing, financing, and distributing groundbreaking films.

To build Zip Cinema into an effective competitor to Myung Film, BOM, and Sidus FnH, Lee recruited a core group of loyal writers, actors, and crew members and produced a steady flow of well-written and well-cast films made on a medium budget. By the end of 2007, Lee had become sufficiently well known for *Variety* magazine to tout her as one of the world's top 10 up-and-coming producers.[27] Zip Cinema's filmography includes Park Jin-pyo's crime thriller *Voice of a Murderer* (2006) and Hur Jin-ho's melodrama *Happiness* (2007); Choi Dong-hoon's choreographed action film *Woochi* (2009, aka *Jeon Woo-chi: The Taoist Wizard* or *Woochi: The Demon Slayer*); and the supernatural action thriller *Haunters* (2010), which added its own powerful punch to the recent boom of Korean horror films, attracting the largest number of advance ticket sales of any domestic film in 2010.[28] More recent films with strong international connections include the romantic comedy *All About My Wife* (2012)—a licensed remake of the 2008 Argentinian hit *A Boyfriend for My Wife*—which generated over 4.5 million admissions and box office takings of $30 million USD; and *Cold Eyes* (2013), a remake of Hong Kong action-adrenaline filmmaker Johnny To's *Eye in the Sky* (2007). The connections forged by Lee with international film financiers, producers, and distributors in 2003—the year that BOM's *Untold Scandal* won co-production support from the Hong Kong Asia Film Financing Forum—have likely contributed to Zip Cinema's ongoing success with its projects in Asia and beyond.

One of Lee's major business coups was the signing in 2007 of a management contract with the Los Angeles-based Creative Artists Agency (CAA), a peak talent agency in the US. As one of the first Korean producers to forge such connections, Lee's move has opened doors for the transnational flow of not only actors, but also technicians and stories across both film industries. In late 2011, the continued success of Zip Cinema attracted investment from the New York and Hong Kong-based investment firm Spackman Group.[29] Following this latest international linkage, two of the company's films, *All About My Wife* and *Cold Eyes*, have benefited from enhanced funding inflows.[30] In 2014 Zip Cinema produced *My Brilliant Life*, based on the bestselling 2011 novel *My Palpitating Life* by Kim Aeran directed by E J-yong (of *Untold Scandal* fame) and co-written by E J-yong and Oh Hyo-jin. *My Brilliant Life* is a drama about a teenage couple (played by

Hallyu stars Song Hye-kyo and Kang Dong-won) whose baby is born with progeria, a rare genetic condition that causes the swift and premature onset of the aging process, beginning in early childhood. As a teenager (trapped in the body of an 80-year-old man), their son attempts to document his parents' love story and their shared family experiences and present his efforts to them as a gift before he dies. On account of its rare theatrical release scheduled for China, as well as Japan and Vietnam in 2015, *My Brilliant Life* already has a significant place in Korean cinema's current wave of expansion into Asia.[31]

Like Lee Eugene, Ahn Soo-hyun (aka An Su-hyeon) began her film career in the mid-1990s. She graduated with a history degree in 1994 from Sungkyunkwan University—the home base of the Jangsangotmae independent film group that flourished in the late 1980s and of which Myung Film co-founder Lee Eun was a member. Following graduation, she worked for ShinCine on the marketing of *The Fox with Nine Tails* (1994) and *Wedding Story II* (1994). After leaving ShinCine in 1997, Ahn completed an MA in media studies at the New School in New York. While in the US, she worked as the production coordinator for director John H. Lee's low-budget neo-cool noir action-crime drama *The Cut Runs Deep* (1999), a film about Korean–American gangsters in Manhattan. Ilshin Investment, which underwrote Kang Je-gyu's *Ginkgo Bed* (1996) and Myung Film's *The Contact* (1997), also produced *The Cut Runs Deep*.

Ahn returned home in 2000—around the time Korean cinema's new wave was breaking—where she worked with director Hur Jin-ho (of *Christmas in August* fame) and executive producer Cha Seung-jae (Sidus) on the award-winning romance drama *One Fine Spring Day* (2001). BOM Productions' Oh Jung-wan then hired Ahn to produce *The Uninvited*, *Three Extremes*, and *You are My Sunshine*, working alongside fellow female producer Lee Eugene (a cousin of Oh Jung-wan's). After a short stint freelance producing films such as *Voice of a Murderer* (2007), produced by Lee Eugene (by now head of Zip Cinema), and director Park Chan-wook's critically acclaimed multi-award-winning horror–thriller drama *Thirst* (2009), Ahn married director–screenwriter Choi Dong-hoon, one of only a handful of Korean directors to have enjoyed an unbroken run of successful genre films.

Choi's box office hits include the action crime film *The Big Swindle* (2004), Sidus FnH's crime comedy *Tazza: The High Rollers* (2006), fantasy martial arts film *Woochi*, and international blockbuster "caper" film *The Thieves* (2012). All these films have performed extremely well in terms of audience numbers: 2.12 million admissions for *The Big Swindle*, 5.68 million for *Tazza: The High Rollers*, 6.13 million for *Woochi*, and around 13 million for *The Thieves*. This latter film, which Choi made with Ahn, was shot on location in Macao, Hong Kong, Seoul, and Busan and was produced by Caper Films, a company founded jointly by Ahn and Choi in 2011. At the time of writing, *The Thieves* has pulled in one of the largest audiences in the history of Korean cinema (12.9 and 13 million), underscoring the value of Ahn's systematized production regime. Caper Films' next blockbuster project *Assassination* (2015), an action thriller set in the 1930s during the Japanese colonial period and telling the story of a group of hitmen who target Japanese collaborators in Seoul and Shanghai, became another 10 million film. As of October 2015, it attracted audiences of more than 12.6 million. The company's track record, as well as the combination of a gripping plot, international cast, and outstanding shooting locations—not to mention the finely honed expertise of the Ahn–Choi production and directing team—helped to set *Assassination*'s new record at the box office.

It is precisely the trend-setting, genre-bending, and audience-pleasing films produced by women such as Shim Jae-myung, Shim Bo-kyoung, Oh Jung-wan, Kim Mi-hee, Lee Eugene, and Ahn Soo-hyun that continue to elevate Korean cinema to ever greater heights. Although space prevents us from discussing all of the female (and male) producers who have made valuable contributions to the Korean film industry, few would dispute that this core group of female producers ranks among the most skilled and visionary members of the domestic film industry and continue to leave their mark on the changing face of cinema in both Korea and the wider world.

Conclusion

In 1984, the Ministry of Culture and Athletics (now the Ministry of Culture, Sports and Tourism) rescinded the PRS, thus opening the industry to new players other than the cartel of government-registered production companies that for years had controlled domestic filmmaking and maintained exclusive rights to import foreign films. New companies such as Lee Jang-ho's Pan Cinema, Hah Myung-joong's HMJ Films, and Lee Doo-yong's Doosung Films rushed into the market and began creating new spaces for commercial expansion. However, scarce production funding and continuing script censorship, as well as limited access to distribution and exhibition channels—yet to be consolidated on a nationwide basis (this was the pre-multiplex era)—restricted the growth and profitability of these new players. Coinciding with this development was a newfound interest in the industry among both family-run Korean conglomerates (*chaebols*) and a new generation of aspiring filmmakers. A flood of Hollywood films and videos, unleashed by the demise of the PRS, threatened the plans of all these parties.

Throughout the 1990s, but increasingly in the latter half of the decade, the *chaebols* began integrating their interests in the entertainment industry vertically across investment, production, and distribution channels, and on an unprecedented scale a new breed of filmmakers was establishing their own small-to-medium production companies, with aspirations to professionalism and diversity. Korea's domestic film industry was reshaped by the energy that flowed from this heady producer mix and also by the near-simultaneous increase in the number of screens, which in turn spawned new directors, stars, and practitioners involved in all aspects of the filmmaking process. Significant improvements in box office reporting procedures and technology, which provided a newfound level of accounting transparency, helped too. A virtuous circle was set in motion that enabled Korean cinema to achieve a renaissance comparable with the Golden Age of the 1960s.

At the time of writing, CJ E&M, Showbox, Lotte Cinema, and N.E.W. are the "big four" corporate players in the industry. Amongst them, CJ E&M and Lotte Entertainment have expanded vertically across all aspects of the film business, exhibiting the kind of cost and market-control strategy for which Hollywood studios were well known in the 1930s.[32] While this transformation of the economic basis of the industry has generated the regularized cash flows needed to sustain continuous production regimes, it has also caused major problems as a result of the monopolization of the market by CJ E&M and Lotte Entertainment. Nonetheless, a 2008 KOFIC directory, *Who's Who in Korean Film Industry: Producers and Investors*, presents biographical data and brief interviews with 47 other major players who have contributed to the so-called renaissance of the Korean cinema beginning in the late 1990s. Not all of the films made by this talented group of producers have been commercial successes, and their combined capacity was undermined by the recession that hit the industry in 2006—largely the result of illegal downloading and piracy and the subsequent erosion of ancillary markets, coupled with a succession of box office failures that contributed to the loss of international pre-sales and a decline in investor confidence. In addition, several of these smaller producers were hit hard by their decision to list their companies on the stock market through backdoor means. Yet, as this chapter discusses, a core group of female producers has not only challenged the hegemony of these larger firms (and their male colleagues), but its members have also developed tested methods of working with them with the aim of improving the creative content of domestic films.

On the surface, the inclusion of only 11 women in *Who's Who in Korean Film Industry: Producers and Investors* (2008, published by KOFIC and made available on its extensive website) suggests that women have played limited roles in the fundamental transformation of the film industry since the late 1980s and increasingly throughout the 1990s and 2000s. However, nothing could be further from the truth: for some time now, the female producers discussed in this chapter, not to mention women working behind the camera and in other roles, have equaled if not outstripped their male colleagues. According to recent industry statistics, women outnumber men working full-time in film importing, as well as public relations and marketing, and also outnumber their male colleagues in part-time and contracted positions in production planning and producing, film importing, distribution, public relations, and marketing, as well as the exhibition side of the industry.[33] This is not to argue that the contributions made by male and female producers to the transformation of the industry have fallen along gender lines, although female producers are often described (at least when it comes to the making of modest-budget commercial and independent films) as being more detail-orientated, more patient, and better communicators than their male colleagues. More to the point—and despite the continued relative neglect of their contributions—by producing arthouse successes as well as mainstream commercial hits, women producers have remained at the core of the domestic industry, often showing a willingness to work with new directors because they believe in them and their stories rather than solely in their potential commercial success. Their energy, vision, and dedication to exploring fresh stories and developing new talent have drawn local and global audiences alike to a constantly innovating national cinema that continues to expand along transnational lines.

Notes

1. One important but brief study is: Kim, Mee-hyun. "Trends in the Structure of the Korean Film Industry". In *Korean Cinema: From Origins to Renaissance*, edited by Mee-hyun Kim, 413–19. 2007. Communication Books, Seoul. 2007.
2. Other smaller *chaebols* that became involved in the film industry in the 1980s included Byucksan, Haitai, Hanbo, SKC, Saehan, and Jinro—all seeking to profit from licensing Hollywood movies for Korea's insatiable videotape market.
3. "US Videotape Distributors Turn their Eyes to Korean Market" (Mi Yeonghwa Teipeusa Hanguk Nundok). *Maeil Gyeongje* (23 August, 1988): 7.
4. See "Large Corporates Entering Media Industry" (Daegieop Yeongsang Saneop Jinchul Baram). *Donga Daily* 3 August: 11; and "Large Corporates Enter the Film Industry – Benefit or Malaise?" (Daegieop Yeonghwagye Jinchul Myoyaginga Dogyaginga). *The Hankyoreh* 26 June, 1993: 9.
5. "Different Views on Long-term Box Office Hits Marriage Story and Mister Mamma" (Janggi Heunghaeng Gyeolhon Iyagi Miseuteo Mamma Ssago Eotgallin Sido). *The Hankyoreh* (24 October, 1992): 9.
6. "Marriage Story" (Gyeolhon Iyagi). *Gyeonghyang Shinmun* (2 July, 1992): 13.
7. "Little Fish Shiri Sank the Titanic" (Jageun Mulgogi 'Shiri' ga Taitanikho Chimmolsikida). *Donga Daily* (9 April, 1999): 21. Shiri is the name of a small fish found in the Han River around the DMZ.
8. The leading figures in Samsung and Daewoo's entertainment divisions—people who later became key drivers during the industry's expansion period—included Choi Geon-yong (former executive director of Lotte Entertainment), Seo Byung-moon (former director of KOCCA), Choi Wan (CEO of IM Pictures), and Kim Ju-seong (former CEO of CJ Entertainment).
9. In 1964, Kwak had established Hapdong Film, and he rapidly amassed the personal connections and financial strength to become a leading member of the local production cartel. During the 1970s and 1980s, he directed several films including *Oh, Frailty* (1972) and *I Want to Go* (1984), moving into the exhibition business after acquiring the Seoul Cinema in the Jongno District—the (literal) center of cinema in Seoul until the large-scale roll-out of multiplexes in the late 1990s.
10. Elley, Derek. "Review: 'Sophie's Revenge'". *Variety* (26 October, 2009). Available: http://variety.com/2009/film/reviews/sophie-s-revenge-1200476676/. Accessed on 12 December 2014.
11. Bingbin, Han. "A Touch of Seoul in Chinese Films". *China Daily USA* (11 December, 2014). Available: http://usa.chinadaily.com.cn/epaper/2014-12/11/content_19066937.htm. Accessed on 11 January 2015.
12. By the beginning of February 2015, the film had gained about 364 million yuan (attracting 11.5 million viewers) at the box office. See Hendriks, Priscilla. "'20, Once Again!' Tops Charts". *On Screen Asia* (11 February, 2015). Available: http://www.onscreenasia.com/article/20-once-again-tops-charts/16657. Accessed 1 June 2015.
13. *Leafie* received international acclaim after winning the Best Sitges Family Film Diploma at the 2011 Sitges Film Festival in Spain, and Best Animated Feature Film at the 2011 Asia Pacific Film Award in Australia.
14. Baek, Eun-ha. "Interview: Shim Jae-Myung 'Lucky to Learn About Lives on the Job'" (Shim Jae-Myung, 'Meokgo Saneun Eobeul Tonghae Sameul Baeundaneun Geon Haengunijyo). *10Asia* (22 July 2010). Available: http://tenasia.hankyung.com/archives/4574. Accessed 16 February 2014.
15. Alford, Christopher. "Eun Lee and Jae-Myung Shim". *Variety* (3 May, 2001). Available: http://variety.com/2001/scene/people-news/eun-lee-and-jae-myung-shim-1117798514/. Accessed 17 February 2014.
16. See *Korean Cinema 2004* 2005: 297–99.

17. See Russell, Mark. "Merger activity continues in Korea film biz". *The Hollywood Reporter* 30 January, 2004.
18. See Mun, Seok. "A New Era for Chungmuro—Listing Companies on the Stock Market (Chungmuro Sangjangsidae)". *Cine21* (22 February, 2006). Available: http://www.cine21.com/news/view/mag_id/36695. Accessed 16 February 2014.
19. Cho, Y. 2005. "The Controversial Scenes of the Movie Should Be Deleted". *Dong-A Ilbo* (January 31). Available: http://english.donga.com/srv/service.php3?biid=2005020157128&path_dir=20050201. Accessed May 1, 2007. Im had created a sequence that blended real and fictitious archival footage of students and citizens in Pusan and Masan holding violent demonstrations in 1979 (about two weeks before Park's death) against the Park regime, demanding democratization. This grainy black-and-white footage also shows tanks subduing the crowds. At the end of the film, a similar style of cinematography is used to show pro-democracy protestors shedding tears in the streets of Seoul during the state funeral for President Park.
20. *King and the Clown* was released in Korea in late December 2005, and it was exhibited until mid-April 2006. Between May and October 2006, the film was released commercially in Taiwan, Singapore, Canada, and Japan and then in Los Angeles in January 2007.
21. US-based Kino Video/Kino International holds the North American distribution rights to *The President's Last Bang* and has yet to release the restored version of the film. The restored film was re-released in Korea in 2008. In early 2009, UK-based distributor Third Window Films released the restored version on DVD; this contained the four minutes of documentary footage cut from the original film.
22. Paquet, Darcy. 'Bang' original Ok'd. *Variety* (11 August, 2006), http://variety.com/2006/film/news/bang-original-ok-d-1200342240/. Accessed 1 May 2007.
23. Yu, Jae-hyeok. "Shim Jae-Myung, CEO of Myung Film: 'Realistic Portrayal of First Love Shakes up Thirty-something Males'" (Shim Jae-Myung Myung Film Daepyo, 'Gwajang Eobsi Pyohyeonhan Cheotsarang Gamseong 30 Dae Namsim Dwiheundreotjyo). *Hanguk Economics (Hanguk Gyeongje)* (4 May, 2012). Available: http://www.hankyung.com/news/app/newsview.php?. Accessed 16 February 2014.
24. "International Power Women: The 12 Execs Making Waves Worldwide". *The Hollywood Reporter* (6 December, 2012). Available: http://www.hollywoodreporter.com/news/international-power-women-12-execs-398898. Accessed 17 February 2014.
25. Jeong, Yang-hwan. "'Big Hand' Controlling Production as well as Distribution ... Need to Protect Diversity in Film" (Jejakeseo Baegeupkkaji 'Keunson' I Jwau ... Dayangseong Yeonghwa Bohohaeya). *Donga.com* (11 February, 2015). Available: http://news.donga.com/3/all/20150211/69585221/1. Accessed 15 February 2015.
26. While Cha (Sidus) produced such memorable films as *Memories of Murder* (2003) and *Save the Green Planet* (2003), Sidus FnH's little-known filmography (2005–2009) includes *Love Me Not* (2006), *South of the Border* (2006), *Miss Gold Digger* (2007), *Love Exposure* (2007), *Radio Dayz* (2008), *The Accidental Gangster* (2008), *The Sword with No Name* (2009), and *Kiss Me Kill Me* (2009).
27. Paquet, Darcy. "Lee Eugene: 10 Producers to Watch". *Variety* (5 September, 2007). Available: http://variety.com/2007/scene/people-news/lee-eugene-1117971414/. Accessed 17 February 2014.
28. Kim, Heidi. "Haunters sees highest advance tickets sales for 2010". *10Asia* (11 November, 2010). Available: www.asiae.co.kr/news/view.htm?idxno=2010111109505165789. Accessed 3 December 2014.
29. See Noh, Jean. "Korea's Opus, Zip secure investment from Spackman Group". *Screen Daily* 7 August 2012; and "Spackman Equities Group Reports Year End Results". *marketwired.com* (1 May 2013). Available: http://www.marketwired.com/press-release/spackman-equities-group-reports-year-end-results-tsx-venture-sqg-1785020.htm. Accessed 17 February 2014.

30. According to KOFIC, *All About My Wife* (2012) and *Cold Eyes* (2013) attracted audiences of 4.6 million and 5.5 million, respectively.
31. Frater, Patrick. "Korean Drama 'My Brilliant Life' Sells to China, Japan". *Variety* (5 November, 2014). Available: http://variety.com/2014/film/news/korean-drama-my-brilliant-life-sells-to-china-japan-1201348012/. Accessed 6 December 2014.
32. Gomery 1986: 84–85. In the 1940s, the US government prohibited the film companies from maintaining monopolies of both production studios and the ownership of theaters, thus curtailing attempts at vertical integration. In Korea, since the early 1990s successive governments have done little to impede or regulate the practice of vertical integration in the film industry.
33. Ministry of Culture, Sports and Tourism and KOCCA. 2014. *2013 Content Industry Statistics* (2013 Kontent Saneop Tonggye). Ministry of Culture, Sports and Tourism and KOCCA, Seoul.

9 The Rise of the Female Writer–Director and the Changing Face of Korean Cinema

This chapter casts the spotlight on six comparatively neglected female writer–directors with a view to illuminating the diversity of this aspect of the nation's filmmaking tradition contributing to a Golden Age of Korean cinema since 1996—the year that the South Korean Constitutional Court declared film censorship to be illegal under Korea's first civilian president, Kim Young-sam. By the early 2000s, high-quality films made by (predominantly male) writer–directors including Lee Chang-dong, Kim Ki-duk, Im Sang-soo, Bong Joon-ho, Park Chan-wook, Hong Sang-soo, and Kim Jee-woon were succeeding in the export market and at major film festivals, showcasing these accomplished filmmakers for international audiences. Despite the attention bestowed on this group of male "commercial auteurs", a number of films made by talented women writer–directors have also made a strong contribution to Korea's contemporary cinema renaissance.

Among the small but growing cohort of both independent and commercial female writer–directors in Korea, the names Lee Jeong-hyang, Byun Young-joo, Park Chan-ok, Lee Soo-yeon, Hong Ji-young, and Roh Deok stand out. All six women undertook formal film studies at different times in their lives, with most entering the field after studying an unrelated discipline such as education, sociology, or law—a common pattern among the first generation of filmmakers in the post-1996 censorship era. Enrolling in a formal film program equipped them with the rudiments of storytelling and the language of film—skills that each used while making short films or documentaries before trying her hand at feature films. Studying at tertiary institutions such as KAFA KNUA, Chung-Ang University, or Dongguk University also enabled these women to develop the personal networks that have helped to shape their diverse approaches to their craft. Yet, despite this circuitous pathway into the industry, their early experiences helped them to develop a mature view of the world. Their considered views of Korean society, and life in general, are reflected in the stories—both original and adapted from existing sources—that they write for the screen. The distinctive perspectives that they developed in their early careers are exemplified in such films as *A Reason to Live* (2011), *Helpless* (2012), *Paju* (2002), *The Uninvited* (2003), *The Naked Kitchen* (2009), and *Very Ordinary Couple* (2012), which between them embrace a wide range of genres.

It is a mark of contemporary Korean cinema that directors—rookies and veterans alike—tend to write or adapt their own screenplays, whether for commercial or independent and arthouse films. Undoubtedly, this has been one of the most effective ways for novice directors to make their mark—provided they have a good screenplay to sell to a producer and potential investors. In taking this approach, many Korean directors have been able to cultivate a sophisticated auteurial style characterized by an innovative narrative and visual aesthetic that expresses a distinctive vision of contemporary society. The six female writer–directors to be considered in this chapter have each made significant contributions to this unfolding process. Each has contributed linkages that bridge mainstream commercial films and self-conscious arthouse productions in her own special way, thus adding some unique contributions to the changing face of Korean cinema.

An Historical Legacy

Female filmmakers in Korea today owe a good deal to the small cohort of women filmmakers who preceded them. As a few previous studies have indicated,[1] these links have been kept alive through two channels in particular: the Seoul International Women's Film Festival (hereafter SIWFF) and the Women in Film Korea group. Both have sought to honor the nation's female film pioneers by unearthing and celebrating their forgotten history.

Since its launch in 1997, SIWFF has provided both practitioners and enthusiasts with an unrivalled space for networking and developing meaningful connections across multiple generations of filmmakers. The opening film of the inaugural festival was *The Widow* (1955), the story of a war widow's attempt to survive in the grim social environment created by the Korean War. Made by Park Nam-ok, one of Korea's very first female directors, *The Widow*'s festival screening showcased the rare and forgotten work of a filmmaker struggling with her own survival in a male-dominated industry, as well as an intensely patriarchal postwar society. As far as we know, the 1997 festival screening was the first time the film had been exhibited in public since its release in 1955; the Korean Film Archive restored the original 16mm negative print (which lacks sound for the final 10 minutes). To celebrate SIWFF's ten-year anniversary in 2008, and to strengthen ties between the various generations of women filmmakers, festival organizers established the Park Nam-ok Award, naming its first recipient as contemporary director Yim Soon-rye. Senior director and actress Choi Eun-hee—aka Choe Eun-hui and wife of Shin Sang-ok—presented the honor to Yim at a glittering ceremony. In 2014, *The Widow* was placed eighth in a list of the top 100 Korean films by the Korean Film Archive, cementing its importance in the nation's film history.

Women in Film Korea (hereafter WIFK) was established in 2000 by a group of active female filmmakers who were concerned about establishing stronger networks and comprehensive training for women in the film industry.[2] Chae Yoon-hee, president and CEO of the film marketing company All That Cinema; Professor Joo Jinsook of Chung-Ang University's film studies program; Shim Jae-myung, founder of Myung Film; and director Yim Soon-rye (aka Lim/Im

Soon-rye) were all instrumental in setting up the group. WIFK also aims to protect the rights and interests of female film workers and to help young women enter the industry. Since 2000, WIFK has pursued these various goals through its annual Women in Film Korea Festival, which celebrates the achievements of women filmmakers and facilitates networking opportunities. The inaugural WIFK festival opened with actress and director Choi Eun-hee's *The Girl Raised as a Future Daughter-in-law* (1965), a film until then thought to be lost but recovered from the vaults of the Korean Film Archive. (Many years later, Choi was invited to add dialogue to parts of the film that were lacking sound.[3]) Also displayed at the event were rare archival materials relating to director Park Nam-ok and Kim Young-hee, a film editor at the state-run Chosun Film Company in the 1940s, as well as other prominent women in film such as actresses Han Eun-jin (*Red Scarf* (1963), *Flame in the Valley* (1967), and *Eunuch* (1968)) and Hwang Jeong-soon (*Romance Grey* (1963), *Seaside Village* (1965), and *Confession of an Actress* (1967)).

Thanks in part to activities sponsored by WIFK, the status of women in Korean cinema was given a tangible boost in the new millennium. Aiming to raise awareness of the issues facing female practitioners and to give women a voice of their own, the group has spearheaded real change by mobilizing both men and women to take individual responsibility for their own actions as a way of improving their working conditions. Through ongoing workshops, training opportunities, and annual formal and informal gatherings, WIFK has encouraged and enabled a new generation of women to enter various sectors of the local industry, including lighting, stunt choreography, cinematography and camera assist, audio recording, post-production, and visual effects—all areas in which women were under-represented.

Through these organizations, the older generation of female filmmakers, such as those discussed below, who worked their way up the ladder without formal training, have joined forces with their younger colleagues, thus ensuring that their important legacy to Korean cinema will not be squandered.[4]

Both SIWFF and WIFK have become vital supports for women working in all sectors of the local film industry. While forging connections across generations is always of value, these two organizations have inspired real change by uniting individuals who have been facing their own challenges in seeking advancement in a male-dominated industry operating within a patriarchal culture. These challenges are part of a wider set of barriers caused by gender prejudice and limited opportunities for women across many sectors of the global film industry. According to a 2014 study of women filmmakers in the US, the leading career obstacles include: gendered financial barriers, male-dominated industry networks, and gender stereotyping of work tasks across the industry.[5] With these hurdles in mind, it is unsurprising that even in the 2010s the reality of working in the film industry is difficult for women filmmakers in most if not all countries. Be that as it may, in 1950s Korea, women film workers would have faced more difficult challenges and obstacles than filmmakers today can imagine—especially given that there were only a tiny handful of female directors working in Korea before the cinematic renaissance of the mid- to late-1990s.

In March 1955, Korean audiences saw what is believed to be the first domestic film directed by a woman: *The Widow*, directed by Park Nam-ok (1923–). In the film, a widow and her little daughter are shown struggling to live as refugees in the aftermath of the Korean War. The widow's struggle to come to terms with her own desire through her search for a lover is one of the primary themes driving the narrative. While this may sound like the story line of a conventional tear-jerking melodrama, the most popular film genre of the time, the film controversially depicts a female protagonist pursuing her own happiness rather than sacrificing herself for the family unit. This understanding of female agency was outside the Confucian mold and highly unconventional for its time. The widow at the center of the story, Lee Shin-ja (played by Lee Min-ja), ends up cohabiting with a younger man. In order to maximize the freedom of their blossoming relationship, Lee sends her daughter to live with an acquaintance, an act that clearly flew in the face of traditional family values.

Aged 32 when *The Widow* was released, director Park was relatively young for someone in her position. Moreover, in order to complete the film, Park took on a number of additional roles, including editor and executive producer as well as fundraiser; the funding she gained from family members (her husband and sister) led to the formation of Jamae Film Co. (aka Sisters Film Co.). Like many of her contemporaries, Park grew up on a steady diet of Hollywood films (until they were banned in the late 1930s) and the Japanese–Korean propaganda pictures exhibited during the colonial period (1910–1945), followed by a renewed flow of Hollywood releases and a smattering of Korean films made in the post-liberation period. Although she was inspired by both local and international productions to make her own films, her dreams were curtailed after making *The Widow*, her only film.

After a short stint with the Daegu News Agency, Park joined the Chosun Film Company immediately following Korea's liberation from Japan in late 1945, learning film editing and script supervision on the job and networking with established practitioners such as actress Kim Shin-jae and director Choi In-gyu. She gained additional experience during the Korean War as part of a film crew with the Ministry of National Defense, shooting war documentaries and newsreels. During this time Park met her husband Lee Bo-ra, who supported her career aspirations and went on to write the script for *The Widow*.[6]

According to a newspaper interview published in 1982, Park shot *The Widow* in the middle of winter 1954 with the aid of around 30 crewmembers, while carrying an infant on her back—she had given birth in June. Industry contacts including director Jeon Chang-geun, actress Lee Min-ja (the heroine of *The Widow*), and fellow woman director Hong Eun-won, whose story is told below, played an essential part in completing the film, enabling her to overcome financial and technical difficulties.[7] The film was advertised with the tagline 'Korea's First Female Director' (see Figure 9.1), and received a positive response from the critics in terms of its shooting technique, music, and sound effects.[8]

Figure 9.1 Film advertisement for *The Widow* (1955). *Gyeonghyang Shinmun* 12 March, 1955: 4.

However, despite the support she received from many quarters, *The Widow* was a commercial failure, and Park's directing career was brought to an abrupt end. Nonetheless, Park's breakthrough in a male-dominated industry inspired other women, albeit in small numbers, to follow her lead. Learning that *The Widow* had been selected as the opening film of the inaugural Women's Film Festival in Seoul, Park (who was living in Los Angeles at the time), conscious of the complex issues surrounding its production and failure at the box office, and the demise of her filmmaking dreams, expressed a mix of excitement and sadness at the film's rediscovery and revival.[9]

Park's colleague Hong Eun-won is a second notable figure from the first generation of woman directors. Over a 15-year period, before her debut as a director, she developed a career as a script supervisor and assistant director working for leading directors Choi In-gyu, Lee Kang-cheon, and Yu Du-yeon. Her first job as assistant director was on the set of *An Innocent Criminal* (1948), directed by Choi In-gyu. After assisting on 10 films, Hong made her directorial debut with the social melodrama *A Woman Judge* (1962), a story about a female judge trying to balance the demands of work and family life. At the time of its release, Hong made it clear that she was interested in making films that depicted the lives of women, but seen through a woman's eyes rather than imagined by male writers and directors.[10] In taking this approach, Hong was boldly challenging the monopoly held by male directors who churned out the endless stream of tearjerkers that characterized Korea's "Golden Age of melodrama" in the 1950s and 1960s. Hong's next two melodramas, *A Single Mom* (1964) and *What Misunderstanding Left Behind* (1966), followed the same lines as *A Woman Judge*: telling women's stories from a woman's perspective. Despite (or perhaps because of) her subversive intentions, however, the films that she directed received little attention from audiences, pushing Hong toward screenwriting as an alternative to directing. Little is known about her later career; she wrote three screenplays after 1966 (the last of which, *Night of Tokyo*, was written in 1970), and then her trail goes cold.[11]

The Rise of the Female Writer–Director   187

The third female director of the older generation to be considered here is Choi Eun-hee, actress and life-long partner of director Shin Sang-ok. In addition to appearing in around 122 films—many of which were directed by Shin—Choi directed a total of three films, the first two of which were produced by Shin Film. According to Choi's memoirs, she ventured into directing at the suggestion of her husband, legendary producer–director Shin Sang-ok.[12] Such powerful backing immediately gave her an advantage over female colleagues such as Park Nam-ok and Hong Eun-won. With Shin's support, she debuted with *The Girl Raised as a Future Daughter-in-law* (1965), an exploration of the Korean tradition of a family "adopting" a girl at an early age and training her to become a domestic worker and their son's wife, in which she also starred. Newspaper advertisements for the film highlighted Choi's reputation as an actress and her high-profile marriage to Shin Sang-ok, rather than her directorial talent (see Figure 9.2). For this film, Choi received the Best Actress Award from the Grand Bell Awards, and the film was later accepted for the 10th San Francisco Film Festival.

Figure 9.2 Film advertisement for *The Girl Raised as a Future Daughter-in-law* (1965). *Gyeonghyang Shinmun* 8 September, 1965: 5.

The second film that Choi made as a director is *One-sided Love of Passion* (1967), a romantic historical drama about the love of a princess for a nobleman. Third, and finally, Choi directed *An Unmarried Teacher* (1972), an "enlightenment" film produced by the Saehan Film Co. The film tells the story of a young male teacher, newly appointed to a high school position, who struggles to provide moral leadership to a class of girls. Given her privileged background, it is fair to say that Choi's directing abilities were overshadowed by her role as a star actress and her position as the wife of a celebrated director; her films disappeared from the public consciousness as rapidly as they had surfaced in the local entertainment news pages.

A striking contrast to Choi was the career of writer–director–producer Hwang Hye-mi, a female filmmaker of exceptional ability. A Seoul National University graduate, Hwang majored in French language and literature. She joined the film industry in 1967 as a producer for director Kim Su-yong's *The Mist* (1967), an award-winning "literary" film in a modernist mold (discussed in Chapter 3). At the time, Hwang was an independent producer under contract with Taechang Heungeop and was often singled out for her ability as a producer and, rather patronizingly, for being "the only girl in the film community".[13] After producing another literary film, *Potato* (1968), directed by Kim Seung-ok—a novelist primarily known for *The Mujin Travelogue*, on which *The Mist* was based—Hwang established her own production company, Bohan Industry Co. With the support of her husband, businessman Kim Dong-su, Hwang became a full-fledged producer–director.

At the time, the professional support offered her by Kim was exceptional, as the idea of a "working wife" was largely alien to traditional norms. Not that this move was planned: for her next project, Hwang stumbled into the role of producer–director after failing to find a suitable person to direct her screenplay *First Experience* (after submitting it to several directors for their consideration). Eager to avoid making the major changes to the story that various (male) directors had suggested, Hwang decided to direct the film herself.[14] She might have approached a female director to direct her film(s) had there been more women working in the industry at the time—in the same way that contemporary women producers such as Shim (discussed in Chapter 8) began employing female directors at the beginning of the 2000s. Despite the difficulties involved, Hwang made three melodramas during her brief career as a director: *First Experience* (1970), *When Flowers Sadly Fade Away* (1971), and *Relationship* (1972).

As her debut film as a writer–director, *First Experience* received positive reviews in the press, which acknowledged her success in tailoring this melodrama to female audiences and using fluid cinematography to create a subtle but distinctive emotional tone.[15] The film depicts a romance between a married man and a younger single woman, for whom this is her first love affair. By depicting their relationship from the woman's perspective, Hwang made the film unique for its time. In addition to writing, directing, and producing these three films in the early 1970s, Hwang composed their original scores, thus showing a level of versatility and creativity virtually unparalleled in the filmmaking community.

Despite her proven abilities, however, these intimate melodramas failed to attract large audiences and thus discouraged Hwang's investors from giving her backing for future projects—a key driver that continues to shape investor confidence and choice today. Besides, in the early 1970s the industry was spiraling downhill in terms of the number of annual productions, box office profits, and audience numbers—all under threat from the rapidly expanding diffusion of television. For the most part, the film industry was subsisting on a host of erotic "hostess" films (a subgenre of the melodrama) and national policy productions including anticommunist and literary films. While Hwang was clearly ahead of her time, and a pioneer for both her own and the next generation of filmmakers, not even the most seasoned directors and producers could have withstood the pressures created by the major downturn experienced by the industry at this time.

Throughout the 1980s, as the industry began to recover from the "dark age" of the 1970s, and as a group of male directors including Lee Jang-ho, Bae Chang-ho, and Im Kwon-taek began to make a name for themselves, one female director stood out above her peers: Lee Mi-rye. Following a well-trodden path, Lee majored in film and theater at Dongguk University and then worked as an assistant director and script supervisor on 17 films, including Yu Hyun-mok's *Rainy Season* (1979) and *Son of a Man* (1980), Jeong So-yeong's *The Carriage Running into the Winter* (1980), and Kim ho-seon's *Three Times Each for Short and Long Ways* (1981). Lee made her own directorial debut with *My Daughter Rescued from the Swamp* (1984), which she followed with *Cabbage in a Pepper Field* (1985), *Forget-me-nots* (1987), *School Days* (1987), *Young-Shim* (1990), and *This Is the Beginning of Love* (1990).

During this period, the number of female Korean feature film directors could still be counted on the fingers of one hand. In 1984, Lee was asked in a newspaper interview to describe the new pathway that she was forging in a male-dominated industry. She replied that she was unaware of any gender discrimination toward her and that her long experience of practical filmmaking standards and skills had given her confidence to be a leader and decision-maker on the set, although this came with a huge responsibility.[16] The leadership role Lee had assumed was a burden not because she was a woman, but because large productions demanded considerable management skills. Unlike the films made by Park Nam-ok, Choi Eun-hee, and Hong Eun-won, Lee's *My Daughter Rescued from the Swamp* was commercially successful, becoming the number five box office hit amongst domestic films of the year—a year in which Hollywood blockbusters such as *Beverly Hills Cop*, *Ghostbusters*, *Indiana Jones and the Temple of Doom*, *Gremlins*, *The Karate Kid*, *Romancing the Stone*, and *Star Trek III: The Search for Spock* drew large audiences to Korean cinemas and to these and other titles on videotape.

In 1986, during the shooting of her third film, Lee gave a further newspaper interview. This time she emphasized the importance of a director providing a creative space for actors to practice their craft, rather than laying down strict rules for the whole crew to follow—a way of working traditionally associated with male directors. For Lee, directing was precisely about developing and maintaining harmony with and among her entire crew, as if everyone on set was an integral part of an orchestra that she was conducting.[17] In these ways, Lee's approach to directing distinguished her from her male colleagues and also shares a good deal with the views expressed by younger female directors today. In fact, Lee's perspectives are broadly shared by all of the women filmmakers that we interviewed for this book and as expressed in their published media interviews.

None of these five women from Korea's first generation of female filmmakers—Park Nam-ok, Choi Eun-hee, Hong Eun-won, Hwang Hye-mi, and Lee Mi-rye—had the opportunity to join an organization such as WIFK. Yet, each has made a lasting impression on all the members of this group and many other filmmakers in all sectors of the domestic film industry. In fact, all five have received the association's highest honor, the Contribution Award, for their dedication to filmmaking, undeterred by the obstacles in their path. (In 2015, Park lives in Los Angeles, while Choi Eun-hi and Lee Mi-rye remain in contact with WIFK.) Today, these five filmmakers are honored among Korean cinema's pioneers, not only for what they achieved, but for the fact that they were able to succeed in a male-dominated industry.

While the contemporary female writer–directors discussed below owe much to these trail-blazing figures, their career trajectories have all followed very different paths.

The Next Generation of Women Filmmakers

As we saw in Chapter 8, in the early 1990s a new generation of producers began changing the fundamental environment of the industry, including workflow practices. Small-to-medium sized companies such as ShinCine and Myung Film, as well as conglomerate Samsung's subsidiary, Samsung Entertainment, created new opportunities for a new generation of female directors to practice their craft.

Female writer–director Yim Soon-rye, who entered the industry shortly after Lee Mi-rye, was one of the first contemporary filmmakers to make a name for herself in this new environment. In 1994 Yim received the Grand Prize at the inaugural Seoul Short Film Festival (sponsored by Samsung Entertainment) for her film *Walking in the Rain* (1994), a piece exploring a day in the mundane life of a ticket attendant at a third-run cinema on the outskirts of Seoul. Yim's talent was acknowledged again in 1996 after her script for *Three Friends* was selected by Samsung Entertainment as the company's first independent film production project. With the company behind her, Yim finished the script and proceeded to direct *Three Friends* (1996) as her debut feature film. It received the NETPAC film award at the first Busan International Film Festival in 1996 and was invited to a number of high-profile international film festivals including Berlin, Vancouver, Seattle, Melbourne, and Karlovy Vary. Since then, Yim has worked closely with Shim Jae-myung (of Myung Film) on two major projects: *Waikiki Brothers* (2001), which she both wrote and directed, and the sports drama *Forever the Moment* (2008).

Waikiki Brothers is a reflective drama following the lives of three high school friends and their band as they meander their way through the 1980s. Interviewed following its release, Yim noted that women had now carved out a legitimate space in which to become directors without having to drink excessively, strike macho poses, and swear incessantly—all stereotypical traits of Korean directors over the past several decades.[18] Her third feature, *Forever the Moment*, was a surprise box office success that became the fifth top performing domestic film of 2008, gaining her the Best Film Award at the Blue Dragon Film Award and the

Baeksang Arts Awards, the Korean equivalent of the Emmy Awards. With this film, Yim was finally recognized as a "commercial" filmmaker in her own right, with an expanding filmography and audience—a status that Yim deeply appreciated.[19] *Forever the Moment* is a sports film inspired by the Korean women's handball team and their winning of the silver medal at the 2004 Athens Olympics. Yim and producer Shim Jae-myung used the Olympics as the backdrop for a social commentary on the lives of female athletes and the daily challenges facing them as wives, mothers, and daughters, as well as professional sportswomen. In 2015, Yim's filmography comprises 12 films—including shorts in omnibus films—and her career is expanding into producing.

Following Yim's path, during the early 2000s, as part of an overhaul of the industry led by a new generation of visionary filmmakers (both men and women) dozens of female directors made their debut. At the time this was seen by women filmmakers in particular as an extraordinary development. As a result of the professionalization of the industry in the mid-to-late 1990s, directors could now enjoy the luxury of concentrating solely on their craft, rather than simply adding directing to the long list of managerial roles demanded of them. In step with these changes came an increasing flow of talented female practitioners, including Lee Jeong-hyang, Byun Young-joo, Park Chan-ok, Lee Soo-yeon, Hong Ji-young, and Roh Deok, who sought advanced training in institutions such as KAFA and KNUA.

The first contemporary writer–director to be discussed is Lee Jeong-hyang (1964–), a member of the first generation of women to enter the domestic filmmaking scene in the post-1996 censorship era and an active member of WIFK. Lee is the writer–director of *Art Museum by the Zoo* (1998), *The Way Home* (2002), and most recently, *A Reason to Live* (2011), starring the popular pan-Asian actress Song Hye-kyo. She studied French language and literature at Sogang University in Seoul and entered KAFA in 1988. After working for Lee Jang-ho—a leading male director who made his name in the mid-1970s with a series of erotic melodramas (see Chapter 7)—as an assistant director on *Declaration of Genius* in 1995, Lee made her writer–director debut with the feature film *Art Museum by the Zoo* (1998). One of only 43 domestic films produced in 1998, it was the fifth top domestic film in terms of annual total attendance.

The film, which is semi-autobiographical, portrays the awkward but heartfelt relationship between two strangers who end up living together due to unexpected circumstances and the promise of saving money. As their entry in a filmmaking contest, the couple co-author a romance film script about a woman working at an art museum and a male zookeeper, thus transforming *Art Museum by the Zoo* into a film-within-a-film. This award-winning story, which Lee began writing in 1995 at a time when government censorship was in full swing, includes some serious reflections on contemporary gender relations and the meaning of friendship between a single man and woman who are cohabitating. The film earned numerous prestigious awards, including Best Actress/Actor (for Shim Eun-ha of *Christmas in August* fame, and Lee Sung-jae) at the Grand Bell Awards, and Best New Actor award for Lee Sung-jae at the Blue Dragon Film Awards and the

Baeksang Arts Awards. Today, local and foreign critics alike consider *Art Museum by the Zoo* a post-censorship (i.e., post-1996) Korean cinema classic.

Interviewed in 1998 when *Art Museum by the Zoo* was released, Lee spoke of the "handicaps" that she and other female filmmakers faced in a male-dominated industry. First, the small number of women interested in pursuing a film career had very few role models to follow and often faced discrimination from a core group of aging male film professors whose attitudes were rarely questioned. Thus, for women of her generation, aspiring to become a director (or producer) before the rise of the "new Korean cinema" in the mid-1990s was a near-impossible task. Second, the pressure to return a profit (or at least recoup most of a film's budget) at a period when funding was severely limited made it especially risky for female filmmakers to experiment with arthouse and independent stories and projects.[20]

Lee's second feature, *The Way Home* (2002) is a semi-autobiographical film about her grandmother that underscores the generation gap as well as the social and cultural divide between Korea's urban and rural communities. It was another box office hit, earning her the status of Korean cinema's "most commercially successful" female director.[21] It also made Lee a beacon of hope for makers of low-to-medium budget films (i.e., films made for under $2 million USD) of either gender.

The Way Home explores the relationship between a seven-year-old boy from Seoul and his mute elderly grandmother who lives deep in the countryside. Through their clashing lifestyles and attitudes, and the boy's eventual warming to her and appreciation of her simple and traditional way of life, the film underscores the social and cultural divide between Korea's urban and rural communities. The film reached the number two spot in the year's list of top 10 domestic films in terms of annual total attendance, drawing audiences of over 1.6 million in Seoul alone. Despite the film's apparent lack of commercial appeal—a simple story without star casting, featuring a child actor and an elderly woman with no previous acting experience—*The Way Home* outperformed Hollywood blockbusters *Minority Report* (2002), *The Lord of the Rings: The Fellowship of the Ring* (2001), and *Spider-Man* (2002), as well as star-driven domestic films such as *Public Enemy* (2002) and *Oasis* (2002).

Following a nine-year hiatus since the release of *The Way Home*, Lee Jeong-hyang wrote and directed her much-anticipated third film, *A Reason to Live* (2011). Reminiscent of Lee Chang-dong's *Secret Sunshine* (2007), *A Reason to Live* offers a range of viewpoints on the theme of forgiveness, a subject with traditional roots in religious practice and belief. The film presents two interwoven stories involving a female television producer whose fiancé is killed by a teenager in a hit-and-run incident and a teenage girl (the producer's friend's sister) who is abused by her father. Ji-Min has little choice but to flee her patriarchal and violently abusive father, a respected judge who is fond of repeating that his daughter has earned the beatings he metes out to her. Other family members treat Ji-Min in the same way, blaming her for everything that goes wrong and beating her to "help her" overcome her perceived shortcomings. This is the only way that her family, which is committed to Confucianism, knows how to show their "love" for her. In the end, Ji-Min breaks free from this cycle of patriarchal and gendered violence by abandoning her family.

Both female protagonists in *A Reason to Live* are at pains to follow Confucian traditions that encourage them to forgive the men who have caused them such deep suffering. Lee focuses on the pain and suffering of family and friends who must deal with the profound emotions occasioned by the loss of a loved one. In so doing, Lee interrogates such formidable topics as the death penalty and Korea's male-dominated society. *A Reason to Live* also questions the role of religion in people's lives as a potential source of strength at times of emotional vulnerability; at the same time, it explores a woman's "purgatorial" function within the religious system as a role abandoned by "providence".[22] Lee's treatment of these weighty themes and the sensitive performance of Song Hye-kyo—who portrays a documentary filmmaker interviewing victims of violence and their families and friends while grieving the loss of her own fiancé in a car accident—attracted critical accolades. *A Reason to Live* was selected as one of the top 10 Asian films of 2011 by the *Wall Street Journal*, demonstrating its wide appeal to Asian and Western audiences alike.[23]

The second contemporary filmmaker, Byun Young-joo (1966 -), is, along with Yim Soon-rye and Lee Jeong-hyang, a key member of the first generation of female directors who have emerged since the 1990s. Byun received an undergraduate law degree from Ewha Womens University and a graduate degree in theater and film from Chung-ang University. Along with Kim So young, Mun Hyae-joo, and Hong Hyo-sook—now all active members of the Korean film community—Byun founded Bariteo ("independent and freedom-loving women"), a feminist film collective, in 1989, with a view to spreading women's film culture and practice. Prior to forming Bariteo, Byun was a member of the mostly male independent filmmakers' group Jangsangotmae, which was founded in 1988 by practitioners including Lee Eun, co-founder of Myung Film, and directors Jang Yoon-hyun, Gong Su-chang, and Choi Ho.[24] Bariteo and Jangsangotmae both provided communal spaces for filmmakers to meet, and they shared the common goal of supporting freedom of expression.

Byun's membership in Bariteo enabled her to enter the film industry as a cinematographer on Kim So-young's *Even Little Grass Has Its Own Name* (1989), an independent short film exploring gender discrimination in the workplace. In 1993 Byun made *Women Being in Asia*, a documentary about the sex trade in Asia and "sex tourism" in Jeju Island, the celebrated Korean honeymoon destination. *Women Being in Asia* was produced by Kim Dong-won of Purn Production, an independent filmmakers' group headed by Kim.[25] Yet, Byun is best known for her critically acclaimed and award-winning documentary series *The Murmuring* (1995), *Habitual Sadness* (1997), and *My Own Breathing* (1999). This poignant and visually compelling trilogy uncovers the painful and suppressed experiences of Korean women who were forced by the Japanese colonial government in Korea to serve as sex slaves or "comfort women" during World War II. Byun's use of film to give a voice to the untold stories of Asian women, as well as her focus on human rights, has made her an iconic mentor for both male and female filmmakers in Korea and beyond.

Byun's first feature, *Ardor* (2002), is an erotic drama that follows the sexual re-awakening of a middle-aged woman, Mi-heun (played by Kim Yunjin of *Lost* and *Shiri* fame), who has suppressed her deepest desires before learning of her husband's affair with another woman. Based on female poet and novelist Jeon Kyongnin's confronting novel *Once in a Lifetime Day* (1999), the story was adapted by director Byun and co-writer Kim Jae-yeon; their film traces Mi-heun's pathway to restored vitality and self-confidence after meeting a young doctor who gives her the emotional support and physical pleasure that she lacked in her marriage. *Ardor* was hailed by both foreign and domestic critics for the progressive way that it portrayed gender roles, sexuality, and class distinctions in Korean society. Byun's second feature, *Flying Boys* (2004), is a romantic coming-of-age story about a boy in his last year of high school who has a crush on a girl from his neighborhood. In order to get close to her, he enrolls in her ballet academy. They end up in the same ballet class, forming a close friendship that gives him the determination to see out the rest of his high school year. Despite the critical acclaim bestowed on *Ardor* and *Flying Boys*, both were unsuccessful at the box office, making it difficult for even an experienced and accomplished filmmaker such as Byun to secure investor support for her next project.

Byun's latest writer–director project *Helpless* (2012) is based on the 1992 crime novel by Japanese author Miyuki Miyabe, *All She Was Worth*. Both the original novel and Byun's version tell the noir story of a woman who mysteriously disappears and the detectives and family members who attempt to find her. During the investigation, the woman's financial problems are uncovered, and a picture of her monstrous transformation emerges. In Byun's adaptation, the female protagonist's dark trajectory, which includes murder and identity theft, is linked to the larger economic woes of Korean society, with its dog-eat-dog ethos. Byun shifts the original story's setting from Japan's precarious bubble economy of the late 1980s and early 1990s to Korea in the late-2000s. This period was marked by the nation's struggles to overcome the damaging impact of the global economic crisis, not to mention the residual hardships instigated a decade earlier by the 1997 Asian economic crisis. Byun's psychological mystery–thriller shows how, despite her efforts to find some sense of normalcy within Korean society her female protagonist is alienated from society and forced to live on its fringes.

Helpless attracted a total audience of 2.4 million, cementing Byun's status as a commercial auteur—a position that needs to be re-secured with each new film, however, as the poor box office performance of her first two features demonstrates. Such uncertainties notwithstanding, *Helpless* was part of a larger cohort of domestic films made and/or produced by women in 2012 that contributed to Korean cinema's groundbreaking achievement in attracting audiences that exceeded the 100 million mark in that year.[26]

As a writer–director, Byun is strongly influenced by current events in everyday society. She is now (in 2015) adapting the popular webtoon *Lamp Shop* (aka *Lighting Fixture Store*)—an online ghost–horror fantasy cartoon serial created by popular Korean webtoonist Kang Full—into a screenplay about ghosts lingering in limbo between heaven and the real world.[27] As Byun demonstrated with her adaptation work for *Helpless*, she is adept at weaving Korean life and culture into stories originating in other settings. According to our interview with the filmmaker in August 2014, her adaptation of *Lamp Shop* will reference real-life Korean tragedies such as the Sewol ferry sinking that killed more than 300 passengers, mostly high school students, in April 2014.[28]

The third writer–director to be considered here is Park Chan-ok (1968–). She studied theater and film at Hanyang University in Seoul as a mature student after quitting her job of four years as an art teacher. Park used her degree as a stepping stone to enter the prestigious Korean National University of Arts (established in 1993 by the Ministry of Culture, Sports and Tourism), where she took her place in the first cohort of graduate students. She made her debut as a short film director with *To Be* (1996), a closing-night film and the recipient of the Excellence Award at the first Women's Film Festival in Seoul in 1997. Her next film *Heavy* (1998) won the Best Short Film award at the 1999 Busan International Film Festival, the largest festival and market in the world for Asian cinema and a key networking location for promoting Asian films to the global film industry. A few years later, she became the assistant director to quintessential male arthouse writer–director Hong Sang-soo on his third film, *Virgin Stripped Bare by Her Bachelors* (2000).

Park gained notoriety as a writer–director following her first feature, *Jealousy Is My Middle Name* (2002), a medium-budget ($1.4 million USD) film produced by Myung Film whose story is told largely through the naïve but observant eyes of a male graduate student, Won-sang (played by Park Hae-il). He works for a magazine publisher–editor who has a Casanova effect on women and also on Won-sang, but in a platonic, homosocial way. The story exposes the reality of infidelity through the figure of a womanizing editor, a married man who has affairs with two women who are both close to Won-sang's heart. Although this situation plunges the young man into a whirlpool of emotions regarding his boss and the women in his life, he still manages to maintain an aloof exterior. Critics applauded Park's ability—strongly reminiscent of Hong—to reflect the banality of everyday life in *Jealousy Is My Middle Name* and the range of subtle moods that she elicited from the actors. For legendary American director Martin Scorsese, this "extremely subtle and emotionally complex" film belongs with the masterpieces of the New Korean Cinema, a body of work that he describes as having quietly "crept up on" him.[29] *Jealousy Is My Middle Name* won the 2002 New Currents Award (for best feature film made by a new Asian director) at the Busan International Film Festival and the 2003 Tiger Award (the best first film award for young filmmakers) at the International Film Festival Rotterdam.

Partly because the critics saw *Jealousy Is My Middle Name* as reminiscent of director Hong's idiosyncratic style, Park was determined to try something new in her next film *Paju* (2009), which she co-wrote with Lee Yu-rim. At the same time, she realized it would be imprudent to turn her back on the distinctive qualities she had gained from Hong's known approach to filmmaking simply because she had worked as his assistant director. In *Paju*, the characters are subdued, which enabled her to place the emphasis on the play of imagery, spaces, and ambiance in each scene. The setting is simultaneously the real city of Paju and the many other places in Korea that have been torn apart by the conflicting demands made by local and federal government and private industry over the issue of forced redevelopment. In this literal and symbolic way, Paju is a main character in the film, and Park presents it as "a city of blind people".[30] To illustrate this myopia, she plays with the multiple layers between real and imaginary space—in particular, by filling spaces with artificial fog and shooting some scenes through semi-translucent surfaces (such as dirty windows or scratched plastic bus stop shelters), making objects and people appear out of focus. This use of symbolism plays a central role in the film, providing a visual analogue for the social and spiritual malaise that afflicts both men and women—or at least provides a thinly veiled excuse for their "clouded" judgment.

The film uses a series of flashbacks and flashforwards to explore the complicated relationship between a young girl (Eun-mo) and her older sister's husband (Joong-shik) that operates along multiple axes including youth, romance, love, hate, suspicion, guilt, ignorance, family, and civic responsibility. Along with an ever-present heavy fog, the city is enveloped in the greed and violence resulting from a real-estate boom. Following her sister's death, and while still a high school student, Eun-mo finds herself living in the same house as her brother-in-law. She begins to experience uncomfortable emotional and sexual feelings for him and decides to leave Paju for a while. After her return, she reunites with Joong-shik, who is involved in an anti-eviction committee that is attempting to prevent a gang of thugs from demolishing a number of residential apartment buildings. An independent young woman, Eun-mo struggles to reconcile her past, marred by the tragic loss of her sister and parents, and her relationship with Joong-shik.

As the film progresses, it weaves together all the non-linear subplots—the suspicious death of Eun-mo's sister Eun-su, the insurance company's reluctance to pay out, protests against corrupt urban renewal initiatives, Joong-shik's leadership of the protest group, and his affection for Eun-mo. (In a harrowing flashback, Eun-su is killed in an explosion resulting from damage to a rubber gas line that Eun-mo had inadvertently caused.) Later, we learn that Joong-shik has been protecting Eun-mo from the truth about her sister's death (he tells her she died in a car accident). While facing a jail sentence for his protest activities, Joong-shik professes his love to Eun-mo, telling her that his feelings for her had begun when she was a high-school student. In the end—and in an un-Confucian display of female agency—Eun-mo makes a deal with the developers and has her brother-in-law arrested, allowing her to keep the family home and forcing him to withdraw from his protest activities. This was her way of protecting Joong-shik from the gangsters at the protest site, who would have had little compunction about killing him.

Critics praised Park for the way in which, in the character of Eun-mo, she had created a young woman of spirit and independence, and had boldly drawn "a realistic picture of modern femininity that's blessedly free of the stereotypes that make up movie women".[31] For these and other reasons, Paju made waves on the international festival circuit as the first South Korean film to open the International Film Festival Rotterdam.[32] Festival director Rutger Wolfson described Paju as "a triumph of resilience and [representing] a powerful female voice from Asia".[33]

Another reviewer praised the film as "first and foremost a humanistic character drama, with multi layered and pleasingly complex relationships between its [male and female] protagonists".[34] To achieve these effects, Park uses the camera frame as a canvas on which to depict particular feelings, enabling the scenes themselves, including natural locations and foggy weather, to speak louder than any dialog.[35] Yet, even as the recipients of such international acclaim, filmmakers like Park have continued to face challenges in an industry where funding for female writer–directors is scarce and potential investors are risk-averse and hard to please—a point made by all of the women (and men) in the film industry to whom we spoke in the course of this study.[36]

One year after Park Chan-ok's debut with *Jealousy Is My Middle Name*, the fourth filmmaker on our list, Lee Soo-yeon (1970 -) debuted as the writer–director of *The Uninvited* (2003, aka *A Table for Four* in Korea), her first feature film. She studied educational technology at Ewha Woman's University and then received her MFA in film studies from Chung-Ang University, known for its robust film program. Lee is also a graduate of KAFA. Before completing her first feature, Lee made four short films, *Survival Game* (1995), *Refrigerator Story* (1998), *La* (1998), and *The Goggles* (2000), honing her skills and creating a personal style in the process. Lee has developed the right mix for success: a solid understanding of film language as well as strong personal networks from her time at KAFA, considerable production experience, and almost 10 years of positive exposure on the national and international film festival circuit.

Following the release of *The Uninvited*, Lee was praised by local and foreign critics alike for her successful casting of both lead actors (popular Korean actors Jeon Ji-hyun and Park Shin-yang) in parts that differed markedly from the types of roles for which they were known.[37] The film, which had a production budget of $3 million USD, won the Best Asian Film and Groundbreaker awards at the 2004 Fantasia International Film Festival, the Best New Director Prize at the 40th Baeksang Arts Awards, and the Citizen Kane Award at the 36th Sitges International Fantastic Film Festival of Catalonia. However, despite this critical acclaim, *The Uninvited* was not included in the top 10 domestic films of the year in terms of total admissions and was considered a box office failure. That is, its "arty mix of belief, guilt, infanticide and madness that slowly self-destructs" failed to satisfy the commercial expectations of its investors.[38]

Despite its shortcomings, *The Uninvited* contributed to the emerging diversity of Korea's longstanding tradition of horror films. In the words of one critic, the film "is a moody and intelligent psychodrama about two bruised souls reaching out for mutual understanding in a world that doesn't understand their supernatural sensitivities".[39] Looking beneath the surface, the film's claustrophobic milieu offers a chilling view of contemporary Korean society, with its strong Confucian culture, in which a sense of foreboding pervades the protagonists as they encounter residual images of dead children. The schizophrenic haze in which the action is played out simultaneously connects the main characters, Jeong-weon (played by Park) and Yeon (played by Jeon, of *My Sassy Girl* (2001) fame), while disconnecting them from society and reality in general. Jeong-won is an anxious soon-to-be married interior decorator, while Yeon, who lives in the same apartment complex, is an introverted clairvoyant whose own baby was dropped from a high-rise apartment balcony by her best friend. Judging by her demeanor, Yeon is either still in shock or heavily medicated; either way, she exemplifies the passive female character who is blamed for society's ills.

One key scene at the film's mid-point shows Yeon (who began living apart from her husband after their baby's death) meeting her mother-in-law in a coffee shop. At first, the older woman appears to console Yeon but quickly begins hounding her about when she plans to begin divorce proceedings. She then lashes out at Yeon, blaming her for her grandchild's death. She causes a scene by throwing a glass of water in Yeon's face and telling her that she should be ashamed for bringing bad luck on her son, the head of the family. Part of the real horror of the film is its depiction of how vulnerable females are blamed for or punished as the result of family breakdown; these include a woman who has killed two children out of the desperation brought on by poverty; another who drops her and Yeon's babies off a high-rise balcony whilst experiencing post-natal depression; and a little girl who is killed accidentally by her older brother (the younger Jeong-weon) during a botched murder/suicide pact aimed at killing their abusive father. By focusing on such scenes of female victimhood, Lee is asking her audience to contemplate the gender inequalities perpetuated by the patriarchal Confucianism to which Koreans are exposed from a very early age.

To date, Lee has yet to make a follow-up feature film. While male directors also face pressure to produce box office hits, women filmmakers are rarely offered a second chance after producing a box office flop, a reality that hit home especially hard for a rookie female filmmaker such as Lee.[40] This gender-biased environment—which Lee discussed during a personal interview with us in 2003—continues to hold back women filmmakers today: Lee's apparent inability to recover from the poor commercial performance of *The Uninvited* is just one example. To date, Lee has been unable to secure sufficient investor support to direct a second feature film, although she has directed single episodes for three omnibus films: *Twenty Identities* (2004), *Ten Ten* (2008), and *Modern Times* (2012).

Stories for a New Generation

Our fifth filmmaker, Hong Ji-young (1971 -), graduated from KAFA in 1999, going on to receive a Master's degree in philosophy at Yonsei University. Before entering KAFA, Hong enrolled at the Hankyoreh Cultural Center in Seoul where she participated in a filmmaking course, a media education program run for students without a film background by the *Hankyoreh* newspaper (the parent company of *Cine21*, Korea's best-known film magazine, published since 1995), gaining invaluable experience. Her classmates on this course included Kim Tae-yong, Im Chan-sang, Cho Geun-sik, and Min Kyu-dong, whom she assisted as the scriptwriter and assistant director on his award-winning short film *Herstory* (1995)—a project that helped her gain subsequent entry into the prestigious KAFA.[41]

Hong made her debut as a feature writer–director with *The Naked Kitchen* (2009), a low-budget production that she co-wrote with Lee Kyoung-eui. On the surface, the film is a light-hearted commentary on adultery and the unpredictability of love. Married woman Mo-rae (played by Shin Min-ah) unexpectedly falls for a stranger (Du-re, played by Ju Ji-hoon) who, unbeknownst to her, is the young French-trained chef whom her husband (Sang-in, played by Kim Tae-woo) has employed to help him launch a new restaurant. Before Sang-in brings Du-re home to their cozy country-style house to stay as their guest while the restaurant is being prepared for opening, Mo-rae has an anonymous sexual encounter with Du-re in a ceramics gallery. Later that night, over dinner at a restaurant, Sang-in tells his wife that he has quit his corporate job in order to concentrate on his new restaurant. While Mo-rae replies that she is happy for him to follow his dream of becoming a chef, her face tells a different story. Wanting to bond with her husband and be honest with him, Mo-rae confesses her transgression, still ignorant of Du-re's name and identity. Following her confession, Sang-in storms out of the restaurant. However, after a few hours of soul-searching, Sang-in forgives Mo-rae and asks that they never speak of the incident again. Predictably, the already fraught situation is exacerbated in comic noir fashion after Du-re is formally introduced to Mo-rae at the couple's home and Sang-in encourages the pair to get to know one another.

In taking a conspicuously non-Confucian approach to this romance drama, director Hong proffers a liberal alternative to a conservative society's view of adultery, which from 1953 until early 2015 was a crime in Korea and punishable by a jail sentence. Against this stern cultural backdrop, Hong constructs a playful story (reinforced with an upbeat musical soundtrack) that shows the audience how a young married couple goes about negotiating the female partner's sexual wants. In the end, after Sang-in finally learns of her extramarital affair, and following a prolonged fistfight with Du-re, the two men give Mo-rae the opportunity to choose the one she wants. In a comic twist, the two men must settle for each other's company after Mo-rae, who is now pregnant with a child fathered by one of them, decides that she wants to be alone (at least for the short term).

As a result of her multiple roles in the making of *The Naked Kitchen*—casting, directing, and supervising set design and post-production work—Hong (along with her husband and brother-in-law, who co-produced the film) was able to maintain control over the core creative process and make the film according to her authorial vision.[42] Her hallmark is the way in which she toys with the audience in terms of genre expectations—it is hard to ignore the dark mood beneath the surface tropes of joy and lightheartedness that constantly nudges *The Naked Kitchen* toward the horror genre. For example, we see Du-re wearing clothes borrowed from Sang-in and occupying spaces (such as the kitchen and shower) in which Mo-rae would expect to find her husband. The young chef becomes increasingly aggressive in his pursuit of Mo-rae, openly revealing his desire to replace her husband. All the complex and competing elements in this bizarre love triangle combine to create a nightmarish emotional trajectory for all three characters. Veering away from black comedy, the film concludes on an upbeat, nostalgic note, titillating the audience with a selfie and audio from earlier in the film revealing two contented men with Mo-rae asleep between them.

After Hong married director and fellow KAFA classmate Min Kyu-dong—who now runs the Soo Film production company with her (and his brother Min Jin-su)—she went to live in Paris. During her time there, she watched as many foreign films as possible at the Forum des images and other cinemas. When we interviewed her in 2015, Hong told us about one special event in 2001 that changed her life: a festival of 100 films that focused on the theme of infidelity, including Luis Buñuel's *Belle de Jour* (1967), Just Jaeckin's *Emmanuelle* (1974), Claude Chabrol's *Une affaire de femmes* (1988), Anthony Minghella's *The English Patient* (1996), Catherine Breillat's *Romance* (1999), and Wong Kar-wai's *In the Mood for Love* (2000). As a result of this experience, Hong conceived the idea of making a film that would follow three people involved in an unconventional (even taboo), but positive and happy relationship.[43] As a result of her exposure to these foreign films, Hong began questioning if the characters involved in the extramarital affairs depicted were really immoral or simply following their hearts.

With these questions in mind, Hong began planning to make a film that would portray love in its purest and most sustained form—and at the same challenge the social norms of Korea's male-dominated society, a culture in which adultery was a crime. If *The Naked Kitchen* unsettled Koreans, it has also created waves beyond Korea's geographic borders. When Hong accompanied the film to the Cairo International Film Festival, one of the male audience members was visibly upset after the screening, questioning her how it was even possible to make this type of film in Korea. The questions about love, female desire, monogamy, male–female relationships, and the so-called sanctity of marriage that are raised by the film could only have been envisaged by a woman who sees things in a highly unconventional way.[44]

The Naked Kitchen came to the attention of European audiences at the 2010 Berlin International Film Festival, when it screened (by invitation) in the late-night culinary cinema section, which celebrates the themes of food, love, nature, and the environment. According to the *Variety* reviewer, Hong's "handsomely shot romantic dramedy" was reminiscent of Korean cinema's "metaphysical" films of the 1990s, represented by well-known male directors such as Bae Chang-ho and Lee Myung-se.[45] Despite these positive reviews, *The Naked Kitchen* failed to shine at the box office, released as it was at a time when the domestic cinema was slowly recovering from a downturn that had made major inroads into total admissions, numbers of films exported, and the proportion of completed films that were actually released. The industry was kept afloat at this time by a small number of high-profile films including Bong Joon-ho's *Mother* (2009), Park Chan-wook's *Thirst* (2009), and the documentary *Old Partner* (2009), as well as two commercial films with heavy special effects content, *Haeundae* (2009) and *Woochi* (2009), and the historical swordplay film *A Frozen Flower* (2008).

Following *The Naked Kitchen*, Hong directed *Secret Recipe,* one of four omnibus films in *Horror Stories* (2012). Her episode is a tale of sibling rivalry in which a woman undergoes facial plastic surgery in order to steal her sister's wealthy and attractive fiancé. Also in 2012, she directed the short film *Star Shaped Stain* for the Korean Ministry of Health and Welfare's omnibus production *Modern Family*

(2012), which explores the social and cultural factors behind Korea's low birth rate. All four episodes were made by female directors.

At the time of writing, Hong's latest directorial project was the light-hearted romantic drama *Marriage Blue* (2013, aka *The Night Before Marriage*)—starring 2PM Kpop idol Ok Teacyeon and Ju Ji-hoon, whom Hong had worked with in *Naked Kitchen*—which follows a series of events preceding the weddings of four couples. Hong adapted the original script by Goh Myeong-ju and completed and directed the screenplay; one reviewer described it as a "Korean Version of *Love, Actually*".[46] Following its release, it was announced that *Marriage Blue* would be remade by Taihe Entertainment in China. For her next project (at the time of writing in 2015), Hong is busy adapting a French novel by Guillaume Musso, *Will You Be There?* into a screenplay, while working on the pre-production for the film.

The sixth and final writer–director to be considered is Roh Deok (aka Nho Deok, 1980 -), a graduate of the Seoul Institute of the Arts' film program and the youngest of the filmmakers in our study. Roh worked as a script assistant on Jang Joon-Hwan's *Save the Green Planet!* (2003), a wildly imaginative sci-fi film, before going on to direct *The Secret Within Her Mask* (2005), an award-winning short film about a girl who wears a mask to hide her facial hair. The story offers a moral about learning to accept and love one's inner beauty, despite what others may see as external flaws.

In 2013 Roh's feature debut, *Very Ordinary Couple* (2013, aka *Temperature of Love*), which she wrote over a seven-year period, won the Best Feature award in the Asian New Talent competition at the 16th Shanghai International Film Festival.[47] The alternative title, *Temperature of Love*, refers to the emotional fluctuations experienced by a couple over the course of their relationship. The film charts the bitter process involved in a couple's break-up, focusing on the final stages of the relationship rather than the early day of a romance with its heart-fluttering excitement. Although the film has many humorous moments, it is not a conventional romantic comedy, instead offering a portrait of a couple who could be found in any office or restaurant. *Very Ordinary Couple* de-romanticizes the fantasy elements surrounding romantic love and, in so doing, invites people to re-think such relationships and what they demand.

Roh often speaks of her nagging sense that both cinema-goers and her fellow filmmakers view her as a woman rather than a director, reaffirming the challenges of succeeding in the macho world of filmmaking in Korea and around the globe. As a survival strategy for overcoming the gender barriers and stereotyping still in force in parts of the industry, Roh maintains a calm and collected "feminine" exterior when interacting with others. She believes that this approach gives her the upper hand as a woman in a male-dominated industry, enabling her to wrong-foot those who underestimate her technical and creative abilities as well as her project management skills. In adopting this stance, and despite experiencing her fair share of obstacles and failures, Roh serves as an example for other women filmmakers to follow—particularly since (as she believes) her patent patience and forbearance stand in stark contrast to the manic behavior of many male filmmakers.[48]

Conclusion

After the Korean government eliminated censorship in 1996, a new breed of writer–directors rapidly created a canon of provocative, visually stunning, and genre-bending hit films, while new and established producers (mostly male) infused unprecedented levels of venture capital into the domestic industry. After the mid-1990s, many female directors gained valuable training while making short films and documentaries before turning their hands to feature films. In making the transition, they frequently made reputations for themselves in the less competitive arena of independent films. For leading female producers such as Shim Jae-myung (Myung Film) and Oh Jung-wan (BOM), who chose to work with and support the increasing number of female directors breaking into the male-dominated commercial side of the film industry, this was a natural progression. In fact, at the turn of the millennium, at least one local commentator felt that Korean cinema was on the cusp of a new era in which female directors would become a major force in the industry.[49]

Today, a slew of savvy female producers, operating independently and also as part of vertically integrated Korean conglomerates, maintain a strong presence in the film industry. All of our interviewees emphasized that it were not for them, fewer female filmmakers would be working in Korea today.[50] Their priorities include backing domestic productions by collaborating with women writer–directors and new, younger male directors who are perceived as easier to manage than their more experienced counterparts. The six writer–directors in our study all emerged from the dynamic period that began in the mid-1990s, underlining both the diversity of contemporary Korean cinema and the multiplicity of viewpoints brought to the screen and to the industry more broadly. Each filmmaker has contributed in her own special way to the expansion and changing face of Korean cinema and in so doing has issued a strong challenge to the gendered nature of the industry. Their invitation to audiences to reflect upon and critique the nature of interpersonal relationships in Korean society—and, more specifically, the impact of traditional Confucian ideals on contemporary gender relations—makes them a source of inspiration to aspiring domestic filmmakers, regardless of gender.

According to female industry leaders such as Chae Yoon-hee, chairperson of Women in Film Korea and president and CEO of All That Cinema, women filmmakers generally show greater attention to detail, are more gentle and sensitive, and are better communicators with both production crews and audiences (a majority of which are female in Korea) than their male colleagues.[51] Furthermore, whilst a majority of both men and women filmmakers follow similar workflow practices, which are international in scope, in the domestic industry a director is often thought of as a 'father', and a producer as a 'mother' figure.[52] However, the most salient difference between men and women filmmakers is that they are not given equal funding for commercial projects; predictably, male producers (and directors) command much larger budgets than their female colleagues. Moreover, whilst there are more commercial female writer–directors (and directors) active today than in the past, a female director—especially one working on a blockbuster—is still a rare thing. Even Shim Jae-myung, one of the top producers in Korea who has worked with more female directors than any of her colleagues, has yet to make a film that has broken the 10 million audience ceiling. (The case is different for documentary and independent films, where women equal if not outnumber men.)

Given the small number of women filmmakers in Korea and the relatively modest size of the domestic market, the writer–directors covered in our study have followed each other's activities with interest. For many, gender does not matter; it is not a "problem" because many female colleagues have already enjoyed a degree of success—particularly in the independent film scene, which employs more female than male practitioners. According to a personal interview with Byun Young-joo, although "Korea is a conservative and male-centered society ... the Korean film industry is unique and progressive when it comes to gender issues—especially compared to other industry sectors".[53] Hence, the micro-society that constitutes Korea's film industry provides a relatively open space where men and women can work together and explore a greater range of gender relations, including gay and lesbian subcultures. These so-called progressive attitudes (which are lacking, for example, in television) make the Korean film industry an island of tolerance within a larger, more traditional social environment.

Be that as it may, the emergence of this influential cohort of woman writer–directors has not been all smooth sailing. Despite the substantial progress and critical acclaim achieved by women filmmakers to date, there is still a need to encourage more promising female writer–directors and screenwriters; the entire domestic industry—including government and quasi-government agencies that support the industry such as KOFIC and KOCCA—needs to develop and facilitate new ways of supporting them. Generous financial support is one approach to solving the problem of finding and nurturing new talent.

Notes

1. See for example Nam 2007.
2. Personal interview with Chae 2015. Chae Yoon-hee (aka Chae Yun-hee and Chai Uni), is Korea's "godmother" of film marketing. She made a name for herself and her company All That Cinema by coordinating the promotional campaigns for hundreds of local and international films. As the first company of its kind in Korea, All That Cinema has become a model for other marketing companies as well as a training facilitator for countless women working in all sectors of the domestic film industry.
3. See "Women in Film Korea Festival: Finding a Film Lost 26 Years Ago Was Something Unbelievable" (Yeoseong Yeonghwain Chukje: 36 Nyeonjeon Pilleum Chaja Mitgiji Anatta). *Hanguk Ilbo* (8 November, 2000). Accessed 10 March 2015. Available at http://entertain.naver.com/read?oid=038&aid=0000032756.
4. See Chae, Yun-hee. "Reason for Gathering of Female Film People" (Yeoseong Yeonghwain-Kkiri Moin Kkadakeun). *Cine21* (6 September, 2003). Available: www.cine21.com/news/view/mag_id/20774. Accessed 30 June 2014; and Shim, Jae-myung. "Association of Female Film People" (Yeoseong Yeonghwain Moim). *Cine21* (8 January, 2003). Available: http://www.cine21.com/news/view/mag_id/16332. Accessed 30 June 2014.
5. See Smith, Pieper, and Choueiti 2014.

6. See Byon 2001b.
7. "Film Director Park Nam-ok: Using a Megaphone While Carrying a One-Year-Old Girl on my Back ... Sorry I Only Made One Film". (Yeonghwa Gamdok Pak Nam-ok, Hansal Ttal Eopgo Megapon, Han Jakpumeuro kkeutna Aswium). *Donga Daily* (28 January, 1982): 11.
8. "*The Widow*, Female Director Park Nam-ok" (Mimangin, Yeoseong Gamdok Pak Nam-ok jak). *Donga Daily* (27 February, 1955): 4.
9. Although no longer working as a director, Park maintained her film industry connections in her role as editor-in-chief of *Cinema-Fan*, a monthly entertainment magazine founded in 1959. See "Launch of Cinema-Fan Magazine" (Sinema Paen Changgan). *Donga Daily* (18 November, 1959): 4.
10. See "Woman Director Portrays a Woman" (Yeoja Geurige Doen Yeogamdok). *Gyeonghyang Shinmun* (22 June 1962): 4; and "Frontline Female Director Hong Eun-won in 1962" (62nyeon Je Ilseon Yeogamdok Hong Eun-won). *Donga Daily* (2 July, 1962): 4.
11. Hong resurfaced in the local press in April 1975 when the experimental filmmaking group Khaidu Cinema (deliberately echoing the name of French film magazine *Cahiers du Cinéma*) invited her to speak at a symposium in Seoul titled "Women and Film World". The event, which was also attended by Park Nam-ok and critics Byon In-sik, Lee Eo-ryeong, and Song Suk-yeong, addressed the current status and future prospects of women filmmakers in Korea. See "Symposium Held at the USIS on 19 April" (USIS seo 19il Simpojieom Gaechoe). *Maeil Gyeongje* (21 April, 1975): 8. In 1974, Han Ok-hee, a graduate of Ehwa Women's University established Khaidu Cinema as a university club. (Today, Han is acknowledged as one of Korea's first generation of independent filmmakers. She directed *Color of Korea* (1976), a 7-minute experimental film listed by KOFA as no. 2 in a list of Korea's 50 best independent films; it contrasts traditional and modern Korea. In 2012, she received WIFK's Lifetime Achievement Award.
12. Choi 2007.
13. "Hwang Hye-mi: The Only Girl in the Film Community" (Yeonghwagyeui Hongiljeom Hwang Hye-mi). *Gyeonghyang Shinmun* (2 Sept, 1967): 8.
14. "Female Producer Hwang Hye-mi: Taking the Megaphone" (Megapon Jabeun Yeo PD Hwang Hye-mi ssi). *Donga Daily* (5 September, 1970): 7.
15. "*First Experience*: Melodrama for Women" (Cheot Gyeongheom Yeoseong Chwihyangui Melleo). *Gyeonghyang Shinmun* (28 November, 1970): 7.
16. "Director Lee Mi-rye: Wishes for 1984" (1984 Nyeone Geonda, Lee Mi-rye Yeonghwa Gamdok). *Maeil Gyeongje* (5 January 1984): 9.
17. "Director Lee Mi-rye: Running Woman" (Yeoseongi Ttwinda, Yeonghwa Gamdok Lee Mi-rye). *Donga Daily* (15 January, 1986): 11.
18. Kim, Hye-ri. "Director Yim Soon-Rye Makes a Come-back with *Waikiki Brothers*" (Waikiki Beuradeoseuro Doraon Yim Soon-Rye Gamdok). *Cine21* (27 March, 2001). Available: http://www.cine21.com/news/view/mag_id/1094. Accessed 10 July 2014.
19. Ju, Seong-cheol. "Yim Soon-Rye: Making This Film was the Most Fun I've Ever Had" (Nae Saengae Gajang Jeulgeopge Mandeun Yeonghwada). *Cine21* (15 January, 2008), Available: www.cine21.com/news/view/mag_id/49811. Accessed 14 April 2015.
20. Nam 2007.
21. Paquet, D. 2002. "Short Reviews: The Way Home". *Koreanfilm.org*. Available: http://www.koreanfilm.org/kfilm02.html. Accessed 12 December, 2014.
22. Lee, Maggie. "A Reason to Live: Busan Film Review". *The Hollywood Reporter* (8 October, 2011). Available: http://www.hollywoodreporter.com/review/a-reason-live-busan-film-245844. Accessed 20 June 2014.
23. Napolitano, Dean. "The Year in Asian Film", *The Wall Street Journal* (29 December, 2011). Available: http://blogs.wsj.com/scene/2011/12/29/the-year-in-asian-film/. Accessed 12 March 2015.

24. Films made under Jangsangotmae's banner, such as *O Dreamland* (1989), *The Night before Strike* (1990), and *Opening the Closed School Gate* (1992), explore the sociopolitical background to the 1980 Gwangju Uprising, labor protest, and inequalities in education respectively. (Bariteo appears in the end credits of *The Night before Strike*, illustrating the solidarity amongst independent filmmakers at the time.) In 1992, because these and other independent films were being screened illegally—that is, without an exhibition permit—at universities and community gatherings, Jangsangotmae's spokesman Kang Heon was arrested for violating the National Film Law. During his trial in 1993, Kang demanded that the Constitutional Court reconsider the legitimacy of censorship; this case played a major role in the court's declaring censorship illegal in 1996.
25. Kim later achieved international recognition for *Repatriation* (2003), a documentary about the return to the North of North Korean soldiers imprisoned in South Korea. This film, which follows the lives of these prisoners-of-war over a 10-year period, received the Freedom of Expression Award at the 2004 Sundance International Film Festival.
26. See Kofic statistics. Available: www.kobis.or.kr/kobis/business/stat/them/findYearlyTotalList.do. Accessed 4 March 2015.
27. Webtoons, a concept developed in Korea, are provided, either free or for a fee, by major Korean search engines such as Naver and Daum, which use the serialized content as a strategy to attract Internet traffic. Specialized webtoon sites such as Lezhin Comics and Toptoon offer paid content only. Kang Full is one of many popular webtoonists known for creating original stories and innovative storytelling techniques. He has sold the remake rights to many of his webtoons to film companies; the following films are based on his work: *Apartment* (2006), *Crush on You* (2008), *BA:BO* (2008), *Late Blossom* (2010), *The Neighbor* (2012), and *26 Years* (2012).
28. Personal Interview with Byun Young-joo. Seoul, 8 August, 2014.
29. Kim, Kyung-hyun. 2011, 'Foreword', *Virtual Hallyu: Korean Cinema of the Global Era*, Duke University Press, Durham, USA, p. x.
30. Ju, S. "Paju, City of Blind People" (Nunmeonjadeurui Dosi Paju). *Cine21* (3 November 2009). Available: <http://www.cine21.com/news/view/mag_id/58429>. Accessed 11 June 2014.
31. Kerr, Elizabeth. Paju. Film Review. *The Hollywood Reporter* (15 October, 2009). Available: http://www1.hollywoodreporter.com/hr/film-reviews/paju-film-review-1004022816.story. Accessed 20 June 2014.
32. Macnab, Geoffrey. "Park Chan-ok's Paju Opens 39th Rotterdam film festival". *Screen Daily* (28 January, 2010), http://www.screendaily.com/park-chan-oks-paju-opens-39th-rotterdam-film-festival/5010166.article. Accessed 3 March 2015.
33. Mundell, Ian. 'Paju' to open Rotterdam Film Festival. *Variety* (12 November, 2009). http://variety.com/2009/biz/markets-festivals/paju-to-open-rotterdam-film-festival-1118011210/. Accessed 5 March 2015.
34. Mudge, James. Paju (2009) Movie Review. *beyondhollywood.com* (20 February, 2010), http://www.beyondhollywood.com/paju-2009-movie-review/. Accessed 5 March 2015.
35. Ju, Seong-cheol. "Park Chan-Ok: I Wanted to Shoot 'A Film Like a Film'" (Park Chan-Ok: 'Yeonghwa Gateun Yeonghwa'reul Jjikko Sipeotta). *Cine21* (3 November 2009). Available: http://www.cine21.com/news/view/mag_id/58430. Accessed 26 November 2014.
36. Personal interviews with: Byun 2014; Chae 2015; Hong 2015; and Kim 2015.
37. Paquet, D. 2003. "Short Reviews: The Uninvited". *Koreanfilm.org*. Available: http://www.koreanfilm.org/kfilm03.html. Accessed 12 December, 2014.
38. Elley, Derek. Review: 'The Uninvited'. *Variety* (23 September, 2003), http://variety.com/2003/film/reviews/the-uninvited-2-1200539043/.

39. Elley, Ibid.
40. Lee 2003.
41. Hong and her husband, director Min Kyu-dong, are deeply involved with each other's work, and the pair is one of the most successful filmmaking couples in Korea today. Soo Film, with which she has been associated since its establishment in 2004, is headed by Min Jin-su, Min Kyu-dong's younger brother. To date, Soo Film has made 14 films with the aid of directors Min and Hong.
42. Personal interview with Hong Ji-young. January 2015.
43. Personal interview with Hong 2015.
44. Interview with Hong. January 2015.
45. Elley, Derek. "Review: 'The Naked Kitchen'", *Variety* (18 January, 2010). Available: http://variety.com/2010/film/reviews/the-naked-kitchen-1117941908/. Accessed 6 March 2015.
46. Lee, ji-young. "Instant Review: Marriage Blues, Touching Emotions: 'Korean Version of Love Actually'". *Max Movie* (21 November, 2013). Available: http://news.maxmovie.com/movie_info/sha_news_view.asp?newsType=&page=&contain=&keyword=&mi_id=MI0099861101. Accessed 13 March 2015.
47. See Conran, P. 'Very Ordinary Couple Wins Prize in Shanghai', *Korean Film Biz Zone*, (24 June, 2013). Available: http://www.koreanfilm.or.kr/jsp/news/news.jsp?mode=VIEW&seq=2560. Accessed 27 April 2014.
48. Roh's comments are reported in: Jo, Ji-young. "Interview with Director Roh Deok of Very Ordinary Couple" (Yeonaeui Ondo No Deok Gamdok). *TV Report* (2 April, 2013), http://www.tvreport.co.kr/?c=news&m=newsview&idx=328383.; and Jo, Yeon-gyeong. Director Roh Deok of Very Ordinary Couple (Yeonaeui Ondo No Deok Gamdok). *Newsen* (23 March, 2013), http://www.newsen.com/news_view.php?uid=201303211358291110.
49. Kim Eun-hyeong. "Is the Era of Female Directors on the Way?" *Hankyoreh 21* (1 November, 2001). Available at: http://h21.hani.co.kr/arti/culture/culture_general/3704.html. Accessed 10 March 2013.
50. Personal interviews with: Byun 2014; Chae 2015; Hong 2015; and Kim 2015.
51. Chae, Ibid.
52. Personal interview with Kim 2015.
53. Personal interview with Byun 2014.

10 Genre Transformations in Contemporary Korean Cinema

In the decades following the rapid economic development of the 1960s, a diverse group of domestic filmmakers, both men and women, have continued to explore a wide range of themes (disability, individuality vs. collectivism, coming of age, man vs. himself, poverty, loyalty, good vs. evil, appearance vs. reality, colonialism, militarism, and challenging authority, etc.), genres (war, crime, prison, period, comedy, horror, road movie, science fiction, and fantasy), and forms (feature, short film, documentary, experimental, animation, claymation, etc.). These are all categories that involve and contribute to genre differentiation, emphasizing the subtleties involved in making and talking about films and the ways in which they subvert expectations associated with particular genres.

In this chapter we focus on three contemporary films representing a variety of genres and genre traditions that have thrust Korean cinema into the global spotlight. Together, these three films illustrate the ways in which Korean cinema has succeeded in integrating both real-life and fictionalized story elements that stem from Korea's experience of accelerated development or "compressed modernity" that began in the 1960s. As one might expect, Korean filmmakers have frequently used their nation's "civilizational condition" as the backdrop for stories that transgress traditional genre boundaries. Although each of the films considered here represents a different genre, the pathways taken by the main characters—inhabiting the fringes of contemporary society where moral ambiguities upset socially constructed boundaries of right and wrong—reveal a shared philosophical outlook.

With these developments in mind, our analyses of three representative genre films, *Mother* (2009), *Late Autumn* (2010), and *The Attorney* (2013), are presented as a guide to understanding contemporary Korean cinema from perspectives that have received little attention in previous studies, while revealing how these films push the boundaries of genre filmmaking in "glocal" ways. Derived from the French, *genre* means a type or kind of classification, in this context denoting the recognizable appearance of an expected arrangement of particular elements in a text. In terms of film genres, these conventional categories include "textual" elements such as plot, motifs, locations, sound design, dialogue, special effects, visual aesthetics, and directing and acting styles—each shaped by the creative choices made by project leaders and their teams (and often by investors) during the pre-production, production, and post-production stages. Outside these textual conventions, the star system—the celebrity status associated with particular actors, firms, and practitioners – as well as the marketing and promotion of a film influence expectations and interpretations of a film's genre.[1] Audience perceptions and the popular discourse associated with film are also key determinants of a film's genre, despite the concerted efforts and playful inventions of industry practices and players.[2] That is, audiences often read films "against the grain", for example viewing poorly made horror, action, or dramatic films as ironic comedies. Of course, filmmakers themselves constantly capitalize on this.

The basic film genres—romance/melodrama, comedy, action/adventure, fantasy, historical, crime/detective, horror/thriller, and the Western—were established over a century ago. These fundamental distinctions enabled an assembly-line approach to producing shorts and serialized films (aka serials) in the well-funded film industries of the US and Europe. Musicals took off after permanent sound took hold in film industries around the world between the late 1920s and early 1930s. Through familiarity with the repeated elements in specific types of films, audiences came to expect particular narratives, settings, characters, and themes that, in turn, enhanced their spectatorial pleasure—at least until they became bored with particular genres and the stereotypes associated with them. Over time, new sub-genres, such as the horror–comedy, romance–comedy, historical–detective, and space–western (a branch of science-fiction), were devised to satisfy changing audience tastes.

Today, thanks to the wide range of stylistic, aesthetic, and creative choices available to filmmakers, and the rapid growth of transnational collaborations, films can no longer be slotted into narrowly defined categories. Simply put, genres overlap, depending on where, when, how, why, and by whom a specific film is made. Despite this, the concept of genre remains useful, offering us a window through which to view social, cultural, and political issues in a variety of contexts: local, global, and glocalized. In this chapter, we present case studies of three representative films to demonstrate how popular film genres have contributed to making Korean cinema what it is today. In particular, we build on the essays published in *Korean Horror Cinema* (2013) as well as the brief comments on gangster films in *Korean Film: History, Resistance, and Democratic Imagination* (2003). In more ways than one, the three films analyzed in this chapter—*Mother*, *Late Autumn*, and *The Attorney*—were inspired by the filmmakers and their genre choices discussed in previous chapters.

A number of domestic film genres and sub-genres have proved especially popular in Korea since government censorship was lifted in 1996: comedy, action, drama, horror, thriller/mystery, and science-fiction/fantasy. Included in this abridged list, which Korea shares with many other countries, are several sub-genres and cross-over categories including romantic comedy, black comedy, and sex comedy, as well as the action–Manchurian Western and the melodrama, many of which developed from Hollywood genre conventions. In national cinemas all over the world genre categories have shown themselves to be dynamic, as this chapter illustrates; they are constantly manipulated, toyed with, and enjoyed in different ways by different audiences. Bong Joon-ho, one of Korea's most renowned filmmakers, has sought to distance Korean cinema from its American antecedents while acknowledging its influence: "Genre is something that has been constructed to fit the Hollywood version of reality and the formulae established by Hollywood, and Korean characters, situations and realities are of course very different from them".[3] A well-known advocate of freedom of expression, Bong expertly weaves sharp political and social commentary into his visually arresting genre-bending story lines.

Thus, given the dominance the Hollywood film industry has maintained in Korea for around a century, genre appropriation and transformation are necessary and constructive processes of development for a national cinema seeking to break from Hollywood's long hegemony.[4] In a globalized and increasingly complex film market—in which Korean cinema now enjoys major status—the transnational flow of film genres is a significant step toward recognizing and celebrating the diversity of contemporary Korean cinema.

While genre-bending is a conspicuous feature of Korea's contemporary cinema—as in Bong's *Mother*—the use of traditional genre conventions is also alive and well. However, a changing production environment calls for novel applications of genre conventions. As a result of the internationalization of Korean cinema, national boundaries and the need to tell "national" stories now have less influence in shaping how a story unfolds, thus liberating Korean filmmakers to explore new terrain. In turn, irrespective of where a particular film is shot, "local flavor" is now seen as a dynamic element that is added to a story line rather than something fixed that restricts its character and development. *Late Autumn*, a classic melodrama of two lost souls who meet by chance—based on director Lee Man-hee's legendary 1966 film of the same title—is an example of this process. Produced by seasoned producer Lee Joo-ik, whose filmography largely comprises international co-productions and is discussed in the next chapter, and starring controversial Chinese actress Tang Wei from Ang Lee's erotic spy–thriller *Lust, Caution* (2007) and Korean television heart-throb Hyun Bin, this ostensibly Korean film is set against the idiosyncratic backdrop of Seattle, Washington, USA.

The third film discussed here is the 2013 courtroom drama *The Attorney*, directed by debut feature director (and co-writer) Yang Woo-seok and released by industry newcomer Next Entertainment World (discussed in Chapter 8). Selling more than 11 million tickets nationwide it was an unexpected hit, earning a place in the short list of Korean films that have attracted audiences of 10 million or more and generating box office takings of nearly 83 billion won (approx. $81 million USD). The success of *The Attorney* illustrates the scale and diversity of Korea's film market, where even a bio-pic inspired by a real person and true events, and never conceived as a blockbuster, can break through the magic "10 million" threshold. Its remarkable success has allowed *The Attorney* to enter the top 10 best-performing Korean feature films of all time, and one of the highest-grossing domestic films of 2013—second only to the family melodrama–comedy *Miracle in Cell No. 7* (2013).[5]

In sum, the continued expansion of Korean cinema has been fueled by an industry that has developed the capacity to constantly reinvent itself and the narrative conventions it has inherited; all three films discussed here display distinctive genre profiles that have little connection with the limited expression of "Koreanness" favored by the nationalist-inspired filmmakers of the past (such as those who made literary films—discussed in Chapter 3). The development of stories that appeal to international audiences and the ongoing transformation of the Korean film industry on both the technical and collaborative fronts illustrate the industry's confidence as it advances into new territory.

And Now For Something Completely Different: *Mother* (2009)

Contemporary Korean directors such as Kim Jee-woon, Jang Joon-hwan, Park Chan-wook, and Bong Joon-ho have become well known as innovative "genre-benders", inspiring filmmakers in other countries in their turn.[6] One of the leading representatives of this new wave of filmmakers is Bong Joon-ho, who has been called a "quiet genre-hopper who's hard to pin down" due to his dexterous blending of comedy, horror, and social commentary in his films.[7] His filmography includes *Barking Dogs Never Bite* (2003), *The Host* (2006), *Mother* (2009), and *Snowpiercer* (2013), a "Korean international film". Based on the French graphic novel *Le Transperceneige*, co-written by Bong and US screenwriter Kelly Masterson, *Snowpiercer* stars a multinational array of actors from the US, UK, and elsewhere, was shot in a studio in Prague and on location in Austria, and post-produced in Korea, Canada, England, Germany, and the Czech Republic.

The origins of the term "genre-bending", which can be found in film magazine and newspaper articles, film festival websites and brochures, and cinephile websites dating back to the early 2000s, can be traced back to a handful of inventive Korean filmmakers who began experimenting with standard Hollywood genre conventions and mixing them freely. Thus, in the Korean context genre-bending results from the creative interweaving of Hollywood genre conventions with distinctively Korean cultural elements, creating a dynamic cinematic dialogue. This mixing of the local and the global to create a cultural and artistic hybrid involves assimilating, modifying, and reformulating existing materials. Filmmakers such as Bong take pleasure in manipulating the visual, thematic, and ideological lessons they learned while growing up on a steady diet of Hollywood films, as well as a smaller number of European (e.g., French and German) and Asian (e.g., Chinese and Japanese) films. Nowhere is this practice displayed to better effect than in Bong's horror–thriller–family drama *Mother*, which explores the complex relationship between a mother and her son against the backdrop of a murder investigation that divides a rural village.

Korean horror (aka K-horror) films began attracting attention in the late 1990s with the appearance of films such as *Whispering Corridors* (1998), *Memento Mori* (1999), and *A Tale of Two Sisters* (2003), which thrilled audiences both at home and abroad. Their trademarks include female ghosts haunting high school campuses and the hysteria born of the extreme levels of stress and pressure that teens experience while preparing for university entrance exams, victims of Korea's "compressed modernity". At the same time, these now classic horror films showcased genre innovations that are now commonly associated with Korean cinema. In short order, the K-horror genre evolved to embrace a variety of sub-genres, such as: historical dramas (*Epitaph* (2007) and *Shadows in the Palace* (2007)); family dramas (*Sorum* (2003), *The Uninvited* (2003), and *Daughter* (2014)); thrillers (*Arang* (2006), *Killer Toon* (2013), and *Manhole* (2013)), and a host of other sub-genres. Many of these films featured a so-called horror queen, a pretty starlet adept at nervous responses and equipped with an impressive scream. Bong's *Mother* turns this convention on its head by featuring a plain, elderly female protagonist with a dim-witted son.

Mother, which sounds like "murder" when pronounced in Korean, is riddled with tropes of remembering, forgetting, and lying, signaling a deep desire to come to terms with the past as well as dealing with the challenges of the present. Because their suffering forces them to repress their true feelings, the coping mechanisms represented by forgetting, lying, or "misremembering" enable each of the characters to live with the deep psychological distress caused by their own transgressions and those of their loved ones. Through depicting ordinary characters in commonplace settings, Bong offers audiences a penetrating if oblique insight into how contemporary Koreans are living under the stresses created by their everyday problems and concerns.

The film's title character is the widowed mother of a not-very-bright young man in his late twenties named Do-joon (played by screen heartthrob Won Bin). When Ah-jeong, a female high school student, is murdered, local police focus their investigation on Do-joon—despite a lack of evidence and a long list of other suspects who include an elderly junk collector; Do-joon's arrogant friend Jin-tae; some of Ah-jeong's male classmates; and a dozen or so men whom Ah-jeong had photographed on her mobile phone following sexual encounters with them. Jin-tae eventually helps Do-joon's mother to investigate the case and clear her son's name, but only after extorting a large sum of money from her and after Do-joon's lawyer proves his incompetence.

In the first five minutes of the film, Do-joon's mother (who is never named) absentmindedly slices her finger while chopping dried herbs after seeing her son knocked down by a car outside the traditional medicine shop she runs. She races outside to help Do-joon, whom she thinks is bleeding, but she (and the audience) quickly realize that the blood on his jacket is hers—a detail that introduces the film's dominant themes of appearance versus reality and numbness to pain. While Do-joon's mother selflessly ignores her own pain and suffering throughout the film, she displays a myopic grasp of reality. Taking self-sacrifice to extreme limits, she becomes immersed in harrowing situations that require her to set aside ethical and legal considerations or to deceive herself and others in order to survive. The ordeals she imposes on herself include committing murder and living with a murderer.

In the opening title sequence, Do-joon's mother performs a melancholy dance to diegetic music among an expanse of gently swaying reeds. In this surreal scene, which shows that "something is not quite right with mom", we cannot tell whether she is smiling or crying, as her hand is covering her eyes. Next, her hand is shown covering her mouth, and all that can be seen of her face is her eyes. Later she turns her back to the camera while continuing to dance. The ambiguity of her movements suggests that she is either drunk, drugged, or that her limbs are being controlled with strings like a marionette. Toward the end of the film, when this scene is revisited, a key part of the puzzle is revealed: she has just murdered the elderly junk collector who, we learn, witnessed her son killing Ah-jeong. Mother, who had visited the old man under the pretense of offering him a free medical check and acupuncture treatment, will stop at nothing to protect her only son.

Despite this key disclosure, the plot continues to thicken. Do-joon is released from jail after the police discover that one of Ah-jeong's suitors—a boy with Down's syndrome who has recently escaped from a sanitarium—has her blood on his shirt and admits to having been in love with the girl. He is the perfect scapegoat for the crime. When Do-joon's mother surprises the police, and the audience, by visiting the boy in jail, she weeps uncontrollably after enquiring if he has a mother of his own. The boy urges her to stop crying—suggesting that either he has no idea what is happening to him or that he has accepted his fate. Either way, the boy is convinced that he has deceived the police (not that they would believe him anyway), and thus he has no choice but to live with the horrible falsehood that he is Ah-jeong's killer. For his part, Do-joon has the equanimity to eat with his mother and sleep next to her, with the audience knowing that she is aware of his heinous crime. Never once does he admit to the truth that his mother learned from the elderly junk collector before viciously killing him.

The film ends with Do-joon, freakishly unflustered, giving his mother a ticket for a special bus tour designed to give hardworking parents a chance to escape the daily grind for a few hours. Before she boards the bus, however, Do-joon returns his mother's acupuncture case which he had found at the scene where the junk collector died in a suspicious fire. She is visibly upset, presumably because Do-joon now knows her brutal secret, thereby making them accomplices. Before she joins the other mothers, who are dancing to loud music in the bus aisle, she administers acupuncture to herself in an apparent attempt to forget the truth about the murders of which she and her son are guilty. She may also be trying to forget about the handicapped boy who has been unjustly incarcerated. Sitting alone on the bus, in near-silence, she inserts an acupuncture needle into her upper thigh in an attempt to escape from reality and achieve a peace of sorts. Only by forgetting—or at least pretending or trying to forget through a self-administered medical procedure—can Do-joon's mother continue living. But the catharsis she has achieved is a false release, as it defies credibility that she could truly forget such a tragedy. Nor can Do-joon or the boy in jail simply shrug off the knowledge of their troubled place in the world.

Mother was released in 2009, one year after the Lee Myung-bak government came to power. Given that the film provided audiences with the opportunity to ponder what it would be like to live a duplicitous and deceitful life, the timing was significant. One of Lee's first acts after taking office in February 2008 was to deliver his "Let us create a new legacy of success" address. In this speech, which commemorated the 89th anniversary of the March First Independence Movement Day, the newly elected president proposed the concept of "open nationalism" as a way of helping Korea reconcile with its painful and complex past and contribute to the contemporary world order. In this important address, President Lee reached out to Koreans both at home and throughout the worldwide diaspora and sought to capture the attention of a non-Korean audience. He presented three simple messages: first, he was the country's new president, offering a fresh vision; second, modern Korea was indebted to its "martyred patriotic forefathers" who had sacrificed everything for independence; and third, rather than retreating into a myopic nationalism, the way forward would involve Koreans in learning to be pragmatic, efficient, and productive, on the political, economic, and diplomatic fronts.

Despite this upbeat message, during Lee's presidency the way forward seemed to involve some backward steps—at least in terms of freedom of expression, which Korean filmmakers had struggled to achieve and maintain from the Japanese colonial period (1910–1945) onward. For many creative artists, the rescinding of government film censorship in 1996 was all but forgotten under Lee's presidency, which gave birth to a new censorship regime of its own. In May 2011, Bong and other leading filmmakers publicly expressed their deep disappointment with the Lee government's classification of graffiti as a crime, thus suppressing a type of public art of which Banksy, David Choe, Shepard Fairey, André, Zevs, and Invader are internationally known exponents. Their particular art form was the focus of the Academy Award-nominated documentary *Exit Through the Gift Shop* (2010).

The story behind the controversy is a complex one. In November 2010, the Supreme Prosecutors' Office (a branch of the Ministry of Justice) jailed part-time university lecturer and painter Park Jung-soo and fined him 2 million won (about $1,800 USD) for spray-painting a Banksy-style rat on posters promoting the forthcoming G-20 Summit in Seoul. The government's decision to censor and punish this form of public expression fueled a fierce—and sometimes farcical—public debate over the regime's intolerance of freedom of expression in its most basic form. Because in Korean the letter 'G' and the word for rat (gwi) sound alike, and because President Lee's nickname was Gwi-bak-I, Park Jung-soo's artwork was seen as a personal attack on the president. However, the regime's intemperate reaction to Park's graffiti spree backfired on the government. In an interview published in the *Wall Street Journal* in May 2011, director Bong criticized what he saw as the government's abuse of power and inflexibility on the issue: "It is an irony that the country [Korea] can't lightly parry this level of satire and humor while holding an internationally big event like G20".[8] In a protest against the government's stance on this issue, which seemed to be at odds with President Lee's vision of Korea as an advanced nation, Bong, Lee Chang Dong, and other Korean filmmakers signed a petition requesting clemency for the so-called Korean rat painter. The domestic and international attention generated about the case through their actions undoubtedly helped Park. Although his jail sentence was eventually overturned, Park was still required to pay the fine and court fees—which his supporters defrayed by selling t-shirts featuring his G20 rat design.

It is precisely these themes of questioning authority and manipulating public perception—two real-life elements of Lee's "open nationalism"—that one can see reflected in Bong's film *Mother*, where the characters are shown struggling to cope with the complex relationship between past and present. While there is no explicit link between President Lee's vision for Korea and the tropes of remembering, forgetting, and deceiving in Bong's film, a number of critics have read *Mother* as an oblique criticism of the Lee Myung-bak government (2008–2013), in particular through the film's portrayal of class differences; one commentator described the film as offering "a dose of 2000s pungent scent, specifically of Lee Myung-Bak's Korea".[9] Explicit or not, Bong's passionate advocacy of freedom of expression may prompt many readers to interpret the adoption by the characters in *Mother* of self-anesthetizing mechanisms for coping with the bleak realities surrounding them as a critique of the social and political environment of Korea in the 2000s.

The Grass is Always Greener ... in *Late Autumn* (2010)

While Korean filmmakers are well known for their experimentation with genre, in recent times a number of international co-productions have returned to classic genre conventions, focusing on simple story lines featuring an international cast and/or exotic locations with wide audience appeal. One film in this mold is the English-language Korea-US-Hong Kong co-production *Late Autumn* (not to be confused with the 1960 film of the same name by Japanese director Ozu Yasujirō), made by Korean producer Lee Joo-ik (whose company Boram Entertainment is at the forefront of Korea's international co-production scene) and writer–director Kim Tae-yong. The film was co-produced by Hong Kong heavyweights Shi Nansun (wife of acclaimed action director Tsui Hark) and Pang Ho-cheung (joined by Japan-based Buddy Marini), along with prominent Korean music director and investor Cho Sung Woo. *Late Autumn* is a remake of Lee Man-hee's lost 1966 arthouse melodrama that explores the relationship between a man on the run and a female prisoner on a three-day prison furlough.[10] Although one critic panned the film's "clumsy ambition to 'internationalise' South Korean cinema",[11] *Late Autumn*'s commercial success outside of Korea points to the domestic industry's growing impact on the Chinese and US markets, where genre films have a strong tradition behind them.

Late Autumn follows three days in the life of a Chinese woman, Anna (played by Tang Wei, who gained notoriety for her controversial role in *Lust, Caution* (2007)), who is serving a prison term in California.[12] After spending seven years in jail for murdering her husband, she is given a weekend furlough in order to attend her mother's funeral in Seattle. During her leave, she falls for a young Korean man, Hoon (played by Korean heart-throb Hyun Bin)—a gigolo doing his best to avoid the outraged husband of one of his wealthy Korean clients.[13] Although Anna and Hoon are both aliens in the US—their mother tongues are Chinese and Korean, respectively—they are able to communicate through eye contact and body language, revealing their inmost feelings and desires. Hoon, who resembles the 1960s "rebel youth" film star Shin Seong-il (discussed in Chapter 4), rekindles feelings buried deep inside of Anna, hinting at a new direction for her turbulent inner life. The film is a classic melodrama that follows the emotional journey of two lonely people who meet at the darkest time of their lives.

While it failed at the Korean box office, *Late Autumn* was a major hit in China. It became the highest grossing Korean film ever released on the Chinese film market, creating a box office record of over $9.5 million USD (60 million RMB) in takings over a two-week period in March 2012.[14] Tang's performance of the movie's theme song (for the Chinese version) was also well received, generating additional publicity prior to the film's release and attracting viewers to the cinema.[15]

In each of the three films he has made to date, director Kim Tae-yong has placed a strong emphasis on human relationships. His debut film *Memento Mori* (1999), co-directed by Min Kyu-dong, is a B-grade high-school horror movie that focuses on the volatile and vulnerable relationships between female students who break down under the pressures they are facing to achieve high academic standards. His second movie, *Family Ties* (2006), deals with the transforming nature of family relationships in modern Korea, changes that go well beyond traditional kinship bonds. Kim's latest feature, *Late Autumn*, is an exploration of human relationships on the fringes of society where a man and a woman meet in a place remote from the comforts of home. This theme and setting recall the Golden Age of Korean melodrama (discussed in Chapter 2).

On the long bus journey to a grey and misty Seattle, Anna's face is empty of emotion, discouraging intrusion into her personal space and the hard shell that life in prison has forced her to build around herself. Almost without thinking, she offers a loan to a newly boarded male passenger, Hoon, who is unable to pay for a ticket. Hoon, who exudes confidence, promises to repay her after they arrive in Seattle, giving her his watch as collateral. At this stage, there is no hint of the emotional roller coaster the pair are about to experience. Arriving in Seattle, Anna visits her brother's house where she is greeted by family members she has not seen in years. Family friend Wang Jing—her former lover—is also present, with his wife and their baby daughter. Wang (played by Korean–American actor Jun-seong Kim) is partly responsible for the murder Anna committed seven years earlier. Meanwhile, Hoon is in an upmarket hotel providing a client with sexual favors. Anna and Hoon meet again near Union Station in downtown Seattle, where they had parted company. Rather than accepting Hoon's proffered repayment of her loan, Anna abruptly asks, "Do you want me?" Desperate for emotional connection, she realizes that even a fleeting liaison with a man like Hoon will grant her a brief reprieve from her oppressive past and empty present. Having checked into a hotel room, they begin undressing each other, until Anna surprises Hoon by calling a halt to proceedings. Despite this hiccup, the reserved playfulness between these two lost souls creates a connection between them and also builds empathy between the characters and the audience.

To kill time, Hoon and Anna explore some of Seattle's tourist landmarks, including the famous farmers market. The pair board an amphibious bus tour, which takes them around the city and explores Lake Union along the waterfront. As the sun appears from behind rain clouds, the tour guide urges his passengers to seize the moment and enjoy the fleeting happiness that life can offer. Next, the couple visits an amusement park in the process of being demolished. After sneaking a ride on a pair of bumper cars, they witness a couple arguing in the distance. To escape from the banality of their own lives, Anna and Hoon act out a movie scene with dialogue set to the quarreling couple's movements. After making amends, and as if on a stage, the couple begins to dance together in slow motion while Anna and Hoon gaze dreamily at them from their bumper cars. The intertwined couple is seen floating in the air and then out of the frame. Without warning, Anna abruptly flees this exaggeratedly romantic scene, which has overwhelmed her carefully constructed defenses.

Back at the now deserted farmers market, Anna reveals her life story to Hoon—in Chinese. He responds occasionally with 'hao' (good) and 'huai' (bad)—the only Chinese words he knows. While married, Anna was in love with another man (Wang, a friend of her older brother), and her jealous husband constantly beat her. This violent abuse eventually led Anna to murder him. As she pours out her heart on Hoon's deaf ears, she surprises him by giving him an affectionate hug followed by a small sum of money, which he refuses with a warm smile. Could Anna be more than a "client" to Hoon? Could Hoon be more than a one-night-stand to Anna? Through a chance encounter, both characters are able to forget about the reality of their situation and the cultural gulf that separates them. Although neither can understand the other's native tongue, Anna is grateful to have found someone willing to listen to her, while Hoon is pleased to have found someone whose interest extends beyond his sexual services.

The next day at the wake, Hoon meets Anna as well as Wang and his wife (who believes Anna has moved to China). Hoon introduces himself as Anna's fiancé to save her the embarrassment of admitting that she has served time in prison. When Hoon accuses Wang of a minor breach of dining etiquette, the two men start fighting. Before Wang can apologize, Anna falls to the floor in tears. Surprised and confused, Wang finally says "sorry"—the word Anna has been longing to hear for all the hardships she has suffered—and Anna's tears offer her a release she has not experienced in years. After the funeral, Hoon escorts Anna to Union Station to catch her bus back to prison. She half-jokingly hands him a $10 bill—practically all she owns—and he offers her his watch to 'remember' him by, but she refuses it. Beaming up at Anna through the bus window, Hoon waves goodbye as if she were a close friend. Then, boarding Anna's bus at the next stop, he sits down next to her and—pretending to be a stranger—introduces himself, saying that he likes her smile. Starting over again, they hope for a brighter future.

However, things don't go their way. At a bus rest stop en route to California, three men accost Hoon and haul him before the husband of his wealthy female client. Eerily calm, he asks Hoon why he robbed and murdered his wife in a hotel room. Immediately, Hoon realizes he is being framed for murder. With the police on their way, Hoon finds Anna and, without telling her of the danger he is in, gives her a long, passionate kiss—a kiss that urges her to embrace life. They make a pact to meet at this same spot when she is released from prison and, while Anna takes a short nap on the bus, Hoon disappears, never to be seen again. Two years later, as the closing credits appear on screen, a whole day passes while Anna waits for Hoon at the rest stop. Although Hoon never appears, Anna pretends to speak with him: "Hi, it's been a long time". Her tense face relaxes, letting the audience know that she has come to terms with herself and her life, and is ready to move on.

Late Autumn is a melodrama in which Anna's three-day sojourn in Seattle is depicted as a healing experience. Faithful to the conventions of the genre, she runs the full gamut of human emotions—feelings she feared had disappeared from her life for good. The frequent close-ups of her face, seemingly devoid of expression yet somehow soft and tender, trace the subtle emotional changes that Anna experiences. Thus, when she breaks down and weeps at her mother's wake, her reaction appears so extreme that everyone around her falls silent. In stark contrast to Anna, Hoon is portrayed as a young, naïve and narcissistic immigrant in full pursuit of the American dream. Although working as a male escort, he still retains the ability to see the good in people. Understanding intuitively what Anna is lacking, he seeks to provide it for her. Underpinning the fictional story is the playful onscreen relationship between lead actors Hyun Bin and Tang Wei, adding an extra dimension of enjoyment to the film for Chinese and Korean audiences.

In conclusion, was the making of *Late Autumn* the result of "clumsy ambition" or a calculated strategy for survival in a highly competitive industry? Time will tell. However, as a Korean melodrama-cum-road movie made in the US by an international crew, *Late Autumn* replaces the 'national' content characteristic of Korean productions with a strong infusion of 'transnational' elements, including stars, locations, and dialogue. This mix of international elements blends seamlessly with the well-established and universal melodrama format, thereby increasing the story's appeal to audiences around the globe. In taking this route, *Late Autumn* can be seen as a Korean transnational film that that takes its place within a larger group of films made in the last two decades that draw on the road-movie, melodrama, and gangster sub-genres in various combinations.

There's One More Thing … It's Been Emotional: *The Attorney* (2013)

Directed by rookie Yang Woo-seok, *The Attorney* is a courtroom drama bio-pic inspired by true events.[16] Produced by N.E.W., also a newcomer to Korea's film industry, the film has attracted audiences in excess of 11 million, earning its place in the exclusive "10 million" club and illustrating once again the pulling power of Korea's market for theatrically released films and the wide appeal of genres other than blockbusters laden with special effects.

Since 2004 only a small number of domestic films have reached the magic 10 million audience mark and achieved the status of a mega-box office hit or *cheonman yeonghwa* ("10 million audience film"). In addition to *The Attorney*, these are *Silmido* (2003), *Taegukgi* (2004), *The King and the Clown* (2005), *The Host* (2006), *Haeundae* (2009), *Masquerade* (2012), *Thieves* (2012), *Miracle in Cell No.7* (2012), *Roaring Currents* (2014), and *Ode to My Father* (2014). In early 2015, only a tiny handful of foreign films released in Korea have achieved this coveted status—*Avatar* (2010), *Frozen* (2013), and *Interstellar* (2014).

Bio-pics based on real people usually identify the protagonist early in the piece. For instance, *Patton* (1970), *Raging Bull* (1980), *The Social Network* (2010), *Behind the Candelabra* (2013), and *Foxcatcher* (2014) are all successful dramatizations of the real lives of US General George S. Patton, Jake La Motta, Mark Zuckerberg, Liberace, and John du Pont, respectively. However, would they have made any sense to the audience without revealing the main character's real name? Possibly; indeed, critically acclaimed films such as *Citizen Kane* (1941) and the television series *Boardwalk Empire* (2010–2014) were both inspired by the lives and times of William Randolph Hearst and Enoch L. Johnson (and the prohibition era in Atlantic City), respectively. Such productions are effective when audiences can readily see points of connection with the real-life personalities behind them.

One celebrated Korean film that elides the central character's name, but which is clearly based on authoritarian President Park Chung Hee, is *The President's Last Bang* (2005) (discussed in Chapter 8). In a similar way, *The Attorney*, while clearly based on the life of former Korean President Roh Moo-hyun (aka Noh Moo-hyun, 2003–2008), never reveals his identity. The film tracks the career of Song Woo-seok (played by experienced actor Song Kang-ho) from the birth of his son in 1971 to his arrest for "initiating disorder" at an "illegal gathering" during a public funeral in 1987. Among a host of other story details, both of these dates match recorded events in Roh's life (1946–2009).

This two-hour film is divided into four parts, each flowing seamlessly into the next, exploring the overlapping themes of birth and re-birth, self-determination and prosperity, social alienation and selflessness, and justice and exoneration and questioning their limits through the conflict and tensions resulting from Korea's experience of "compressed modernity". Through its interlocking story lines, *The Attorney* reveals the yawning gulf between national security and human rights in contemporary Korea.

The film opens in Busan in 1978—one year before President Park Chung Hee was assassinated by his own security chief, the director of the KCIA. Easy-listening music sets a lighthearted tone as Song boards a public bus to visit a senior legal colleague. Wearing a suit, Song is the best-dressed person on the bus. Like his real-life counterpart Roh, he has recently resigned his position as a judge in Daejeon, and he is seeking to launch a new real estate registration (notary) company to capitalize on Korea's property boom. (The bubble created by Korea's 1970s real estate boom was the subject of the 2015 noir action film *Gangnam Blues* (aka *Gangnam 1970*).)

In the first part of the film, Song is portrayed as a warm-hearted family man who is focused on making money. Although shunned by his peers, he maintains a happy-go-lucky view of the world despite the social and political turmoil unfolding around him, including President Park Chung Hee's 1972 declaration of martial law and his promulgation of a constitutional amendment giving him powers to govern the nation in perpetuity. Increasing tensions with North Korea were also felt during this period, fueled by the 1974 assassination of First Lady Yuk Young-soo and the 1976 axe murder incident in the Panmunjom demilitarized zone. Fuel was added to the flames of civil unrest by the assassination of Park Chung Hee himself and the subsequent military coup of General Chun Doo-hwan in October and December 1979 respectively, as well as the 1980 Gwangju

Massacre in which around 200 students and civilians were killed by troops during a rally calling for democracy. The main part of the story that follows, that is, the Burim Incident, is the outcome of the social-political environment resulting from the abovementioned events.

However, far from being cowed by the upheaval and disorder enveloping the country, Song sets his sights resolutely on the future—revealing the inner strength and remarkable survival instincts for which the young Roh was also known. While many of Song's peers mock him for failing to progress beyond high school and for peculiarities such as his unconventional use of business cards, these minor irritations cause him little concern; he is more concerned with servicing the legal clients who have flocked to him in such large numbers that he and his wife are hard put to spend the profits generated by his business.[17]

Comic relief is provided by the sub-plots that proliferate in the first part of the film, such as the scene in which Song's future business partner (played by prolific actor Oh Dal-su) chokes on a scalding cup of coffee during his job interview. Later at their house Song and his wife joke about the noisy rats in the roof, taking turns at making meowing noises in a comic attempt to scare the rodents away. The incident gives Song the idea of moving to a high-rise apartment with panoramic sea views. This proves to be no ordinary apartment. Renovations reveal the slogan "never give up" inscribed on the cement wall, and Song explains to his family that he had built this apartment for them with his bare hands, brick by brick. A flashback to the day when his son was born seven years earlier reveals Song working as a construction laborer on this very site, around the time he began studying for the Bar exam—hence the motivational slogan. The phrase becomes both a personal mantra and an aspirational catchphrase for Korean society as a whole, urging its slow but methodical development one building block at a time.

A fierce pro-democracy protest, spiraling out of control on the streets fronting Song's office, signals the beginning of the film's second part, which is set in March 1981. Song goes out to investigate the commotion, involving students and others who are part of a nationwide movement determined to bring about social and political change. Without warning, the streets are enveloped in thick clouds of teargas fired by faceless military policemen clad from head to toe in protective black riot gear. One of them advances out of the haze, approaching Song in slow motion with club in hand. Will Song suffer a beating or arrest for being in the wrong place at the wrong time? The shot fades to black, leaving us to ponder the outcome of this pro-democracy rally turned violent.

We next see Song as he enters his favorite restaurant with a group of classmates from his old high school. Worse the wear for drink, boasting about his financial success, and argumentative, Song forces his way into the restaurant after it has officially closed for the night. During the meal, he argues with one of his old schoolmates (a reporter) about the ethics of the pro-democracy protests and the prosecution of protesters for violating the National Security Law (introduced in 1948 and still in force today). The reporter admits that he is a coward for not supporting the protests against the Chun military government but is concerned about keeping his job. Song, who has been traumatized by his earlier encounter with the riot police, condemns the "socialist radicals" behind the protest for causing a public disturbance and failing to make the effort to find solutions to Korea's (and the world's) problems. He attacks the protestors' "privileged" university lifestyle (they are mainly university students), which stands in stark contrast to the independent path that he has carved out for himself. While Song may not have been physically harmed during his encounter with the riot police, something inside him has been damaged, and he remains out of synch with the social and political tensions that accompany Korea's "compressed modernity". While the light-hearted subplots in the first half of the film offer some relief from its weightier concerns, and generous acts such as Song's assisting his neighbors with their tax returns make him appear saintly, such tropes are absent from the second half of *The Attorney*.

The second part of the film opens with the KCIA converting a deserted motel and public bathhouse into a secret interrogation facility, creating a grim torture chamber which they populate with local youths suspected of reading subversive literature, supporting anti-government organizations and activities, showing an interest in communist ideology, and committing pro-communist "thought crimes". While rounding up some of these "social radicals", plain-clothes KCIA officers arrest Jin-woo, son of the owner of Song's favorite restaurant. Jin-woo's distraught mother spends over a month looking for the abducted boy. For his part, Song shows no interest in a case relating to the National Security Law that is being prepared in Busan, turning down an opportunity (offered by a senior colleague and friend) to join the defense team. This Burim Incident case, which is regarded by local lawyers as tantamount to career suicide, is certain to be lost against state prosecutors who have framed the issues in black-and-white terms without any regard for due process. Song, who in his own eyes is simply a money-grubbing tax attorney with no formal education, prefers to focus on the business side of his legal career and to serve Korea in other ways, such as qualifying (in sailing) for the 1988 Summer Olympics. Seoul's bid for the Games (voted on in September 1981) is another significant real-life event in the story of Korea's accelerated development path that is referenced by the film.

Near the film's halfway point, Song's character (and the story) makes a dramatic about-face after Jin-woo's mother pleads with him to defend her son. Surely Jin-woo is innocent of carrying out orders from Communist North Korea, which is technically still at war with the South? Despite her pleas, Song remains unconvinced that taking the case will be to his advantage; in addition, he is about to land the biggest and most lucrative commercial real estate development client of his career. However, after seeing Jin-woo in custody, mentally and physically shattered from weeks of torture and abuse by the secret police, Song undergoes a radical change of attitude. With less than two days to prepare for the trial, Song takes his reputation in his hands and joins the defense team—against the fervent pleas of his friends and colleagues, and also his wife, who is intimidated deeply by the case and what it might mean for them. Others simply think that Song must be "tired of making money". In taking this step, he veers from the road to riches that has hitherto shielded him from the harshness of social reality and takes the worthier path of defending the oppressed—in this case, alleged communists. The film presents this binary opposition—capitalism vs. communism—as if they were the only choices available to Koreans at this time.

Part three opens with Song's courageous decision to defend Jin-woo and eight other "communist sympathizers" on trial for illegal assembly (under cover of a book club) and studying subversive literature, as well as spreading communist ideology and anti-national propaganda. Absurdly, they are also accused of fomenting a secret plot to incite a revolt on behalf of the North Koreans. Fundamentally, the nine students are on trial for violating Korea's National Security Law—and the judge, prosecutors, and even the defense counsel act as if the outcome is a *fait accompli*. (Warning Song to back down, the senior defense counsel tells him that the trial is about "negotiating penalties" rather than proving guilt or innocence. Song ignores his advice, arguing that in a "normal" situation, all nine defendants would be found innocent due to insufficient evidence.) From this point on, the film focuses on the trial with its predetermined outcome, portraying Song's tireless efforts to advocate for the defendants' constitutional and human rights after taking over the case from his senior (and less daring) colleague. Risking charges of contempt of court and obstruction of justice, Song challenges the prosecutor's charges as well as the judge's apparent bias at every opportunity, demanding that the court recognize the defendants' right to innocence until proven guilty—an ironic message coming from the mouth of a character portraying Roh at a time when Korea's president Chun Doo-hwan was unequivocally guilty of military insurrection.[18]

In the final part of the film, Song uncovers the KCIA's secret torture facility; for this disclosure, in addition to his thorough defense efforts despite the farcical nature of the trial, he is labelled as a communist sympathizer by the authorities and the press and verbally abused in front of the courthouse by his fellow lawyers. To lend weight to the sheer inhumanity of the regime's actions, a series of harrowing flashbacks portray the relentless torture meted out to Jin-woo and other students by the KCIA to make them sign false confessions. At one point, KCIA chief Cha takes the stand, giving incomplete and misleading testimony in order to protect the state security apparatus. Although he fails to intimidate Song, he succeeds in making him look like a communist sympathizer in the eyes of the court. Just when all seems lost for the defense, the young military doctor assigned to the torture facility to keep the prisoners alive appears as a "whistle blower", offering truthful testimony that contradicts Cha's evidence. However, his testimony is stricken from the record after he is accused of leaving his post without approval. Despite these determined attempts to pervert the course of justice, Song refuses to waver from his course, emphasizing the idea that every citizen, including the poor, deserves justice—even under the all-powerful National Security Law, which remains in force today and is still susceptible to being abused.[19]

Finally, in a flash-forward to 1987, a year before the Seoul Olympics, Song is seen leading a protest march in memory of Park Jong Cheol, an actual student who was tortured to death by the KCIA. Once again, Song is enveloped in a cloud of teargas, but this time he is seen taking up a position between the crowd and heavily armed riot police, shouting "we must fight for democracy". Song is arrested for instigating civil disorder at an illegal public gathering. In the film's final scene,

Song appears in handcuffs before a judge who is being asked by his lawyer to read out all of the names of Song's legal counsel; 99 out of a total of 142 lawyers in Busan had agreed to represent Song at the trial, demonstrating overwhelming support for the embattled lawyer and illustrating the level of pro-democratic solidarity amongst the legal community and society at large.

As a result of his popularity among Korea's "386 Generation"—people in their thirties during the early 1990s who had studied at university in the 1980s and were born in the 1960s—Roh (for whom Song is an obvious cipher) never gave up the struggle for justice and democracy, even after losing a number of local and national contests for public office, eventually winning the presidential election in 2002.

Although *The Attorney*'s opening inter-title states that "while this story is based on a real person and real events, the film is a work of fiction", and the end credits are lacking the conventional disclaimer that all persons depicted in the film are fictitious, the filmmakers deliberately chose to distance themselves from the film's unmistakable parallels with the career of Roh Moo-hyun, his aspirations to become a lawyer and to serve the public interest, and his repeated challenges to the authoritarian military regime that ruled the country in the 1980s. Were *The Attorney*'s backers seeking to avoid the type of political controversy that director Im Sang-soo and his producers MK Pictures became embroiled in with the release of *The President's Last Bang* in 2005?

Despite the many achievements of his presidency, Roh's name is associated now only with controversy. Politically speaking, people either love him or hate him. According to a 2014 survey on the standing of Korean presidents conducted by Gallup Korea, Roh is the most popular president (32%), followed by Park Chung Hee (28%), and Kim Dae-jung (16%).[20] Roh aptly named his administration the 'Participatory Government', emphasizing the importance of openness and communication in ways that would have been unthinkable for his predecessors. However, his non-authoritarian approach was soon overshadowed by Lee Myung-bak after he took office in 2008, wresting political power from the liberals to the conservatives after a decade of liberal-controlled governments. Roh took his own life in May 2009 during a state investigation and prosecution involving bribery charges that also included his family and friends. In mid-2013, Roh (and his administration) were retrospectively portrayed in a negative light when the South Korean spy agency, the National Intelligence Service—operating under newly elected President Park Geun-hye—controversially leaked classified transcripts from Roh's private meetings with North Korean leader Kim Jong-il during an unprecedented summit in Pyongyang in 2007.[21] Since his death, Roh Moo-hyun has become a politically charged name with the potential to polarize Koreans.

Given the controversy that continues to swirl around Roh's reputation, it is easy to understand why almost all of the film's cast and production crew avoided the explicit use of his name during live interviews for *The Attorney*. Song may be a thinly disguised version of Roh, but the film must be judged on its own merits. Lead actor Song Kang-ho must take much of the credit for the film's success. In the title role, he powerfully conveys the sincerity, courage, and compassion of a man who believed he had no choice but to take his own life after fighting for so long to help the nation overcome the negative fallout of over-rapid development. Seen in this light, *The Attorney* sheds much of the political baggage associated with the real Roh Moo-hyun, enabling the audience to reflect on a universal human story, one that inspires both laughter and tears. In addition, Song Kang-ho's association with the film enabled its producers (including Withus Film CEO, Choi Jae-won) to solicit investment and recruit additional cast members with ease, thus transforming the project from a potentially small arthouse film into a well-funded commercial hit.[22]

Song's contribution to this film extends beyond his role as the title character; he is a quintessential actor whose name has become synonymous with contemporary Korean cinema. Since the late 1990s, Song has featured in some of the highest-grossing and critically acclaimed Korean films and has become recognized internationally for his craft. His numerous product endorsements, ranging from the national lottery and financial services to the traditional Korean alcohol *Baekseju*, have been vigorously promoted through broadcast, print, and online media campaigns; advertisements featuring him adorn buses, billboards, and the walls of busy pedestrian precincts across urban and rural Korea. To date, he has played the central character role in 31 films, and his three most recent films—*Snowpiercer*, *The Face Reader* (2013), and *The Attorney*—have drawn combined audiences of nearly 30 million. His films have attracted many more millions of viewers across the globe who have either purchased or rented them, downloaded them from the Internet, or seen them at an international film festival or on general release in their own countries. In addition, *Cine21* and *Film2.0*, two of Korea's most popular film magazines, have featured Song on their covers on numerous occasions. It is no exaggeration to say that Song Kang ho represents the changing face of the Korean cinema of the 2000s.

Through his diverse roles and performances, Song has elicited a positive response from audiences of all ages and critics alike. Since the early 2000s, he has shown his ability to capture the basic human instinct for laughter and tears, making his characters humane and down to earth, but without exaggerating and thus caricaturing the emotions they express. Most of Song's characters have their roots in the middle and lower-middle classes, enabling him to represent the common man with believable personality flaws, a sense of humor, and a range of everyday concerns that embrace family, work colleagues and neighbors. His filmography contains as many serious roles as comic ones, each creating a unique portrait of Korean manhood in its various aspects. This image of the common man or anti-hero, which Song has developed by means of his repertoire of idiosyncratic physical movements and facial pantomime, has grown in power and complexity as his reputation has increased. To celebrate its 1000th issue in April 2015—and 20 years of publication—*Cine21* published a major article on Song Kang-ho, whose career began in 1995, the same year the magazine was founded.[23]

This complexity of character, and Song's charismatic ability to project it on screen, reflects not only the depth of his talent but also the mentoring that he has received while working with many of Korea's leading directors. His versatility and mass appeal reaches beyond that of other popular Korean actors such as Lee Byung-heon, Jang Dong-gun, Won Bin, and Hyun Bin, all of whom have a certain "look" that appeal to viewers around the globe. Considered both actor and movie star, Song has successfully made the transition from the local to the international context, beginning with his performance in Bong Joon-ho's *The Host* and more recently with *Snowpiercer*. In his seemingly effortless ability to embrace both comedy and tragedy in a single performance, he has also transformed the ways in which we think about Korean cinema.

Conclusion

In this chapter, we have sought to throw new light on approaches to the question of genre by contemporary Korean filmmakers by exploring some of the themes, styles and industrial concerns relating to three very different films. Bong Joon-ho's *Mother* illustrates the expansion of traditional genre categories with an eye on the domestic market, maximizing the film's simultaneous appeal to local and international audiences with the wrenching twists and turns of the plot. Although limited space has prevented us from analyzing more of his films in detail, Bong's directorial approach to *Snowpiercer*, a science-fiction action film, shows how he—and Korean cinema in general—has continued to push genre boundaries and seek new opportunities for international collaboration. *Late Autumn*, the second film discussed here, demonstrates how Korean cinema continues to reach out beyond its national borders, as well as ethnic and language boundaries, while seeking to appeal to international audiences with its use of melodramatic conventions that are understood and enjoyed around the globe. The seemingly eccentric pairing of a Chinese woman with a Korean man in the American Northwest uses a familiar story type to transform an unpromising situation into a heartwarming love story between two lost and lonely souls. Our final film, *The Attorney*, joins a very short list of "10 million audience" films, demonstrating that reflecting on the nation's sensitive past, and touching some very raw nerves in the process, can result in unexpected—even overwhelming—success at the box office.

In sum, the continuing success of contemporary Korean cinema is the result of many factors; these include—but are by no means limited to—genre formats and the endless variations that can be played on them. Genre conventions, innovations, and appropriation continue to extend and enrich Korean cinema beyond the local flavors popularized by 1960s festival films, while also reflecting and stimulating an unprecedented level of international collaboration. The three films discussed in this chapter demonstrate the ongoing transformation of an industry that continues to make Korean cinema worthy of study and discussion.

Notes

1. See Gledhill 1991; McDonald 1995; Schatz 1981; and Neale 1980.
2. Mittell 2003.
3. Kim *et al.* 2007: 33.
4. See Yecies and Shim 2011.
5. In 2013 N.E.W. released 5 of the top 10 performing domestic films: *The Attorney, Miracle in Cell No. 7, Hide and Seek, Cold Eyes,* and *New World.*

Genre Transformations 225

6. In 2011, for instance, *Variety* magazine reported that a new wave of filmmakers in Morocco were claiming to have been inspired by Korean genre films. See Dale, Martin. "New-gen Genre Benders". *Variety* (January 2011): 3. In an earlier issue, director Kim Jee-woon was characterized as a 'genre-bending helmer' for his continued experimentation in this area since debuting with the gothic–horror–comedy *The Quiet Family* (1997). See Elley, Derek. "Review: 'The Good the Bad the Weird'". *Variety* (24 May, 2008). Available: http://variety.com/2008/film/markets-festivals/the-good-the-bad-the-weird-1200522089/. Accessed 1 June 2015.
7. See Bordwell, David. "A Welcome Influenza". *David Bordwell's website on cinema* (29 September, 2009). Available at www.davidbordwell.net/blog/2009/09/. Accessed 5 October 2014.
8. See Woo, Jaeyeon. "Rat Graffiti Becomes a Political Stew". *The Wall Street Journal – Korea Real Time* (31 May, 2011). Available at: http://blogs.wsj.com/korearealtime/2011/05/31/rat-graffiti-becomes-a-political-stew. Accessed 4 May 2015.
9. See Bechervaise, Jason. Koreafilm.org.uk. (2009) "London Film Festival Reviews: *Mother*". Available: http://koreanfilm.org.uk/64.html. Accessed 5 May 2015; and "TIFF 09: MOTHER Review".twichfilm.com (14 September, 2009). Available: http://twitchfilm.com/reviews/2009/09/k-film-reviews-mother.php. Accessed 5 May 2015.
10. Although Lee Man-hee's *Late Autumn* is no longer extant, more than 170 still images from the film are available on the KMDB, and numerous interviews have been conducted with its film crew over the years. Lee's original film is said to have utilized a daring story, sparse dialogue, and striking visuals that were ahead their time. Apparently, producer Ho Hyun-chan sent the master print to an importer in Spain who had asked to view it before agreeing to distribute it in Europe. On its return to Korea, airport customs impounded the print, and Ho had insufficient funds to pay the customs tax for its release. Its loss has inevitably given rise to speculation about its contents, giving the film something of the status of a lost masterpiece.
11. Elley, Derek. "Late Autumn" *Film Business Asia* (21 October, 2010). Available: www.filmbiz.asia/reviews/late-autumn. Accessed 3 February 2014.
12. For her role in *Late Autumn*, Tang received best actress award at the Baeksang Arts Awards and gained the same honor at the Korean Association of Film Critics Awards. Tang is the first foreign actor to be honored in this way at either of these Korean award ceremonies.
13. In the original 1966 film, the man the heroine meets (on a train) is played by Shin Sung-il of *Barefoot Youth* fame.
14. Hwang, Hei-rim. "Late Autumn Becomes the All-Time Highest Grossing Korean Film in China". *Korean Cinema Today* (13 April, 2012). Available at: http://koreanfilm.or.kr/webzine/sub/news.jsp?mode=A_VIEW&wbSeq=106#sthash.jd8Q5pw2.dpuf. Accessed 6 April 2015.
15. "Tang Wei Sings 'Late Autumn' Theme". *China.or.cn* (19 March 2012). Available: http://www.china.org.cn/arts/2012-03/19/content_24933338.htm. Accessed 7 May 2014.
16. Yang is the writer for the critically acclaimed webtoons *If Thou Must Love Me* (2008) and *Steel Rain* (2011), which begins with the (then) fictitious death of Kim Jeong-il and the imminent threat of war between North and South Korea. *Steel Rain* became increasingly popular after the real-life Kim Jeong-il died in December 2011.
17. Roh graduated from Busan Commercial High School in 1966, eventually becoming a lawyer after passing the bar exam in 1975 (after failing it four times). After defending the Burim case in 1981, which is recreated in *The Attorney*, Roh embarked on a career as a human rights lawyer. Then as now (and until a projected law change in 2017), the Bar exam was open to all, including those without a university degree in law.
18. Sentenced to death in 1996 for conspiracy and his part in the May 1980 Gwangju Massacre, Chun was pardoned by President Kim Young Sam and President-elect Kim Dae Jung in 1997.

19. According to Amnesty International, "One of the most important human rights issue[s] in South Korea continues to be the National Security Law, which is used arbitrarily to curtail the right to freedom of expression and association, providing long sentences or the death penalty for loosely defined 'anti-state' activities. ... In 2010, 34 people were charged under the NSL". See http://www.amnestyusa.org/our-work/countries/asia-and-the-pacific/south-korea.
20. The survey was conducted among 1,700 people over the age of 13. Further down the list is Park Geun-hye (5%) and Lee Myung-bak (3%). In 2004, a similar survey showed Park Chung Hee as the most popular president (48%), with Kim Dae-jung (14%) and Roh Moo-hyun (7%) trailing behind. See Shim, Hye-ri. "People's Favorite President Is Roh Moo-Hyun ... Winning over Park Chung Hee" (Gungmini Gajang Joahaneun Daetongryeong-eun No Mu-Hyeon ... Park Chung Hee Jecheo). *Gyeonghyang Shinmun* (12 March, 2015). Available: http://news.khan.co.kr/kh_news/khan_art_view.html?artid=201503122208235&code=91010. Accessed 10 May 2015.
21. Jun, Kwangwoo. "In South Korea, Spy Agency Is the Leaker". *The Wall Street Journal* (25 June, 2013). Available: http://blogs.wsj.com/korearealtime/2013/06/25/in-south-korea-spy-agency-is-the-leaker/. Accessed 10 May 2015.
22. Kim, Seong-hun. "The Film's Attorney is the Audience Themselves" (I Yeonghwa-ui Byeonhoineun Gwangaekida). *Cine21* (17 Dec, 2013). Available: www.cine21.com/news/view/mag_id/75277. Accessed 10 May 2015.
23. The article was based on a discussion among Song Kang-ho and four leading directors with whom he has worked: Park Chan-wook, Bong Joon-ho, Kim Jee-woon, and Han Jae-rim. See Ju, Seong-cheol. "Someone We May Think We Know Well, but is Actually One of a Kind" (Uriga Jal Aneun Saram Gateun Dongsie Geu Modeun Paeteoneul Bikkyeoganeun). *Cine21* (21 April 2015). Accessed 10 May 2015. Available at http://www.cine21.com/news/view/mag_id/79630.

11 Korean Transnational Cinema and the Renewed Tilt Toward China[1]

From the perspective of the international aspects of cinema, or more specifically the "internationalization" of the film industry, transnational flows among companies and practitioners, stories and ideas, location and production services, and co-investors—as well as audiences and their fan practices—have long characterized the global film business. Once upon a time, most of these people, things, and services flowed toward the US, because "Hollywood" spelled the dream destination for industry workers and aspiring actors alike. However, with the general decline of the working environment in the US film industry since the 1990s, and the global industry's transition to digital production, distribution, and exhibition in the early-to-mid-2000s, there has been a sharp diverting of these flows away from Hollywood toward new centers of transnational cultural production, also known as global media capitals.[2] Korea (Seoul and Busan) and indeed China (Beijing, Shanghai, and many other first and second tier Chinese cities) are now among the growing list of global media capitals into which transnational cultural production is flowing. In particular, China has become the new and largest wild frontier, a stimulating environment where film companies and practitioners are now heading in droves.[3] As we showed in Chapter 8's discussion of CJ Entertainment's increasing interest in China since the late 2000s and N.E.W.'s cementing of ties with Chinese investors in late 2014, developments in the Chinese market are central to the changes now sweeping across the Korean film industry.

With these developments in mind, in this chapter we explore some recent examples of collaboration and technological transfer between the Korean and Chinese film industries; because much of this joint activity has occurred behind the scenes, the sheer volume of these efforts has frequently gone unrecognized. More and more Korean filmmakers are opening new doors by looking beyond the limitations of the local market to the wider Asian region, especially to China, and are thus aspiring to internationalize Korean cinema. The internationalization of the Korean film industry, and thus the evolution of a "Korean transnational cinema", is leading to new kinds of collaboration with Chinese colleagues and firms and on an increasing scale, although not without teething problems. Cultural understanding between players on both sides has surfaced as a critical challenge to further developing these collaborative relationships. To cite one example: *Mr. Go* (2013), a baseball film starring a CG gorilla and young Chinese actress Xu Jiao, was planned to become a simultaneous hit in Korea and China, but it failed to do so—not least because baseball is not a popular sport in China. This was a critical point that Korean filmmakers had overlooked from the start. How would the film have fared had there been more consultation with the project's Chinese partners? Perhaps basketball would have been selected as the more realistic alternative.

To shed more light on this important and growing trend in international filmmaking, in this chapter we specifically investigate the increasing levels of cooperation in co-productions and post-production work between Korea and China since the mid-2000s, following a surge in personnel exchange and technological transfer. We explain how a range of international relationships and industry connections is contributing to the consumption strength and expansion of Korea's domestic market and synergistically transforming the shape and style of Korean cinema.

The *Guanxi* Snowball Effect

Notwithstanding the limited view offered by bald statistics and earlier studies, over the last five years a small number of Korean film companies has contributed to the making of nearly one-third of the top-performing films at the Chinese box office. At the center of this development, at least initially, have been a handful of Korean nationals who studied directing, producing, editing, and theory at the Beijing Film Academy (hereafter BFA), beginning in the early 1990s. These students were part of the first wave of Koreans allowed by their government to study in China after bilateral relations began to thaw in the post-Cold War era. Among the earliest cohort of BFA graduates—who also learned valuable language and cultural skills in China—are Yi Chi-yun (aka Edward Yi Chi-yun, a producer who by his own admission aspires to become the "Jerry Bruckheimer of Asia"), director Kim Jeong-jung, Chloe Park (producer, CJ E&M China), Kim Pil-jeong (manager, KOFIC China), film critic Do Seong-hi, and Peter Ahn (VFX producer, Dexter Digital), to name only a few.

In their own ways, all these figures have been central to the creation of new personal and industry networks (*guanxi* in Chinese) between the two countries. (In China, *guanxi* can enable things to be done, or undone.) Throughout the 1990s, these Korean students studied alongside and developed close relationships with critically acclaimed Sixth Generation Chinese filmmakers such as Jia Zhangke, Wang Xiaoshuai, and Zhang Yuan.[4] During their time at the BFA, they also befriended aspiring film and television actors studying at the academy's performance institute including Jiang Wu, Huang Lei, Li Yixiang, Xu Jinglei, Zhao Wei, Huang Xiaoming, Chen Kun, and Zu Feng, all of whom have become major names in the Chinese entertainment industry. These Korean and Chinese classmates, who are now at the helm of their respective industries, were taught by some of the most distinguished Fourth and Fifth Generation Chinese filmmakers (as professors as well as guest lecturers), including Xie Fie, Tian Zhuangzhuang, Chen Kaige, and Zhang Yimou—many of whom were themselves graduates of the BFA.

As we saw in Chapter 8, this period (the early-to-mid 1990s) coincided with the advancement of a new breed of producers, directors, and investors who sought operational efficiency and economies of scale, as well as international standards of business transparency. In addition to lapping up Hollywood films, aspiring Korean filmmakers of the 1990s had grown up on a steady diet of landmark Fifth Generation Chinese films such as Chen Kaige's *Yellow Earth* (1984), *King of the Children* (1987), *Life on a String* (1991), *Farewell My Concubine* (1993), and Zhang Yimou's *Red Sorghum* (1987), *Ju Dou* (1990), *Raise the Red Lantern* (1991), and *The Story of Qiu Ju* (1992). These films were shown on television and in cinemas and also distributed more widely on videotape. Xia Jin's *Hibiscus Town* (1986) and *Red Sorghum* were among the first mainland Chinese films officially released in Korea in 1989, introducing this new wave of Chinese cinema to eager filmmakers and audiences alike. Given these films' popularity in Korea and the universal acknowledgement of their artistic merit, it is little wonder that aspiring Korean filmmakers were drawn to Beijing to study at the BFA, Asia's most prestigious film institute. After completing their studies, these Korean graduates returned home and applied their training to improve the quality and diversity of the local industry, as well as the sheer quantity of domestic films produced. After proving themselves at home and becoming recognized for their craft, they began filtering back to China to assist the rise of the new wave of Chinese cinema through their established networks there.

Ultimately, the depth of *guanxi* that Korean filmmakers had nurtured in China in the early-to-mid-1990s led to the flowering of relationships with both the state-controlled *and* budding commercial sectors of the Chinese film industry. As a result, when the Pusan International Film Festival (hereafter PIFF, but known today as BIFF)—the largest festival and market in the world for Asian cinema and a key networking location for promoting Asian films to the global film industry—was launched in 1996, established linkages with the Chinese film industry proved invaluable. Festival programmers tapped into established personal networks and also began building new networks of their own—to the benefit of the industry as a whole.

During the 1990s, members of the inner circle of the mainland Chinese film industry added new layers to the networks developing between Korean and Chinese filmmakers. Major directors including Xie Jin, Zhang Ming, Zhang Yimou, Jia Zhangke, Zhang Yuan, Wang Xiaoshuai, and their entourages visited Korea under the auspices of the Busan International Film Festival, networking with Korean industry figures attending the festival. In 1996, Chinese film and television director and producer Zhang Yuan (a BFA graduate) was invited to be a jury member for the New Currents Award at the inaugural PIFF. In 1997, Shan Dongbing of China Film Export & Import Corporation—the single largest (state-run) company of its kind—sat on the jury for PIFF's NETPAC (Network for the Promotion of Asian Cinema) Award, while Sixth Generation director Zhang Ming was a jury member for the New Currents Award, which he had himself won the previous year for his contemporary social drama *In Expectation* (1995, aka *Rainclouds over Wushan*). In addition to these three, the festival was attended by numerous guests from all sectors of Greater China's film and entertainment industries during the 1990s. PIFF festivals continue to provide unrivalled opportunities for networking. Around-the-clock formal festival events and ad hoc gatherings at screening venues, hotels, and cafes have frequently been translated into long-term friendships and industry relationships—not only for Korean and Chinese practitioners but for national film industries around the globe.

In the East Asian context, the development of these *guanxi* networks has provided the seedbed for the rapid growth of collaboration between Korean and Chinese filmmakers after 2001 and for the Korean film industry's tilt toward China more generally.

Blazing New Trails

Today, the world's major film industry players—whether from Hollywood, Korea, East Asia, or China itself—are jockeying for a share in the rapidly unfolding economic and cultural dream that is the Chinese market: a privileged position that up until a few years ago was open only to filmmakers and firms within mainland China. Unquestionably, the "opening up" of the burgeoning Chinese film market has played a significant part in writing the latest chapter of the Korean film industry's expansion into international markets. Since China joined the WTO in 2001, cooperation between the Korean and Chinese film industries has gradually generated a momentum that has drawn them increasingly closer together, enabling Korean filmmakers to become "wider, deeper, more tightly [enmeshed] with China".[5] In recent years, this relationship has blossomed in a number of areas, including a handful of formal co-productions overseen by KOFIC and a much larger number of informal collaborations, including the use by Chinese companies of Korean post-production and visual effects (aka VFX) firms, co-financing, the sharing of casts and crews, and the shooting of particular scenes or even entire films on location in one or both countries.

It is especially notable that the number and kinds of bilateral collaborations have multiplied steeply since 2009, following the establishment of a Korean Film Council (KOFIC) branch office in Beijing. In 2011 the newly appointed KOFIC chairman, Kim Ui-seok, publicly underscored the necessity of pursuing globalization activities of this kind.[6] Although the bulk of Korean–Chinese collaborations were occurring outside of this official channel, nevertheless, under Kim's leadership, in 2011 KOFIC and KAFA launched a small and exclusive (but nevertheless high-profile) industry networking event known as KAFA China Pre-biz. This annual event has brought a select group of Korean film people to Beijing to make new contacts in China (primarily with an eye to their own future projects) and to learn more about the Chinese film market. The Korean Film Business Center, established near the Beijing KOFIC office in 2012, has also played a role in this transforming arena by providing office space and administrative support specifically for co-production projects. Partly as a result of the significant networks established in these spaces (as well as the continued hosting of Chinese industry delegates at the annual Busan International Film Festival), the value of official

Korean film exports to China has taken off: $730,809 in 2012; $1,757,100 in 2013; and a massive $8,206,702 in 2014.[7]

A sharp upturn for the Korean film industry (and industries around the globe) occurred in early 2012, when the Chinese government increased the number of foreign feature films permitted to share in domestic box office profits from 20 to 34; as a result, the market for Korean films in China expanded even further. [8] At the same time, multiplex screens have continued to rise in China, reaching around 23,600 at the end of 2014: in 2014 alone 1,015 new cinemas and 5,397 new screens were added, revealing a truly remarkable acceleration in growth (up from an estimated 1,500 modern multiplex screens in 2008).[9] According to *The Hollywood Reporter*, mainland Chinese cinemas showed a 'tenfold increase' between 2002 and 2012: from 1,300 to 13,000.[10] This trend is bound to continue given the size of China's population, which now is reaching 1.4 billion. The number of films exhibited in 3D has risen sharply too, and new box office revenue-sharing records have been set in this area. (The 4,000-screen release of Korea's 3D sci-fi action-thriller *Sector 7* in China at the end of 2011 was very well timed, filling the void created by the shortage of Chinese 3D films during this period.)[11] Most importantly, in mid-2014 Korea and China signed a co-production treaty that classified co-produced films as local films, thus further increasing Korea's share of the massive Chinese box office. Bilateral collaborations can only increase following the signing of this landmark treaty. Although the number of foreign feature imports to China has been increased to 34, many industry insiders feel that Hollywood films will grab most of this quota, thus leaving co-productions as an especially attractive option for other competitors. In short, a large slice of the contemporary Korean film industry—regardless of whether they are consciously a part of the current wave of globalization—has become part of the "China dream". China has become a unique stepping stone for the further globalization, and perhaps continued survival, not only of Korean cinema but of major sectors of the Korean film industry as well.

The Korean film industry's recent tilt toward China is the product of a long sequence of developments. With the growing popularity of Korean cultural contents in Asia—the so-called Korean Wave or *Hallyu*—one of the most notable areas of film collaboration in the 2000s was the export of acting talent. Since 2003, an increasing number of Korean actors, including Kwon Sang-woo, Kim Hee-sun, Song Hye-kyo, Jung Woo-sung, and So Ji-seup, have accepted invitations to appear in Chinese productions, eager to expand their profiles among new pan-Asian audiences.[12] In turn, directors such as Jackie Chan have increased the potential commercial value of their films by casting these popular stars. *Seven Swords* (2003) and *The Myth* (2005) starred leading ladies Kim So-yeon and Kim Hee-sun, respectively, while popular singer and television actress Jang Na-ra appeared in *Girls' Revolution* (2007), directed by San Dao and co-staring Jaycee Chan (Jackie Chan's son). Other actresses and television stars including Lee Jung-hyun, Jang Seo-hee, and Chu Ja-hyeon (aka Choo Ja-hyun) have boosted flagging careers by appearing in Chinese TV dramas. Chu decidedly made a career decision to come to China in 2007, where she has starred in multiple TV dramas;

she has developed a strong focus on working in China, all but leaving Korea behind.[13] Unlike many other *Hallyu* stars who have worked in China on one-off projects, Chu has mastered Chinese in order to communicate effectively with both colleagues and fans, separating her from other Korean actors who rely on translators and/or dubbing on Chinese TV and films. Most recently, Chu starred in the crime thriller film *The Boundary* (2014), directed by Wang Tao.

On the other side of the set, a number of established directors in Korea have also been able to re-boot their careers in China. Korean director Hur Jin-ho (aka Heo Jin-ho), well known for *Christmas in August* (1998) and *One Fine Spring Day* (2001), has directed two Chinese films, *A Good Rain Knows* (2009, aka *Season of Good Rain*) and *Dangerous Liaisons* (2012). Both films were produced by Beijing-based Zonbo Media, blending the commercial acumen of Zonbo's president Chen Weiming with the artistic vision of director Hur. Around the same time, Ahn Byung-ki, Korea's leading horror film director (and founder of Toilet Pictures)—best known for *A Nightmare* (2000), *Phone* (2002), and *Bunshinsaba* (2004) and also the producer of *Speed Scandal* (2008, a box office hit in China) and *Sunny* (2011, among the top 10 films released in Hong Kong in April 2012)—entered the Chinese market. He has directed a Chinese trilogy based on his 2004 hit film—*Bunshinsaba* (2012), *Bunshinsaba* 2 (2013), and *Bunshinsaba* 3 (2014)—one of the earliest domestic horror series released in China. In 2015, Korean director Chang Yoon-hyun, known for the thriller *Tell Me Something* (1998), is directing the transnational thriller *The Peaceful Island*, a co-production produced by CJ E&M, China's C2M and Huace Media, and Hong Kong's Media Asia Group. Finally, in 2015 Kang Je-gyu and Feng Xiaogang, two leading directors from both countries, gave a further boost to the cross-industry linkages they had established through their joint work on *Assembly* by producing the action black comedy *The Bad Man Must Die*. The film is set in Jeju Island, which has become a very popular destination for Chinese tourists. Although these are all seasoned directors with strong track records, their reputations had faded in Korea after a cohort of younger, ambitious directors pushed them out of the spotlight. As a result, they struggled to find new projects at home and turned their attention to China where more than 600 films were produced in 2014—signalling a need for experienced directors to capitalize on the opportunities presented by the burgeoning Chinese film industry.

Despite these developments, it is not widely known that the Korean–Chinese collaborations of the early 2000s included Fifth Generation Chinese director Chen Kaige—celebrated for directing *Yellow Earth* (1984), *Farewell My Concubine* (1993), *Temptress Moon* (1996), and *The Emperor and the Assassin* (1998)—in two very different types of projects. First was the drama *Together* (2002, aka *Together With You*), which was shot by Korean cinematographer Kim Hyung-gu—known for *Beat* (1997), *Peppermint Candy* (1999), and *Musa* (2001)—and produced by Lee Joo-ik, president of Korean production company Big Bang Creative and a key player in the Korea–China co-production scene. *Together* also involved contributions by well-known Korean costume designer Ha Yeong-su and Korean TV actress Kim Hye-ri (playing Professor Yu's wife).

Together tells the story of a small-town teenage violin prodigy who is taken by his father to study music in Beijing, where he finds the fame (and wealth) of which his poor father could only dream. Once established in the big city, the boy is shuffled between two well-known but very different teachers, and among these three competing father figures (not to mention a materialistic young female neighbor who befriends him) he discovers a deeper meaning to life. This early transnational collaboration resulted from networking meetings and detailed conversations between Lee Joo-ik and director Chen. At the time, Lee Joo-ik was planning to make a pan-Asian film—to be called *Mong-u-do-won-do*, based on Choi In-ho's bestselling love story—with director Chen Keige. Chen made a special visit to Korea in July 2001 where he made an official announcement about this collaborative project to the local press.[14] Impressed by Chen's films, Lee Joo-ik sent him the project proposal, and his persistent pitching of the film to Chen was rewarded by his agreement to join the project.[15] Although this big-budget Korean–Chinese blockbuster failed to eventuate, Korean filmmakers had made another good friend in China, resulting in strong Korean contributions to *Together* as well as for Chen's next pan-Asian project, *The Promise* (2005). This historical fantasy was submitted by China to the 2006 Academy Awards for Best Foreign Language Film, and was nominated by the Golden Globes for Best Foreign Film in the same year.[16]

An official co-production film according to KOFIC records, *The Promise* was made with contributions from members of the Korean, Chinese, Japanese, US, and Australian film industries, behind as well as in front of the camera, and starred popular actors Jang Dong-gun (from Korea), Cecilia Chung and Nicholas Tse (from Hong Kong), and Sanada Hiroyuki (from Japan). After leaving Big Bang Creative, producer Lee Joo-ik established Boram Entertainment in 2004. Lee, who is fluent in Mandarin, Cantonese, Japanese, and English, rejoined Chen for this project, providing one-third of the budget. US-based Moonstone Entertainment provided additional financing, and Australian post-production company Soundfirm contributed to the film from its newly opened Beijing studio. There can be little doubt that, with this project, this international crew was hoping to replicate the runaway success of transnational blockbuster Ang Lee's Chinese–Hong Kong–Taiwanese–US co-production *Crouching Tiger, Hidden Dragon* (2001), which still loomed large in the minds of industry workers and audiences alike.[17]

Given that Korean cinema was experiencing a boom in the mid-2000s, additional opportunities to work closely with Chinese and other international colleagues offered new pathways for expansion, while spreading the risk of producing a box office sleeper by dividing funding among multiple international partners. For Lee, and the other industry pioneers discussed in this chapter, language skills and strengthening industry and personal networks in China have continued to produce dividends. These include Lee's historical action war drama *Battle of Wits* (2005, aka *Battle of the Warriors*) featuring Andy Lau and Ahn Sung-ki (aka Ahn Sung-kee), who are mega-stars in Greater China and Korea, respectively. Five years later, Lee produced two more international co-productions: the Korea–New Zealand Western–action film *The Warrior's Way*, starring Jang Dong-gun and Kate

Bosworth; and director Kim Tae-yong's *Late Autumn* (2010), an English-language melodrama (a remake of the lost 1966 Korean film directed by Lee Man-hee) co-produced by Korea, Hong Kong, and the US. Set in Seattle, *Late Autumn* starred Korea's Hyun Bin opposite China's Tang Wei, who later married director Kim Tae-yong.

Korean executive producers such as Lee Joon-ik (aka Lee Jun-ik) of Cineworld Entertainment—and director of the immensely successful *King and the Clown* (2005)—have also looked to China to provide the varied locations that are unavailable at home—a trend that Chinese filmmakers had first exploited during the 1960s and 1970s (see Chapter 4). The hard-boiled historical gangster drama *Anarchists* (2000), produced by Lee, co-written by celebrated director Park Chan-wook, and directed by KAFA (and Yonsei University) graduate Yoo Young-sik, tells the story of five Koreans in mid-1920s Shanghai bent on overthrowing the Japanese colonial government. This $3 million USD-budget film (well above average for films made before 2000) starred Jang Dong-gun, Jung Joon-ho, Lee Bum-soo, Kim Sang-joong, and Kim In-kwon. It was shot at Shanghai Film Studio's newly built 62-acre film production and theme park complex, with heavy assistance from local art director Zheng Changfu and producers Zhong Zheng (of *Purple Butterfly* (2003) fame) and Fu Wenxia. The latter pair coordinated the three-month shoot involving production and set design, as well as recruiting local acting talent and coordinating hundreds of extras on location in and around Shanghai and at the studio. Through these activities, that is, the relatively simple conjoining of separately produced parts of a film, Korean filmmakers began accumulating a little *guanxi* in China. As a result, the working relationship between the two industries entered a formative collaborative stage.

Over time and as Korean cinema's local and global profile continued to expand, the nature and scope of joint Korean–Chinese projects became increasingly sophisticated. Following *Anarchists*, Korean productions featuring Chinese locations (primarily for historical tales and particular scenes in other genre films) include: the fantasy–action swordplay movie *Bichunmoo* (2000, aka *Out Live*), directed by Kim Young-jun and co-produced by CJ Entertainment and Taewon Entertainment and shot on location at Hengdian World Studio; and the historical–action swordplay epic *Musa* (2001, aka *The Warrior*). *Musa* was written and directed by Kim Sung-soo (aka Kim Sung-su) and produced by Cha Seung-jae (Sidus) with Chinese partner Zhang Xia (deputy managing director of the Beijing Film Studio), with major support from CJ Entertainment and the state-run China Film Group, and shot on location in the desert lake area of Zhongwei, the Liaoning highlands, and the ancient city of Xingcheng. Also on this list are: CJ Entertainment's fantasy–action drama *The Legend of Evil Lake* (2003); the historical–action swordplay movie *Shadowless Sword* (2005), directed by Kim Young-jun and co-financed by Taewon Entertainment and US-based New Line Cinema (also shot at Hengdian World Studio); and the historical action–adventure drama *Demon Empire* (aka *The Restless*, 2006), produced by Nabi Pictures and directed by its co-CEO Kim Sung-soo, with visual effects by Seoul-based Macrograph. *Demon Empire* was also shot at Hengdian World

Studio, which was built in 1996 and incorporates replicas of historic buildings such as the Qin Imperial Palace and the palaces of the Ming and Qing Dynasties. In addition, we must not neglect to mention Kim Jee-woon's Manchurian Western–action–adventure–black comedy *The Good, The Bad, and The Weird* (2008)—shot almost wholly in China on the outskirts of Dunhwang city, with unprecedented numbers of Korean and local crewmembers working together on its various outdoor and studio sets. *The Good, The Bad, and The Weird* ranks at number five in terms of all-time Korean film production budgets, coming in at $10 million USD.

In this growing list of genre films shot wholly or in part in China, *Musa* stands alone in incorporating all of the key ingredients necessary for a major cross-over Korean blockbuster. This epic historical drama is set near the end of the Koryo Dynasty (935–1392), one of Korea's golden eras, when the ruling house began developing cultural traditions distinct from those found in other parts of East Asia. In the film, a band of soldiers, diplomats and their servants is sent to China to make contact with the emperor of the newly established Ming Dynasty. En route, the delegation is accused of spying and is attacked by an army of well-armed Chinese soldiers. Adding to their burdens, the Koreans are joined by a Ming princess (played by Chinese star Zhang Ziyi of *Crouching Tiger, Hidden Dragon* fame), who promises them riches if they can protect her and escort her home. The members of the Korean party who survive the attack, as well as local Chinese refugees who join them along the way, seek refuge in an abandoned seaside fort, hoping to defeat their unrelenting pursuers and escape to safety.

Musa contains the high production values, universal story, talent, and visual effects that also marked Ang Lee's screen-grabbing, box-office giant *Crouching Tiger, Hidden Dragon* (2000). The film's total budget was around $8 million USD—more than double the average cost ($3 million USD) of all Korean feature films and animations made in 2001, but still only a fraction of the cost of a comparable Hollywood blockbuster (and less than half of the budget for *Crouching Tiger, Hidden Dragon*). At the time, *Musa* was by far the most expensive Korean film ever made, establishing Cha Seung-jae's reputation as one of Korea's most influential and ambitious producers. However, the unfortunate timing of *Musa*'s release in Korea—four days before the September 11 tragedy in the US in 2001—prevented it from attracting the international audiences and box office success that *Crouching Tiger, Hidden Dragon* had enjoyed.[18] Nevertheless, by investigating how *Musa* was produced outside of Korea, we can gain some valuable insights into the international affiliations of Korean cinema and their importance for its continuing rise. The film was shot by cinematographer Kim Hyung-gu (whose next project, Chen Kaige's *Together*, was filmed a year later) over a five-month period on location in Liaoning—the southern part of northeast China bordering North Korea—and Mongolia. It features massive battle sequences and dialogue recorded in three languages. Following the success of *Shiri*, Korea's "first" blockbuster, industry, market, and audience conditions were judged to be ripe for further large-scale productions, and director Kim Sung-soo began pre-production and location hunting in China in September 1999. Chinese producer Zhang Xia, who had worked with Chen Kaige as a line producer for *Farewell My Concubine* (1993), and Japanese composer Shirō Sagisu, known for his work on the celebrated Japananimation *Neon Genesis Evangelion* (1997), joined director Kim on this massive and pioneering undertaking. *Musa* was truly a global project led by a core of Korean pathfinders.

Filming in a Chinese desert during the summer months was challenging to say the least, with daily temperatures reaching over 40°C. Nights were cooler, with temperatures dipping below 30°C. Changing weather patterns, including intense dry heat, lightning, and heavy rainfall, added to the difficulties of working in this scenic but harsh region. Nevertheless, the dynamic backdrop provided by the desert landscape of Liaoning, including sandstorms that were used as natural special effects, enabled the filmmakers to create a production unrivalled in contemporary Korean cinema.

In undertaking this highly ambitious venture, the Korean crew succeeded only with the help of their Chinese colleagues; both were dependent on a coterie of translators who bridged the technical and cultural gaps between Korean and Chinese working practices. On a project on the scale of *Musa*, a Korean director would normally employ six or seven assistant producers, who would help oversee day-to-day production processes. As one might expect, a venture on this scale requires decisive direction and strict workflow patterns in order to stay on schedule and on budget. Director Kim Sung-soo and producer Jo Min-hwan worked effectively with their Chinese producer, Zhang Xia, forming a tight bond cemented by mutual trust. Jo oversaw production tasks that were delegated to the Korean crew, while Zhang was responsible for those assigned to the Chinese crew (which included seasoned actor Yu Rongguang and a slew of extras, as well as costume designer Huang Bao Rong and production designer Huo Tingxiao). Given a large amount of responsibility for the project, Zhang further delegated tasks through her own employee networks, thus easing workflows within the cross-cultural production teams.[19] Later in 2006 *Musa* producers Jo and Kim established a Beijing office of Nabi Pictures, and employed their former Chinese co-producer Zhang Xia to develop and oversee local projects to add to their portfolio. After four years in the movie business, in 2010, Nabi Pictures co-produced the romantic comedy *My Ex-wife's Wedding* (2010) with Chinese–Hong Kong partner October Pictures (with support from Korea's iHQ, the Beijing Poly-bona Film Distribution Company, and Hong Kong newcomer Sundream Motion Pictures).

In short, *Musa* stands as a watershed production, a film that has inspired further collaborative ventures between the Korean and Chinese film industries. Since *Musa*, the links between the two industries have continued to grow both in strength and scope. Deeply impressed by Korean cinematographer Kim Hyung-gu's work on the film, and immediately following its release, Chen Kaige invited Kim and established Korean producer Lee Joo-ik, whom he had gotten to know on the aborted project *Mong-u-do-won-do* in 2001, to collaborate on the multi-award-winning feature *Together* (2002). Further collaboration between Korean and Chinese filmmakers followed these successes, including the casting of actors from both countries. In addition, a growing number of Korean firms began to provide production and digital post-production services in China, at a fraction of the cost of similar work undertaken for most Hollywood blockbusters.

In 2007, as Korean cinema began to recover from the downturn that had hit the industry the previous year, a new watershed in international film collaboration was celebrated when BIFF (then known as PIFF) screened Feng Xiaogang's *Assembly* (2007) as the festival's opening offering. The prominent position given to this action–war drama—a co-production of China, Hong Kong and Korea—at BIFF represented a new level of recognition for the collaborative efforts of the Korean and Greater Chinese film industries. Not only were *Assembly's* producers, the Huayi Brothers and Media Asia Films, the largest and most progressive film companies in China, but the festival screening also showcased the close involvement in the film of Korean action and post-production digital effects specialists (coordinated by Edward Yi Chi-yun for MK Pictures)—features that would soon come to typify Korea's deepening contribution to Chinese cinema.

From this moment on, the large-scale sharing of technical staff and technological transfer between Korea and China signalled the birth of an advanced form of film collaboration. Replacing the patterns of the recent past, where one partner commonly maintained leadership of a co-production project, Korea and China were showing how it was possible for groups of international crewmembers to be brought together through personal and industry networks to complete creative projects as a team. This is not to claim that colleagues from both countries shared intimate details of every aspect of the film during the pre-production, production, and post-production stages of *Assembly*, rather that levels of collaboration, mutual respect, and *guanxi* had reached unprecedented heights since members of both film industries had worked alongside each other on *Anarchists* in 1999.

The varied types of international collaboration that Korean filmmakers have pursued with colleagues in China and elsewhere are by no means a new trend, as transnational film encounters have become increasingly common since non-US media conglomerates dramatically increased their investment in Hollywood entertainment companies in the early 1990s. Examples are Sony's purchase of Columbia Pictures Entertainment in 1989, Matsushita Electric/Panasonic's acquisition of MCA/Universal Pictures in 1990, and CJ Entertainment's founding investment in DreamWorks in 1995 (see Chapter 8).[20] Korean and other national cinemas are increasingly being shaped by a range of international collaborations that have resulted from this global shift in ownership; the result has been an accelerated number of high-concept genre films involving a wide range of co-production and assisted production arrangements, as well as visual effects and post-production services provided by highly skilled practitioners from around the globe.

Ever since the production and release of *Assembly* in 2007, Korean practitioners have become a larger part of this global trend. Nevertheless, one of the least known aspects of Korean cinema—or what we can now justly call Korean transnational cinema—is the industry's extensive engagement in post-production work for many Chinese films after this period. Put simply, a range of Korean post-production practitioners have contributed to the professionalization of Chinese cinema while enhancing the domestic film industry's capacity for change—that is, its ability to integrate advanced skills, techniques, and manpower from outside.

Listing the numerous films made in China with input from Korean practitioners following the release of *Together* and *Assembly* is a near-impossible task, although to our knowledge this chapter contains the most comprehensively researched and consolidated listing available to date. What the list does show is that Koreans have left their mark on a plethora of genres—*wuxia* (martial arts) comedies and fantasies, contemporary and period dramas, romantic and black comedies, thrillers and horror films, and war films. The list also includes Chinese remakes of Korean films, such as *20 Once Again* (2015)—a remake of the Korean fantasy–comedy–musical *Miss Granny* (2014).[21] In reality, the number of Korean–Chinese film encounters of all varieties far exceeds the list of coproductions offered by KOFIC and other studies of Korean cinema in international markets.[22]

The Transnational Post-production Trail

In early 2006, when Feng Xiaogang was conceiving the war film *Assembly*, he and his core production and planning team looked to Kang Je-gyu's Korean War blockbuster hit *Taegukgi* (2004, aka *Brotherhood of War*) as a model. Not only did *Taegukgi* look, sound, and feel like the Hollywood blockbuster *Saving Private Ryan* (1998), which was made on a budget of around $70 million USD (not including prints and advertising), but it was produced for around 18 percent of that figure. To help bring "*Taegukgi*" to China, Feng and his team collaborated with Korea's MK Pictures (Myung Film and Kang Je-gyu Film, see Chapter 8), which was exploring ways of capitalizing on the momentum generated by the production of *Musa* in China five years earlier.

Although it failed to produce a film of its own, MK Pictures assisted the project by connecting Feng with producer Edward Yi Chi-yun, a BFA graduate who coordinated the work of specialized teams from Korea. Yi had extensive networks in both the Korean and Chinese film industries and had developed an intimate knowledge of their inner workings. In addition to speaking Chinese and understanding Chinese culture, he knew the right people for this project: the key executives and crewmembers who had worked on *Taegukgi*. In 1996, on returning to Korea after completing his studies at BFA, Yi was appointed production manager on director Kang Je-gyu's *Gingko Bed*. Then in 1999, he was involved in the pre-production of *The Anarchists*, scouting locations in Shanghai and line producing during production. As one of the active producers on *Assembly*, Yi was responsible for bringing together and supervising a Korean team of action and stunt coordinators, as well as technical experts in special effects, make-up, sound effects, and sound editing—teams that had worked together previously on *Taegukgi*. Given that this was the first time such a large number of Korean technicians and other specialists had worked on a Chinese blockbuster, there was much for both sides to learn from each other. As a result, the Korean film industry was made aware of the burgeoning need in the Chinese industry for the type of expertise and advanced technical skills and training that Korean practitioners had amassed since *Shiri* splashed across the big screen in 1999.

Since *Assembly*, Yi has continued to work as a producer with some of China's leading commercial directors and has introduced an increasing number of fellow Korean film practitioners to Chinese film projects. At the same time, he has served in various leadership and liaison positions, including special effects supervisor for John Woo's *Red Cliff I* (2008), post-production producer for Tsui Hak's *Flying Swords of Dragon Gate* (2012), special effects and action producer for Wei Te-Sheng's *Warriors of the Rainbow: Seediq Bale* (2013), and action producer for Hu Guan's *The Chef, The Actor, The Scoundrel* (2013). While working on these and additional projects, Yi (and others following in his footsteps) came to appreciate that Korea was far ahead of China in terms of advanced digital production and post-production technology and techniques. As a result, Korean companies and practitioners began following the post-production trail in China, concentrating their activities in this lucrative frontier territory.

In 2008 and 2009, Korean special effects and make-up company MAGE, in concert with special effects company Demolition and the Seoul-based Dolby film sound-mixing studio Bluecap Soundworks, worked extensively on John Woo's *Red Cliff I* (2008) and *Red Cliff II* (2009), helping to realize the director's full creative vision for the series. In 2010, these same three firms, along with other Korean action consultants and stunt coordinators, helped to re-create the striking disaster sequences and soundscapes in Feng Xiaogang's *Aftershock* (2010), a film about the 1976 Tangshan earthquake and its devastating aftermath. In addition, Busan-based AZ Works (headed by CEO Lee Yong-gi) received the visual effects award at the Hong Kong Film Awards for its contribution to Tsui Hark's *Detective Dee and the Mystery of the Phantom Flame* (2010).

Between 2009 and 2015, Korean practitioners working in China continued to consolidate their skills while gaining valuable experience in the rapidly expanding Chinese film industry. During this period, Seoul-based Digital Idea and Beijing-based Lollol Media worked on the visual effects and digital intermediary (aka DI or color grading) work for Tsui Hark's top-performing 3D film *Flying Swords of Dragon Gate* (2011) as well as *CZ12* (aka *Chinese Zodiac*, directed by Jackie Chan, 2012) and *The Chef, The Actor, The Scoundrel*.[23] In addition, Korea's CJ Powercast, Next Visual Studio, and Lollol Media (along with Chinese firm Phenom Film) played major roles in the VFX and 2D/3D digital intermediary work on director Wuershan's supernatural fantasy–action romance *Painted Skin 2: The Resurrection* (2012), inspired by the classic Liao Zhai Zhi Yi collection of supernatural tales.[24]

In addition, Forestt Studios—a full-service post-production company based in the Qikeshu Innovation Park area of Chaoyang District in Beijing and run by experienced Korean national and former HFR Co. DI expert Ethan Park[25]—completed a series of films of its own. Forestt specializes in color grading for feature films (to which it has recently added full-scale sound post-production), and (without sounding overly promotional) is genuinely one of the few Chinese companies that can meet the highest international standards for 2D and 3D high-resolution (4K real-time) digital intermediate service (at least at the time of writing). The firm's filmography includes the romance *My Lucky Star* (2013), a prequel to the 2009 official Chinese–Korean co-production *Sophie's Revenge* (produced by Beijing Perfect World Co. and CJ Entertainment), directed by US-born Dennie Gordon and starring Zhang Ziyi and Leehom Wang; and the Chinese–Hong Kong action crime thriller *A Chilling Cosplay* (2013, aka *-197°C Murder*), by director Wang Guangli and producer Wong Jing. Forestt Studios completed around 20 films in 2014 and another 15 in the first quarter of 2015, and there are another 10 films in the pipeline for completion before the end of 2015.

Thus far, the biggest box office sensation resulting from Chinese–Korean collaboration is Stephen Chow's *Journey to the West: Conquering the Demons* (2013), an action–comedy directed by Stephen Chow and Derek Kwok Chi-Kin, which returned a gross profit of $192 million USD. For this action-packed 3D production, Korean companies Macrograph and Moneff, in concert with the Korean VFX farm run by Los Angeles-based Venture 3D, completed the spectacular visual effects; Seoul-based Locus Corp. was responsible for key CGI scenes as well as the film's ancillary character-licensing products. The next big collaborative hit was *The Monkey King* (2014), which conquered the box office with $168 million USD. A total of 28 Korean companies worked on this film, including CG firms Dexter Digital, Digital Studio 2L, Digital Idea and Macrograph, helping *The Monkey King* to become the second runner-up at the box office in 2014, behind *Transformers: Age of Extinction* and the Chinese romantic comedy/road movie *Breakup Buddies* directed by Ning Hao.[26] In their respective credits, *Journey to the West* and *The Monkey King* boast the longest list of Korean companies and practitioners of any films produced in China, demonstrating the increasing scope of the ongoing internationalization of Chinese cinema. *Journey to the West* and *The Monkey King* mark watersheds in Korean and Chinese cinema and film history if only because, in 2013 and 2014 respectively, they took their place among the highest grossing domestic films ever screened in China. Confirming a local market trend, both films made a significant proportion of their total revenues at the box office within the first few days of their release, and both outperformed a majority of the Hollywood films released in China in the same year.[27] Little wonder that in 2015 the major US film companies and foreign critics alike have their eyes firmly fixed on the Chinese film market.

Other recent bilateral collaborations include the 3D baseball fantasy film *Mr. Go* (2013), directed by Kim Yong-hwa (known for the 2006 film *200 Pounds Beauty*, a box office hit in China and Korea) and produced by Korea's Dexter Studios with Yi Chi-yun in the role of the 'Chinese' producer; and CJ E&M China's romance drama *Wedding Invitation* (2014) and the romantic fantasy comedy *Miss Granny* (2014). The list of Korean companies and individuals contributing to Asian blockbusters that exemplify Chinese cinema's upward technological trajectory is burgeoning. In 2015, Yi and director Kang Je-gyu are working together on the Korea–China co-production *The Bad Man Must Die*. Korean actress Son Ye-jin and actor Shin Hyun-jun, as well as Taiwanese actor Chen Bolin have been cast in the main roles for the film, which has received investment funding from China's Huayi Brothers and New Power Film.[28] Yi has also overseen several Myung Film remakes in China, including the popular romance dramas *Cyrano Agency* (2010) and *Architecture 101* (2012).[29] Where other Koreans have failed to secure a foothold in the Chinese market in the past, Yi and other producers, who have stayed and worked in China as long-termers, are now setting their sails to catch the winds of change blowing across China—changes that have come about as a result of government regulations that have opened up the film industry and that may or may not continue in the same direction in the future.

The Changing Face of Chinese–Korean Cinema

Since 2002, China's annual film production figures have soared, with an average annual growth rate of 20%; in 2010, with 526 productions to its credit, China became the third largest producer of films in the world.[30] In 2014 this figure had reached 618. The rapidly expanding number of films being produced on an annual basis in China is ensuring that there is no shortage of DI and visual effects work for both domestic and international practitioners and firms.[31] Having said this, Chinese directors and producers inspire Korean DI and visual effects technicians in different ways from their Korean counterparts, pushing them to satisfy a different set of aesthetic values and production needs. Simply put, China's landscape color palette is unlike that found in Korea; in particular, the colors of land and sky, the shapes of mountains and rivers, and people's reaction to the natural world all differ in significant respects from their Korean equivalents, further challenging Korean professionals to explore alternative artistic and creative terrain.

This trend has been strengthened by the relaxation of official censorship regulations. In July 2013, China's State Administration of Press, Publication, Radio, Film, and Television (formerly known as the State Administration of Radio, Film, and Television or SARFT) announced that it would confine its scrutiny to inspecting a story summary prior to granting a filming permit, thereby eliminating 20 distinct components requiring government approval, including the thorough assessment of film scripts.[32] With this changing policy landscape in mind, the somewhat surprising censorship approval granted to the psychological mystery–thriller–drama *Double Xposure* (2012) offers a timely opportunity to assess the potential for technical and artistic creativity in the Chinese film industry under a relaxed censorship regime. A case study of its post-production context offers insights into how and where Korean practitioners are making a mark on Chinese cinema in a potentially volatile policy environment.

Double Xposure (2012), director Li Yu's fifth and most aesthetically ambitious feature film to date, is a quintessential example of an evolving transnational cinema—one that is being created through a range of international collaborators drawn from multiple production networks. Her exploration of thriller and road movie conventions, which marks a departure from her earlier documentary and realist style, makes the film a significant new addition to "China's genre revolution".[33]

In this visually stunning film, Li uses the flashbacks, illusions and hallucinations involving sex, adultery, violence, and murder experienced by the protagonist Song Qi (played by Fan Bingbing) to disorient the audience. Song Qi, an ambitious cosmetic surgeon, experiences emotional turmoil after learning that her closest friend is having an affair with her boyfriend. Her life becomes more disjointed when she discovers that she has a psychological disorder. Song embarks on a road trip in search of her past and as a means of uncovering her deeply repressed thoughts. The second half of the film in particular is marked by a sense of ambiguity, detracting from the overall cohesion of the story. Despite its provocative content—or perhaps *because* the film's controversial scenes are presented as the protagonist's paranoid delusions—*Double Xposure* managed to evade government censorship.[34]

Double Xposure is an excellent example of the ways in which, in contemporary Chinese cinema, film genres are being expanded with the aid of the sophisticated technical support and creative input offered by Korean practitioners. Even for a veteran colorist like Ethan Park, with almost a decade of experience in the industry—which he has shared with us in multiple interviews—the DI process made *Double Xposure* the most challenging and interesting film he had worked on to date. The film was shot on five different formats: primarily with the Alexa digital film camera, but with flashback, helicopter, and underwater sequences shot on a combination of 35mm (for aerial photography) and Super 16mm analogue, and Canon 5D, GoPro (for CCTV footage), and RED MX (for high-speed shots) digital film cameras. This approach was similar to the use of multiple film stocks, for example, in Oliver Stone's *JFK* (1991) and *Natural Born Killers* (1994, using techniques suggested in Quentin Tarantino's original script), as well as in Tarantino's *Kill Bill* (2003).[35] The crisp, clean, cold look that these filming techniques created for the scenes set in the present day reflected the sterile atmosphere of the cosmetic surgeons' operating theater, to give one example. This aesthetic forms an effective contrast to the aged, analogue-style appearance of the flashbacks and historical sequences—initially replicated through digital film noise, but eventually given a more authentic "grainy" look through the use of Super 16mm film stock. Specifically, the DI was used to enhance the "cold" feeling of the appropriate sequences by increasing the blue and green tints, and then to create a desaturated and low-contrast color effect near the end of the film when Song Qi emerges from her delusions and into a more natural but still ethereal setting on a beach.

Once the footage had been digitized using state-of-the-art equipment, DI specialist Ethan Park, working on the project exclusively in Beijing, created artificial scratches and dust spots on the film, removed grain from other shots, and applied motion and edge blur for the dream sequences as well to simulate camera shake and add "highlight glow" to close ups of Song Qi. Park's attempts to differentiate sequential shots, while using particular colors to signal emotions displayed by the characters, provided additional challenges.[36] The shared vision that marked the pair's relationship—along with Li Yu's confidence in Park's talent and ability, as seen in his work on her previous film *Buddha Mountain* (2010)—enabled Park to experiment freely with color grading and correction techniques—processes that were not only new to him as one of Korea's most experienced DI experts, but also to Chinese cinema. Park dedicated 20 days to completing the DI for *Double Xposure* over a three-month period, taking breaks between processing each quarter of the film in order to maintain a fresh perspective on the work and to push his (and cinematographer Florian Zinke's) ideas even further, achieving just the kind of creative response to the material producer Li Fang had hoped for.[37]

For *Double Xposure*, Park and German-born cinematographer Florian Zinke, a graduate of the Beijing Film Academy, pushed their joint creative endeavors in a new direction. Building on their combined track record, the team developed a unique visual style honed over three months' worth of DI, resulting in an aesthetic that veered away from the direction taken by recent unconventional Korean thrillers such as the horror–thriller *H* (2002, about an urban serial killer), Kim Jee-woon's *A Tale of Two Sisters* (2003), and Park Chan-wook's *Thirst* (2009).

More recently, Forestt Studios, under Ethan Park's creative direction, completed the post-production and digital effects for Sixth Generation arthouse director Lou Ye's Chinese–French co-production *Blind Massage* (2014), a drama told from the perspective of blind masseurs and masseuses. In order to create an innovative look for the film, and also to manage the multiple grading applied to nearly every single shot, Park required 60 days (about six times as long as a film with more conventional DI) to color it, guided in each scene by the tempo of the background music and the natural sound layer. This was a novel approach for Park and for DI more generally (certainly in Korea and China, but also internationally), given that conventional DI involves a single consistent grading for each shot. Furthermore, many colorists turn off the audio while working to avoid the soundtrack influencing their coloring style. As a result, in *Blind Massage* the soundtrack and the color palette flow in unison as if they were two halves of a single breathing rhythm, raising provocative questions about what blind people "see" in their imaginative world. To gain further understanding of this synesthetic rhythm in a real-life setting, Park visited numerous "blind massage" parlors in an attempt to experience this world for himself.

Working behind the scenes, Ethan Park is a key figure in understanding the nature of the collaborative relationship between the Korean and Chinese film industries and the ways in which the institution of Korean cinema is being absorbed by the Chinese film industry, at least in part. Park studied film editing at Dongguk University and in 2006 joined post-production company HFR, where he specialized in color grading and DI, skills in high demand as a result of the ongoing transition to digital workflow practices. Here he experienced firsthand the explosive growth of the Chinese market, which was happening at the same time as the downturn in Korea's domestic film industry—the number of local DI projects had begun to plateau. Park's English-language skills landed him a key role as a DI producer on CJ E&M's first co-production project, *Sophie's Revenge* (2009). In the same year he urged HFR to open a Beijing branch, and Park moved to China to apply the skills he had mastered while working on several dozen top-grossing Korean films.[38] After leaving HFR, he teamed up with Yi Chi-yun at rival post-production firm Lollol Media in Beijing, thus gaining further experience in the local market and expanding his industry and personal networks. Park is currently

CEO of Forestt Studios, known for both its commercial work and highly creative arthouse genre-bending films.

Post-production practitioners like Ethan Park are pioneer digital colorists, that is, they manipulate the colors of a film during the post-production and final printing processes, which are now completely digitized (and known as digital intermediary or DI). DI, which has become an essential medium for filmmaking around the globe, enables filmmakers to manipulate a film and prepare it for digital projection before it is distributed to cinemas or processed for other screen formats. Other leading names in the field include Lee Yong-gi – Korean cinema's "grandfather of color grading"; Peter Ahn, a translator and marketer for HFR Beijing, and now VFX producer at the Paju and Beijing-based firm Dexter Digital; and Kim Hyeong-seok, now working at 4th Creative Party in Korea, but previously with Phenom Film, a newcomer formed by the merger of HFR-Beijing, Lollol Media, and a local Chinese VFX company. Between them, these practitioners have "colored" and—following the industry's transition from analog to digital equipment—digitized the bulk of Korean feature films, both commercial and independent, made by the leading producers discussed in Chapter 8. They are also responsible for much of the DI work done on the films made by leading directors such as Bong Joon-ho, Park Chan wook, Kim Jee-woon, and Lee Myung-se, and by the female directors discussed in Chapter 9. This remarkable achievement has come hard on the heels of their role in pioneering Korean cinema's transition to digital equipment and workflow processes between 2002 and 2005.

While working in China, Park and these other Korean practitioners have explored numerous opportunities offered by new types of film projects that have enabled them to enhance their skills. The pathways they have taken, and the timing of their entry into the Chinese market, have coincided with the large-scale transformation of the Korean film industry. At the same time, limited opportunities at home have pushed them in this international direction. Against the backdrop of the changes discussed above, and bearing in mind that international film co-productions have become commonplace around the globe, fine-tuning the working relationships between international partners still presents a challenge for both Korean and Chinese cinema. In the cases of *Double Xposure* and *Blind Massage*, a pinch of Korean technical skill and ingenuity has proven to be a key ingredient in producing a successful dish, especially where the creation of original and dynamic colorscapes has been a critical factor. Just as a new breed of Korean films produced after the success of *Shiri* achieved a high level of production values and narrative diversity, contemporary Chinese films are becoming known for their innovative visual styles and growing diversity of genres and stories. The increasing collaboration between the two countries, especially cooperation in post-production work, is raising the bar in terms of technical quality, leading to increased value in the marketplace.

As a result, a wave of change is sweeping through the Chinese film industry, although some practitioners are yet to appreciate the rapidly changing policy environment in which they are now operating. Be that as it may, there is no doubt that this transformation of the Chinese film scene is being driven by commercial imperatives and achieved in large part by the leveraging of creativity from outside China—notably from Korea, one of the country's most significant trading partners. In this way, new avenues are being created for alternative production and distribution ventures within China's independent cinema as well as the mainstream commercial environment. But, one still needs to ask how long will Korean practitioners be part of this wave, and where is the wave heading?

Conclusion

Whilst industrial and technological change is always the product of multiple factors and variables, it is undeniable that a handful of Korean technicians, as well as a range of contract workers from Korea (with and without Chinese language skills), have created new pathways that have smoothed the Chinese film industry's transition to digital workflow practices to advanced international standards. Through interviews with these specialists and some of their Chinese colleagues conducted for this study, it is clear that Chinese practitioners and firms appreciate that Koreans are: 1) technically competent; 2) hardworking and ethical; 3) geographically nearby, and always available for work; 4) more affordable than their Chinese (and Western) counterparts; 5) culturally closer than workers outside of Greater China; and 6) willing to state hard truths about quality and offer practical, creative solutions during the pre-production, production, and post-productions stages. In the recent past, DI was a cost-prohibitive luxury offered by a small number of US, Canadian, and Australian firms working with a select group of leading Chinese directors and their big-budget films. However, the arrival of Park and Lee and other Korean practitioners (working for Korea-based companies such as CJ Powercast, Dexter Digital, Digital Idea, Digital Studio 2L, Macrograph, Moneff, and SK Independence, etc.), coupled with lower costs and a high level of technical capability, has enabled both established and emerging Chinese filmmakers to utilize this key process. These technical specialists have provided a set of readily transferable and economical resources—in the form of core skills, knowledge, and technological expertise that are a match for the high-end infrastructure and capabilities generally associated with Hollywood productions—while complementing and strengthening the existing capabilities of Chinese filmmakers and technicians.

The opportunity for Korean film practitioners to work on the long list of Chinese films discussed in this chapter has grown from tiny seedlings—the contacts and friendships (aka *guanxi*) that a handful of aspiring Korean filmmakers made while studying at the Beijing Film Academy during the early-to-mid-1990s. The professional inroads made by these now major Korean industry players have enabled them and others throughout the Korean film industry to become some of the most active practitioners (and companies) in China today. In this way, Korean cinema is continuing to expand its boundaries, leveraging talent and expertise deployed outside of Korea's national borders. More than happenstance, Koreans are closer to China in terms of cultural and geographical proximity, sharing a common cultural and historical background, at least in part. This has given Korean practitioners some key competitive advantages over their competitors from the West. In addition, many (including BFA graduates) have mastered or are learning Chinese in order to communicate directly with their clients and colleagues. As a result of these cultural and linguistic factors, an expanding core of Korean practitioners is being seamlessly absorbed by the Chinese film industry, along with their creative ideas and practices.

Assuming that the Korean practitioner or firm involved has succeeded in developing a strong and long-term relationship with a reputable Chinese partner—one practiced in negotiating official government channels, including the censorship apparatus—*guanxi* will continue to be the single most important factor in the bilateral collaborative relationship. As our interviews with practitioners such as Park, Yi, Lee, Ahn, and Kim have repeatedly emphasized, just being in China—establishing a continuous presence there—underpins one's credibility. Having a physical base in China in itself demonstrates a commitment to achieving success there as a long-term goal. Despite the fact that not all Korean companies with an interest in the Chinese market have the ability (or the desire) to establish a presence in the country, Korean film workers are contributing invaluable technical and creative resources to the very nerve center of China's expanding global production network.

The cooperation between the two nations has unfolded on multiple levels, bringing together producers, directors, and actors as well as action, visual effects, and post-production specialists and cinematographers on an unprecedented scale. In 2015, the situation looks like a promising situation for both countries. Koreans have contributed to the expansion of Chinese cinema in terms of the refinement of genres, themes, and story lines, as well as technical maturity, and Chinese film companies have enabled Korean cinema to increasingly internationalize its approach to overseas markets. In other words, in 2015 Korean cinema has well and truly embraced the concept of "glocalization". In these ways, both Korean *and* Chinese national cinemas are undergoing a major makeover as Chinese filmmakers and firms leverage the fresh aesthetic qualities and export-oriented expertise for which Korean cinema has become celebrated around the globe since the censorship of domestic films was ended by the Korean government in 1996.[39] In this new cultural and commercial arena, Korea's global experience and success with its own brand of soft power has been instrumental in developing its collaborative relationship with China.

In sum, the collaborative ventures that Korean producers and directors pursued in tandem with their Chinese colleagues throughout the 2000s have entered a new stage with the advent of a host of new opportunities in the post-production arena. In 2015 China is still the new wild frontier, a stimulating environment that nevertheless presents Korean practitioners with many challenges, including opportunity costs: the sharing of trade secrets and intellectual property, among other things. If industry headlines are anything to go by, however, this is a small price to pay given that there seems to be "No End in Sight for China Film Sector's Rapid Expansion".[40] Nonetheless, one has to wonder what lies ahead on this long and winding road.

Notes

1. This chapter draws on research currently being conducted in association with 2014–2016 Australian Research Council Discovery project, *Willing Collaborators: Negotiating Change in East Asian Media Production* DP 140101643.
2. See Curtin 2003.
3. Since the end of 2012 the Chinese market has become the second largest in the world after the US, and it has taken only three years for box office takings (primarily from locally produced films) in China to overtake US returns. See Pulver, Andrew. "China Confirmed as World's Largest Film Market Outside US". *The Guardian* (22 March, 2013). Available: www.theguardian.com/film/2013/mar/22/china-largest-film-market-outside-us. Accessed 20 February 2015; and Qin, Amy. "China Overtakes U.S. at the Box Office". *New York Times* (2 March 2015). Available: http://sinosphere.blogs.nytimes.com/2015/03/02/china-overtakes-the-u-s-at-the-box-office/?_r=0. Accessed 5 April 2015.
4. Given these personal networks between Korean and Chinese practitioners, it comes as no surprise that experienced Korean DI colorist and CEO of Forestt Studio, Ethan Park, made major contributions to Wang Xiaoshuai's *Red Amnesia* (2014) and *Chongqing Blues* (2010), as well as Zhang Yuan's celebrated *Beijing Flickers* (2012).
5. *Korean Cinema Today 2012*: 30.
6. Kim, Hyeol-lok. "Kofic Chairman Kim Ui-Seok, 'Globalisation Is Not a Choice, but a Necessity" (Kim Ui-Seok Yeongjin Wiwonjang 'Geullobeoreun Seontaek Anira Pilsu'). *Star News* (14 April, 2011). Available: http://star.mt.co.kr/view/stview.php?no=2011041408173701359&type=1&outlink=1. Accessed 1 March 2015.
7. According to a major KOFIC report, film exports to Hong Kong are listed separately from those to mainland China; the value of exports to Hong Kong also increased from $832,700 in 2012 to $2,755,624 in 2014. Taken together, these figures show an unprecedented increase in total exports to Greater China. See KOFIC 2015: 48.
8. The government also allows a small number of flat-fee foreign films on China's big screens. Between 2012 and 2014, more than 100 additional films were approved for import—each recouping a one-off payment without taking a cut of the box office revenue. One advantage of the flat-fee system is that the film's original foreign producer/distributor receives the fees up-front and is not dependent on a local partner to report box office income accurately—a besetting problem for parts of the global film industry today.
9. Jibu, Bian. "China Passes US at Movie Box Office". *China Daily* (3 March, 2015). Available: http://m.chinadaily.com.cn/en/2015-03/03/content_19709880.htm. Accessed 3 March 2015.
10. Tsui, Clarence. "Why More Movie Theaters in China Could Be Bad News for Hollywood". *The Hollywood Reporter* (7 December, 2012). Available: http://www.hollywoodreporter.com/news/chinese-movie-theaters-why-more-399173. Accessed 2 March 2015.
11. During its one-month run in China, *Sector 7* earned around $3.5 million USD, which was about one-third of the production budget, keeping in mind that its Korean producers and investors only received a proportion of this amount.
12. Other recent cases of Korean actors working in China include Jung Woo-sung starring alongside Michelle Yeoh in *Reign of Assassins* (2010), Kim Hee-sun in *The Warring States* (2011), Kwon Sang-woo in *Chinese Zodiac* (2012), Song Hye-kyo in *The Grandmaster* (2013), *The Crossing* (2014), and *The Crossing 2* (2015), as well as K-pop boy band Super Junior singer and actor Choi Si Won, in *Dragon Blade* (2015).
13. Chu debuted in Korea as a fashion model at the age of 17 and began acting in 1996. Failing to get steady work in Korea, despite receiving the Best New Actress Award at The Grand Bell Awards and Best Supporting Actress Award at the Korean Film Award for her performance in *Bloody Tie* (2006), Chu sought to restart her career in China.

Her big break came in 2011 after the runaway success of Chinese TV drama *Temptation to Go Home*, a remake of the popular Korean television drama *Temptation of Wife*. The story of her success in China was documented in the SBS television documentary *New Year Special: China, Secret of Wealth— Survival in the Larger China* (20 January, 2015).

14. Composer *Ryuichi Sakamoto* of *Last Emperor* fame; special effects director John Bruno of *Cliffhanger* (1993), *The Abyss* (1998), and *Titanic* (1997); screenwriter Cheung Tan of *Dragon Inn* (1992) and *Once Upon a Time in China III* (1993); Korean actor Lee Jeong-jae; and designer Ha Yeong-su had also been shoulder-tapped for this project, creating high hopes for its international success. See Anonymous. "Who Makes Mong-U-Do-Won-Do" (Mong-U-Do-Won-Do Reul Mandeuneun Saramdeul). *Cine21* (20 July, 2001). Available: http://www.cine21.com/news/view/mag_id/3225. Accessed 20 March 2015.
15. Cho, Sun-hi. "Cho Sun-Hi Met Chen Kaige" (Cho Sun-Hi-Ga Mannan Chen Kaige). *Cine21* (20 July, 2001). Available: http://www.cine21.com/news/view/mag_id/3223. Accessed 20 March 2015.
16. See Paquet, Darcy. "Chen Kaige to direct big-budget Korean epic". *Screen Daily* (11 July, 2001). Available: www.screendaily.com/chen-kaige-to-direct-big-budget-korean-epic/406265.article. Accessed 5 May 2014.
17. International box office takings for the "fusion" *wuxia* blockbuster *Crouching Tiger, Hidden Dragon* were around $213,500,000 USD. It attracted Asian and Western audiences alike with its blend of Eastern and Western narrative traditions and visual styles, taking Chinese cinema to a new level by totally eclipsing the well-known auteur and underground films made by Fifth and Sixth Generation Chinese filmmakers respectively. See *Box Office Mojo* <www.boxofficemojo.com/movies/?id=crouchingtigerhiddendragon.htm>.
18. Nevertheless, the *Musa* DVD has continued to sell well through commercial online sites such as Amazon, YesAsia, *Netflix*, and Madman Entertainment, and it is also available on all of the giant Chinese online and mobile video-on-demand (VOD) platforms such as Sohu, Youku, Sina Video, Tencent Video, and LeTV.
19. *Musa*'s producers used the Sydney firm Audioloc for post-production audio work, looking to benefit from the Australian film industry's solid record in this area. Audioloc's managing director and sound-team leader, John Dennison, and *Musa*'s production manager, Kim Yang-il, had worked together on the *Gingko Bed* in 1996.
20. See Miller *et al.* 2001.
21. The co-production list includes: *Tracing Shadow* (2009), *Lan* (2009), *Buddha Mountain* (2010), *My Belle Boss* (2010), *In a Tangle* (2010), *Color Me Love* (2010), *Driverless* (2010), *Love in Cosmo* (2010), *A Big Deal* (2011), *The Warring States* (2011), *House Mania* (2011), *Love on Credit* (2011), *Legendary Amazons* (2011), *One Mile Above* (2011, aka *Kora*), *The Sword Identity* (2011), and *The Purple House* (2011). It also includes Wilson Yip's *A Chinese Ghost Story* (2011, aka *A Chinese Fairy Tale*) and *Magic To Win* (2011), which were both completed by Seoul-based Digital Studio 2L, and *Love in Space* (2011), a Hong Kong romantic comedy produced by Fruit Chan and Indian-born Australian filmmaker Anupam Sharma. In 2012 and 2013, the list of Chinese films made with Korean input expanded to include: *The Locked Door* (2012), *To My Wife* (2012), *Son of the Stars* (2012), *Falling Flowers* (2012), *Happy Hotel* (2012), *The Zodiac Mystery* (2012), *Wu Dang* (2012), *Full Circle* (2012), *An Inaccurate Memoir* (2012), *Guns and Roses* (2012), *Beijing Flickers* (2012), and *Midnight Train* (2013).
22. On the Kobiz (Korean Film Business Zone) website run by KOFIC, a total of 28 films are listed in the Korea–China co-production category, beginning with *Seven Swords* in 2005. The co-production areas listed include co-producing, co-financing, location, production services and talent exchanges. See <www.kobiz.or.kr/jsp/production/productionCaseList.jsp>.

23. The total gross profit earned by *The Flying Swords of Dragon Gate* was $100 million USD. See Marsh, James. "China Beat: Tsui Hark & Bona Exploring 3D Together". *Twitchfilm* (12 May 2012). Available: http://twitchfilm.com/2012/05/china-beat-tsui-hark-bona-3d-projects.html. Accessed 31 March 2015.
24. *Painted Skin 2*'s box office takings exceeded $108 million USD, overtaking Jiang Wen's *Let the Bullets Fly* ($106 million USD) and Feng Xiaogang's *Aftershock* ($106 million USD) and becoming the highest-grossing Chinese film of 2012. See Anonymous. "Painted Skin 2 Becomes Highest-Grossing Chinese Film Ever". *Screen Daily* (28 July, 2012). Available: http://www.screendaily.com/territories/asia-pacific/painted-skin-2-becomes-highest-grossing-chinese-film-ever/5044809.article. Accessed 31 March 2015.
25. Aka Park Sang-soo, not to be confused with the colorist Ethan Park working in the US industry.
26. See www.boxofficemojo.com/intl/china/yearly/.
27. According to industry website *Box Office Mojo*, *Journey to the West* beat Hollywood blockbusters *Iron Man 3*, *Pacific Rim*, *Fast & Furious 6*, and *Man of Steel* in China's annual box office rankings. And *The Monkey King* overtook Hollywood blockbusters *Interstellar*, *X-Men: Days of Future Past*, *Captain America: The Winter Soldier*, *Dawn of the Planet of the Apes*, *Guardians of the Galaxy*, and *The Amazing Spider-Man 2*.
28. See Kil, Sonia. "Feng Xiaogang, Kang Je-Gyu Team up for 'the Bad Man Must Die'". *Variety* (26 February, 2015). Available: http://variety.com/2015/film/news/feng-xiaogang-kang-je-gyu-team-up-for-the-bad-man-must-die-1201442889/. Accessed 2 March 2015.
29. Kim, Seong-hun. "Catching the Beijing Express" (Beijing Teukgeup Yeolchareul Taryeomyeon). *Cine21* (11 December, 2014). Available: http://www.cine21.com/news/view/mag_id/78645. Accessed 3 March 2015.
30. Entgroup. "China Film Industry Report 2010–2011". Entgroup, 2012.
31. Frater, Patrick. "China Surges 36% in Total Box Office Revenue". *Variety* (4 January, 2015). Available: http://variety.com/2015/film/news/china-confirmed-as-global-number-two-after-36-box-office-surge-in-2014-1201392453/. Accessed 26 Feb 2015.
32. The easing of restrictions only applies to films dealing with "ordinary" subjects—those avoiding matters connected with "diplomacy, ethnic topics, religion, military, judiciary, historical figures, and cultural celebrities" Xinhua News Agency, 2013.
33. Elley, Derek. "China's genre revolution". *Film Business Asia* (23 July, 2013). Available: http://www.filmbiz.asia/news/chinas-genre-revolution. Accessed 26 Feb 2015.
34. Earlier, the cuts to Li's *Lost in Beijing* demanded by the censors had fundamentally altered the story written by Li and her co-writer and producer Li Fang. (The film was later banned outright.).
35. Prior to shooting the principal sequences for *Double Xposure*, the team shot test scenes on these state-of-the-art film cameras as well as a generous selection of older cameras available in China, including the iPhone 4, and projected the resulting images onto a large screen to assess their effect.
36. In post-production, Park's DI work on the film was supplemented with a small number of additional elements including computer graphics and around 50 special effects shots.
37. In the digital environment, the DI process normally takes around seven days to complete, or five days for a rush job. Not only did Park's work on *Double Xposure* amount to more than double the number of working days usually spent on the DI for a film (which usually involves around 80 percent grading and 20 percent adjusting the work according to feedback received from the director and/or producer), but it also marked an innovative approach to the workflow process.
38. For HFR's China branch, Ethan Park and Lee Yong-gi purchased and installed state-of-the-art digital post-production equipment, costing upwards of $500,000 USD (depending on the film scanner, recorder, and digital projector chosen, as well as upgrades and options, but not including the cost of building a suitable studio space, a project they

also oversaw). The pair have transferred state-of-the-art technology by overseeing the purchase of new equipment with which they familiarized themselves by attending key annual industry trade shows such as the National Association of Broadcasters (NAB) Show or the Cine Gear Expo Los Angeles. Park and Lee relocated to Beijing in 2009 and 2011, respectively, and in 2015 they and a growing number of Korean colleagues are among the most sought-after DI and visual effects experts in China.
39. For more details on film censorship in Korea, see Yecies 2008.
40. Coonan, Clifford. "No End in Sight for China Film Sector's Rapid Expansion". *The Hollywood Reporter Busan Daily*, no. 3 (6 October, 2013): 2.

Conclusion
Welcome to Planet Hallyuwood

This study began by posing some very basic questions about how official film policy was developed in Korea and how it impacted production, direction, and genre development. We also asked: what were the hallmarks of the Golden Age of the 1960s, and how was it achieved; who were the major industry players, and how did their roles transform over time; how did government policy shape the progress and direction of the film industry; and where do the achievements of the 1960s stand in relation to the ongoing development of Korea's national *and* transnational cinema?

Part I of the book addresses these questions by documenting and analyzing the nexus of production, direction, genre, and internationalization initiatives with a special emphasis on the fundamental impact that policy has made on all four areas. Against this background, we explore the fundamental impact of the production cartel and major company system on the film industry. With the increasing power of these producers, a range of dynamic production strategies—including creative responses by filmmakers to heavily interventionist government policies—contributed to an industry "boom" in the 1960s, the likes of which was not to be seen again until the 2000s. In the mid-to-late 1960s Korea was experiencing rapid and wide-scale growth in terms of industrialization and the internationalization of trade through policy development across all industry sectors. These included agriculture and food production, defense, education, finance (attracting flows of foreign currency and investment), public infrastructure (with an emphasis on railroads and ports), heavy industry (especially cement, fertilizer, and steel plants), manufacturing, and energy (electricity and coal), as well as the introduction of technology and the promotion of the arts, culture, and entertainment for the masses.

In this rapidly evolving environment representative director Yu Hyun-mok developed his own style. At the same time he used *The Empty Dream* (1965) to distance himself and the art of filmmaking from the forced popularization of state ideology and the capitalist social order demanded by the government's film policy regime. Although *The Empty Dream* borrowed heavily from the Japanese film *Day Dream*, it differs significantly from its source, particularly in regard to art direction, cinematography, and editing style. After 14 years of bi-lateral talks, the *Treaty on Basic Relations between Japan and the Republic of Korea* was formalized and signed in mid-1965. Expectations that importers in both countries would benefit from the treaty and its internationalization effect by gaining access to each other's markets were high. While Yu (and other directors) benefited from Korea's new relationship with Japan after his producers acquired the remake rights to *Day Dream*, the much-anticipated relaxation of film imports and market barriers failed to eventuate; at the end of 1965, the MPI announced a permanent ban on Japanese films in Korea—an embargo that would last until 1998.[1] Despite exploiting a brief window of opportunity presented by the treaty, *The Empty Dream* fell from grace when the state prosecutor's office intervened to pull the film from cinemas for violating national obscenity laws.

As a near-ironic result of continual government intervention, producers and directors began to create festival-type films that embraced ideas of cultural nationalism and traditionalism. Redefining "art film" from a Korean perspective, we highlight the marked political character of "literary films" as cultural propaganda during the 1960s. On the one hand, films based on literary adaptations were tailored to appeal to the masses rather than to art-house audiences, out of commercial motives. On the other hand, filmmakers found themselves in a politically compromising situation that pressured them to "collaborate" with the government. Hence, the literary films produced during this period could be called "political art cinema". The film discussions in this first part of the book present a broad picture of the complex conditions involved in the making of these films and their social and political implications.

Part I concludes by showing how Korean filmmakers engaged in a variety of state-endorsed internationalization strategies that involved a range of co-productions with regional partners and a host of remakes. Shin Film's close links with Shaw Brothers in Hong Kong enabled the two companies to pool resources and make a series of historical epics, most notably *Last Woman of Shang*. Partnering with an experienced practitioner like Shin meshed in with Shaw Brothers' overall business approach—choosing long-term foreign partners whose national companies (big name, well established) could provide matching investments and unique industry skills.[2] On top of such legitimate arrangements, the potential profits to be made from international co-productions lured producers like Shin Sang-ok into making a string of fake co-productions, which led to the tainting of his company and eventually undermined the Korean film industry as a whole. The MPI's ever-increasing requirements for maintaining company registration and high levels of productivity also contributed to the industry's downfall—motivating producers like Shin to do whatever was necessary to meet annual production quotas (and to chase easy money). Hence, while genuine co-production initiatives with Hong Kong got off to a positive start, "internationalization" soon came to mean little more than the pursuit of bogus co-productions.

Alternatively, during the late 1950s and over the next two decades, Korean filmmakers worked on numerous remakes of Japanese films, forging strong, if irregular, connections between the two film industries. Clearly, despite the ban on Japanese films, Korean filmmakers were being inspired by Japanese cinema. In turn, "remade" films such as *Barefoot Youth* and *The Empty Dream* stimulated

Korean audiences because they connected them with the outside world. Korean youth films followed in the footsteps of Japanese "sun tribe" films, reflecting the attitudes of the "angry young man" generation in Korea and across many parts of the globe. Although *Barefoot Youth* and many other similar films were derivative of Japanese productions, they accurately reflected the frustrations of a generation born after the Second World War, an era marked by rapid industrialization and widespread urbanization. These films also mirrored the younger generation's engagement with Western culture and explored the ways in which it was negotiating these international cultural crosscurrents.

Today, it is difficult to separate out the genuine Hong Kong co-productions and official Japanese remakes from the bogus collaborations and plagiarized films that were produced between the late 1950s and the early 1970s. However, what is certain is that during this period there was a marked lack of awareness and appreciation of copyright. To make matters worse, the MPI showed little interest in intervening in this particular issue and educating filmmakers about avoiding infringement on creative content. There can be little doubt that this peculiar flirtation with internationalization was one of the primary reasons behind the onset of Korean cinema's dark age in the 1970s. These surreptitious activities generally lacked creative and stylistic vision; while offering an easy way out of the troubles besetting the industry, they demonstrated a lack of commitment to the art and practice of filmmaking.

In taking this particular approach with part one, we offer readers a useful framework for understanding the ways in which the complex interplay of local, national, regional, and global forces have impacted on the comparatively rapid development of Korean cinema. We show how a similar nexus of production, direction, genre, and internationalization initiatives in the post-1996 renaissance enabled Korea to position itself as an important contributor to both the world economy and international culture.

Part II analyzes some of the key trends in film producing, directing, and genre development that transformed Korean cinema in the 1970s during the industry's "dark age", through to the 1980s when producers and directors struggled to develop a distinctive voice in Hollywood's shadow. We show how Korean cinema continued to re-invent itself by opting to take particular, if narrow, pathways that were different from their senior colleagues. The filmmakers active through these two decades developed new strategies to survive under Park Chung Hee's authoritarian government, which was aggressively engaged in Cold War politics and then to respond to the succeeding Chun Doo-hwan military government. The sexploitation hostess and "ero" genre films marked out a small but important creative space that challenged the suppression of democracy and limitations on freedom of expression. This was at a time when Korea was continuing to experience rapid economic growth and industrialization alongside a newly emerging consumer culture (driven by the conspicuous consumption and spread of popular culture from the US) and a growing urban population. While filmmakers may not have engaged in the same type of clandestine practices as they had followed in the 1960s, the demands for high productivity levels made by the state forced them into a kind of collaborative relationship with the government of the day in order to survive during a major downturn.

While previous scholars point to 'policy failure' as the major cause of the decline of the industry between the late 1960s and early 1980s, our archival research shows that national film policy had a different effect, at least in part, by facilitating the industrialization of the sector during a tumultuous social, cultural, and political period.[3] As part two shows, larger questions including the development path of a national cinema and genre studies are also involved in the producer–director–policy nexus, especially when determining where the Korean cinema stands in the story of world cinema.

In Part III we show how many of the most active members of the contemporary film industry surfaced in the early 1990s. Drawn from outside the ranks of the PRS, which ran the film industry in the 1960s, they worked with new directors and created new types of films. While the 1960s had begun with a sense of freedom and hope after the 1960 April Revolution, the political turmoil that followed the 1961 military *coup d'état* led by Park Chung Hee changed everything. Similarly, the early 1990s began with a sense of liberation and hope for democratization after Kim Young-sam won the presidential election in 1992. The domestic film industry began to transform itself in unforeseen ways through the business strategies employed, for instance, by the entertainment arms of the Samsung and Daewoo *chaebols*. However, the Asian financial crisis of 1997 and Korea's subsequent IMF bailout changed everything—particularly after Samsung and Daewoo restructured by selling off their entertainment divisions. Around this time, the Kim Dae-jung government's (1998–2003) proactive support of the local industry without intervention, that is, without impeding the freedom of expression and creativity released after government censorship was eliminated in 1996, was critical to the changing face of Korean cinema.

As a result, a new cartel of corporate/executive producers brought a ruthless efficiency to the industry by maintaining and fine-tuning the core elements of "high-concept" filmmaking, while generating new venture capital and ensuring accountability to their shareholders and customers (cinema audiences) rather than pandering to the whims of auteur filmmakers. Their business acumen and the diverse strategies employed have reduced the risks associated with previous financial strategies involving self- or family funding, private loans, and pre-sales from regional distributors and exhibitors, thus leading the industry into new and profitable areas. In sum, as shown in this part, the so-called power of the producer—as opposed to the power of writer–directors such as Im Sang-soo, Kim Jee-woon, Hur Jin-ho, Lee Chang-dong, Park Chan-wook, Bong Joon-ho, and Kim Ki-duk—has reached new heights through producers' willingness to finance globally marketable films and encourage talented young directors to make them.

A significant part of the producer mix today is the powerful, vertically integrated group of investor–distributors—CJ E&M, Showbox, and Lotte Entertainment—that monopolize the commercial (and thus the predominant) side of industry. They have effectively excluded small-to-medium producers (like the female producers discussed in Chapter 8) by choosing to distribute only certain kinds of commercial films and also by forming close relationships with both established and newer directors. As a result of their size, ownership of exhibition chains, and ties to the corporate media and financial institutions, together these corporate producers are able to exert more influence over the industry than any single producer. In particular, CJ E&M, which launched a branch in China in mid-2012, now leads the pack with its corporate production, distribution and sales, and actor management services, as well as ownership of a growing number of multiplex cinemas in Korea and a smaller but increasing number in China (as well as in the US and Vietnam)—including IMAX and 4DX screens—under the brand-name CGV.

As we show, however, an emerging number of female producers and writer–directors involved in both the independent and commercial sides of the industry have begun impacting the growth and sustainability of Korean cinema—precisely by challenging this corporate domination. More to the point, their contributions have been made in an industry where male directors, producers, and investors have historically controlled the content and dissemination of film and continue to do so, despite the relatively large number of female producers and crewmembers currently working in the industry. Although traditional Korean culture continues to privilege men over women, in part through the country's long history of Confucianism, the emergence of the female writer–director represents an open challenge to the industry's existing structures. In fact, in 2012, four of the year's biggest hits were *Thieves, A Werewolf Boy, All about My Wife,* and *Architecture 101*—all produced by women: An Su-hyeon of Caper Film, Kim Su-jin of Bidangil Pictures, Lee Yu-jin of Zip Cinema, and Shim Jae-myung of Myung Film. Each film represented a different genre—a star-studded caper film, fantasy melodrama, romantic comedy, and romance, respectively. Our discussion of these and other female filmmakers adds an important dimension to the changing face of Korean cinema by illustrating how women producers and female writer–directors have achieved outstanding successes in both feature and independent filmmaking.

Finally, Part III concludes by showing how, since the mid- to late-2000s, the Korean film industry has engaged in a love affair with China. Shooting on location in China's vast and inspiring landscapes, casting stars for pan-Asian or international audience appeal, and pursuing a range of official (joint and assisted) and unofficial co-productions have all helped the Korean film industry gain access to China's massive and fast-growing market. The personal networks (*guanxi*) developed by Korean students at the Beijing Film Academy from the early 1990s—serving as local liaison personnel and consultants for both industries—have been invaluable to this process. As a result, Korean film companies and individual practitioners have made stronger inroads into China than anything thus far achieved by Hollywood, once regarded as the sole center of cinematic fame and success. These internationalization strategies, which Korean practitioners have increasingly pursued in China since collaborating on Feng Xiaogang's *Assembly* in 2007, have become a vital ingredient in the continuing rollout of

Korea's soft power throughout the region and around the globe. These contemporary co-productions share at least one thing in common with the earlier collaborations between the Shaw Brothers and Shin Film: the favor shown by Chinese production companies toward Korean actors and actresses, attractive Hallyu stars who have already made reputations throughout the Asian region following their exposure in K-dramas.

Increasingly since 2007, Korea's VFX and DI technicians, whose technical achievements were celebrated in part three, have been looking for new opportunities in the Chinese post-production industry, a sector they are helping to develop and bring to maturity. In addition to their competence and experience, Korean technicians have a good understanding of Chinese culture compared to their Western colleagues, and their rates are more affordable than those of competing Western companies. After years of collaboration, the two national industries have engaged in a range of co-productions, including films that have been pre-produced, shot, and/or post-produced in either country by domestic firms and practitioners, as well as films made with international funds, and using local casts and crews or productions that have utilized locations in Korea, China, or third countries to shoot specific scenes or entire films. These combinations and permutations are all part of international production trends that have become commonplace since the end of World War II. In this way, Korean companies have provided their Chinese partners with a level of visual quality associated with Hollywood blockbusters, but at a fraction of the cost involved in using Hollywood firms, thus pushing Korean cinema into new territory.

Welcome to Planet Hallyuwood

To conclude, while the achievements of the historical and contemporary Korean cinema have been widely discussed in the relevant literature, the historiographical approach taken in the present book attempts to break new ground.[4] We have seized on the designation of Korean cinema as "Planet Hallyuwood", not only with a view to building on these previous studies, but also to link its astonishing transformation with the complex economic, historical, industrial, technological and political factors that have defined "Planet Hollywood" (Kipen 1997; Stenger 1997; Olson 1999), "Planet Hong Kong" (Bordwell 2000), and "Planet Bollywood" (Desai 2005; Dwyer 2006). While these studies show that these three national cinemas formed gradually over time, so too has "Planet Hallyuwood": through a series of critical and complex moments in an unfolding story about Korean national *and* transnational cinema. The construction and development of Korean cinema's foundations, and its subsequent flourishing during the dynamic decade of the 1960s, forms the cornerstone of this history. Building on this base, we tell a story that begins with a film industry molded by state intervention, but also offered practical support, and ends with an industry that, while lavished with government intervention lacks effective support.

That is to say that, despite all of its glory, the film industry is still not free from government intervention. In 2005, newly formed MK Pictures, in conjunction with CJ Entertainment, co-produced *The President's Last Bang* (2005), directed by Im Sang-soo. The film became the subject of legal action by the family of former president Park Chung Hee (i.e., the brother of current President Park Geun-hye). While MK Pictures fought these proceedings with a will, CJ Entertainment responded to the negative publicity and political pressure generated by Park's family by reneging on its investment (20% of the film's total production budget) and withdrawing its pre-arranged distribution deal for the film. CJ Entertainment's attempts to distance itself from the controversy over *The President's Last Bang* sent a clear message about the limits of artistic freedom that the largest corporate producers are willing to extend to a director and their lack of support (and the government's matching disinterest in providing assistance) to fight attempts at censorship.

Even today, the Korean film industry is not immune from attacks on freedom of expression from official quarters, and the government crackdown that Lee Myung-bak re-invigorated (discussed in Chapter 10) has continued under the administration of President Park Geun-hye (2013 -). In 2014, the Busan International Film Festival committee became embroiled in a row with Busan mayor Seo Byung-soo—who also happened to be chairman of BIFF—over the screening of *Diving Bell* (2014), a documentary that was heavily critical of the national government and its ineffectual handling of the *Sewol* ferry disaster in April 2014. Although the controversial film was screened at the festival, BIFF director and co-founder Lee Yong-kwan was forced to resign his position following pressure from Mayor Seo.[5] Seo's actions were widely seen as interference with freedom of expression, prompting the Korean film community to speak out about the government's apparent abuse of power.[6] As a government representative, KOFIC also hit back, slashing its funding of film festivals in half and leaving BIFF in a particularly vulnerable position.[7] This type of intervention without policy support is one of the biggest challenges Korean filmmakers and Korean cinema more broadly faces today.

Nevertheless, Korean cinema has benefited greatly from the efforts of high-profile directors such as Bong Joon-ho and other writer–directors whose auteurial and genre films bridge mainstream commercial films and minority-interest arthouse productions. Today the industry presents a complex web of producers, directors, writers, post-production specialists, policymakers, and others—a more dynamic picture than could be gleaned from either the trade and popular press or previously published academic studies. The films and filmmakers discussed in this book have made strong contributions to the development and internationalization of the domestic industry by taking conventions established by Hollywood and injecting them with Korean characters and storylines that diverge from those used in mainstream American films. Korean writer–directors are at pains to avoid replicating the uniformity of the global Hollywood industry. Their work can thus be read as running counter to the trend of worldwide cultural standardization by global media, and as a localized form of "cultural proximity" created by the use of local culture, language, market strength, and other factors, mixing Hollywood genre conventions with domestic linguistic elements, stories, and other aspects of Korean culture.

The cinema driven by this new breed of writer–directors is thus a hybrid of the local and the global—irrespective of the messages or social commentary it seeks to convey. While this type of analysis can be applied to any national cinema, it carries a special resonance in Korea's case because its film history has been poorly preserved as the result of over a century of historical dislocation, from Japanese colonial rule (1910–1945), the US army occupation (1945–1948), and the Korean War (1950–1953) to over three decades of military dictatorship (1961–1993).[8] Thus, it is hoped that our re-examination of Korean cinema from the 1960s through to the present day will enable a better understanding of its historical lineage and rich cultural legacy and facilitate a re-inscription of it into the larger history of world cinema—even if the final shape of Planet Hallyuwood remains a work in progress.

Notes

1. "Censure of Japanese Film Importation" (Ilyeonghwa-ui Su-ip Bulheo). *Gyeonghyang Shinmun* (27 December, 1965): 5.
2. Kar, Bren, and Ho 2004: 222.
3. On the role of policy failure in the downturn of the film industry in the 1970s see, for example: Ho 2000; Byon 2001a; Lee 2004; and Park 2005.
4. See, for instance: Lee 2000; Kim and James 2002; Kim K. 2004; Shin and Stringer 2005; Jackson et al. 2006; Jin 2006; Lee 2006; Paquet 2009; and Yecies and Shim 2011. Many readers might also know there is also a dearth of discussion of Korean cinema in reference books on world cinema history. For example, there is almost no mention of Korea in Geoffrey Nowell-Smith's 'comprehensive' *Oxford History of World Cinema* (1996); and the second edition of Kristin Thompson and David Bordwell's *Film History: An Introduction* (2003) devotes less than 1,000 words to Korea and its film pioneers. Although the third edition of Thompson and Bordwell sheds some light on the development of South Korea's contemporary cinema, including its key directors, it has little to say about the rich and complex history of cinema in Korea.
5. See Lee, Hyo-won. "Busan City Government under Fire amid Debate over Film Festival's Independence". *The Hollywood Reporter* (28 January, 2015). Available: www.hollywoodreporter.com/news/busan-debates-independence-film-festival-767864. Accessed 6 May 2015.
6. Noh, Jean. "South Korean Film Groups Protest for Freedom of Expression". *Screen Daily* (13 February, 2015). Available: http://www.screendaily.com/screenasia/south-korean-film-groups-protest-for-freedom-of-expression/5083268.article. Accessed 6 May 2015.
7. Yu, Yeong-seok. "'Being Defiant?' KOFIC Slashes Funding to the BIFF" ('Gwaessimjoe?' Yeongjinwi, Busan Gukje Yeonghwaje Jiwongeum Daepok Sakgam). *Nocutnews* (5 May, 2015). Available: http://www.nocutnews.co.kr/news/4408368. Accessed 7 May 2015.
8. As of 2007, the Korean Film Archive (KOFA) held 3,771 out of the 5,795 films produced in Korea. For the 1960s, only 581 out of 1,506 films—one third—are preserved. The recent discovery of four Korean films from the 1940s (*An Angel without a House* (1941), *Spring in the Korean Peninsula* (1941), *Volunteer* (1941), and *Straits of Joseon* (1943)) through its overseas film archive networks has rewarded KOFA's relentless efforts to preserve the nation's film heritage. For more information, see http://www.koreafilm.or.kr/index.asp (Accessed 20 October 2007); and Yecies and Shim 2011.

Bibliography

Abelmann, N. 2005. "Women's Lives, Movies, and Men". In: McHugh, K. and N. Abelmann (eds.) *South Korean Golden Age Melodrama: Gender, Genre and National Cinema*, Wayne State University Press, Detroit, Michigan. 43–64.
Ahn, Cheol-hyeon. October 2005. Seoul. (Personal interview.)
Ahn, J. 2005. "Film Policy after the 5th Revision of the Motion Picture Law: 1985–2002" (Je 5-cha Yeonghwa-beop Gaejeong Ihu-ui Yeonghwa Jeongchaek: 1985–2002). *A History of Korean Film Policy (Hanguk Yeonghwa Jeongchaeksa)*, Nanam Publishing, Seoul, Korea.
Ahn, J. 2007. *Shin Sang-ok Collection, KOFA,* Seoul, Korea.
Ahn, Peter. December 2013. Beijing. (Personal interview.)
Anderson, J. L. and D. Richie. 1982. *The Japanese Film: Art and Industry,* Princeton University Press, Princeton, New Jersey.
Baek, Gyeol. October 2005. Seoul. (Personal interview.)
Baek, M. 2003. "Screenplay In the Form of Literary Adaptation in the Late 1950s" (1950nyondae huban 'munye'roseo sinario-ui euimi). *Time of Attraction and Confusion: 1950s Korean Cinema (Maehok-gwa Hondon-ui Sidae: 50yondae-ui Hanguk Younghwa),* Sodo Publishing, Seoul, Korea.
Berry, C. 2003. "What's Big about the Big Film?": "De-Westernizing" the Blockbuster in Korea and China. In Stringer, J. (ed.) *Movie Blockbusters,* Routledge, London, England.
Bordwell, D. 2000. *Planet Hong Kong: Popular Cinema and the Art of Entertainment,* Harvard University Press, Cambridge, Massachusetts.
———. 2004. "The Art Cinema as a Mode of Film Practice". In Braudy L. and Cohen M. (eds.) *Film Theory and Criticism: Introductory Readings*, Oxford University Press, New York, New York and Oxford, England. 774–82.
Byon, J. 2001a. Film (Yeonghwa). In The Korean National Research Center for Arts (ed.) *Korean Modern Art History III: 1960s (Hanguk Hyeondae Yesulsa Daegye III: 1960nyeondae),* Sigongsa, Seoul, Korea.
———. 2001b. Park Nam-ok. In Joo, J., Jang, M. and J. Byon (eds.) *Korean Film Dictionary 1: Dictionary of Women Film Industry People (Hanguk Yeonghwa Sajeon 1: Yeoseong Yeonghwain Sajeon),* Sodo Publishing, Seoul, Korea.
Byun, I. 1995. "Description of the Last Romantist" (Majimak Romaentiseuteu-ui Somyo). *Yu Hyun-mok: Cinematic Life (Yu Hyun-mok: Yeonghwa Insaeng),* Hyegwadang, Seoul, Korea.
———. 2007. "Metaphors of Resistance during Devastation: Yeong-ja's Heydays and The March of Fools". In Kim, M. (ed.) *Korean Film History: From the Origins to Renaissance,* Communication Books, Seoul, Korea.
Byun, In-shik. October 2005. Seoul. (Personal interview.)
Byun, Young-joo. 8 August 2014. Seoul. (Personal interview.)
Cha, Yun. October 2005. Seoul. (Personal interview.)

Chae, Yoon-hee. January 2015. Seoul. (Personal interview.)
Chang, K. 1998. "Risk Components of Compressed Modernity: South Korea as Complex Risk Society". *Korea Journal,* 38, 207–28.
———. 1999. "Compressed Modernity and Its Discontents: South Korean Society in Transition". *Economy and Society,* 28, 30–55.
Cho, Y. 2004. "From Golden Age to Dark Age, A Brief History of Korean Co-production". *Rediscovering Asian Cinema Network: The Decades of Co-production between Korea and Hong Kong.* PIFF, Pusan, Korea.
Choi, E. 2007. *Confession of Choi Eun-hee (Choi Eun-hi-ui Gobaek),* Random House, Seoul.
Choi, J. 2010. *The South Korean Film Renaissance: Local Hitmakers, Global Provocateurs,* Wesleyan University Press, Middletown, Connecticut.
Choi, J., Wi, O., Kim, S., Kim, H., Noh, J., Kim, D., Son, Y. and H. Cho 1994. *Current Flow and Prospects of Korean Film Policy (Hanguk Yeonghwa Jeongchaek-Ui Heureumgwa Saeroun Jeonmang),* Jimmundang Publishing Company, Seoul, Korea.
Chung, H. 2005. "Toward a Strategic Korean Cinephilia: A Transnational Detournement of Hollywood Melodrama". In McHugh, K. and N. Abelmann (eds.) *South Korean Golden Age Melodrama: Gender, Genre and National Cinema,* Wayne State University Press, Detroit, Michigan.
Collins, S. M. and W. Park 1989. "External Debt and Macroeconomic Performance in South Korea". *NBER Chapters.* National Bureau of Economic Research, Inc., Cambridge, Massachusetts.
Crofts, S. 2006. "Reconceptualizing National Cinema/s". In Vitali,V. and Willemen, P. (eds.) *Theorising National Cinema.* BFI Publishing, London, England.
Cumings, B. 1997. *Korea's Place in the Sun: A Modern History,* W.W. Norton & Company, New York, New York.
Curtin, M. 2003. "Media Capital: Towards a Study of Spatial Flows". *International Journal of Cultural Studies,* 6, 202–28.
Desai, J. 2005. "Planet Bollywood: Indian Cinema in Asian America". In: Dave, S., Nishime, L. and Oren, T. (eds.) *East Main Street: Asian American Popular Culture,* New York University Press, New York, New York. 55–71.
Desser, D. 2004. "The Kung Fu Craze: Hong Kong Cinema's First American Reception". In Fu, P. and D. Desser (eds.) *The Cinema of Hong Kong: History, Arts Identity,* Cambridge University Press, New York, New York.
Diffrient, D. S. 2005. "Hanguk Heroism: Cinematic Spectacle and the Postwar Cultural Politics of Red Muffler". In McHugh, K. and N. Abelmann (eds.) *South Korean Golden Age Melodrama: Gender, Genre, and National Cinema,* Wayne State University Press, Detroit, Michigan.
Dissanayake, W. 1994. "Introduction: Nationhood, History, and Cinema: Reflections on the Asian Scene". In Dissanayake, W. (ed.) *Colonialism and Nationalism in Asian Cinema,* Indiana University Press, Bloomington, Indiana.
Doherty, T. August 1984. "Creating a National Cinema: The South Korean Experience". *Asian Survey,* 24, 840–51.
Dwyer, R. 2006. "Planet Bollywood: Hindi film in the UK". In: Ali, N., Karla, V. and Sayyid, S. (eds.) *Postcolonial people: South Asians in Britain,* C. Hurst and Co, London, England. 366–75.
Eckert, C. J., Lee, K., Lew, Y., Robinson, M. and E. W. Wagner 1990. *Korea Old and New: A History,* Ilchokak Publishers, Seoul, Korea.
Elliott, K. 2003. *Rethinking the Novel/Film Debate,* Cambridge University Press, Cambridge, Massachusetts.

Elsaesser, T. 1991. "Tales of Sound and Fury". In Landis, M. (ed.) *Imitiations of Life: Explorations of Melodrama*. Wayne State University Press, Detroit, Michigan. 68–92.
Entgroup 2012. China Film Industry Report 2010–2011. Entgroup.
Gledhill, C. 1991. "Signs of Melodrama". In Gledhill, C. (ed.) *Stardom: Industry of Desire*, Routledge, London, England.
Gomery, D. 1986. *The Hollywood Studio System*, St. Martin's Press, New York, New York.
———. 2005. *The Hollywood Studio System: A History*, British Film Institute, London, England.
Goto-Jones, C. S. 2009. *Modern Japan: A Very Short Introduction*, Oxford University Press, Oxford, England.
Gwon, Y. 2006. "Overview of Korea's Modern Literature" (Hanguk Hyeondae Munhak Gaegwan). In Gwon, Y. (ed.) *Encyclopedia of Korea's Modern Literature (Hanguk Hyeondae Munhak Daesajeon)*. Seoul National University Press, Seoul, Korea. 1108–43.
Han, D. 1999. "Structure of the 1960s Rural Society and Its Transformation" (1960-nyeondae Nongchon Sahoe-ui Gujowa Byeonhwa). *Study on Social Transformation in the 1960s: 1963–1970 (1960nyondae Sahoi Byonhwa Yeongu: 1963–1970)*, Baiksan Seodang Publishing, Seoul, Korea.
High, P. B. 2003. *The Imperial Screen: Japanese Film Culture in the Fifteen Years' War, 1931–1945*, University of Wisconsin Press, Madison, Wisconsin.
Hilmes, M. 1996. "Cinema in the Age of Television". In: Nowell-Smith, G. (ed.) *Oxford History of the Cinema, 1895–1995*, Oxford University Press, London, England. 466–75.
Ho, H. 2000. *100 Years of Korean Cinema (Hanguk yeonghwa 100 nyeon)*, Moonhak Sasang Press, Seoul, Korea.
Hong, Ji-young. January 2015. Seoul. (Personal interview.)
Hong, S. 2003. *A Study on the Masculinity in the Literary Adaptaion Film: Focusing on the Korean Cinema from 1966 to 1969 (Munye Yeonghwa-eseoui Namgseongseong Yeongu: 1966~1969ggajiui Hanguk Yeonghwa-reul Jungsim-euro)*. MA, Chung-Ang University.
Hwang, Nam. October 2005. Seoul. (Personal interview.)
Im, Kwon-taek. October 2004. Busan. (Personal interview.)
Im, Won-sik. October 2005. Seoul. (Personal interview.)
Jackson, A. D., Gibb, M. and D. White. (eds.) 2006. *How East Asian Films Are Shaping National Identities: Essays on the Cinemas of China, Japan, South Korea, and Hong Kong*, The Edwin Mellen Press, New York, New York.
James, D. E. and K. KIM. (eds.) 2002. *Im Kwon-taek: The Making of a Korean National Cinema*, Wayne University Press, Detroit, Michigan.
Jang, Gyeong-ik. October 2004/2005. December 2011/2012/2013/2014. Seoul. (Personal interview.)
Jarvie, I. 1992. *Hollywood's Overseas Campaign: The North Atlantic Movie Trade, 1920–1950*, Cambridge University Press, Cambridge, Massachusetts.
Jeong, H., Yun, J. and S. Han 2000. "Literature" (Munhak) In The Korean National Research Center for Arts (ed.) *Korean Modern Art History III: 1950s (Hanguk Hyundae Yesulsa Taegye III: 19650nyondae)*, Sigongsa, Seoul, Korea. 27–152.
Jo, H. 2003. *The History and Prospect of Broadcasting in Korea (Hanguk Bangsong-ui Yeoksa-wa Jeonmang)*, Hanul Academy, Seoul, Korea.
Kang, J. 2001. "Novel in Literature" (Soseol—Munhak). In The Korean National Research Center for Arts (ed.) *Korean Modern Art History III: 1960s (Hanguk Hyeondae Yesulsa Daegye III: 1960nyeondae)*, Sigongsa, Seoul, Korea. 75–110.
Kar, L. 2004. "Korean and Hong Kong Interflows in the 1950s & 1960s". *Rediscovering Asian Cinema Network: The Decades of Co-production between Korea and Hong Kong*, PIFF, Pusan, Korea.

Kar, L., Bren, F. and S. Ho 2004. *Hong Kong Cinema: A Cross-cultural View*, Scarecrow Press, Langham, Maryland.

Kim, B. Hwang, J. and S. Lee 2003. "Novel in Literature" (Soseol—Munhak). In The Korean National Research Center for Arts (ed.) *Korean Modern Art History III: 1960s (Hanguk Hyeondae Yesulsa Daegye III: 1960nyeondae)*, Sigongsa, Seoul, Korea.

Kim, Dong-ho. October 2005. Busan. (Personal interview.)

Kim, Erin. August 2014. Seoul. (Personal interview.)

Kim, Hyae-joon. October 2004/2005. December 2011/2012/2013/2014. Seoul. (Personal interview.)

Kim, Hyeon-jung. October 2004/2005. Seoul. (Personal interview.)

Kim, H. 1994. "Reading Policy through Development of Film Regulations" (yeonghwa beopgyuwa sichaek-euro bon jeongchaek-ui heurum). In *Current Flow and Prospects of Korean Film Policy (Hanguk yeonghwa jeongchaek-ui heureumgwa saeroun jeonmang)*, Jimmundang Publishing Company, Seoul, Korea. 145–214.

Kim, H. 2002. *Korean Film History Viewed Away from the Screen (Screen Bak-ui Hanguk Yeonghwasa)*, Inmulgwa Sasangsa, Seoul, Korea.

Kim, H. 2002. "South Korea: The Politics of Memory". In Vasudev, A., Padgaonkar, L. and R. Doraiswamy (eds.) *Being & Becoming: The Cinemas of Asia*, Macmillan India, Delhi, India. 281–300.

Kim, H. 2004. *Korea's Development under Park Chung Hee: Rapid Industrialization, 1961–79*, Routledge, London, England.

Kim, In-gi. September 2005. Seoul. (Personal interview.)

Kim, Ji-heon. October 2005. Seoul. (Personal interview.)

Kim, Ji-yeon. December 2014. Seoul. (Personal interview.)

Kim, J. and J. Jeong 2001. *100 Years of Our Film (Uri Yeonghwa 100nyeon)*, Hyonam Publishing, Seoul, Korea.

Kim, K. 2004. *The Remasculinization of Korean Cinema*, Duke University Press, Durham, North Carolina.

Kim, M. (ed.) 2006. *Korean Film History: From the Origins to Renaissance (Hanguk Yeonghwasa: Gaehwagi-eseo Gaehwagi-ggaji)*, Communication Books, Seoul, Korea.

———. 2007. "Trends in the Structure of the Korean Film Industry". In Kim, M. (ed.) *Korean Cinema: From Origins to Renaissance*, CommBooks, Seoul, Korea. 413–19.

Kim, K. 2011. *Virtual Hallyu: Korean Cinema of the Global Era*, Duke University Press, Durham, North Carolina.

Kim, M., Jung, J. and S. Jang. 2003. *Study on History of Motion Picture Distribution in Korea (Hanguk Baegupsa Yeongu)*, KOFIC, Seoul, Korea.

Kim, Mee-hyeon. October 2004/2005. Seoul. (Personal interview.)

Kim, P. and H. Shin. 2010. "The Birth of 'Rok': Cultural Imperialism, Nationalism, and the Glocalization of Rock Music in South Korea, 1964–1975". *Positions: East Asia Cultures Critique*, 18, 199–230.

Kim, Soyoung. October 2004. Seoul. (Personal interview.)

Kim, S. 2002. *Korean Film Directors 1 (Hanguk Yeonghwa Gamdongnon 1)*, Jisik Publishing, Seoul, Korea.

———. 2003a. *Korean Auteur Theory 2: 14 Directors from the Liberation to the 1970s (Hanguk Yeonghwa gamdongnon 2: Haebang Duibuteo 1970nyeondaeggaji Hanguk yeonghwajakga 14in)*, Jisik Saneupsa, Seoul, Korea.

———. 2003b. *Korean Literary Adaptation Film (Hanguk Munye Yeonghwa)*, Salleem Publishing, Seoul, Korea.

———. 2005. *Korean Film Directors 3: Korean Film Movement by 14 Korean Directors In the 1980–90s (Hanguk Yeonghwa Gamdonnon 3: 1980–90nyeondae Yeonghwagandok 14in-ui Hanguk Yeonghwa Undongsa)*, Jisiksaneuo Publisher, Seoul, Korea.

Kim, Tae-hoon. October 2004. Seoul. (Personal interview.)

Kipen, D. 1997. "Planet Hollywood: The Death of the American Film". *World Policy Journal*, 14, 59–66.

KMPPC 1977. *Korean Film Data Collection (Hanguk Yeonghwa Jaryo Pyeollam)*, KMPPC, Seoul, Korea.

KOFA. 2007. *Speaking of Korean Cinema: Renaissance of Korean Cinema 2 (Hangunk Yeonghwareul Malhanda: Hangunk Yeonghwaui Reunesangseu 2)*, Yiche, Seoul, Korea.

KOFIC 2001. *Korean Cinema 2001*, KOFIC, Seoul, Korea.

KOFIC 2005. *Korean Cinema 2004*, KOFIC, Seoul, Korea.

KOFIC 2007. *Korean Cinema 2006*, KOFIC, Seoul, Korea.

KOFIC 2010. *Korean Cinema 2009*, KOFIC, Seoul, Korea.

KOFIC 2015. *Korean Cinema 2014*, KOFIC, Seoul, Korea.

Kwak, Jeong-hwan. October 2004. Seoul. (Personal interview.)

Lee, G. 2001. "Modernism Appeared in Korean Cinema" (Hanguk Yeonghwa-eh Natanan Modeoniseum Gyeonghyang). In Cha, S. (ed.) *Korean Film History Seen through Props: Modern Landscape (Sopumeuro bon Hanguk Yeonghwasa: Geundae-ui Punggyeong)*, Sodo Publishing, Seoul, Korea.

Lee, Hyeong-pyo. October 2004/2005. Seoul. (Personal interview.)

Lee, H. 2000. *Contemporary Korean Cinema: Identity, Culture, and Politics*, Manchester University Press, Manchester, New York.

———. 2004. "Korean Cinema in the 1970s" (1970nyeondae Hanguk Yeonghwa). In KOFA (ed.) *Studying Korean Film History 1960–1979 (Hanguk Yeonghwasa Gongbu 1960–1979)*, Yiche, Seoul, Korea. 87–142.

———. 2005. History of Korean Film Support Organization (Hanguk Yeonghwa Jinheunggigu-ui Yeoksa). *History of Korean Film Policy (Hanguk Yeonghwa Jeongchaeksa)*. Nanam, Seoul, Korea. 350–459.

———. 2006. "Film on Global Stage". In: Ciecko, A. T. (ed.) *Contemporary Asian cinema: popular culture in a global frame*. Berg, Oxford, England. 182–206

Lee, Jang-ho. October 2005. Seoul. (Personal interview.)

Lee, K. (ed.) 2003. *2003 Looking for Film Locations: Interviews (2003 Yeonghwa-ui Gohyang-eul Chajaseo)*, KOFA, Seoul, Korea.

Lee, N. 2011. "The Automobile Industry". In Kim, B. and E. Vogel. (eds.) *The Park Chung Hee Era: The Transformation of South Korea*. Harvard University Press, Cambridge, Massachusetts. 295–321.

Lee, S. "Park Chan-ok: 'As I Am Not Park Chan-ho, I Am Not Hong Sang-soo.' (Park Chan-ok: 'Naega Park Chan-ho Anideun Nan, Hong Sang-soo Anio.')". *Cine21* (19 November 2002). Available: <http://www.cine21.com/news/view/mag_id/15139>. Accessed 26 November 2014.

Lee, Soo-yeon. October 2003. Busan. (Personal interview.)

Lee, W. 2003. *A Study on the Building of Youth Film Genre in the 1960s (1960nyeondae Cheongchun Yeonghwa Hyeongseong Gwajeong-eh Gwanhan Yeongu)*. MA., Chung-Ang University.

Lee Woo-seok. November 2005. Seoul. (Personal interview.)

Lee, Yong-gi. July 2014; and June 2015. Beijing. (Personal interview.)

Bibliography

Lee, Y. 1995. "Contemplation over Yu's Aesthetics (Yu Hyun-mok Mihagui Seongchal)". In: *Yu Hyun-mok: Cinematic Life (Yu Hyun-mok: Yeonghwa Insaeng)*. Hyegwadang, Seoul, Korea. 192–202.

———. 1988. *Introduction to Cinema (Yeonghwa Gaeron)*, Hanjin Publishing, Seoul, Korea.

———. 2004. *History of Korean Cinema (Hanguk Yeonghwa Jeonsa)*, Sodo Press, Seoul, Korea.

———. 2007a. "The New Military Regime's Rule over Culture and the Advent of the New Film Culture". In Kim, M. (ed.) *Korean Cinema: From Origins to Renaissance*. CommBooks, Seoul, Korea. 271–72.

———. 2007b. "The 3S Policy and Erotic Films". In Kim, M. (ed.) *Korean Cinema: From Origins to Renaissance*. CommBooks, Seoul, Korea. 277–79.

Lee, Y. and Y. Choe. 1998. *The History of Korean Cinema*. Jimoondang Publishing Company, Seoul, Korea.

Ma, I. 1999. "Democratic Movement in the Late 1970s and the Collapse of Yusin System (1970 Nyeondae Hubangiui Minjuhwa Undonggwa Yusin Chejeui Bunggoe)". In: Academy of Korean Studies. (ed.) *The Socio-political Change of Republic of Korea in the Late 1970s (1970 Nyeondae Hubangiui Jeongchi Sahoe Byeondong)*. Baeksan-Seodang Publishing, Seoul, Korea. 259–322.

Maliangkay, R. 2008. "Staging Korean Traditional Performing Arts Abroad: Important Intangible Intercultural Performance Issues". *Sungkyun Journal of East Asian Studies*, 7, 49–68.

McDonald, P. 1995. "Star Studies". In Hollows, J. and M. Jancovich. (eds.) *Approaches to Popular Film*, Manchester University Press, Manchester, New York. 79–97.

McHugh, K. and N. Abelmann (eds.) 2005. *South Korean Golden Age Melodrama: Gender, Genre and National Cinema*, Wayne State University Press, Detroit.

Michelle, H. 1996. "Cinema in the Age of Television". In Nowell-Smith, G. (ed.) *Oxford History of the Cinema, 1895–1995*, Oxford University Press, London, England. 466–75.

Miller, T., Govil, N., Mcmurria, J., Maxwell, R., and T. Wang. 2001. *Global Hollywood*, British Film Institute, London, England.

Min, E., Joo, J. and H. J. Kwak. 2003. *Korean Film: History, Resistance, and Democratic Imagination*, Prager, Westport, Connecticut.

Minkahyup Human Rights Group. Feb. 2004. "Human Rights Condition under the National Security Law" (Gukga boanbeop jeogyongsang eseo natanan ingwon siltae), National Human Rights Commission of Korea, Seoul, Korea.

Mittell, J. 2003. "Audiences Talking Genre: Television Talk Shows and Cultural Hierarchies". *Journal of Popular Film and Television*, 31, 36–46.

Moon, C. and B. Jun. 2011. "Modernization Strategy: Ideas and Influences". In Vogel, E. F. (ed.) *The Park Chung Hee Era: The Transformation of South Korea*, Harvard University Press, Cambridge, Massachusetts.

Nam, I. 2007. "Korean Woman Directors". In Kim, M. (ed.) *Korean Cinema: From Origins to Renaissance*, CommBooks, Seoul, Korea. 161–68.

National Statistics Office. 1995. *Trace of Korea Looking through Statistics (Tonggye-ro Bon Hangugui Baljachue)*, National Statistics Office, Seoul, Korea.

Neale, S. 1980. *Genre*, British Film Institute, London, England.

Nelmes, J. 2003. *An Introduction to Film Studies*, Routledge, New York, New York.

Nichols, B. Spring 1994. "Discovering Form, Inferring Meaning: New Cinemas and the Film Festival Circuit". *Film Quarterly*, 47, 16–30.

Nowell-Smith, G. 1996. "Art Cinema". In Nowell-Smith, G. (ed.) *The Oxford History of World Cinema: The Definitive History of Cinema Worldwide*. Oxford University Press, Oxford, England. 567–75.

Olson, S. 1999. *Hollywood Planet: Global Media and the Competitive Advantage of Narrative Transparency,* Erlbaum, Mahwah, New Jersey.
O'Regan, T. 1996. *Australian National Cinema,* Routledge, London, England.
Paquet, D. 2009. *New Korean Cinema: Breaking the Waves,* Wallflower Press, London, England and New York, New York.
Park, C. 1963. *The Country, the Revolution and I,* Hollym Corp., Seoul, Korea.
———. 1970. *Our Nation's Path: Ideology of Social Reconstruction,* Hollym Corporation: Publishers, Seoul, Korea.
Park, Ethan. July 2011; December 2013; July 2014; and June 2015. Beijing. (Personal interview.)
Park, J. 2005. "Between the Establishment of the Motion Picture Law and its 4th Revision (1961–1984) (Yeonghwabeop Jejeongeseo Je 4 Cha Gaejeongkkajiui Yeonghwa Jeongchaek (1961–1984 Nyeon))". In: *A History of Korean Film Policy (Hanguk Yeounghwa Jeongchaeksa).* Nanam Publishing, Seoul, Korea. 186–268.
Park, Kwang-su. October 2004. Seoul. (Personal interview.)
PIFF. 1999. "Interview with Yu Hyun-mok". In: *Yu Hyun-mok: The Pathfinder of Korean Realism.* PIFF, Pusan, Korea. 86–113.
Raine, M. 2001. "Ishihara Yujiro: Youth, Celebrity and the Male Body in Late 1950s Japan". In Washburn, D. and C. Cavanaugh. (eds.) *Word and Image in Japanese Cinema,* Cambridge University Press, New York, New York.
Rayner, J. 2000. *Contemporary Australian Cinema: An introduction,* Manchester University Press, Manchester, New York.
Rayns, T. 1994. *Seoul Stirring: 5 Korean Directors,* Institute of Contemporary Arts, London.
Rhyu, S. and S. Lew. 2011. "Pohang Iron & Steel Company". In Kim, B. and E. Vogel. (eds.) *The Park Chung Hee Era: The Transformation of South Korea,* Harvard University Press, Cambridge, Massachusetts. 322–44.
Richie, D. 2001. *A Hundred Years of Japanese Film,* Kodansha International, Tokyo, Japan.
Rubin, B. November 1971. "International Film and Television Propaganda: Campaigns of Assistance". *Annals of the American Academy of Political and Social Science,* 398, 81–92.
Sarris, A. 2004. "Notes on the Auteur Theory in 1962". In Simpson, P., Utterson, A. and K. J. Shapherdson, (eds.) *Film Theory: Critical Concepts in Media and Cultural Studies,* Routledge, London, England. 21–33.
Schatz, T. 1981. *Hollywood Genres: Formulas, Filmmaking, and the Studio System,* Temple University Press, Philadelphia, Pennsylvania.
———. 1988. *The Genius of the System: Hollywood Filmmaking in the Studio Era,* Pantheon Books, New York, New York.
———. 1996. "Hollywood: The Triumph of the Studio System". In Noel-Smith, G. (ed.) *The Oxford History of World Cinema,* Oxford University Press, New York, New York. 220–34.
Sharp, J. 2008. *Behind the Pink Curtain: The Complete History of Japanese Sex Cinema,* FAB Press, Godalming, England.
Shin, C. and Stringer J. (eds.) 2005. *New Korean Cinema,* Edinburgh University Press, Edinburgh, Scotland.
Shim, A. 2011. "Anticommunist War Films of the 1960s and the Korean Cinema's Early Genre-bending Traditions". *Acta Koreana,* 14, 175–96.
Shim, A. & Yecies, B. November 2012. "Asian Interchange: Korean-Hong Kong Co-productions of the 1960s". *Journal of Japanese & Korean Cinema,* 4, 15–28.
———. 2012. "Power of the Korean Film Producer: Dictator Park Chung Hee's Forgotten Film Cartel of the 1960s Golden Decade and Its Legacy". *The Asia-Pacific Journal: Japan Focus* 10:52. http://www.japanfocus.org/-Brian-Yecies/3875.

Shin, K. 2007. "The Cultural Center Generation and the Growth of Film Buff Culture". In Kim, M.-H. (ed.) *Korean Cinema: From Origins to Renaissance*. CommBooks, Seoul, Korea. 258–60.

Singer, B. 2001. *Melodrama and Modernity,* Columbia University Press, New York, New York.

Smith, S., Pieper, K. & Choueiti, M. 2014. "Exploring the Barriers and Opportunities for Independent Women Filmmakers Phase I and II". *Sundance Institute and Women in Film Los Angeles Women Filmmakers Initiative.* Media, Diversity & Social Change Initiative Annenberg School for Communication & Journalism University of Southern California, Los Angeles, California.

Staiger, J. 1997. "Consuming the Planet: Planet Hollywood, Stars, and the Global Consumer Culture". *Velvet Light Trap* (Fall): 42–55.

Standish, I. 1994. "Korean Cinema and New Realism". In Dissanayake, W. (ed.) *Colonialism and Nationalism in Asian Cinema.* Indiana University Press, Bloomington, Indiana. 65–89.

Tadashi, I. 1939. "Japanese Films in Review 1938–9". In The Society for International Cultural Relations (ed.) *Cinema Yearbook of Japan 1939.* Tokyo, Japan. 19–22.

Thompson, K. 1985. *Exporting Entertainment: America in the World Film Market 1907–34,* British Film Institute, London, England.

Thompson, K. and D. Bordwell. 2003. *Film History: An Introduction,* McGraw Hill, New York.

Valenti, J. 1968. "The 'Foreign Service' of the Motion Picture Association of America". *The Journal of the Producers Guild of America.* MPEA collection. MPEA-AMPTP 2000, Additions b.2. AMPAS (March): 1–4.

———. 1976. Testimony Regarding the Role of Congress in Regulating Cable Television and the Potential for New Technologies in the Communications System. Hearings before the Subcommittee on Communications of the Committee on Interstate and Foreign Commerce. House of Representatives. 94th Congress, Second Session (27 July): 634–65.

———. 1977. Testimony Regarding International Communications and Information. Hearings before the Subcommittee on International Operations of the Committee on Foreign Relations. United States Senate. 95th Congress, First Session (9 June): 192–232.

———. 1986. Testimony Regarding Trade Reform Legislation. Hearings before the Subcommittee on Trade of the Committee on Ways and Means. House of Representatives. 99th Congress, Second Session (15 April): 989–1008.

———. 1987. Testimony (on Behalf of the MPAA and the International Intellectual Property Alliance) Regarding Comprehensive Trade Legislation. Hearings before the Committee on Ways and Means. House of Representatives and its Subcommittee on Trade. 100th Congress, First Session (20 February): 446–52.

———. 1989. Testimony Regarding Unfair Foreign Trade Practices. Hearings before the Subcommittee on Oversight and Investigations of the Committee on Energy and Commerce. House of Representatives. 101st Congress, First Session (1 March): 8–121; 237–60.

Vasey, R. 1997. *The World According to Hollywood, 1918–1939,* University of Wisconsin Press, Madison, Wisconsin.

Wade, J. March 1969. "The Cinema in Korea: A Robust Invalid". *Korea Journal*, 9, 5–12.

Xinhua News Agency (2013), "China cuts 20 approval items for film, TV sectors". *China Daily US Edition* (ChinaDaily.com.cn) (17 July). Available at: http://usa.chinadaily.com.cn/china/2013-07/17/content_16789815.htm.

Yang, Gi-hwan. October 2004/2005. Seoul. (Personal interview.)

Yecies, B. 2005. Systemization of Film Censorship in Colonial Korea: Profiteering from Hollywood's First Golden Age, 1926–1936. *The Journal of Korean Studies,* 10, 59–84.

———. 2007. "Parleying Culture against Trade: Hollywood's Affairs with Korea's Screen Quotas". *Korea Observer* Vol. 38, No. 1 (Spring): 1–32.

———. 2008. "Planet Hallyuwood's Political Vulnerabilities: Censuring the Expression of Satire in *The President's Last Bang* (2005)" *International Review of Korean Studies* 5(1): 37–64.

———. 2008. "Sounds of Celluloid Dreams: Coming of the Talkies to Cinema in Colonial Korea". *Korea Journal*, 48, 16–97.

———. 2010. "Inroads for Cultural Traffic: Breeding Korea's CinemaTiger". In Black, D., Epstein, S. & Tokita, A. (eds.) *Complicated Currents: Media Production, the Korean Wave, and Soft Power in East Asia,* Monash E-Press, Melbourne.

Yecies, B. and A. Shim. 2011. "Contemporary Korean Cinema: Challenges and the Transformation of 'Planet Hallyuwood'". *Acta Koreana* 14, 1–15.

———. 2011. *Korea's Occupied Cinemas, 1893–1948,* Routledge, New York, New York.

Yecies, B., Shim, A., and Goldsmith, B. 2011. "Digital Intermediary: Korean Transnational Cinema". *Media International Australia* #141 (November): 137–45.

Yi, C. 2002. "Formation of Ideology in Park Chung Hee Era: Focusing on Historical Origin" (Park Chung Hee sidae Chibae ideology-ui Hyongsong: Yoksajok Giwon-up Chungsimuro). In Hanguk Chongsin Munhwa Yonguwon (ed.) *Study on Park Chung Hee Era,* Baeksan Seodang, Seoul, Korea.

Yi, Edward Chi-yun. 2011 Busan; and July 2014. Beijing. (Personal interview.)

Yi, Hyoin. October 2004. Seoul. (Personal interview.)

Yi, H. 2002. "Evolving Aesthetics in Korean Cinema: From 'Literary' to 'Art' Films". *Getting to Know Korea: Resource Book for K-12 Educators,* 69–75.

———. 2003. *Social and Cultural History of Korea Reflected in Films (Yeonghwaro Igneun Hanguk Sahoe Munhwa-Sa),* Gaemagowon, Seoul, Korea.

———. 2005. "1960s Korean Cinema". *A History of Korean Cinema: from Liberation through the 1960s,* Korean Film Archive, Seoul, Korea.

———. 2008. *Shin Sang-ok,* KOFIC, Seoul, Korea.

Yi, H., Jung, J. and J. Park. 2005. *A History of Korean Cinema: from Liberation through the 1960s,* KOFA, Seoul, Korea.

Yi, P. 2003. "Political Economy of Developmental Dictatorship and Korea's Experience" (Kaebal Tokche-ui Chongch'igyongjehak-kwa Han'guk-ui Kyonghom). In Yi, P. O. (ed.) *Developmental Dictatorship and Park Chung Hee Era: Political and Economic Origin of Our Time (Kaebal Tokchewa Park Chung Hee Sidae: Uri Sidae-ui Chongch'igyongje-jok Kiwon),* Changbi, Seoul, Korea. 16–65.

Yim, H. 2003. *The Emergence and Change of Cultural Policy in South Korea,* Jinhan Book, Seoul, Korea.

Yoo, S. & Lee, S. M. Summer 1987. "Management Style and Practice of Korean Chaebols". *California Management Review,* XXIX, 95–110.

Yu, Hyun-mok. October 2005. Pusan. (Personal interview.)

Yu, H. 1995. *Yu Hyun-mok: Cinematic Life (Yu Hyun-mok: Yeonghwa Insaeng),* Hyegwadang, Seoul, Korea.

Yu, H. and H. Cho. 2009. "Yu Hyun-mok" (Yu Hyeon-mok). *Oral History of Korean Arts: Performing Arts (Gusullo Mannaneun Hanguk Yesulsa: Gongyeon Yesul).* Available: <http://oralhistory.arko.or.kr/oral/main.asp>. Accessed 14 December 2012.

Yu, In-taek. October 2004. Seoul. (Personal interview.)

Yun, Il-bong. September 2004. Seoul. (Personal interview.)

Selected Filmography

Aimless Bullet (오발탄), Yu Hyun-mok, Daehan Film Company, 1961.
Art Museum by the Zoo (미술관 옆 동물원), Lee Jeong-hyang, Cine2000, 1998.
Assembly (集結号), Feng Xiogang, China Film Co-Production Corporation, 2007.
Barefoot Youth (맨발의 청춘), Kim Ki-duk, Geukdong Heungeop Co. 1964.
Blind Massage (推拿), Ye Lou, Dream Factory/Les Films du Lendemain, 2014.
Children of Darkness Part 1 (어둠의 자식들), Lee Jang-ho, Hwacheong Gongsa, 1981.
Deaf Samryong (벙어리 삼룡이), Shin Sang-ok, Shin Film, 1965.
Double Xposure (二次曝光), Yu Li, Laurel Films, 2012.
Eoudong (어우동), Lee Jang-ho, Taegeung Film Company, 1985.
Evergreen Tree (상록수), Shin Sang-ok, Shin Film, 1961.
Good Windy Day (바람불어 좋은 날), Lee Jang-ho, Donga Export Co., 1980.
Habitual Sadness (낮은 목소리 2), Byun Young-joo, Boim Pictures, 1997.
Heavenly Homecoming to Stars (별들의 고향), Lee Jang-ho, Hwacheon Gongsa, 1974.
Helpless (화차), Byun Young-joo, Boim Pictures, 2012.
Late Autumn (만추), Kim Tae-yong, Boram Entertainment/Film Workshop/North by Northwest Entertainment, 1966.
Madam Freedom (자유부인), Han Hyeong-mo, Samseong Film Company, 1956.
Marines Who Never Returned (돌아오지 않는 해병), Lee Man-hee, Daewon Film Company, 1963.
Marriage Blue (결혼전야), Hong Ji-young, Soo Film, 2013.
My Own Breathing (낮은 목소리 3 -숨결), Byun Young-joo, Boim Pictures, 1999.
Paju (파주), Park Chan-ok, TPS Company, 2009.
Rice (쌀), Shin Sang-ok, Shin Film, 1963.
Last Woman of Shang (달기), Shin Sang-ok, Shin Film. 1964.
Love with an Alien (aka *An Exotic Garden* 이국정원), Tu Gwang-qi/Jeon Chang-geun/Mitsuo Wakasugi, Hanguk Yeongye/Shaw Brothers, 1958.
Madam Aema (애마부인), Jeong In-yeop, Yeonbang Film Co., 1982.
Mist (안개), Kim Su-yong, Taechang Heungeop Co., 1967.
Monkey Goes West, Meng Hua Ho, Shaw Brothers, 1966.
Mother (마더), Bong Joon-ho, Barunson Entertainment, 2009.
Seong Chunhyang (성춘향), Shin Sang-ok, Shin Film, 1961.
Reason to Live (오늘), Lee Jeong-hyang, Poison Sky Company, 2011.
Red Scarf (빨간 마후라), Shin Sang-ok, Shin Film, 1964.
Seaside Village (갯마을), Kim Su-yong, Daeyang Film Company, 1965.
Seven Female POWs (칠인의 여포로), Lee Man-hee, Haptong Film Company, 1965.
Shiri (쉬리), Kang Je-gyu, Samsung Entertainment, 1999.
Snowpiercer, Bong Joon-ho, CJ Entertainment, 2013.
The Attorney (변호인), Yang Woo-seok, Withus Film/Will Entertainment, 2013.
The Empty Dream (춘몽), Yu Hyun-mok, Segi Sangsa, 1965.
The Host (괴물), Bong Joon-ho, Showbox Entertainment/Chungeorahm Film/Boston Investments, 2006.
The Martyrs (순교자), Yu Hyun-mok, Haptong Film Company, 1965.
The Murmuring (낮은 목소리 -아시아에서 여성으로 산다는 것), Byun Young-joo, Boim Pictures, 1995.
The Naked Kitchen (키친), Hong Ji-young, Su Film/Yeoubeak Entertainment, 2009.
The Testimony (증언), Yu Hyun-mok, KMPPC, 1973.
The Uninvited (4인용 식탁), Lee Soo-yeon, BOM Productions/Sidus HQ, 2003.

The Way Home (집으로), Lee Jeong-hyang, Tube Pictures, 2003.
Very Ordinary Couple (aka *Temperature of Love* 연애의 온도), Roh Deok, Vanguard Studio, 2012.
Youngja's Heydays (영자의 전성시대), Kim Ho-seon, Taechang Heungeop Co., 1975.

Additional Resources

Websites

KTV (Korean government's Internet website): http://www.ktv.go.kr/
Korean Film Biz Zone: http://www.koreanfilm.or.kr/jsp/index.jsp
Korean Film Council (KOFIC): http://www.kofic.or.kr/
Korean Film Database (KMDB): http://www.kmdb.or.kr/
Korean Film Archive (KOFA): http://www.koreafilm.or.kr/
The Oral History of Korean Arts: http://oralhistory.arko.or.kr/oral/main.asp
Media Gaon (Media Portal Service from Korea Press Foundation): http://www.mediagaon.or.kr/
Korean History Database: http://db.history.go.kr/
Ministry of Government Legislation: www.moleg.go.kr
Korean Cinema Website by Darcy Paquet: *Koreanfilm.org*
Film Business Asia: http://www.filmbiz.asia/
Korea Creative Contents Agency http://eng.kocca.kr/en/main.do
Newspapers (Paper/Online)

Chosun Daily (Chosun Ilbo)
Donga Daily (Donga Ilbo)
Gyeonghyang Shinmun
Hanguk Daily (Hanguk Ilbo)
Joongang Daily
Maeil Gyeongje
Seoul Newspaper (Seoul Shinmun)
The Hankeoreh

Magazines

Cine21
Gendae Yeonghwa (Modern Movie)
Gukje Yeonghwa (International Film)
Jugan Hanguk (Weekly Korea)
Korean Cinema (published monthly by KMPPC)
Korean Cinema Today (published bi-monthly by KOFIC)
Screen Daily
Screen International
Silver Screen (Silver Screen)
Shin Dong-a (Shing Donga)
Shin Sajo (Shin Sajo)
Shin Yeonghwa (*New Films*)
The Hollywood Reporter
Yeonghwa TV Yesul (*Film TV Art*)

Yeonghwa Munhwa Yeongu (Film Culture Studies)
Yeonghwa Japji (Movie Magazine)
Yeonghwa Segye (Cinema World)
Yeonghwa Yesul (Film Art)
Yeonye Japji (Entertainment Magazine)
Wolgan Hanguk (Weekly Korea)
Wolgan Yeonghwa (Monthly Film)
Wolgan Yeonye (Weekly Entertainment)
Variety

Index

10 million audience film; *see cheonman yeonghwa*
12 Angry Men 92
20 Once Again 166, 238
200 Pounds Beauty 240
386 Generation 222
3S Policy 148; *see also* sexuality in films

Affair, An 175
Affection of the World, The 84
Aftershock 239
Ahn Byeong-seop 70
Ahn Byung-ki 232
Ahn Soo-hyun 11, 161, 167, 174, 176, 177
Ahn Sung-ki 233
Ahn, Peter 228, 244
Aimless Bullet 6, 7, 20, 42, 45–51, 59–60, 64, 143–4
All About My Wife 175
All She Was Worth 194
All That Cinema 183, 202–203; *see also* Chae Yoon-hee
Altar for a Tutelary Deity 64
American Forces Korea Network (AFKN) 96, 129
Americanization 7, 63; *see also* Hollywood
American fashion, culture, and ideas 96
Anarchists 234, 237–238
Another Public Enemy 164, 171
anticommunist films 8, 56, 62, 109, 111
Anticommunist Law 41, 54, 122, 152
Anyang Film 26, 83, 87, 89
April Revolution 45, 84, 100, 130, 131, 254
Arahan 174
Arang 211
Architecture 101 167, 172, 240
Ardor 174, 194

Arirang 64
Art Museum by the Zoo 191–2
arthouse films 42–4, 64–5, 77–8;
   characteristic features 64;
   government subsidies 65;
   political nature 77
Asia Film 83, 87
Asian Film Festival 30, 32, 68, 72, 75, 149; 9th 81–2, 91–3, 98–9;
   linkages created by 82–3; 13th 88
Asian financial crisis 2, 10, 158, 159, 254;
   IMF bailout 158; IMF crisis 163
Assassination 4, 176–7
Assembly 232, 237, 238
Asung Film 35
Attack the Gas Station! 174
Attorney, The 4, 11–12, 207, 208, 209, 217–24
audience reception 5
auteur(s) 42–5, 55–56, 58, 66, 99;
   commercial auteurs 11, 138, 182, 194
authorial expressivity 64–65
Avatar 217
AZ Works 239

Bad Man Must Die, The 232, 240–1
Bae Chang-ho 135, 136, 189
Baek Gyeol 97–8
Baek Yun-shik 169
Baeksang Arts Awards 191, 192, 197
Bae Chang-ho 135–6, 138, 189, 200
Bandits, The 97
Barefoot Youth 8, 94–6
Bariteo 193
Barking Dogs Never Bite 210
Batteries not Included 118
Beat 232
Beijing Film Academy 12, 228–229, 238, 246

Bergman, Ingmar 43, 75, 94
Between the Knees 136–8, 150
Bichunmoo 234
Big Bang Creative 232–33; *see also* Lee Joo-ik
Big Swindle, The 176
Bittersweet Life, A 173, 175
BK Pictures 172; *see also* Shim Bo-kyoung
Black Gloves 93
Blind Massage 12, 243, 244
Bloody Rain 174
Blue Days 147
Blue Dragon Film Awards 32, 190, 192
Boardwalk Empire 218
Bohan Industry Co. 188
BOM Productions 173, 175–6, 202
Bong Joon-ho 119, 138, 167, 173, 182, 200, 208, 209, 210–14, 224, 244
Boo Ji-young 172
Boram Entertainment 214, 233
Bordwell, David 64
Boundary, The 232
Boyfriend for My Wife, A 175
British Free Cinema 128
Bucheon International Fantastic Film Festival 13, 55
Buddha Mountain 242
bungei-eiga film movement 63
Bunshinsaba 232
Burim Incident 219–20
Busan International Film Festival (BIFF) 3, 13, 14, 43, 117, 190, 195, 229–30, 237, 257; *see also* Pusan International Film Festival (PIFF) 229–30, 237
Buy My Fist 95
Byon In-sik 56, 128
Byun Young-joo 11, 15 174, 182, 191, 193–5, 203

Cabbage in a Pepper Field 189
Cairo International Film Festival 200
Carriage Running into the Winter 189
Cart 172
Catch One Cable 159, 161
censorship 21, 26, 35, 42, 43, 45, 48, 54, 121, 136, 144; battles 45, 48, 50, 54; lifting of 2, 158, 182, 208; *see also* sexuality in films
CGV multiplex cinemas 159, 162, 164–66, 171; *see also* CJ E&M; in China 255
Cha Seung-jae 161, 174, 176, 234, 235
Chae Tae-jin 95
Chae Yoon-hee 183, 202

chaebols 10, 15, 33, 120; involvement in film industry 158–63, 169, 174, 177
Chan, Jackie 231
Chan, Jaycee 231
Changsu's Heydays 147
Chaser, The 174
Chef, the Actor, the Scoundrel, The 239
Cheil Communications 161
Chen Bolin 240
Chen Kaige 228, 229, 232, 233, 235, 236
Chen Kun 228
cheonman yeonghwa (10 million audience film) 4, 171, 176–7, 217
Children of Darkness Part 1 136, 138
Chilling Cosplay, A 240
China Film Group 234
China: 3D films in 231, 239–40; 4DX cinemas in 255; bilateral ventures 12, 227, 232; changing face of Chinese–Korean cinema 241–5; co-productions with 12; IMAX cinemas in 255; Korean Film Business Center (Beijing) 230; *see also* KOFIC Beijing office; Korean film exports to 231; membership of World Trade Organization 230; opening up of film market 230; post-production technology transfer 237–8
Cho Moon-jin 118
Cho Seon-jak 130
Cho Sung Woo 214
Choi Dae-hyeon 54
Choi Dong-hoon 175, 176
Choi Eun-hee 30, 68, 81, 85, 183, 184, 187–8, 189, 190
Choi Gyeong-ok 89
Choi Ho 193
Choi Hyeon-min 34–5, 71
Choi In-gyu 43, 88, 185, 186
Choi In-ho 130, 131
Choi Jae-won 223
Choi Mu-ryong 46
Chosun Film Company 184, 185
Chosun Film Law 21
Chow, Stephen 240
Christmas in August 176, 191, 232
Chu Ja-hyeon 231–2
Chun Doo-hwan 1, 8, 9, 107, 115, 117, 134, 135, 149, 151, 158, 218, 221, 222
Chung Chang-hwa 88, 89, 97
Chung Ji-young 128
Chung Sung-ill 128
Chung, Cecilia 233
Chungmuro 6, 24, 157, 162
Cine Poem Club 50–1

cinema of perseverance 12
Cinema Service 159, 160, 163, 164, 173; see also Kang Woo-seok
Cineworld Entertainment 234
Citizen Kane 218
CJ E&M 11, 165–6, 167, 177, 178, 240; CJ Entertainment 159, 164, 165, 166, 167, 171, 234; CJ Powercast 239, 245; interest in China 227
Classroom of Youth, The 93, 94, 95
co-production 81–90, 173; bogus arrangements 83, 88–90; fake co-productions 8, 25, 255
Coalition for Cultural Diversity in Moving Images (CDMI) 120
Cold Eyes 175
Colorful Rainbow, The 97
Come Drink with Me 88
Come Rain, Come Shine 173
compressed modernity 5, 12, 135, 207, 210, 218, 220
Confession of an Actress 184
Confucian values 11, 70, 73, 143, 150–1, 185, 192–3, 196–9, 202, 255
Contact, The 10, 160, 168, 176
Countdown 173
Crazed Fruit 94
Creative Artists Agency (CAA) 175
Crossroad 44–5
Crouching Tiger, Hidden Dragon 233, 235
Cuckoo's Dolls 147
cultural nationalism 7, 62–3, 65–70, 76–8, 252
Cultural Properties Protection Law 67
Cut Runs Deep, The 176
Cyrano Agency 172, 241
CZ12 239

Dad, Please Get Married 98
Daedong Film Company 35
Daehan Film Company 46, 49
daemyeong jejak system 33–4, 36; ban on 35
Daewoo 10, 120, 158, 159, 163, 254
Dangerous Liaisons 232
dark age of Korean cinema 8–9, 127, 129
Daughter 211
Daughter of Government General 96
Daughters of Kim's Pharmacy 95
Daydream 96
Deaf Samryong 7, 31, 64, 68–70, 71, 74; awards 68; film festival invitations 68
Declaration of Genius 191
Demon Empire 234–5
Descendants of Cain 56

Desire 36
Devils, The 133
Dexter Digital 228, 240, 244, 245
digital work practices 245; see also post-production
distribution arrangements with US studios 163–4
Do Seong-hi 228
Do You Know Kkotsuni 147
domestic market: dominance of Korean film in 3, 119
Dong-A Export Co. 149, 173
Donga Heungeop 6, 32, 83
Dorodarake no junjō 8
Double Xposure 12, 241–3, 244
Dream 64
Dreambox 158, 161
DreamWorks 159, 165, 237
Drifting Story, A 64

E J-yong 173, 175–6
Early Rain 95
Electronic Industry Promotion Act 141
Emperor and the Assassin, The 232
Empty Dream, The 6–7, 42, 44, 51–5, 98, 144–5; censorship trial 58
enlightenment films 65, 109, 132, 187
Eom Aeng-ran 94
Eoudong 136–8
Epitaph 211
erotic (ero) melodramas 10, 136–7, 142, 148–51
Eunuch 145, 184
Even Little Grass Has Its Own Name 193
Evening Bell, The 129
Evergreen Tree 26, 27, 67, 81
Evil Night 44, 64
Extra Mortals, The 50
Eye in the Sky 175

Face Reader, The 223
Family Ties 215
Fan Bingbing 242
Farewell 128
Farewell My Concubine 229, 232, 236
Fatal Attraction 118, 151
Fearless Foreign Region 137
female producers, 11, 157, 167–77
female writer-directors 182–203
historical legacy 183–90
Feng Xiaogang 232, 237–9
Fifth Generation filmmakers 228
Film Quarterly Young Sang Shi Dae 130
First Experience 188

274 Index

Fists of Vengeance 89
Five Fingers of Death 88–9
Five Marines 95
Flame in the Valley 184
Flu, The 119
Flying Boys 194
Flying Swords of Dragon Gate 239
FnH Pictures 173–4; *see also* Kim Mi-hee
Forestt Studios 239–40, 243–4; *see also* Park, Ethan
Forever Only You 84
Forever the Moment 167, 190–1
Forget-me-nots 189
Foul King 173
Fourth Generation filmmakers 228
Fox with Nine Tails, The 160, 176
Freedom, Madam 64
French Cultural Center 128, 167
French New Wave, *see* Nouvelle Vague
Frozen Flower, A 200
Fu Wenxia 234

Gate of Chastity 31
gender relations 11
General's Moustache, The 65, 75
Genji Keita 98
genre 208; bending of 210; differentiation 207, 208; transformations 7, 207–24
German Cultural Center 128
Geukdong Heungeop 23, 83, 94–6
Ghost 163
Gingko Bed 10, 160, 162, 176, 238
Girl at My Door, A 165
Girl Raised as a Future Daughter-in-law 184, 187
Girls' Revolution 231
Glocalization 246; *see also* internationalization
Go Go 70s 133
Godzilla 92
Goggles, The 197
golden age of Korea cinema 19, 37, 182
Golden Harvest 88, 89
Gong Su-chang 193
Good Lawyer's Wife, A 167
Good Rain Knows, A 232
Good Windy Day 9–10, 134–6, 137, 138
Good, the Bad and the Weird, The 235
Gordon, Dennie 240
Grand Bell Awards 27, 32, 68, 71, 75, 136, 187, 191
Great Monster Yongary, The 95, 129
guanxi 12, 228–30, 234, 237, 245–6, 255

Guests of the Last Train, The 56, 75
Guk Kwae-nam 51, 96
Guns and Talks 164
Gwak Gyeong-taek 2
Gwangju Massacre 135, 218–19
Gwangseong Film Co. 84

H 243
Ha Gil-jong 128, 130, 147
Ha Yeong-su 232
Habitual Sadness 193
Hae Jae-yeong 133
Haeundae 4, 200, 217
Hah Myung-joong 177
Hallyu, *see* Korean Wave
Han Eun-jin 184
Han River, The 128
Han Suk-gyu 170
Han Un-sa 30
Han Wu-jeong 97–8
Hand 51
Hanguk Yeonye 82, 83, 84
Hanguk Yesul 6, 23, 32
Hanryu, *see* Korean Wave
Hanyang 23
Hapdong 23
Happiness 175
Happy End 167
Haunters 175
Hayworth, Rita 81
Heartless 67
Heavenly Homecoming to Stars 9, 129, 131–2, 134, 137, 145
Heavy 195
Helpless 182, 194
Hengdian World Studio 235
Herstory 198
Hibiscus Town 229
Hide and Seek 119, 174
Ho Hyeon-chan 34–5, 71, 72, 145
Hole, The 163
Holiday in Seoul 163
Hollywood, influence of 1, 13, 107–21; increased access to Korean market 118
Homebound 97
Hometown in Heart, A 64
Hong Eun-won 185, 186, 189, 190
Hong Gi-seon 118
Hong Ji-young 11, 182, 191, 198–201
Hong Kong Asia Film Financing Forum 173, 175
Hong Kong: co-productions with 8, 81–99; fake co-productions 25, 83, 88–90, 252

Hong Pa 128, 130
Hong Sang-soo 2, 121, 173, 182
Hong Seong-gi 88
Horror Stories 200
Host, The 4, 210, 217, 224
"hostess" melodramas 9, 10, 129, 131, 136–7, 142, 144–51, 189, 253
How to Top My Wife 163, 173
Hu Guan 239
Huang Lei 228
Huang Xiaoming 228
Huayi Brothers 237, 241
Huh Jung 119
Huh Moon-young 128
Human Condition, The 97
Hur Jin-ho 167, 175, 176, 232
Hwacheon Film 83, 87, 130, 173
Hwajang 172
Hwang Gi-seong 118
Hwang Hye-mi 75, 188–9, 190
Hwang Jeong-lee 90
Hwang Jeong-soon 184
Hwang Jin Yi 164
Hwang Sun-won 67
Hyun Bin 214, 223

I am Lady Number 77 147
I Look Up When I Walk 82, 91–2
I Will Be a King of the Day 95
I Won't Cry 109, 111
Idiot Adada, An 64
Ilshin Investment 176
Im Chan-sang 198
Im Hi-suk 130, 133
Im Hwa-su 83, 84
Im Kwon-taek 9, 99, 110–11, 167, 189
Im Sang-soo 2, 121, 167, 169–71, 173, 182
Import License Reward System (ILRS) 23–4, 33, 55, 62, 65, 78
Import Recommendation System 78
In Expectation 229
industrialization of Korea 5, 81
internationalization 1, 2, 3, 5, 12, 83, 227; *see also* film exports
Interstellar 217
Ishihara, Shintarō 94
Ishihara, Yujirō 94
Isle, The 167, 168
It Rained Yesterday 147

Jaeckin, Just 200
Jamae Film Co. 185
James Bond films 8, 90

Jang Dong-gun 223, 233–34
Jang Gil-soo 128
Jang Il-ho 88, 89, 97
Jang Jin 121, 164
Jang Joon-Hwan 201, 210
Jang Na-ra 231
Jang Seo-hee 231
Jang Sun-woo 118, 135, 136
Jang Yoon-hyun 193
Jansangotmae independent film group 176, 193
Japan: co-productions with 8; influence on Korean film 88; plagiarizing of Japanese film 91, 97–8; remakes of films from 8, 81, 90–98
Japanese colonial period 7, 44–45, 63–4, 67–69, 91–2; comfort women during 193
Japanese–Korean propaganda pictures 185
Jealousy is My Middle Name 195, 197
Jeon Chang-geun 84, 185
Jeon Ji-hyun 197
Jeon Kyongnin 194
Jeon Woo-chi: The Taoist Wizard, see *Woochi*
Jeong Jin-woo 95, 135
Jeong Ju-ri 166
Jeong Seong-il 168
Jeong so-yeong 34, 189
Jeong U-taek 81
Jia Zhangke 228, 229
Jiang Wu 228
Jo Min-hwan 236
Joint Security Area (*JSA*) 167, 168, 172
Journey to the West: Conquering the Demons 240
Ju Dou 229
Ju Ji-hoon 199, 201
Jung Bi-seok 64
Jung Woo-sung 231

K-horror films 210–11
K-pop 3
Kanako, Michi 96
Kang Dae-jin 133–4
Kang Dae-seon 118
Kang Dong-wan 175
Kang Full 194
Kang Han-sup 128
Kang Je-gyu 2, 138 162, 168, 176, 232, 238
Kang Je-gyu Film 160, 169
Kang Seong-jin 174
Kang Woo-seok 138, 163, 164, 173

Kang Woo-seok Productions 160, 173; see also Cinema Service
Kidnapping Granny K 164
Kido Shiro 92
Killer Toon 211
Kim Dae-jung 163, 222
Kim Dong-ho 117
Kim Dong-in 67
Kim Dong-won 193
Kim Hak-seong 46
Kim Hee-sun 231
Kim Ho-seon 128, 130, 147, 189
Kim Hong-joon 128, 135
Kim Hye-ri 232
Kim Hyung-gu 232, 235, 236
Kim In-gi 88
Kim Jae-yeon 194
Kim Jee-woon 2, 121, 138, 167, 168, 173, 175, 182, 210, 225, 235, 243, 244, 254
Kim Jeong-hyeok 113
Kim Jeong-jung 228
Kim Ji-yeon 97
Kim Jin-kyu 30, 46, 49, 68, 83
Kim Ki-duk 56, 57, 94, 95, 96, 121, 167, 168, 182
Kim Ki-young 5, 42, 45
Kim Mi-hee 11, 167, 173–4, 177; see also FnH
Kim Mu-ryeong 161
Kim Pil-jeong 228
Kim Sang-Jin 121
Kim Seok-min 84
Kim Seong-chun 46
Kim Seong-hong 163
Kim Seong-min 44, 93
Kim Seung-ok 68, 74, 75, 188
Kim Shin-jae 185
Kim So-yeon 231
Kim Su-jin 255
Kim Su-yong 39, 56, 57, 64, 71, 74, 75, 135, 144, 188
Kim Sung-soo 234–6
Kim Tae-woo 199
Kim Tae-yong 198, 214, 215
Kim Ui-seok 160, 163
Kim Woo-hyung 170
Kim Woo-taek 165
Kim Yong-ho 90
Kim Yong-hwa 240
Kim Young-hee 184
Kim Young-jun 234
Kim Young-sam 10, 120, 157, 158, 182
Kim Yu-jeong 67
Kim Yunjin 194
Kim's Daughters 50, 64
King and the Clown 4, 171, 217, 234
King Hu 88
King of the Children 229
Korea Amateur Filmmakers Association (KAMA) 56
Korea Broadcasting System (KBS) 145
Korea Creative Contents Agency (KOCCA) 203
Korea Entertainment Corporation, see Hanguk Yeonye
Korea National University of Arts (KNUA) 166, 182, 191
Korean Academy of Film Arts (KAFA) 160, 166, 182, 191, 197, 198, 230
KAFA China Pre-biz 230
Korean Central Intelligence Agency (KCIA) 27, 58, 220
KOFIC (Korean Film Council, formerly known as Korean Film Commission) 9, 109, 120, 127, 178, 203, 257; Beijing office 230
Korean Film Directors Association 118
Korean film industry: professionalization 1, 10; reduction in film exports 4; value of film exports 3, 75, 231; see also internationalization
Korean Film Union (KFU) 113
Korean Motion Picture Promotion Corporation (KMPPC) 9, 108; formation 115, 127; involvement in film production 100–11; national policy films 9, 141
Korean Motion Pictures Producers Association (KMPPA) 9, 24–5, 32, 35–6, 55, 81, 108, 109–12, 114–5, 128, 141, 144
Korean New Wave 14, 134–8
Korean War: film setting 109, 143; impact of 113
Korean Wave 2, 3, 12, 141–2, 175, 231–32, 256
Kurosawa, Akira 82
Kusakabe, Kyūshirō 92
Kwak Jeong-hwan 163–4, 168
Kwon Byeong-gyun 161
Kwon Sang-woo 231

La 197
Lamp Shop 194
Last Flight to Pyeongyang, The 127
Last Present 166

Last Woman of Shang, The 8, 82, 85, 87, 90
Late Autumn 11–12, 97, 207, 208, 209, 214–17, 224, 234
Lau, Andy 233
Leafie, a Hen into the Wild 167, 172
Lee Beom-seon 45
Lee Bum-soo 234
Lee Byung Chull 165
Lee Byung-heon 223
Lee Byung-il 45, 113
Lee Chang-dong 121, 167, 182, 192
Lee Chang-yong 113
Lee Doo-yong 177
Lee Eugene 11, 167, 174–6, 177
Lee Eun 168, 176, 193
Lee Gwang-su 63
Lee Gyeong-son 63
Lee Gyu-hwan 43, 44
Lee Ho-geol 147
Lee Hyeong-pyo 145, 149
Lee Jang-hee 130, 139
Lee Jang-ho 9–10, 128–34, 135, 138, 147, 177, 189, 191
Lee Jang-ho's Baseball Team 137
Lee Jeong-hyang 11, 191–3, 121
Lee Joo-ik 209, 214, 232, 233, 234, 236
Lee Joon-ik 168, 234
Lee Jung-hyun 231
Lee Kang-cheon 186
Lee Man-hee 6, 42, 54, 57–8, 99, 110, 129, 209, 214, 234
Lee Mi-rye 189–90
Lee Min-ja 185
Lee Mun-wung 151
Lee Myeong-won 97–8
Lee Myung-bak 212–14, 222, 257; graffiti aimed at 213
Lee Myung-se 121, 200, 244
Lee Seong-gu 64, 135
Lee Soo-yeon 11, 175, 182, 191, 197
Lee Sung-gu 42, 71
Lee Sung-jae 174, 191
Lee Tae-won 118
Lee Won-se 128, 130, 131–2
Lee Woo-seok 149
Lee Yeong-ho 133, 137
Lee Yong-gi 239, 244
Lee Young-il 97
Lee, Ang 209, 214, 233, 234, 235
Lee, Dragon 90
Lee, John H. 176
Lee, Miky 165, 167
Legend of Evil Lake 234

Li Yixiang 228
Li Yu 241–3
Life on a String 229
Lin Dai, Linda 85
Lines 51
literary films 7, 62–78; links with art films 64; origins of genre 63–8; use as propaganda 62
Lollol Media 239, 243
Lost 194
Lost Sun, The 94, 95
Lotte Entertainment Group 11, 159, 164–5, 167, 172, 177, 178
Lou Ye 243
Love and Hatred 84
Love of Shadow, The 84
Love with an Alien 82, 83–4
Lover of a Friend, The 150
Lust, Caution 209, 214

Macquarie Group 164–5
Madam Aema 148, 149–50, 151
MAGE 239
Maki, Noriko 92
Male Housekeeper, A 36
Man and a Woman, A 75
Manchurian Westerns 90, 208, 235
Manhole 211
Marathon 171
March First Independence Movement 67, 212
March of Fools 132–3, 147
Marines Who Never Returned 97–8
Marriage Blue 201
Marriage Story 160–1, 173
martial arts films 8, 90; *see also wuxia*
Martyrs, The 50
Masaki, Kobayashi 97
Masquerade 4, 217
Masumura, Yasuzō 82, 98
May 16 Revolution and Changed Society 20–1
McCann, Richard 48
Media Asia Films 237
melodrama 10; female audiences 143; female themes 142–3; Golden Age of 142–4; *shinpa* 143; *see also* erotic (ero) melodramas; "hostess" melodramas
Memento Mori 210, 215
Memories of Murder 174
Meng Hua Ho 87
Mie, Kitahara 94
Mifune, Toshirō 92

Min Jin-su 200
Min Kyu-dong 198, 200, 215
Ministry of Culture and Public Information (MCPI) 114, 116, 117
Ministry of Public Information (MPI) 19–20; co-production guidelines 84–5; import limitations 144; leniency to Japanese filmmakers 93; shared production quota system 87
Miracle in Cell No. 7 4, 209, 217
Miss Granny 166, 238, 240
Miss Rhino and Mr. Korando 137
Mist 7–8, 56, 65, 74–7, 198
Miyabe, Miyuki 194
MK Buffalo 168–9
MK Pictures 169–72, 222, 237–8, 257
Modern Boy 164
Modern Family 200–01
Modern Times 198
modernity 7, 50, 63, 65–6, 74–8
Mong-u-do-won-do 236
Monkey Goes West 8, 87–8
Monkey King, The 240
Moon Jeong-suk 46
Mother 11–12, 95, 200, 207, 208, 209, 210–14
Mother and a Guest 31, 68, 81
Motion Picture Association of America (MPAA) 32, 120
Motion Picture Association of Korea (MPAK) 24, 35, 36, 90
Motion Picture Ethics Committee 45
Motion Picture Export Association (US) (MPEA) 9, 15, 108, 112–19
Motion Picture Law (MPL) 9, 20, 21, 107, 117, 127; stricter criteria 21–3, 62; campaign against 36;
Mountain Strawberries 150, 151
Mr. Go 227–8, 240
Mr. Mamma 160
Mrs. Kim Mari 150
Mujin Travelogue 75, 188
Mulberry 148
multiplexes 4, 10, 25, 120, 159, 162, 164–6, 169–72, 177, 255; *see also* CGV
Mun Hyae-joo 193
Munhwa Broadcasting Corp (MBC) 108, 145
Murmuring, The 193
Musa 232, 234, 235–6
My Brilliant Life 175–6
My Daughter Rescued from the Swamp 189
My Dear Enemy 173

My Ex-wife's Wedding 236
My Lady 145
My Lucky Star 240
My Own Breathing 193
My Sassy Girl 197
My Wife is Confessing 98
Myong-ja Akiko Sonia 137
Myth, The 231
Myung Film 160, 161, 167–72, 175, 176, 183, 190, 193, 202, 238, 241; *see also* Shim Jae-myung; MK Buffalo; MK Pictures

Na Ung-gyu 43
Nabi Pictures 236
Naises 161
Nakahira, Kō 8, 95–6
Naked Kitchen, The 11, 182, 199–200
Nation's Light 59
National Film Production Center (NFPC) 6, 19–20, 48
national policy films 9, 109–12, 141
National Security Law 219–21
Neon Genesis Evangelion 236
New American Cinema 128, 130, 167
New Korean Cinema 2, 13, 138, 160, 192, 195
New Village Movement 57; *see also* Park Chung Hee's rural development campaign
Next Entertainment World (N.E.W.) 11, 159, 165, 167, 177, 209, 227
Next Visual Studio 239
Night and Day 173
Night Before Marriage, The 201
Night Before Strike, The 168
Night of Burning Bone and Skin, A 148, 150
Night of Tokyo 186
Nightmare, A 232
Nikkatsu Studio 91
Ning Hao 240
Nouvelle Vague 65, 128, 130

Obaltan, see *Aimless Bullet*
Obscenity Law 54, 144–45, 252
OCN 159
Ode to My Father 4, 217
Oh Dal-su 219
Oh Jung-wan 11, 161, 167, 173, 174, 175, 176, 177, 202
Oh Ki-hwan 166–7
Omongnyeo 64
Oh Young-jin 97

Oh Young-su 68, 71
Ok Teacyeon 201
Okawa, Hiroshi 92
Old Park 133–4
Old Partner 200
Once in a Lifetime 194
One Fine Spring Day 176, 232
One-Armed Swordsman 90
One-Legged Man 90
One-sided Love of Passion 187
Orion Group 164, 165
Over that Hill 36
Ozu, Yasujirō 214

Pacemaker 174
Painted Skin 2: The Resurrection 239
Paju 11, 172, 182, 195–6
Pan Film Co. 137, 177
Pang Ho-cheung 214
pansori 142
Parade of Wives 109, 111
Park Chan-ok 11, 172, 182, 191, 195–7
Park Chan-wook 2, 119, 121, 138, 167, 168, 171–2, 176, 182, 200, 210, 234, 243, 244
Park Cheol-su 118
Park Chung Hee 1, 4, 5, 8, 9, 15, 19, 26, 30, 107, 113, 114, 128, 132, 151, 169–71, 218, 222; ascent to power 19, 81, 130; assassination 112, 134, 135, 218; control of film production 19–20, 35; cultivation of nationalism 65–6; documentary about 59; Emergency Measure No. 9 128; industrialization plan 25, 81; rural development campaign 6, 26, 27–30; on "youth menace" 133; *see also The President's Last Bang*
Park Dong-ho 164
Park Geun-hye 171, 222, 257
Park Hae-il 195
Park Ji-man 170, 171
Park Jin-pyo 175
Park Jong Cheol 221
Park Jong-ho 145
Park Jung-soo 213
Park Kwang-su 128, 135, 136
Park Nam-ok 183, 184, 185, 189, 190
Park No-sik 87
Park Shin-yang 197
Park, Chloe 228
Park, Ethan 239, 242–4
Peaceful Island, The 232

Peppermint Candy 232
Performance Ethics Committee 116, 136–7
Phenom Film 244
Phone 232
Pil li Quan 89
pink films 51, 91, 96, 98, 148; *see also* erotic (ero) melodramas; "hostess" melodramas; sexuality in films
Pioneer, The 63
piracy 178
plagiarism 8, 91, 97–8
Planet Bollywood 256
Planet Hallyuwood 2, 4, 251, 256–58
Planet Hollywood 256
planned films (*gihoek yeonghwa*) 160
post-production 237, 238–41, 246
Potato 68, 188
President's Last Bang, The 167, 169–71, 218
Prince Yeonsan 81, 82, 85
Private Tutor 93, 94, 95, 98
Producer Registration System (PRS) 6, 21, 32, 33, 37, 55, 108, 115, 158; abolition 116, 137, 177; importers becoming producers 24; role of pre-sales 24–5; *see also daemyeong jejak* system
producer-distributors 163
producers: 1960s 23; 1990s 157–78; cartel 6, 24–7; independent 65; *see also* female producers; Producer Registration System (PRS)
Promise, The 233
propaganda: film as 1, 6, 7, 20–4, 62; soft vs hard 20, 62
Prostitution 151
Pulgasari 26
Purn Production 193
Pusan International Film Festival (PIFF) 229–30, 237; *see also* Busan International Film Festival (BIFF)

Q Channel 161
Quiet Family, The 167, 168
Quirino, Jose 75

Rainy Season 189
Raise the Red Lantern 229
Rayns, Tony 136
Reason to Live, A 182, 191, 192–3
Rebel without a Cause 94
Red Cherry 148
Red Cliff I 239
Red Cliff II 239

Red Scarf, The 6, 21, 30–2, 184
Red Sorghum 229
Refrigerator Story 197
Relationship 188
Rice 6, 21, 27–30
Roaring Currents 4, 217
Roh Deok 11, 182, 191, 201
Roh Moo-hyun 117, 218, 222, 223
Romance Grey 184
Room in the Forest, The 137
Ruffians, The 97

Saehan Film Co. 187
Saehan Media 158
Samsung 2, 10, 120, 158, 159, 160, 161, 163, 254
Samsung Entertainment 120, 161–2, 190
San Francisco Film Festival 48–50, 70
Sanjuro 82, 92
Save the Green Planet! 201
Shochiku Studio 92
School Days 189
Screen Quota System 3, 9, 108–9, 115–16, 117, 120; halving of 119; "quota quickies" 62
Screen Quota Watch Group 120; *see also* Coalition for Cultural Diversity in Moving Images (CDMI)
Sea Wind 44
Seaside Village 7, 71–4, 184
Secret Recipe 200
Secret Sunshine 192
Secret Within Her Mask, The 201
Sector 7 231
Segi Sangsa 23, 51, 83, 96, 97
Seizure of Life, The 45
Sejong Film Company 93
Seo Yoon-seong 94–5
Seong Chunhyang 26, 85, 92
Seorabeol Art College 44
Seoul Cinema 118, 149, 163, 168; *see also* Kwak Jeong-hwan
Seoul International Women's Film Festival (SIWFF) 13, 183, 184, 195
Seoul Olympics 117, 148, 158, 163, 220, 221; protests 118
Seoul Spring 135
Seven Swords 231
Sewol ferry disaster 195, 257
sexploitation 10, 145, 149, 151, 253; *see also* erotic (ero) melodramas; "hostess" melodramas
sexuality in films 10, 136–7, 141–52

Shadowless Sword 234
Shadows in the Palace 211
Shanghai Film Group 166
Shaw Brothers 8, 82, 83–90, 97
Shaw, Run Run 82, 84
Shi Nansun 214
Shim Bo-kyoung 11, 167, 168, 172, 177
Shim Eun-ha 191
Shim Hun 67
Shim Jae-myung 11, 161, 167–72, 174, 177, 183, 190, 202
Shim San 150
Shim, Jaime, *see* Shim Jae-myung
Shin Chul 128, 167, 168, 173
Shin Film 6, 23, 25–7, 32, 36–7, 68, 81, 83, 85, 93; *see also* Shin Sang-ok; expansion 86; financial problems 87; links with Park Chung Hee 26–7; multiple studios 26
Shin Hyun-jun 240
Shin Jung-hyeon 133
Shin Min-ah 199
Shin Sang-ok 5, 6, 19, 21, 25–30, 42, 44, 56, 57, 68, 74, 81, 82, 83, 85, 88, 92, 97, 99, 129, 135, 145, 187
Shin Seong-il 94, 96, 214
Shin Yeong-gyun 30, 81, 85, 96
Shina Film 26, 87, 89
ShinCine Communications 160, 161, 168, 173, 176, 190; *see also* Shin Chul
Shingwang Film Co. 84
Shiri 1, 2, 10, 160, 162–3, 169, 194, 235, 244
Shirō Sagisu 236
Showbox 11, 159, 167, 177
Sidus 169, 174–6; *see also* Cha Seung-jae
Sidus FnH 174–6
Silmido 4, 164, 217
Shin Il-ryong 111
Single Mom, A 186
SKC 158
Slope in the Sun, A 93–4
Snowpiercer 119, 210, 223, 224
So Ji-seup 231
"soft power" 12
Son of a Man 189
Son Ye-jin 240
Song Chang-sik 130
Song Hye-kyo 175, 191, 193, 231, 247
Song Kang-ho 222, 223
Song Neung-han 121
Soo Film 200
Sophie's Revenge 240, 243

Sorum 211
South and North 95
spaghetti Westerns 8, 90;
  see also Manchurian Westerns
Spring, Spring (1935) 67
Spring, Spring (1969 *mustache*) 68
Spy Remained Behind, A 109, 111
Star Shaped Stain 200
Starmax 158, 161
state film policy 5, 9, 19, 21
  control of film production 19–20
Stolen Apple Tastes Good, The 148
Story of Chunhyang 44
Story of Qiu Ju, The 229
Story of Sim Cheong, The 26, 93
Studio Dreamcatcher 174
studio system 23, 32–5
Summer with Monica 94
"sun tribe" movies 91, 93–7
Survival Game 197
Suzuki, Akira 111
Syngman Rhee 15, 28, 45, 130

Tadashi, Iizima (Iijima) 63
Taebaek Mountain, The 109
Taechang Heungeop 23, 188
Taegukgi 4, 217, 238
Taewon Entertainment 234
Tale of Two Sisters, A 173, 210, 243
Tang Wei 209, 214, 217, 234
Tazza: The High Rollers 176
telecommunications companies:
  involvement in film industry 174
television: as bedroom cinema 141; impact on film 141; as propaganda tool 141
Tell Me Something 232
Tell Me, Earth! 97
Temperature of Love, see Very Ordinary Couple
Temptress Moon 232
Temptress with Thousand Faces 88
Terror, Live, The 119
Testimony, The 9, 109, 110–1
Tetsuji, Takechi 96, 98
Thieves 4, 176, 217
Thirst 176, 200, 243
This is the Beginning of Love 189
Thousand Year Old Fox 129
Three Days of their Reign 129
Three Extremes 176
Three Friends 190
Three Times Each for Short and Long Ways 148, 189

Tian Zhuangzhuang 228
Titanic 1, 2, 162
To, Johnny 175
Together 232, 233, 235, 236, 238
Toho Studios 92, 93
Toilet Pictures 232
Tomotaka, Tasaka 94
Tongyang Broadcasting Company (TBC) 145
trade wars 115–18
transnational cinema 227; see also China; co-production; Hong Kong; Japan
Treaty on Basic Relations between Japan and the Republic of Korea 93
Tse, Nicholas 233
Tsui Hark 168, 214, 239
Tu Gwang-qi 84
Twenty Identities 198
Two Cops 160, 163
Two Cops II 163, 173
Two Cops III 173
Two Thieves in Love 127
Tyrant Yeonsan 85

Uji, Misako 92
Uninvited, The 175, 176, 182, 197–8, 210
Unmarried Teacher, An 187–8
Untold Scandal 173, 175
US Army Military Government in Korea (USAMGK): approach to art and culture 113; curfew 149
US films screening in Korea 3

Valenti, Jack 113, 114, 117, 118, 119; see also Hollywood; MPEA
Venus Talk 172
vertical integration 6, 163
Very Ordinary Couple 182, 201
Veteran 4
Virgin Stripped Bare by Her Bachelors 195
Visual Age group 128, 129–34, 138, 147, 167; adaptation of novels 130
Voice of a Murderer 175, 176

Waikiki Brothers 172, 190
Wakasugi, Mitsuo 84
Walking in the Rain 190
Wang Ziaoshuai 228, 229
Warrior's Way, The 233–4
Warriors of the Rainbow: Seediq Bale 239
Way Home, The 191, 192
Wedding Invitation, A 166, 240
Wedding Story II 176

Wei Te-Sheng 239
What Misunderstanding Left Behind 186
When Flowers Sadly Fade Away 188
When the Buckwheat Flower Blossoms 68
When the Sun Rises 64
Whispering Corridors 210
Widow, The 183, 185–6
Wife Confesses, A 82, 92
Wild Flowers in the Battle Field, The 109, 111
Winter Woman 147
Woman and the Rain, The 150
Woman in the Wall, A 145
Woman Judge, A 186
Woman on the Beach 173
Woman Who Lives on Night, The 148
Woman, Woman 150
Women Being in Asia 193
women directors, *see* female writer-directors
Women Don't Fear the Night 148; Women in Film Korea (WIFK) 14, 183–4, 190, 191, 202
Women in Film Korea Festival 184
Women of Yi-Dynasty 129, 145
women producers, *see* female producers
Won Bin 211, 223
Wong Jing 240
Woo, John 168, 239
Woochi (aka *Jeon Woo-chi: The Taoist Wizard*) 175, 176, 200
Wooil Yeongsang 158
wuxia films 36, 88, 90, 238

Xia Jin 229
Xie Fie 228
Xie Jin 229
Xu Jiao 228

Y's Experience 137
Yagi, Masao 111
Yang Woo-seok 209, 217
Yellow Earth 229, 232
Yeom Bok-sun 147

Yes, Good-Bye Today 134
Yi Cheong-jun 74
Yi Chi-yun 228, 238, 240, 243
Yi Hyoin 149–50
Yi Kwang-su 67
Yim Soon-rye 121, 172, 183, 190, 193
Yojimbo 92
Yōjirō, Ishizaka 93, 98
Yoo Oh-sung 174
Yoo Young-sik 234
Yoshimura, Kōzaburō 98
You are My Sunshine 173, 175, 176
Young Sang Shi Dae, *see* Visual Age group
Young-Shim 189
Youngja's Heydays 133, 146–7
Your Name is Woman 145
youth films 93, 130, 132–3; *see also* "sun tribe" films
Yu Du-yeon 84, 186
Yu Hyun-mok 5, 6–7, 20, 34, 42–59, 64, 71, 95, 97, 98, 100, 127–8, 135, 143–5, 189; as auteur 42–4; *The Country, The Revolution and I* 67; early years 44–5; later career 55–9; legal action against 54–5
Yu In-taek 161
Yu Ji-tae 174
Yu Productions 57
Yun Hyeong-ju 133
Yushin system 9, 122, 128, 133, 145, 151

Zhang Ming 229
Zhang Xia 234, 235, 236
Zhang Yimou 228, 229
Zhang Yuan 228, 229
Zhang Ziyi 235, 240
Zhao Wei 228
Zheng Changfu 234
Zhong Zheng 234
Zinke, Florian 243
Zip Cinema 175, 176
Zonbo Media 232
Zu Feng 228